HAND
ROAD ATLAS
GREAT BRITAIN

© EDITION 1 1993 Copyright of the publishers
Geographers' A-Z Map Company Limited
Head Office: Fairfield Road, Borough Green, Sevenoaks, Kent. TN15 8PP Telephone 0732-781000
Showrooms: 44 Gray's Inn Road, London WC1X 8LR Telephone 071-242 9246

CONTENTS

REFERENCE

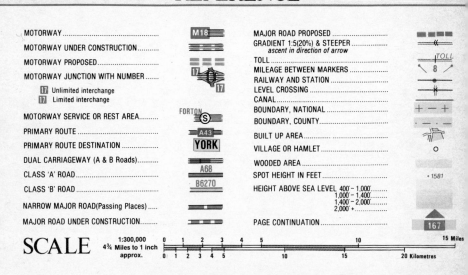

MOTORWAY M18

MOTORWAY UNDER CONSTRUCTION ....

MOTORWAY PROPOSED.................

MOTORWAY JUNCTION WITH NUMBER ....

    17 Unlimited interchange

    17 Limited interchange

MOTORWAY SERVICE OR REST AREA......... FORTON S

PRIMARY ROUTE A43

PRIMARY ROUTE DESTINATION .... YORK

DUAL CARRIAGEWAY (A & B Roads)...........

CLASS 'A' ROAD A68

CLASS 'B' ROAD B6270

NARROW MAJOR ROAD(Passing Places) .....

MAJOR ROAD UNDER CONSTRUCTION........

MAJOR ROAD PROPOSED ....

GRADIENT 1:5(20%) & STEEPER ....
ascent in direction of arrow

TOLL ...... TOLL

MILEAGE BETWEEN MARKERS 8

RAILWAY AND STATION ....

LEVEL CROSSING ....

CANAL...............

BOUNDARY, NATIONAL ....

BOUNDARY, COUNTY.............

BUILT UP AREA...................

VILLAGE OR HAMLET................. o

WOODED AREA ....

SPOT HEIGHT IN FEET .... • 1581

HEIGHT ABOVE SEA LEVEL 400´ – 1,000´........
      1,000´ – 1,400´........
      1,400´ – 2,000´........
      2,000´ +........

PAGE CONTINUATION.................. 167

SCALE

1:300,000
4¾ Miles to 1 inch approx.

0 1 2 3 4 5 .... 10 .... 15 Miles

0 1 2 3 4 5 .... 10 .... 15 .... 20 Kilometres

Tourist Information

AIRPORT ....

AIRFIELD ....

HELIPORT ....

BATTLE SITE & DATE............................. 1066

CASTLE...................

CASTLE WITH GARDEN (Open to Public) ....

CATHEDRAL, ABBEY, PRIORY etc....................

COUNTRY PARK ....

FERRY (VEHICULAR) ....
    (FOOT ONLY)

GARDEN (Open to Public) ....

GOLF COURSE 9. 18.

HISTORIC BUILDING (Open to Public) ....

HISTORIC BUILDING WITH GARDEN(Open to Public) .....

HORSE RACECOURSE.......................

INFORMATION CENTRE ....

LIGHTHOUSE ....

MOTOR RACING CIRCUIT ....

MUSEUM ....

NATIONAL & FOREST PARK ....

NATIONAL TRUST PROPERTY   (Open) .... NT
    (Restricted Opening)............. NT
    (National Trust of Scotland)........... NTS NTS

NATURE RESERVE & BIRD SANCTUARY ....

NATURE TRAIL & FOREST WALK ....

PLACE OF INTEREST ....

PICNIC SITE ....

RAILWAY, STEAM or NARROW GAUGE ....

TELEPHONE, PUBLIC (Selection) ...   AA or RAC ..

VIEW POINT ....

WILDLIFE PARK....................

WINDMILL...................

ZOO or SAFARI PARK.................

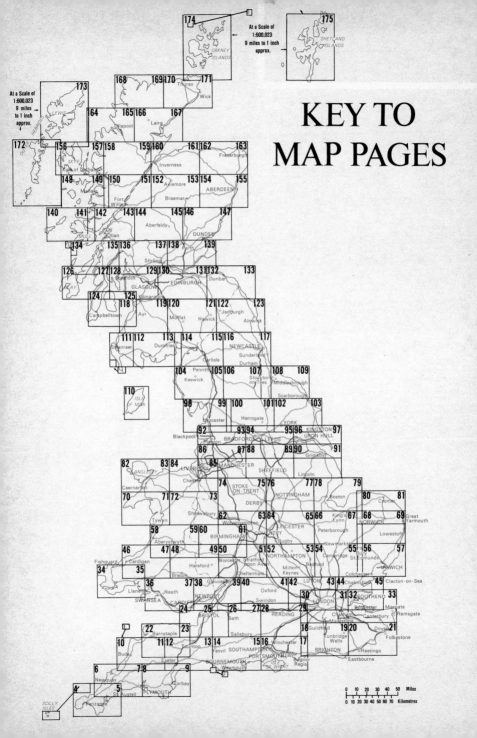

KEY TO MAP PAGES

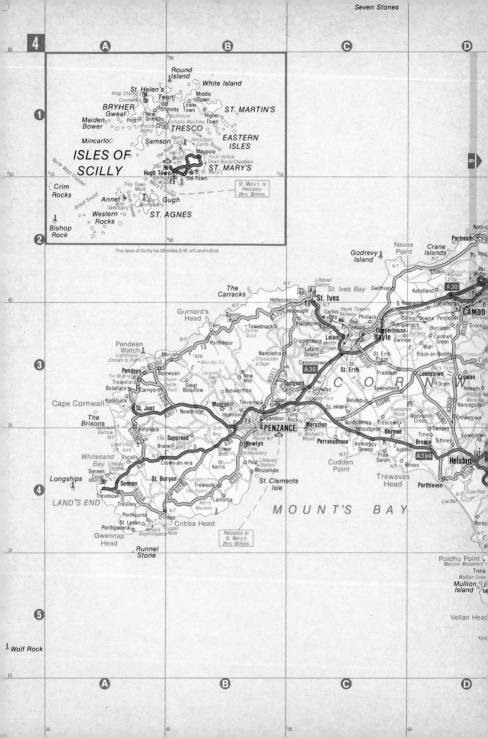

Seven Stones

4

60

4

Ⓐ   Ⓑ   Ⓒ   Ⓓ

⁹0

Round Island

White Island

❶

St. Helen's
King Charles'   Tean
Cromwell   Middle Town
BRYHER   Old   Lower Town
Gweal   Grimsby   Town
New   Brockhouse   Higher **ST. MARTIN'S**
Maiden   Grimsby   Valhalla Maritime   Town
Bower   Pool **TRESCO**
Abbey

Mincarlo   Samson   **EASTERN ISLES**

Bant's Carn
Innisidgen Carns

ISLES OF SCILLY   The Road
Harry's   Maypole
Bar   Porth Hellick
Down Burial Chambers
Star   **St. Mary's**
⁰10

⁰50   North West Channel   Hugh Town   Old Town   ⁰10

Garrison
St. Mary's Sound

St. Mary's to
Penzance
2hrs. 30 mins.

Crim Rocks   Troy Town Maze   St. Mary's Sound

Broad Sound   Smith Sound   Gugh
Annet   Bird Sanctuary   Observatory
Western Rocks   **ST. AGNES**

❷ Bishop Rock

⁹0

The Isles of Scilly lie 28 miles S.W. of Land's End

Navax Point   Crane Islands
Godrevy Island   NT   **Portreath**
NT   Roman   Par Botto
A30   **CAMBO**
Lifeboat Station
The Carracks   NT   St. Ives Bay   Gwithian   Kehelland   Kenidjack

❸

Hellesveor   **St. Ives**   Roseworthy   Loswittian
Gurnard's Head   Penbeagle   Carbis Bay   Hayle Towans   Connor Downs   Penponds   Troon
Zennor   The   Phillack   Angarrack   Barripper
Treen   Towednack   Halsetown   Towans   **HAYLE**   Gwinear   Carnhell Green
Porthmeor   Zennor Quoit   Lelant   Copperhouse   Railway   Praze-an-Beeble
Pendeen Watch   Nancledra   Cripplesease   Lelant   St. Erth Praze
Lighthouse   Morvah   Chysauster Village   Downs   Canonstown   A30   Fraddam   **CROWAN**
(Shown to Public)   Men-An-Tol   St. Erth   Townshend   Releath
Foage   B28   Lanyon   New   Ludgvan   **CORNW**   Drym   Nancegollan
Pendeen   Lanyon Quoit   Mill   Crowlas   Leedstown
Tin Mining   Bojewyan   Chun   Great   Boswarthen   Long Rock   Relubbus
Trewellard   Castle (Iron)   Bosullow   Crowlas   St. Hilary
Botallack   Carnyorth   Boskenna   Goldsithney   Godolphin   Carleen
Kenidjack   Madron   Trevarrack   Gulval   Marazion   Cross   **Crowntown**   Lowertown
St. Just   Heamoor   Relubbus   Rosudgeon   Ashton   B3302
Cape Cornwall   Newbridge   Tryandour   **PENZANCE**   St. Michael's   **Germoe**   Trew   Breage   A394   **Helston**
The Brisons   **NEWLYN**   Mount NT   **Perranuthnoe**   Kenneggy   Sithney
Ballowall Barrow   Kelynack   Drift Rest   Long Rock   Cudden   Downs   Praa Sands   Porthleven
Land's End (St. Just)   Sancreed   Egyptian   Point   Hinsey   Loe Bar
Whitesand Bay   Brane   Lower   House NT   St. Paul   Trewavas
Sennen   Escalls   Drift   Tidal   Lifeboat   Head   Poldhu Point
Longships   Sennen Cove   Crows-an-wra   Kerris   Observatory   Station   Mousehole   Marconi Monument
❹   **Sennen**   St. Buryan   Trewoofe   **St. Clements Isle**   Trena   Mullion Cove
Trevescan   The Pipers   Lamorna   **M O U N T ' S   B A Y**   **Mullion Island**
LAND'S END   Trevilley   Merry Maidens
Porthcurno   Treen   Cribba Head   Penzance to St. Mary's   Vellan Head
St. Levan   Logan Rock   2hrs. 30 mins.
Gwennap Head   Porthgwarra   Minack Amphitheatre
Runnel Stone

❺

⚓ **Wolf Rock**

Ⓐ   Ⓑ   Ⓒ   Ⓓ

30   40   ⁵0   60

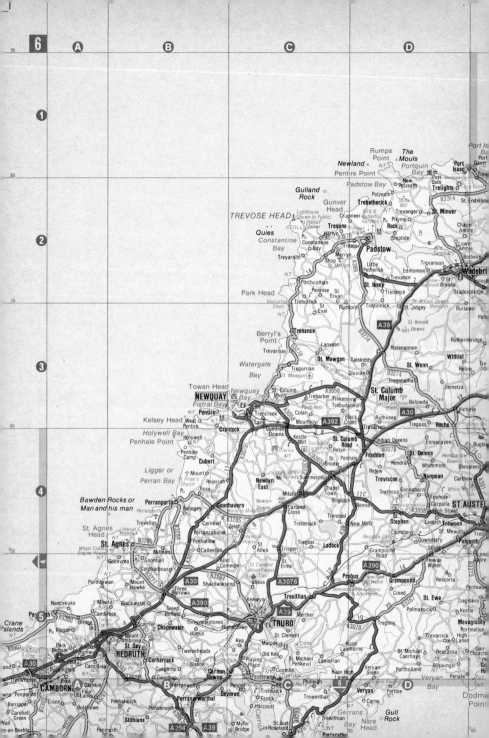

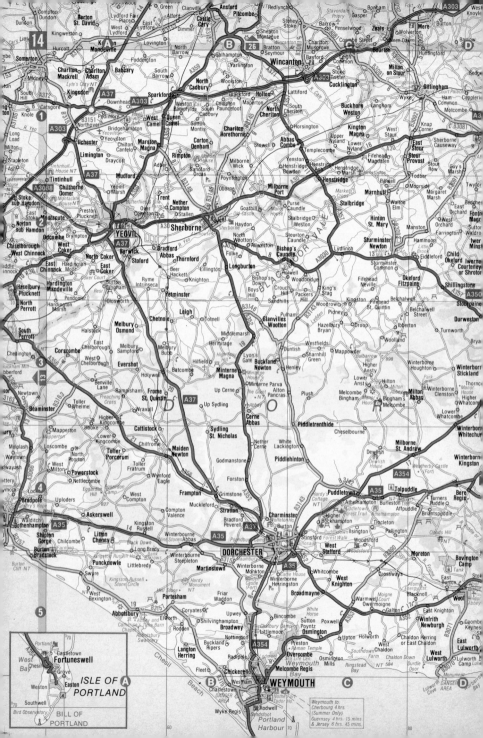

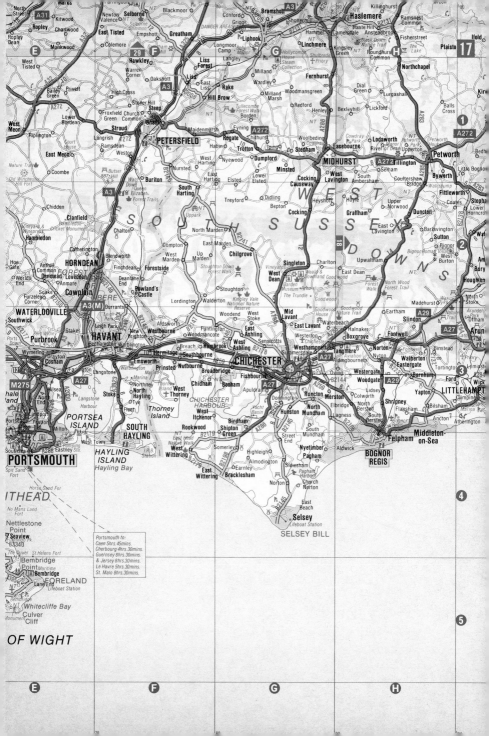

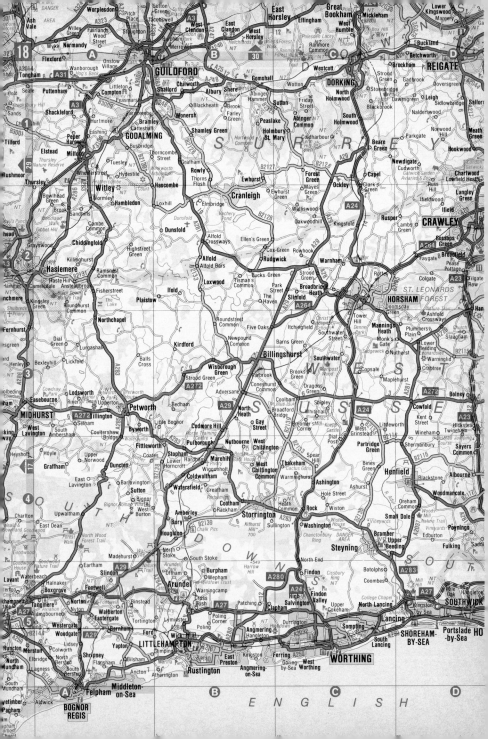

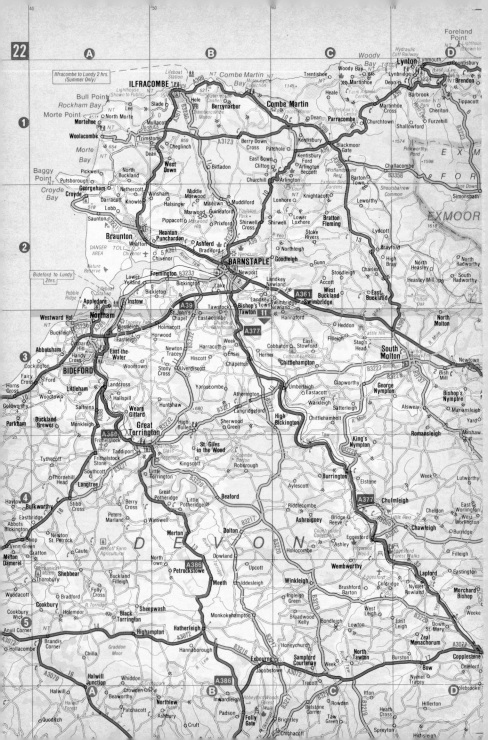

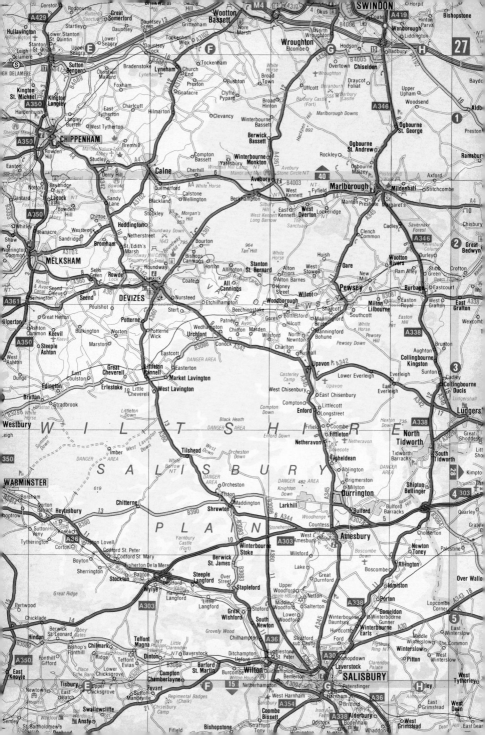

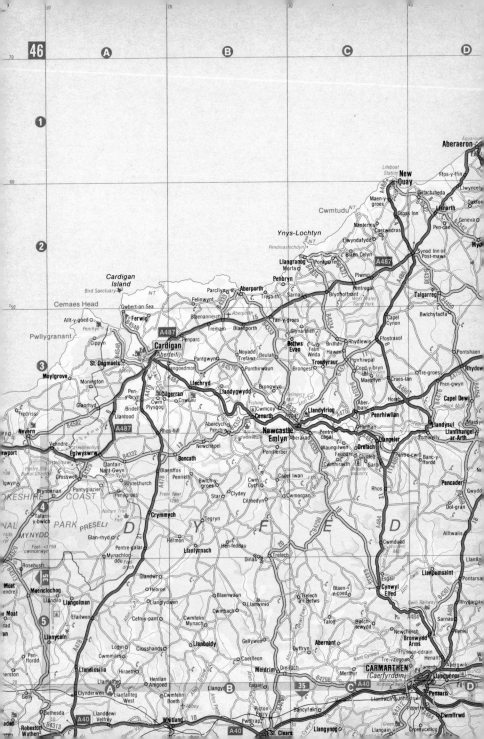

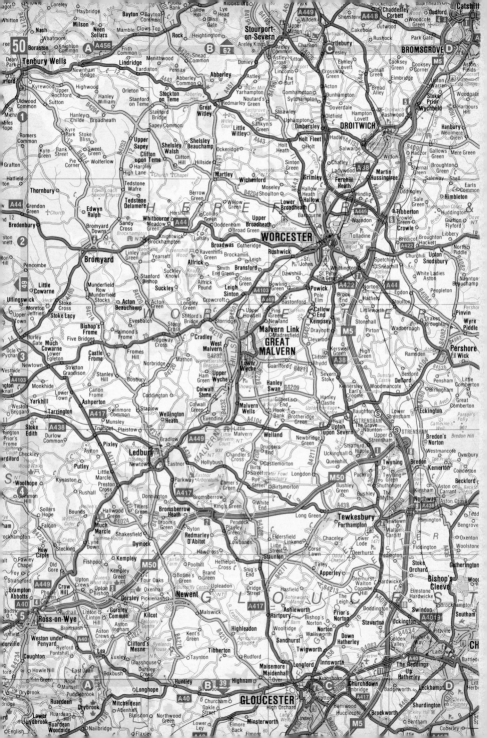

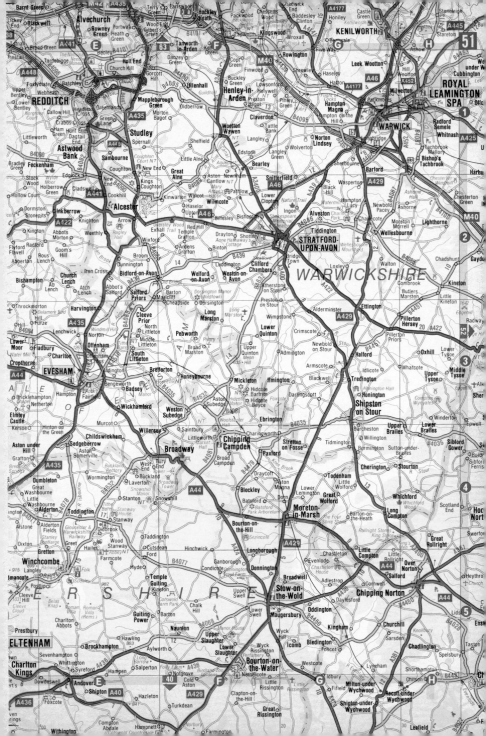

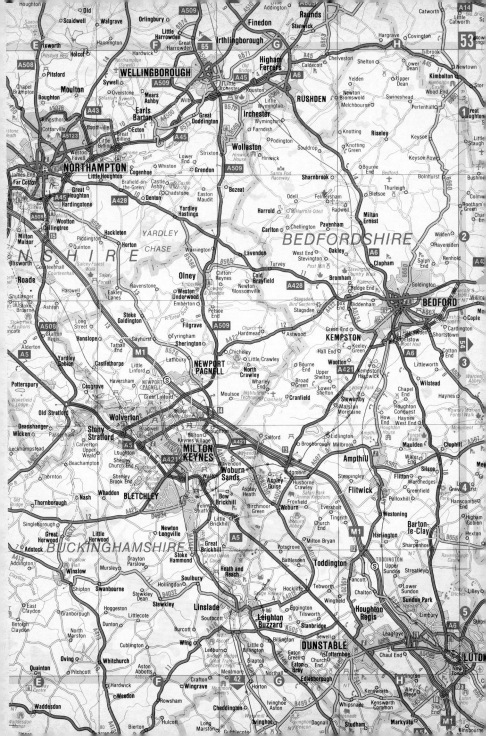

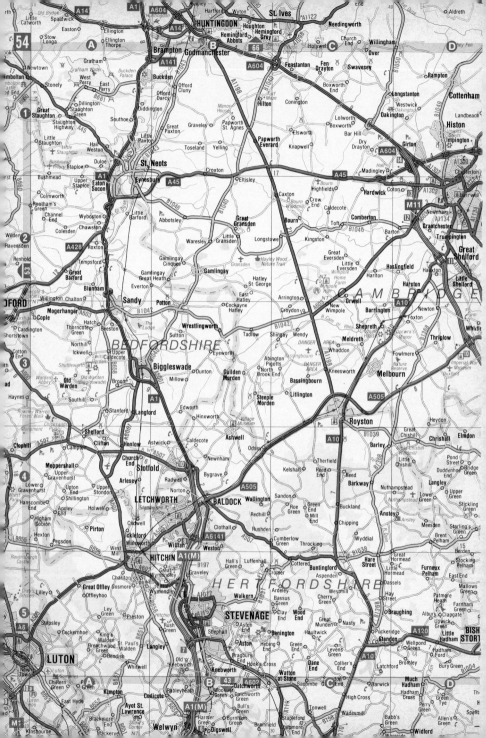

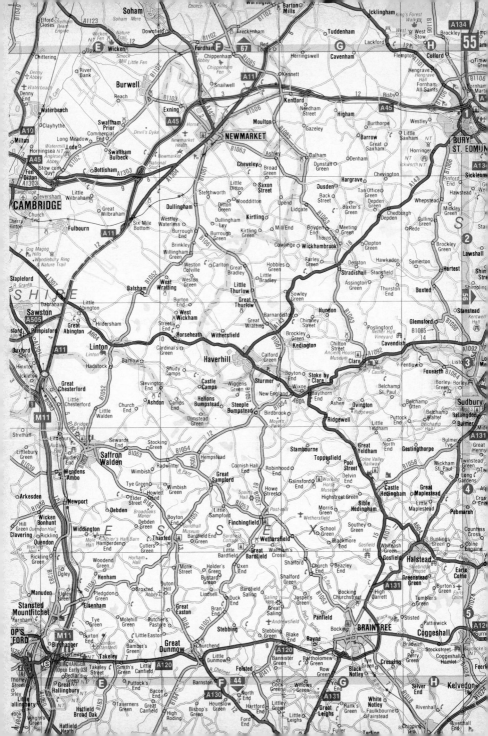

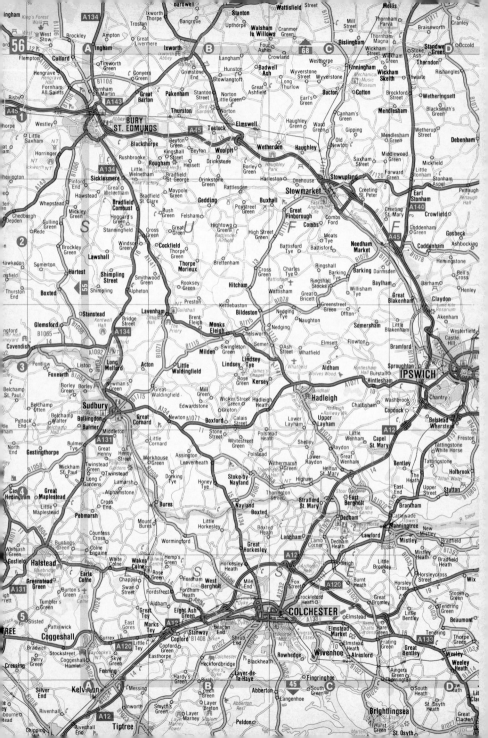

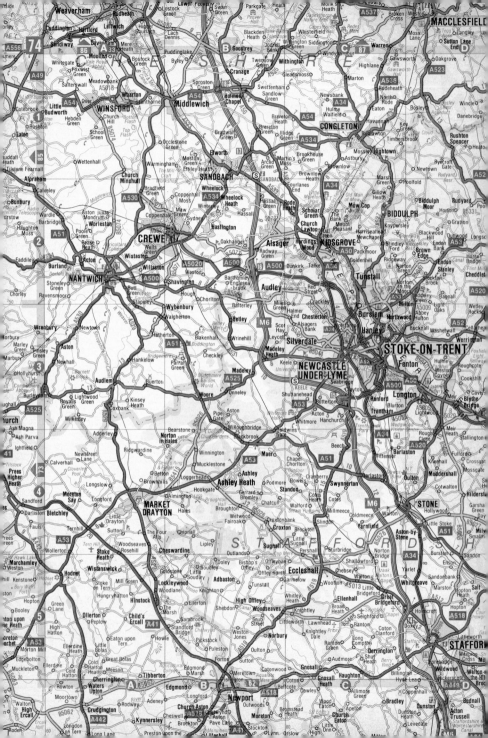

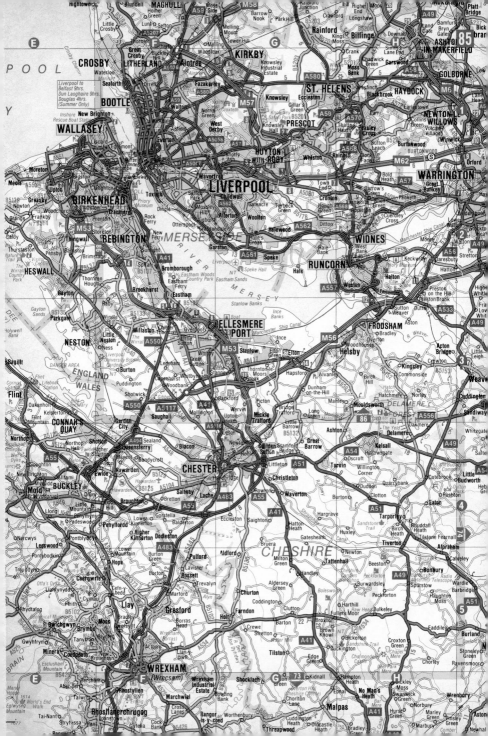

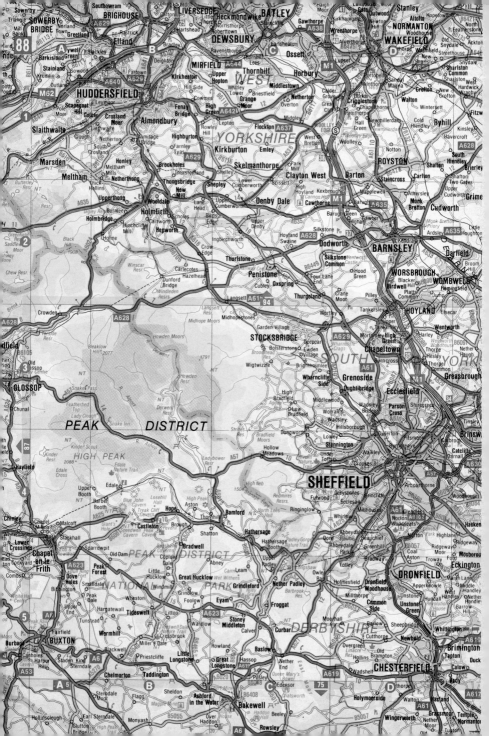

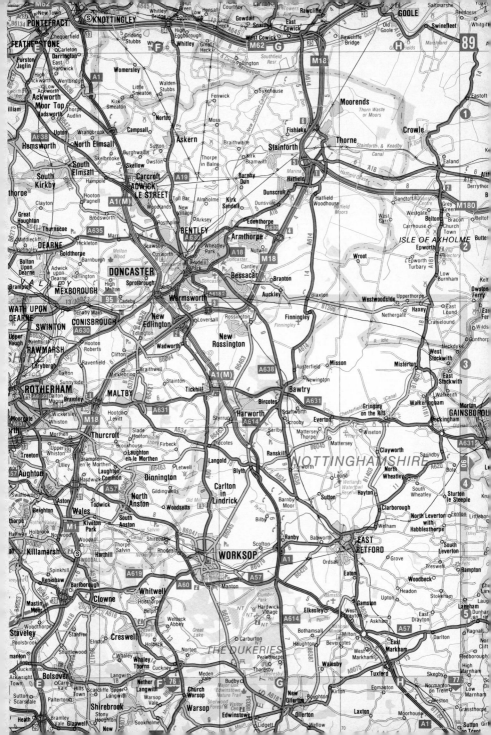

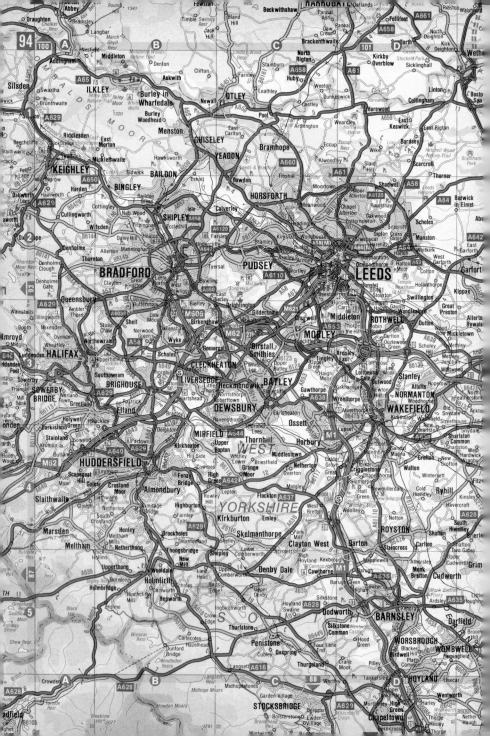

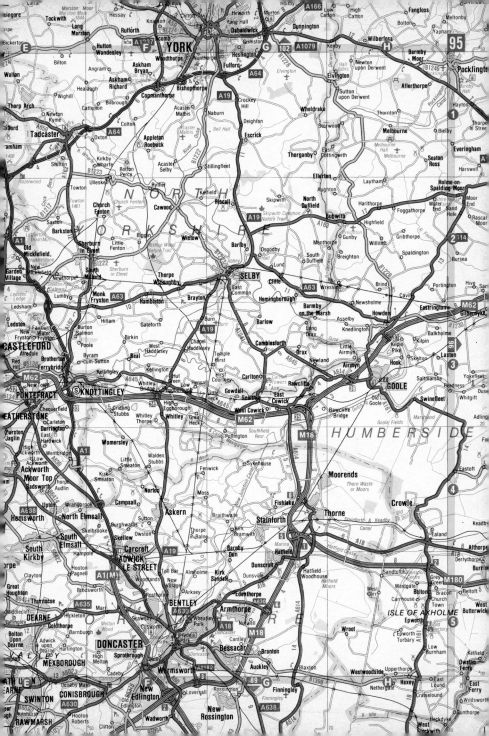

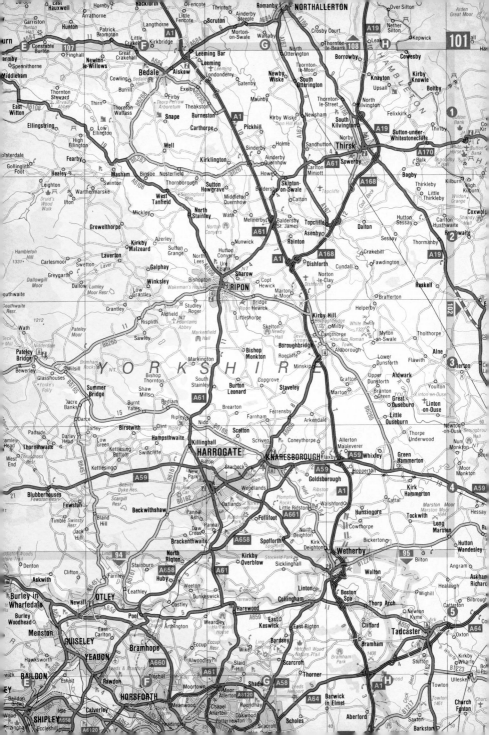

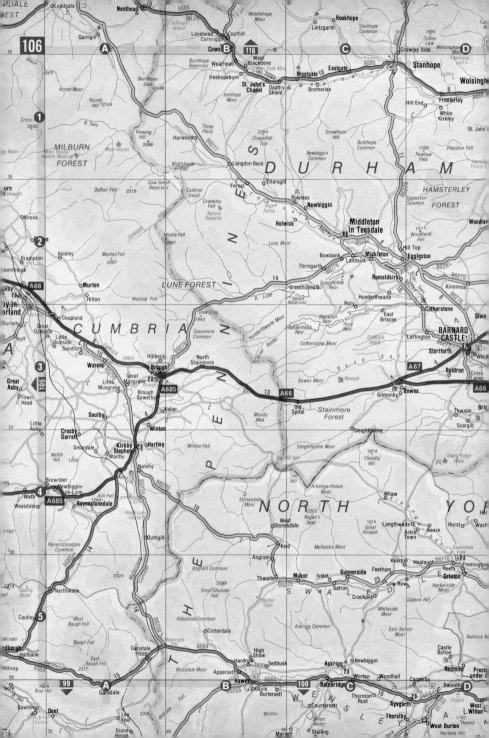

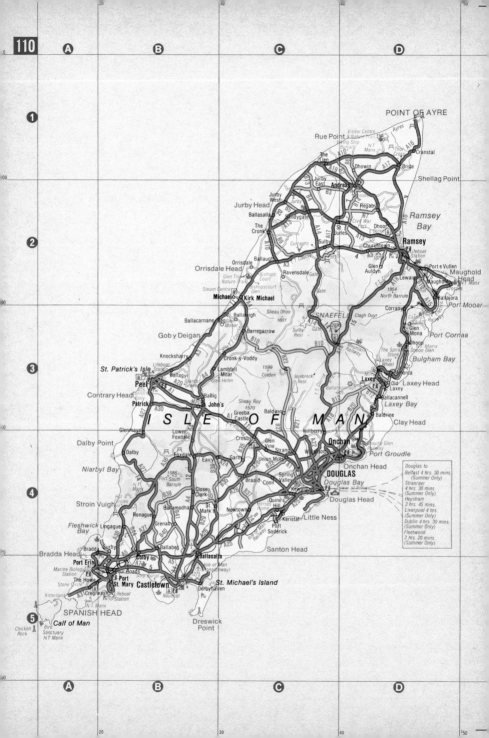

A **B** **C** **D**

1

POINT OF AYRE

Rue Point & Nature Trail The
Viking Ship
NT
Manx

Visitor Centre
Ayres
Cranstal
Thor
The
Glen
Dhowin
Bride
Shellag Point

Jurby
East
Andreas
Regaby
**Ramsey
Bay**

Jurby
West
Jurby Head
Ballasalla
Sandygate
St. Jude's
Civil War
Fort
Dhoon
Churchtown
Ramsey

2

The
Cronk
Curraghs
Sulby
Lifeboat
Station
Port e Vullen
**Maughold
Head**

Orrisdale
Ballaugh
Glen
Auldyn
Lewaigue
Maughold
NT Manx

Orrisdale Head
Bishops
Court
Ravensdale
Gate
1854
North Barrule
Ballajora
Port Mooar

Glen Trunk
Nature Trail
Bishopscourt
Glen
Corrany
Michael **Kirk Michael**

Steam Centre
Slieau Dhoo
SNAEFELL
Clagh Ouyr
Glen
Mona
Dhoon
Manx
Dhoon Glen
Port Cornaa

Ballaleigh
Moar
1601
Sulby
Resr.
The Spiral
Stone
Laxey
Wheel
Bulgham Bay

Ballacarnane
Gob y Deigan
Barregarrow
Mountain
Railway
Corrany

Knocksharry
Cronk-y-Voddy
1599
Colden
Injebreck
Resr.
Ballaglonney
Laxey **Old
Laxey Head**

St. Patrick's Isle
Lifeboat
Station
Lambfell
Moar
Glen Helen
Laxey
Ballacannell
Laxey Bay

3

Peel
Ballagyr
Ballig
St. John's
Greeba
Castle
Slieau Roy
1570
Baldwin
Baldrine

Contrary Head
Patrick
ISLE OF MAN
Clay Head

Glenmaye
Lower
Foxdale
Crosby
Glen
Vine
Strang
Hillberry
Groudle Glen
Railway

Dalby Point
Dalby
Foxdale
Eairy
Garth
Union Mills
Onchan
Onchan Head
Port Groudle

Niarbyl Bay
1586
Mt South
Barrule
Closed
Clark's
Braaid
Cooil
Spring
Valley
Keppington
DOUGLAS
Douglas Bay

4

Stroin Vuigh
Ronague
Ballamodha
St
Mark's
Newtown
Quine's
Hill
Horses
Home
Douglas Head

*Fleshwick
Bay*
Lingague
Grenaby
Keristal
Port
Soderick
Little Ness

Bradda
Surby
Ballabeg
Ballasalla
Santon Head

Bradda Head
Port Erin
Colby
Ballasalla
Isle of Man
(Monastery)

Marine Biology
Station
Stone Circle
The Howe
Four Roads
Port
St. Mary
Castletown
St. Michael's Island

Kitterland
Cregneash
Lifeboat
Station
Derbyhaven

5

SPANISH HEAD
Calf of Man
NT Manx
Nautical
Dreswick
Point

Chicken
Rock
Bird
Sanctuary
NT Manx

Douglas to
Belfast 4 hrs. 30 mins.
(Summer Only)
Stranraer
4 hrs. 30 mins.
(Summer Only)
Heysham
3 hrs. 45 mins.
Liverpool 4 hrs.
(Summer Only)
Dublin 4 hrs. 30 mins.
(Summer Only)
Fleetwood
3 hrs. 20 mins.
(Summer Only)

A **B** **C** **D**

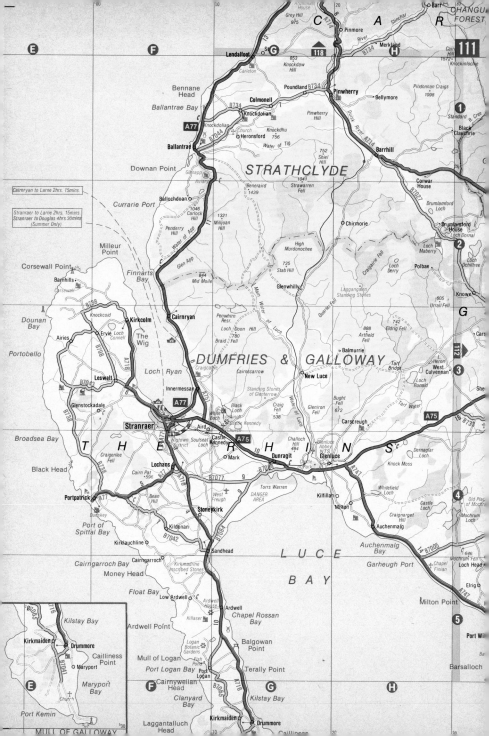

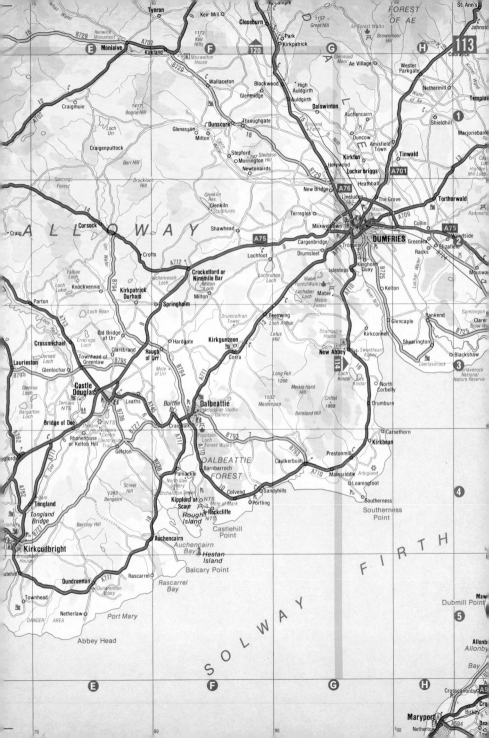

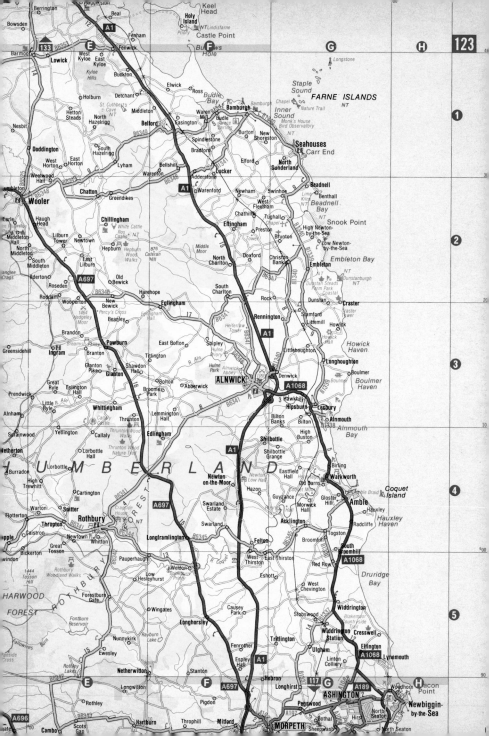

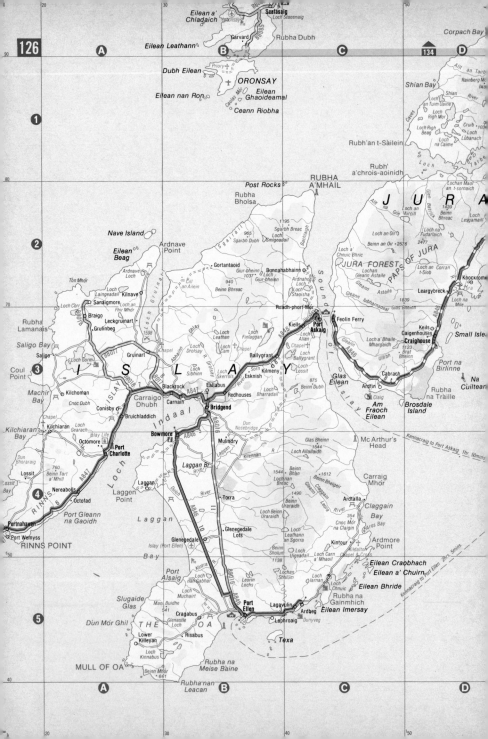

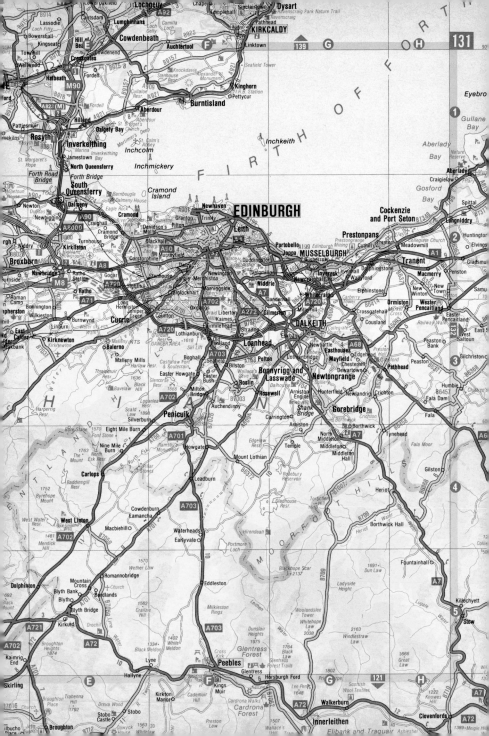

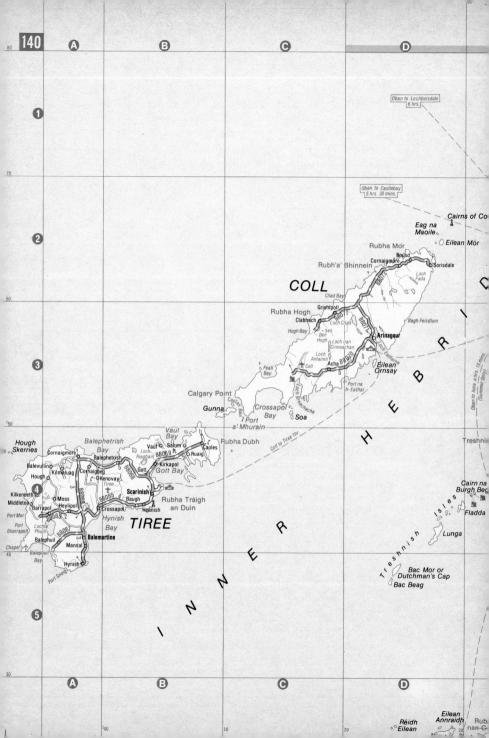

Oban to Lochboisdale
6 hrs.

Oban to Castlebay
5 hrs. 30 mins.

Cairns of Co

Eag na
Maoile

Eilean Mór

Rubha Mór

Bousd

Cornaigmore

Sorisdale

Rubh'a' Bhinnein

Loch
Fada

COLL

Rubha Hogh

Grishipoll

Cliad Bay

Clabhach

Loch Cliad

Bagh Feisdlum

Hogh Bay

·340
Ben
Hogh

Arinagour

Loch nan
Cinneachan

Loch
Anlaimh

Acha

Feall
Bay

Loch
Fannuna

Coll

Eilean
Ornsay

5

Calgary Point

Port na
h-Eathar

Gunna

Caolas Bay

Crossapol
Bay

Soa

Port
a' Mhurain

Loch Breachacha

Rubha Dubh

Coll to Tiree 1hr.

**Vaul
Bay**

**Hough
Skerries**

Cornaigmore

Balephetrish
Bay

Vaul

Salum

Caoles

Balevullin

Balephetrish

Loch
Riaghain

BB069

Ruaig

Kilmaluag

Cornaigbeg

Kirkapol

Rubha Tràigh
an Duin

Hough

Tiree

Kenovay

Gott

**Gott
Bay**

Kilkenneth

Moss

Scarinish

Middleton

Heylipol

Baugh

Barrapol

Crossapol

Heanish

Port Mor

Lochia
Phuill

BB065

**Hynish
Bay**

TIREE

Port
Bharrapol

Balephuil

Mannal

Balemartine

Chapel

Balephuil
Bay

Hynish

Oban to Iona 4 hrs. 15 mins.
(Summer Only)

Treshni

Treshnish
Isles

Cairn na
Burgh Beg

Fladda

Lunga

I N N E R

H E B R I D

Bac Mor or
Dutchman's Cap

Bac Beag

Port Snoig

Réidh
Eilean

Eilean
Annraidh

Rub
nan-C

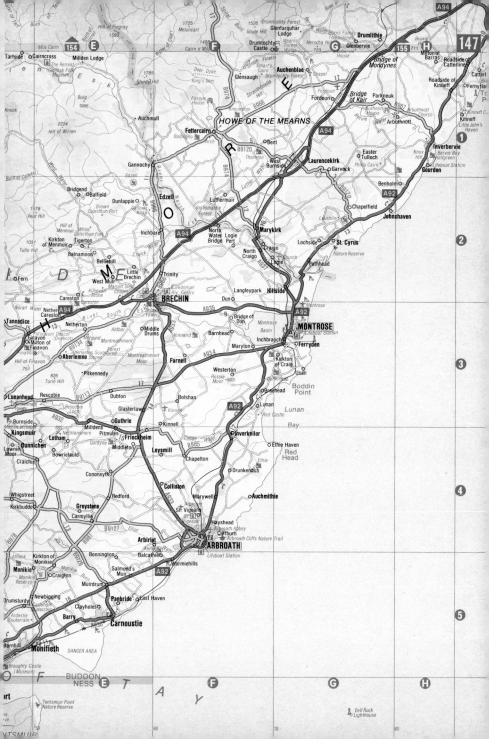

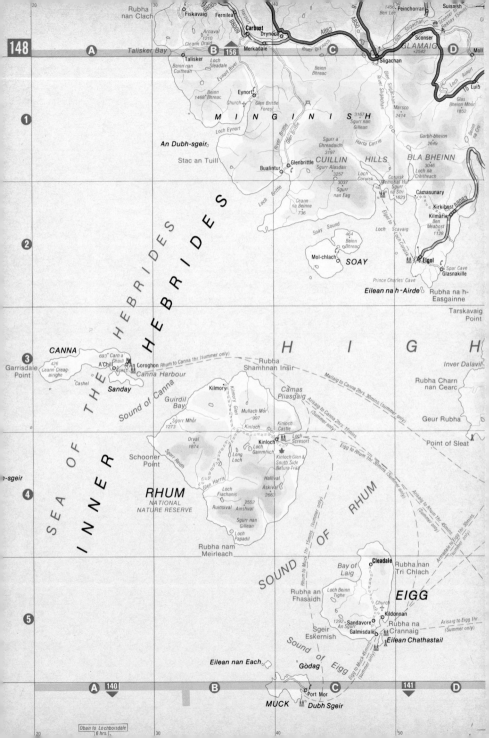

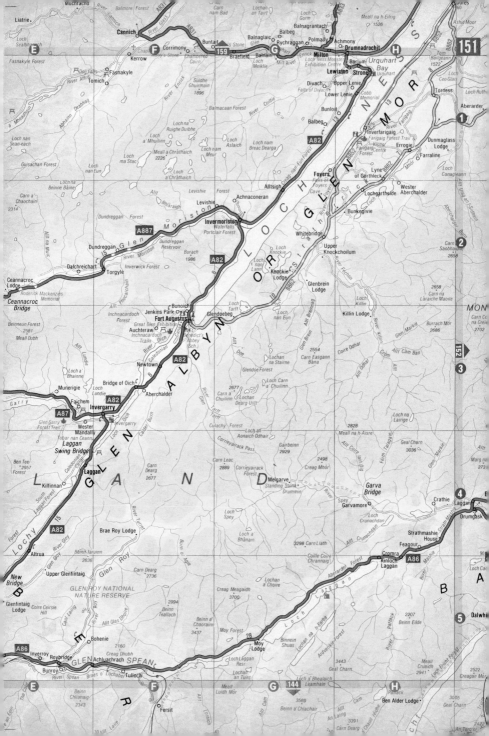

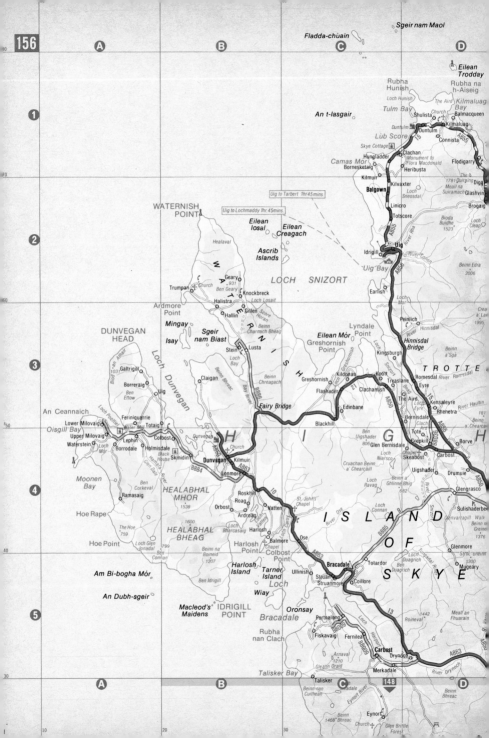

A   B   C   D

1

2

3

4

5

Sgeir nam Maol

Fladda-chùain

Eilean Trodday

Rubha Hunish
Loch Hunish
Tulm Bay
An t-Iasgair

Rubha na h-Aiseig
The Aird
Kilmaluag Bay
Shulista
Church
Balmacqueen
Kilmaluag

Duntulm   Duntulm
Lùb Score
Skye Cottage
Clachan
Monument to Flora Macdonald
Connista
Flodigarry

Camas Mòr
Hungladder
Bornesketaig
Heribusta

Kilmuir
Kilvaxter
Loch Sneosdal

1781 Quiraing
Meall na Suiramach
Digg
Glashvin

Balgown
Linicro
Totscore

Bioda Buidhe 1523
Loch Cleap

Brogaig

WATERNISH POINT

Uig to Tarbert 1hr 45mins.

Uig to Lochmaddy 1hr 45mins.

Eilean Iosal
Eilean Creagach

Ascrib Islands

Uig

Uig Bay
River Conon

Beinn Edra 2006

LOCH SNIZORT

Healaval
Geary 931
Ben Geary
Trumpan   Church
Knockbreck
Halistra
Loch Losait
Gillen
Sgeir Horan
Hallin

Earlish

Loch Mòr

Peinlich
River Hinnisdal

Crea a' Lai 1995

Ardmore Point
Mingay
Isay
Sgeir nam Biast

Beinn Charmach Bheag

Lusta
Stein
Loch Bay

Lyndale Point
Eilean Mòr
Greshornish Point

Hinnisdal Bridge

Kingsburgh

Beinn a' Sga

Beinn Edra

DUNVEGAN HEAD

Loch Dunvegan

Claigan
Beinn Bhreac
Bay River
Beinn Chreagach

Greshornish
Flashader

Kildonan
Klott
Treaslane
Eyre

Romesdal River Romesdal
The Aird

TROTTE

Galtrigill
Borreraig
Ben Ettow
Uig
Feriniquarrie
An Ceannaich
Lower Milovaig
Upper Milovaig
Waterstein
Oisgill Bay
Loch Mòr
Borrodale
Lephin
Holmisdale
Skinidin
Black House
Glen Dale

Totaig
Water Mill

Dunvegan
Church
Kilmuir
Lonmore

Fairy Bridge
Edinbane
Blackhill

Clachamish
21

The Aird
Loch Eyre
Bernisdale
Glen Bernisdale
Tote
Skeabost
Chapel
Carbost
Crepkill

Kensaleyre
Rhenetra
River Haultin

Borve

Drumuie
Uigshader

Moonen Bay
Ramasaig
Hoe Rape
The Hoe 759
Hoe Point

HEALABHAL MHOR 1538
HEALABHAL BHEAG
1600
Loch Glen Jonadal
Ben Connan
799

B884
Colbost

Roskhill
Roag
Orbost
Ardroag
Vatten

St. John's Chapel
Ose

Loch Bharcasaig
Harlosh
Balmore
Harlosh Point
Colbost Point
Harlosh Island
Tarner Island
Loch Bracadale

Am Bi-bogha Mòr
An Dubh-sgeir
Beinn na Boineid 1207
Ben Idrigill

ISLAND OF SKYE

River Ose
Ullinish
Struan
Struanmore
Bracadale
Totardor
Coillore

Loch Ravag
Cruachan Beinn a' Chearcaill

Loch Duagrich
Ben Duagrich

Glenmore
Mugeary

Stroc-bheinn

Macleod's Maidens
IDRIGILL POINT

Wiay
Oronsay

Rubha nan Clach
Fiskavaig
Ferniiea

Bracadale
Portnalong

13
1442 Roineval

Meall an Fhuarain

Carbost
Drynoch
Merkadale

River Drynoch

Meall an

Talisker Bay
Talisker

148

Beinn Breac

Arnaval 1210
Gleann Oraid

Eynort
Church
Beinn 1468 Bhreac
Glen Brittle

A   B   C   D

E   F   164   G   H

Peterburn   962   Naast   Inverewe

Port Erradale   North   River Sand   Loch na nan Liagh   Loch Bad a' Chreamh   Poole   157

Loch na Curra   A832   Loch Ewe   Kerr

Big Sand   Caolas Beag   Lonemore   Mial   Loch Tollaidh   Tollie Farm

Longa Island   B8021   Strath   Loch Airigh a' Phuill   Flowerdale Walks   Meall an Doirein   1381   1

Smithstown   Gairloch   Starbhach Forest Walk   Tollie Path

Loch Gairloch   Heritage   Eilean Horrisdale   Charlestown   A832

Port Henderson   Airdo   B8056   Loch Shieldaig   River Kerry   Loch Bad an Sgalaig   Abhainn a' Gharbh Choire

Badachro   Loch nan Eun   Shieldaig

Opinan   Loch Clair   Loch Gaineamhach

South Erradale   River Erradale   Loch Braigh Horrisdale   W   E   S   T

Redpoint   Allt a' Ghiubhais   Loch Gaineamhach

Sgeir Eirin   Baosbheinn   2869

Eilean Flodigarry   Sgeir Ghlas   Meall na h-Uamha   Shieldaig   Beinn Bhreac   2031   Loch a' Bhealaich   2

Staffin Island   Sgeir na Trian   Lochan Sgeireach   Beinn Alligin   2

enscholl   Garrafad   Craig   Craig River   Lower Diabaig   Loch na h-Uamhaig

Staffin   Loch Torridon   Upper Diabaig   Loch Diabaigas Airde   158

Kilt Rock   Rubha na Fearn   Fearnmore

iachan   Elishader   Meall Waterfall   Arinacrinachd   Allt na Diabaig   Inveralligin   Rechullin

Maligar   Valtos   Loch a' Bhraige   Fearnbeg   Kenmore   Loch a' Chracaich   Balgy   3

Marishader   Rubha nam Brathairean   PORT an FHEARAINN   RONA   Cuaig   Alltan Dubh   Ardheslaig   Shieldaig Island   Shieldaig   NTS

Garros   Rubha Chuaig   Allt an t-Strathain   Loch Shieldaig   Torridon

Leac Tressirnish   Kalnakill   Croic-bheinn   Coire   Ben-damph

THE STORR   Eilean Garbh   Lonbain   1619   Glensheildaig Forest

ISH   2358   Old Man of Storr   Garbh Eilean   An Dubh-loch

Bearreraig Bay   Eilean Tigh   Loch a' Sguirr   Loch nan Eun   Loch Lundie

Holm Island   Eilean Fladday   River Applecross   Loch Coire Attadale   Loch Gaineamhach

Loch Leathan   Loch Fada   Manish Point   Loch Arnish   Torran   Chapel   Applecross Forest   2938   Beinn Bhan   Loch Coultrie   4

Arnish   Sgurr a' Chaorachain   2539   Rassal Nature Reserve

hachirk   Brochel   Applecross Bay   Applecross   Milton   Kishorn

Torvaig   Chapel   Glame   RAASAY   Camusteel   Camusterrach   Ardarroch

Portree   Penifiler   Ben Tianavaig   1355   Culduie   Loch Braigh an Achaidh   Achintraid

Heatherfield   Dun Caan   1455   Ard-dubh   Loch Kishorn

Camastianavaig   Holoman Bay   Rubha na Leac   Toscaig   Loch Maol Fharochaid   Kishorn Island   Stromeferry   5

Conordan   Tianavaig Bay   Oskaig   St Molnag's Chapel   Raasay Walks   Eilean na Bà   Ardaneaskan   Plockton   Stromeferry

Lower Ollach   Clachan   North Fearns   Eilean Beag   Meall Loch Airigh Alasdair   Loch Carron   Craig   Achmore

Upper Ollach   Inverarish   Suishnish Hill   CROWLIN ISLANDS   Uags   Plockton   Drumbuie

Gedintailor   Balmeanach   Eyre   Eyre Point   Eilean Mor   Duirinish

Peinchorran   Suisnish   Caolas Mòr   Sgeir Dhearg   Longay   Black Island   Erbusaig   Badicaul   Auchtertyre

GLAMAIG   Sconser   Moll   Scalpay House   SCALPAY   Pabay   149   Kyle of Lochalsh   Balmacara   Kirton

Sligachan   Guillamon Island   Plock of Kyle   Kyleakin   Loch Alsh

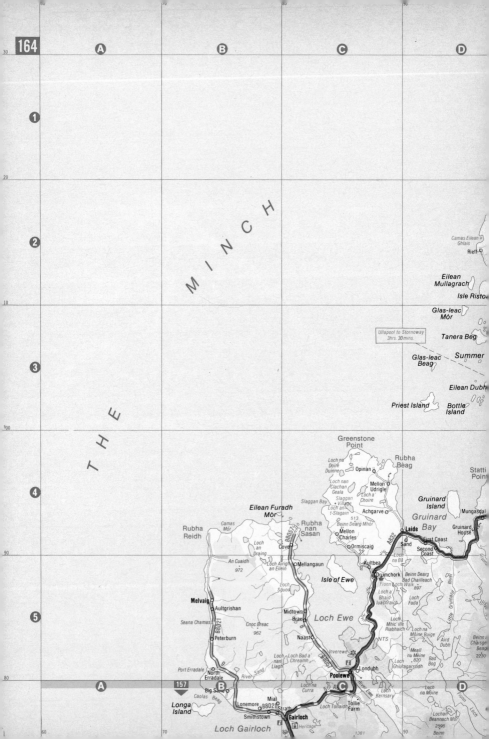

A   B   C   D

1

20

2

T H E   M I N C H

10

3

Ullapool to Stornoway
3hrs. 30 mins.

00

4

Camas Eilean
Ghlais

Rieff

Eilean
Mullagrach

Isle Risto

Glas-leac
Mòr

Tanera Beg

Glas-leac
Beag

Summer

Eilean Dubh

Priest Island

Bottle
Island

Greenstone
Point

Rubha
Beag

Statti
Point

Loch na
Doire
Duimne

Opinan

Loch nan
Clachan
Geala

Mellon O
Udrigle

Loch a'
Choire

Gruinard
Island

Slaggan Bay

Slaggan
Village

Achgarve

Mungasdal

Eilean Furadh
Mòr

Loch an
t-Slagain

Beinn Dearg Mòr

Gruinard
Bay

Rubha
nan
Sasan

513

Mellon
Charles

Laide

First Coast

Gruinard
House

Rubha
Reidh

Camas
Mòr

Loch an
Draing

Cove

Ormiscaig

Sand

Second
Coast

Loch
na Bâ

An Cuaidh
972

Loch Airigh
an Eilein

Mellangaun

Aultbea

Druimchork

Beinn Dearg
Bad Chailleach
897

5

Melvaig

Aultgrishan

Isle of Ewe

Loch
Squod

Fionn Loch Walk

Loch a'
Bhaid-
luachraich

Loch
Fada

Seana Chamas

Midtown

Brae

Loch Ewe

Loch
Mhic'ille
Riabhaich

Loch na
Mòine Buige

Aird
Dubh

Beinn a'
Chaisge
Beag
2230

Peterburn

Cnoc Breac
962

Naast

NTS

Meall
na Mèine
820

Bad
Bog

90

80

Port Erradale

North
Erradale

River

Sand

Loch
nan
Liagh

Loch Bad a'
Chreamh

Inverewe

Loch
Ghiuragarstidh

Poolewe

Londubh

A

B

C

D

157

Longa
Island

Big Sand

Caolas
Beag

Lonemore

Mial

Strath

B802

Loch na
Curra

Loch Tollaidh

Tollie
Farm

River Ewe

Loch
Kernsary

Loch
na Mòine

Lochan
Beannach Mòr
2595

Smithstown

Gairloch

Heritage

Loch Gairloch

1381

Beinn

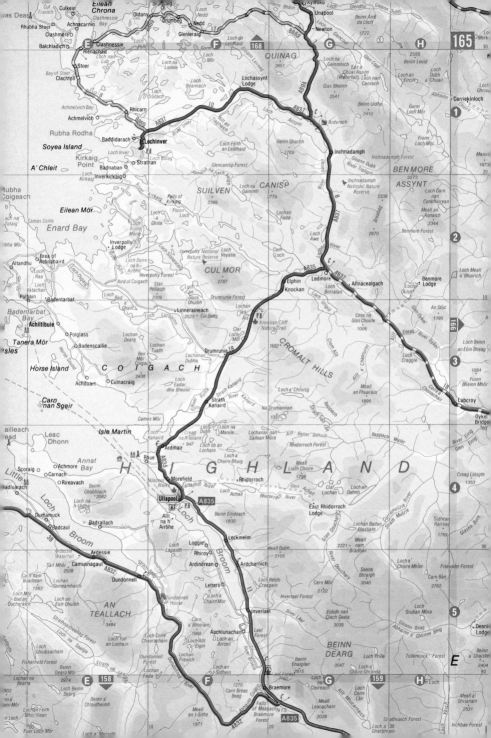

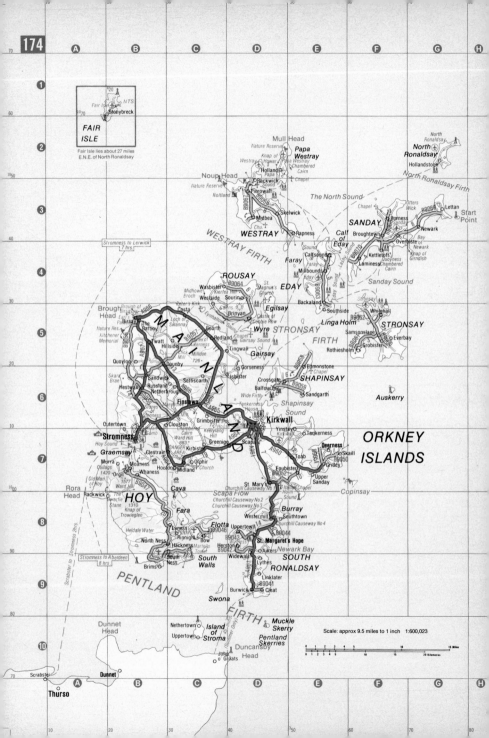

FAIR
ISLE

Fair Isle lies about 27 miles
E.N.E. of North Ronaldsay

ORKNEY
ISLANDS

Scale: approx 9.5 miles to 1 inch   1:600,023

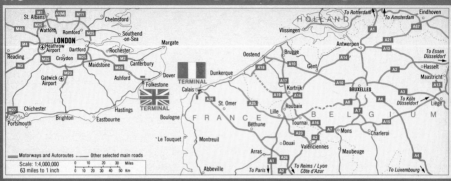

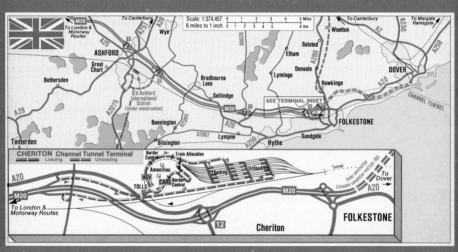

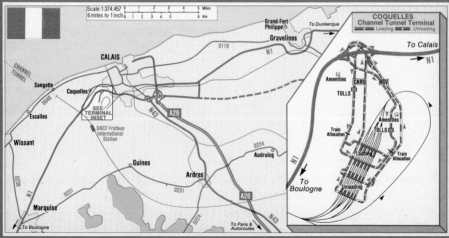

ROUTE PLANNING

| 180 | 181 |
| 178 | 179 |

Thurso

Inverness Aberdeen
Fort William
Perth
GLASGOW
Edinburgh
Ayr
Carlisle Newcastle
Kendal Middlesbrough
Bradford Leeds York Hull
Holyhead Liverpool MANCHESTER Doncaster Lincoln
Sheffield Nottingham
Shrewsbury Derby Leicester Norwich
Aberystwyth BIRMINGHAM Coventry Cambridge Ipswich
Worcester Gloucester Oxford Harwich
Swansea LONDON Southend
Cardiff Bristol Reading Dover
Salisbury Brighton
Exeter Southampton Portsmouth
Plymouth
Penzance

Mileage Chart

PRIMARY ROUTES, Shown in green throughout this Atlas, are a national network of recommended through routes which complement the motorway system. Selected places of major traffic importance are known as Primary Route Destinations and on road signs have a green background.

The distances for the mileage chart have been compiled by using a combination of Primary Routes and Motorways between any two towns shown.

To find the distance between any two Towns shown.
Follow the horizontal line of one Town and the vertical line of the other, at the intersection read off mileage.

i.e.: Horizontal—LONDON
Intersection 205 miles
Vertical—LIVERPOOL

ABERDEEN
439 ABERYSTWYTH
175 314 AYR
403 116 275 BIRMINGHAM
326 169 193 124 BRADFORD
566 257 463 169 263 BRIGHTON
503 125 368 88 215 139 BRISTOL
451 213 366 102 156 117 167 CAMBRIDGE
513 109 389 106 233 180 43 201 CARDIFF
218 224 91 193 107 370 275 256 278 CARLISLE
437 134 303 19 124 157 102 84 129 215 COVENTRY
404 137 274 39 88 188 134 99 159 184 43 DERBY
340 192 339 95 39 232 184 117 210 147 94 57 DONCASTER
570 315 464 169 284 77 194 118 233 393 180 208 244 DOVER
125 340 73 284 198 466 374 326 367 91 303 266 212 441 EDINBURGH
569 199 442 161 282 166 75 232 118 351 166 213 257 242 439 EXETER
186 422 136 391 305 566 478 456 493 198 413 382 345 591 132 548 FORT WILLIAM
145 322 35 291 205 468 378 355 393 98 313 282 245 497 46 449 102 GLASGOW
450 108 326 52 171 152 35 132 56 240 60 86 149 189 331 107 438 338 GLOUCESTER
515 281 434 170 224 130 203 64 234 326 152 167 185 129 394 262 524 419 179 HARWICH
443 107 316 151 158 322 207 232 209 225 167 156 169 358 316 279 423 323 180 331 HOLYHEAD
357 235 250 134 68 259 216 134 239 157 122 100 46 254 230 290 357 255 195 204 216 HULL
104 480 202 449 353 620 538 481 551 246 458 421 367 595 154 607 63 167 496 549 481 384 INVERNESS
505 267 420 156 210 125 206 55 240 311 138 155 171 127 381 264 510 409 177 21 307 169 536 IPSWICH
262 182 135 151 62 324 235 215 232 44 170 136 94 344 135 307 242 142 200 279 180 127 290 268 KENDAL
316 171 202 120 9 256 209 144 226 111 117 75 30 275 190 279 311 208 167 208 162 60 345 197 68 LEEDS
407 155 305 43 90 163 118 70 140 214 24 28 73 183 262 189 412 312 83 134 182 96 431 125 166 97 LEICESTER
372 206 269 88 78 307 170 89 192 178 76 52 41 206 247 341 376 276 135 152 196 44 402 132 140 70 92 LINCOLN
333 102 206 99 67 267 170 179 169 115 113 87 89 294 306 240 313 213 142 243 95 126 361 236 75 73 110 118 LIVERPOOL
335 126 208 67 37 252 167 159 188 117 99 59 50 273 208 239 315 215 122 223 121 98 363 71 72 43 95 85 33 MANCHESTER
271 232 185 174 68 316 265 196 267 94 175 130 82 316 146 337 278 192 200 262 224 87 300 253 80 62 154 125 134 104 MIDDLESBROUGH
232 261 149 209 98 345 300 232 312 58 209 165 115 350 105 369 237 139 263 296 257 123 259 287 89 96 188 153 167 136 38 NEWCASTLE
476 270 371 163 185 174 229 62 256 280 142 136 142 169 351 284 478 378 193 72 289 145 505 43 249 178 112 110 217 177 221 252 NORWICH
381 155 279 53 78 191 140 84 165 188 50 15 46 210 256 332 386 286 108 148 177 83 410 140 141 172 28 37 103 67 128 159 118 NOTTINGHAM
485 151 358 61 167 106 72 92 106 267 56 99 136 143 358 151 465 365 50 134 207 169 513 128 223 162 71 153 168 157 218 253 159 102 OXFORD
680 310 553 273 394 279 181 343 230 463 278 325 369 355 551 111 663 561 219 374 340 401 715 379 419 391 301 353 342 351 449 481 396 324 361 PENZANCE
84 362 92 336 245 486 412 370 415 137 346 309 245 485 43 487 104 58 377 439 362 271 112 424 181 233 326 290 262 254 169 148 394 298 404 598 PERTH
616 241 485 203 325 206 113 274 159 394 209 253 300 284 485 43 592 490 150 305 322 332 648 305 348 323 231 283 282 281 379 412 328 255 193 74 529 PLYMOUTH
575 217 448 147 254 47 92 132 138 357 132 175 231 123 448 122 555 455 114 161 291 253 603 158 308 247 166 209 254 237 315 360 192 191 82 235 486 163 PORTSMOUTH
526 181 399 103 213 79 79 90 103 308 90 136 184 170 402 138 506 406 71 129 247 209 559 146 264 295 149 141 25 250 445 181 58 READING
525 178 400 121 228 92 51 140 96 309 113 159 207 158 400 91 502 407 75 177 248 233 555 177 265 302 132 187 213 195 287 318 200 152 65 204 443 132 41 57 SALISBURY
355 173 235 79 41 225 166 121 191 156 50 30 26 268 230 345 292 139 185 164 65 384 176 96 36 64 40 100 133 142 17 361 273 293 228 186 203 SHEFFIELD
390 73 263 46 100 209 102 140 107 172 62 67 114 246 363 175 370 276 78 204 104 163 418 195 125 104 77 123 65 67 170 200 196 84 103 286 309 218 195 147 151 85 SHREWSBURY
543 198 410 108 235 61 74 129 122 357 124 170 226 111 477 118 529 429 110 106 273 233 572 162 273 336 120 136 235 221 268 303 162 165 81 217 461 146 20 46 25 209 147 SOUTHAMPTON
520 258 431 152 220 85 177 63 211 340 129 168 185 98 395 236 526 438 151 61 313 200 549 97 279 296 150 192 99 160 106 331 238 226 155 162 154 127 SOUTHEND
368 112 241 44 73 217 127 137 140 150 92 32 74 236 241 202 348 248 94 94 133 71 396 179 121 75 55 87 56 38 141 176 171 50 105 313 267 224 147 159 11 35 183 192 STOKE
504 74 377 124 220 218 81 236 41 286 139 163 209 284 377 154 484 384 91 279 202 260 532 229 241 325 163 212 106 138 422 453 273 210 167 289 302 330 275 277 139 72 SWANSEA
212 588 310 557 461 728 644 589 659 354 563 539 470 703 263 715 170 276 604 657 589 492 108 644 398 453 637 610 518 621 623 221 756 710 662 865 492 526 680 667 504 640 THURSO
431 95 304 30 135 163 119 213 43 68 117 197 284 314 411 317 29 181 151 166 458 174 146 66 57 248 350 177 146 95 105 165 105 48 124 158 69 97 567 WORCESTER
312 211 207 129 34 269 187 289 314 211 213 184 37 342 214 81 213 194 437 254 216 47 108 73 96 46 83 176 84 474 400 230 231 267 223 214 114 256 449 164 YORK
497 205 396 118 202 53 117 57 151 305 107 126 163 73 372 170 503 403 102 79 260 185 527 76 264 195 101 132 205 185 245 276 114 126 54 182 416 214 74 39 97 165 188 160 76 43 165 188 634 106 207 LONDON

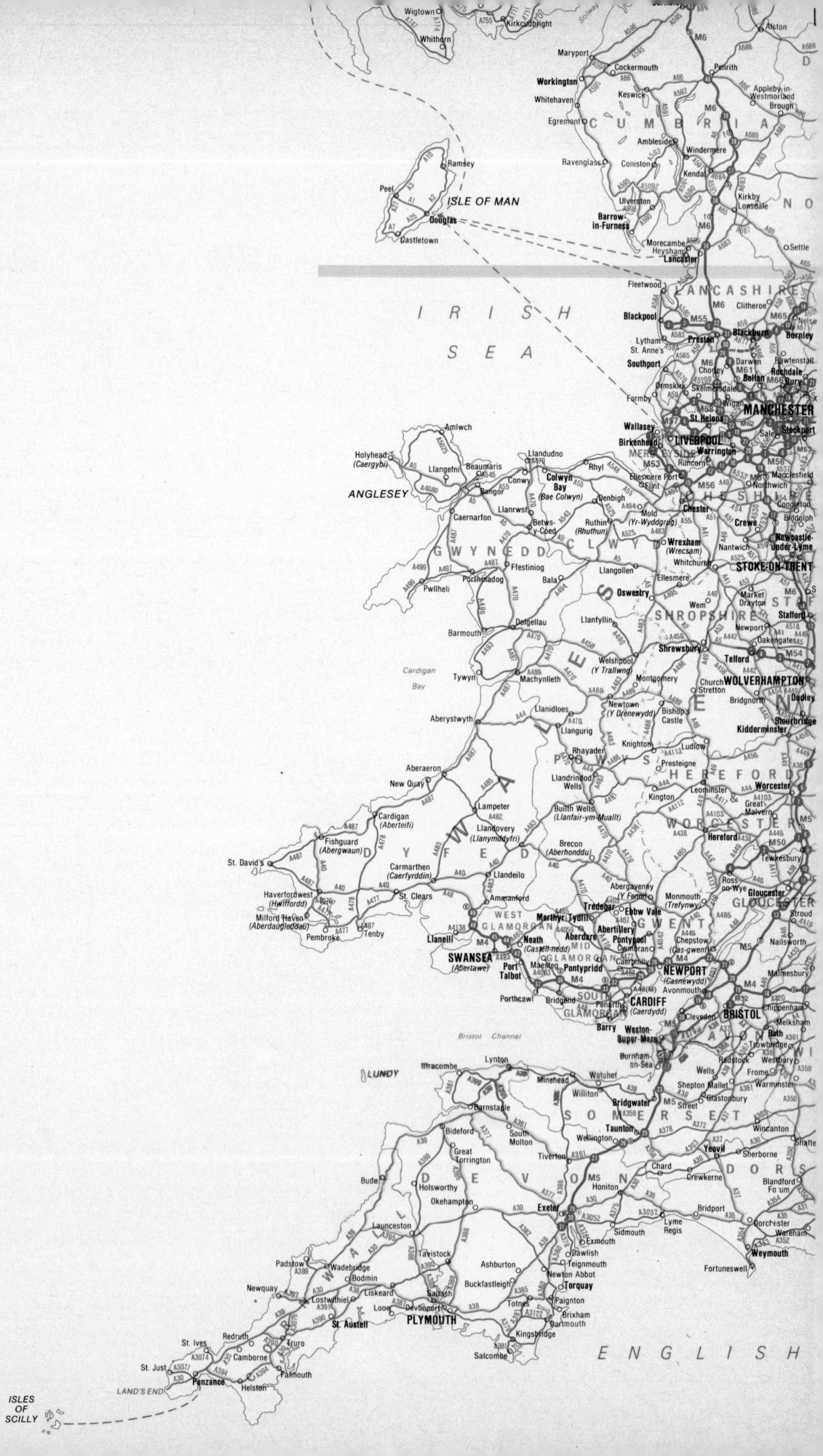

Wigtown
Kirkcudbright
Whithorn
Maryport
Cockermouth
Penrith
Appleby-in-Westmorland
Brough
Workington
Keswick
Whitehaven
Egremont
C U M B R I A
Ambleside
Windermere
Ravenglass
Coniston
Kendal
Kirkby Lonsdale
Ramsey
Peel
ISLE OF MAN
Ulverston
Barrow-in-Furness
Morecambe
Heysham
Lancaster
Settle
Douglas
Castletown

I R I S H   S E A

Fleetwood
L A N C A S H I R E
Blackpool
Clitheroe
Burnley
Lytham St. Anne's
Preston
Blackburn
Darwen
Rawtenstall
Rochdale
Southport
Chorley
Bolton
Bury
Skelmersdale
Formby
St. Helens
MANCHESTER
Stockport
Wallasey
Salford
Birkenhead
LIVERPOOL
Warrington
Amlwch
Holyhead (Caergybi)
Llandudno
Rhyl
Runcorn
Macclesfield
Northwich
Llangefni
Beaumaris
Colwyn Bay (Bae Colwyn)
Ellesmere Port
Chester
Crewe
ANGLESEY
Bangor
Conwy
Denbigh
Flint
Mold (Yr Wyddgrug)
Newcastle-under-Lyme
Caernarfon
Llanrwst
Betws-y-Coed
Ruthin (Rhuthun)
Wrexham (Wrecsam)
G W Y N E D D
C L W Y D
Whitchurch
STOKE-ON-TRENT
Porthmadog
Ffestiniog
Bala
Llangollen
Oswestry
Ellesmere
Wem
Market Drayton
Stafford
Pwllheli
S H R O P S H I R E
Newport
Oakengates
Barmouth
Dolgellau
Llanfyllin
Welshpool (Y Trallwng)
Shrewsbury
Telford
Cardigan Bay
Tywyn
Machynlleth
Montgomery
Church Stretton
WOLVERHAMPTON
Dudley
P O W Y S
Llanidloes
Newtown (Y Drenewydd)
Bishop's Castle
Bridgnorth
Stourbridge
Aberystwyth
Llangurig
Rhayader
Knighton
Kidderminster
Llandrindod Wells
Presteigne
H E R E F O R D
Worcester
New Quay
Aberaeron
Leominster
Great Malvern
WORCESTER
Lampeter (Llanbedr Pont Steffan)
Builth Wells (Llanfair-ym-Muallt)
D Y F E D
Cardigan (Aberteifi)
Llandovery (Llanymddyfri)
Brecon (Aberhonddu)
Hereford
Tewkesbury
Fishguard (Abergwaun)
Ross-on-Wye
St. David's
Carmarthen (Caerfyrddin)
Llandeilo
Abergavenny (Y Fenni)
Monmouth (Trefynwy)
Gloucester
GLOUCESTER
Haverfordwest (Hwlffordd)
St. Clears
Ammanford
Merthyr Tydfil
Tredegar
Ebbw Vale
Chepstow (Cas-gwent)
Milford Haven (Aberdaugleddau)
WEST GLAMORGAN
Llanelli
Neath (Castell-nedd)
Aberdare
Abertillery
Pontypool
Stroud
Nailsworth
Pembroke
Tenby
SWANSEA (Abertawe)
Port Talbot
MID GLAMORGAN
Pontypridd
Caerphilly (Caerffili)
NEWPORT (Casnewydd)
Malmesbury
G W E N T
M4
Porthcawl
Bridgend (Penybont)
SOUTH GLAMORGAN
CARDIFF (Caerdydd)
Avonmouth
Clevedon
BRISTOL
Bath
Chippenham
Barry
Weston-Super-Mare
Bristol Channel
Portishead
Melksham
Ilfracombe
Lynton
Burnham-on-Sea
Radstock
Westbury
LUNDY
Minehead
Watchet
Williton
Wells
Shepton Mallet
Glastonbury
Frome
Warminster
Barnstaple
Bridgwater
Taunton
S O M E R S E T
Wincanton
South Molton
Wellington
Yeovil
Sherborne
Great Torrington
Bideford
Tiverton
Chard
Crewkerne
D O R S E T
Bude
Holsworthy
Honiton
Blandford Forum
Okehampton
Exeter
Axminster
Bridport
Dorchester
Wareham
Launceston
D E V O N
Sidmouth
Lyme Regis
Weymouth
Fortuneswell
Tavistock
Ashburton
Dawlish
Teignmouth
Padstow
Wadebridge
Newton Abbot
Torquay
Newquay
Bodmin
Liskeard
Saltash
Totnes
Paignton
Brixham
C O R N W A L L
Lostwithiel
Looe
Devonport
PLYMOUTH
Kingsbridge
Salcombe
St. Ives
Redruth
Truro
St. Austell
E N G L I S H
St. Just
Camborne
Penzance
Falmouth
Helston
ISLES OF SCILLY
LAND'S END

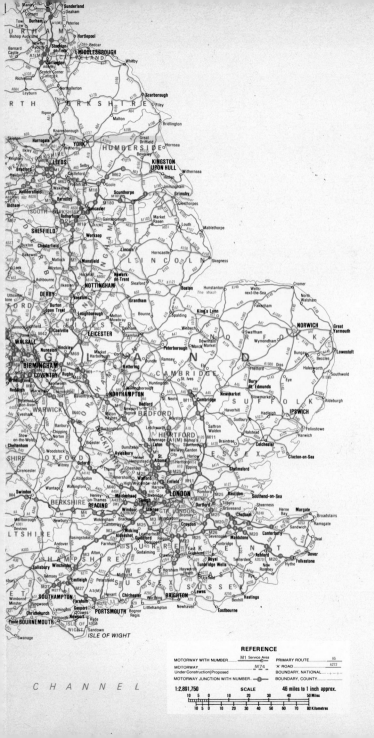

REFERENCE

MOTORWAY WITH NUMBER	M1 Service Area	PRIMARY ROUTE A5
MOTORWAY M74		'A' ROAD A272
Under Construction/Proposed		BOUNDARY, NATIONAL. _._._._._
MOTORWAY JUNCTION WITH NUMBER...		BOUNDARY, COUNTY..........

1:2,891,750   SCALE   46 miles to 1 inch approx.

10   5   0   10   20   30   40   50 Miles
10   5   0   10   20   30   40   50   60   70   80 Kilometres

CHANNEL

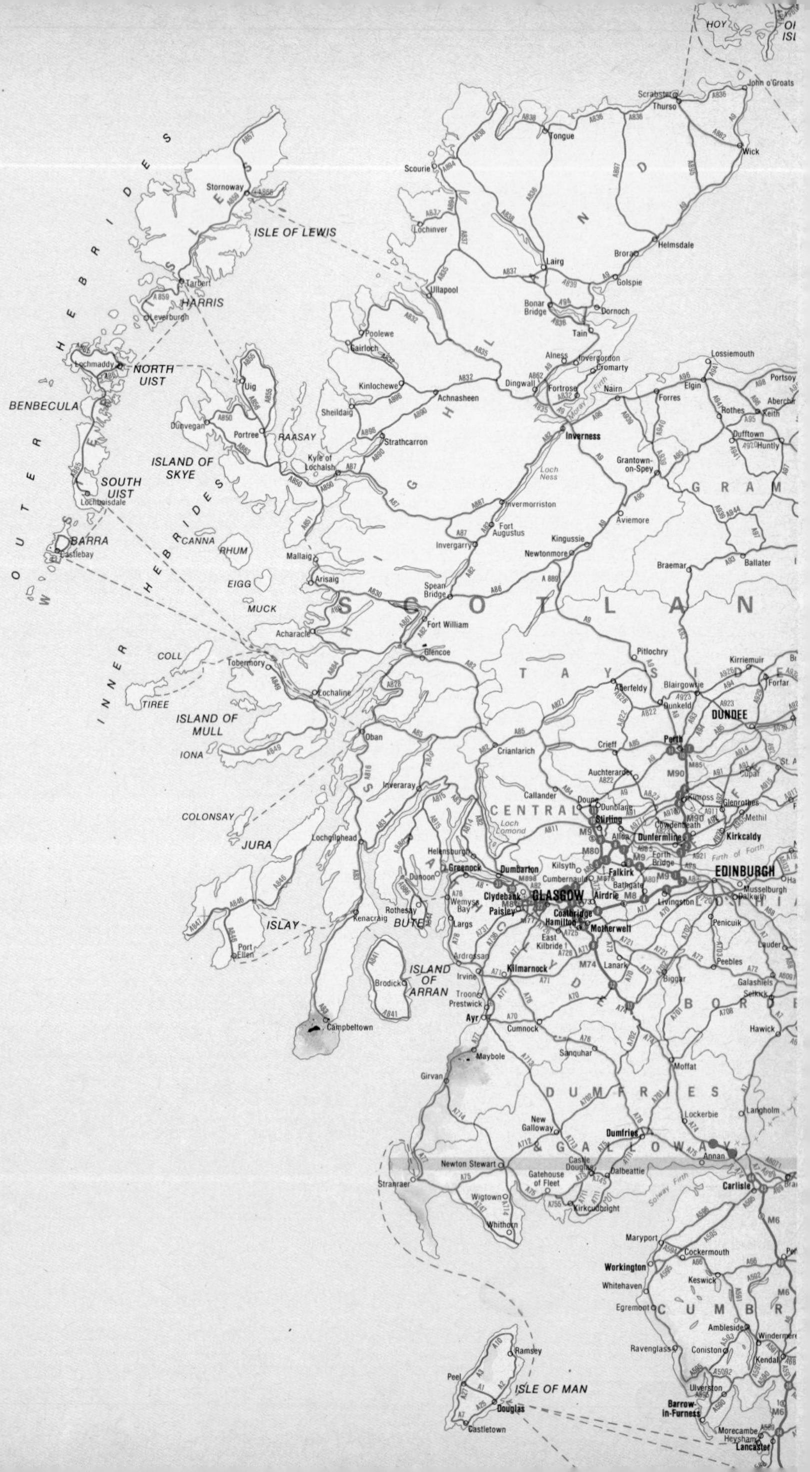

HOY

ISL

John o'Groats

Scrabster
Thurso
Wick

Tongue

Scourie
Lochinver
HIGHLAND

Stornoway
ISLE OF LEWIS
Ullapool
Brora
Helmsdale

Lairg
Golspie

TARBERT
HARRIS
Leverburgh
Poolewe
Bonar
Bridge
Dornoch
Tain

Gairloch
Alness
Invergordon
Cromarty
Lossiemouth
Portsoy

NORTH
UIST
Uig
Kinlochewe
Dingwall
Nairn
Forres
Elgin
Aberchy
Keith

BENBECULA
Dunvegan
Sheildaig
Fortrose
Rothes
Dufftown
Huntly

Portree
RAASAY
Strathcarron
Inverness

SOUTH
UIST
ISLAND OF
SKYE
Kyle of
Lochalsh
Loch
Ness
Grantown-
on-Spey
GRAM

Lochboisdale
Invermorriston
Aviemore

BARRA
Castlebay
CANNA
RHUM
Fort
Augustus
Kingussie

Invergarry
Newtonmore
Braemar
Ballater

EIGG
MUCK
Mallaig
Arisaig
Spean
Bridge

Acharacle
Fort William
SCOTLAND

COLL
Tobermory
Glencoe
Pitlochry
Kirriemuir
Forfar

TIREE
Lochaline
Aberfeldy
Blairgowrie
Dunkeld
DUNDEE

IONA
ISLAND OF
MULL
Oban
Crianlarich
Crieff
Perth

COLONSAY
Inveraray
Auchterarder
CENTRAL
Callander
Doune
Methil

JURA
Lochgilphead
Loch
Lomond
Stirling
Dunfermline
Kirkcaldy

ISLAY
Helensburgh
Dumbarton
Kilsyth
Cumbernauld
Falkirk
EDINBURGH
Musselburgh

Port
Ellen
Greenock
Clydebank
GLASGOW
Airdrie
Bathgate
Livingston
Penicuik

Dunoon
Wemyss
Bay
Paisley
Coatbridge
Hamilton
Motherwell

BUTE
Rothesay
Largs
East
Kilbride
Lanark
Biggar
Peebles
Galashiels
Selkirk

ISLAND OF
ARRAN
Brodick
Ardrossan
Irvine
Kilmarnock
M74
Lauder
Hawick

Kenacraig
Troon
Prestwick
Ayr
Cumnock
Moffat
Lockerbie
Langholm

Campbeltown
Maybole
Sanquhar
DUMFRIES
& GALLOWAY
Dumfries
Annan

Girvan
New
Galloway
Castle
Douglas
Dalbeattie
Carlisle

Newton Stewart
Gatehouse
of Fleet
M6

Stranraer
Wigtown
Kirkcudbright
Maryport
Cockermouth

Whithorn
Workington
Keswick
CUMBR

Whitehaven
Egremont
Ambleside
Windermere

Ramsey
Ravenglass
Coniston
Kendal

Peel
ISLE OF MAN
Ulverston
Barrow-
In-Furness

Douglas
Morecambe
Lancaster

Castletown

SHETLAND
ISLANDS

UNST

YELL

FETLAR

WHALSAY

FOULA

Scalloway Lerwick

BRESSAY

FAIR ISLE

WESTRAY

EDAY

SANDAY

ROUSAY

STRONSAY

SHAPINSAY

Stromness Kirkwall

ORKNEY
ISLANDS

HOY

SOUTH
RONALDSAY

Scrabster John o' Groats

Thurso

Banff Fraserburgh

Turriff Peterhead

Oldmeldrum Ellon

Inverurie

ABERDEEN

Banchory Peterculter

Stonehaven

Inverbervie

Montrose

Arbroath

Carnoustie

ndrews

ittenweem

orth Berwick

Dunbar

ddington

Eyemouth

Duns Berwick-upon-Tweed

Coldstream

NORTH

SEA

HOLY
ISLAND

Kelso

Wooler

Jedburgh

Alnwick

Amble

NORTHUMBERLAND

Ashington

Morpeth

Bedlington

Blyth

Whitley Bay

NEWCASTLE
UPON TYNE

Tynemouth

South Shields

Hexham

Gateshead

Washington

Stanley Sunderland

Seaham

Alston

Consett

Durham

Peterlee

Tow Law

Bishop Auckland

Hartlepool

Appleby-in-
Westmorland

Brough

Barnard
Castle

Redcar

Stockton-
on-Tees

MIDDLESBROUGH

Whitby

Darlington

Richmond

Scotch Corner

Catterick

Scarborough

Kirkby
Lonsdale

Leyburn

Northallerton

Filey

Settle

Ripon

Thirsk

NORTH YORKSHIRE

Malton

Bridlington

Skipton

Knaresborough

Great
Driffield

Harrogate

YORK

Hornsea

Cities, Towns, Villages, Hamlets & Locations INDEX

(1) A strict alphabetical order is used e.g. Abbotstone follows Abbots' Salford but precedes Abbots Worthy.

(2) The map reference given refers to the actual map square in which the town spot or built-up area is located and not to the place name.

(3) Where two places of the same name occur the appropriate County or Region is added. However, where two places of the same name occur in the same County or Region, the nearest large town is also given e.g. Acharn—4E 145 (nr. Aberfeldy, Tayside) indicates that Acharn is located in square 4E on page 145 and is situated near Aberfeldy in the Region of Tayside.

(4) Only one reference is given although due to page overlaps the place may appear on more than one page.

COUNTIES and REGIONS with the abbreviations used in this index

Avon	Derbyshire : Derbys.	Greater London : London	Isles of Scilly : Scilly	Nottinghamshire : Notts.	Surrey
Bedfordshire : Beds.	Devon	Greater Manchester : Manchester	Kent	Orkney	Tayside
Berkshire : Berks.	Dorset	Gwent	Lancashire : Lancs.	Oxfordshire : Oxon	Tyne & Wear
Borders	Dumfries & Galloway	Gwynedd	Leicestershire : Leics.	Powys	Warwickshire : Warwicks.
Buckinghamshire : Bucks.	: Dum & Gall.	Hampshire : Hants.	Lincolnshire : Lincs.	Shetland	Western Isles : Western I.
Cambridgeshire : Cambs.	Durham	Hereford & Worcester	Lothian	Shropshire : Shrops.	West Glamorgan : W Glam.
Central	Dyfed	: Here & Worcs.	Merseyside	Somerset : Som	West Midlands : W Midlands
Cheshire : Ches.	East Sussex : E Suss.	Hertfordshire : Herts.	Mid Glamorgan : Mid Glam.	South Glamorgan : S Glam.	West Sussex : W Suss.
Cleveland	Essex	Highland : H'land	Norfolk : Norf.	South Yorkshire : S Yorks.	West Yorkshire : W Yorks.
Clwyd	Fife	Humberside	Northamptonshire : Northants.	Staffordshire : Staffs.	Wiltshire : Wilts.
Cornwall : Corn.	Gloucestershire : Glous.	Isle of Man	Northumberland : Northmb.	Strathclyde : S'clyde	
Cumbria	Grampian	Isle of Wight : I.O.W.	North Yorkshire : N Yorks.	Suffolk : Suff.	

Abbas Combe.—1C 14
Abberley.—1B 50
Abberley Common.—1B 50
Abberton.—1G 45
(Essex)
Abberton.—2D 51
(Hereford & Worcester)
Abberwick.—3F 123
Abbess Roding.—1B 44
Abbey.—2E 13
Abbeycwmhir.—3F 59
Abbeydale.—4D 88
Abbeydale Park.—4D 88
Abbey Dore.—4F 49
Abbey Hulton.—3D 74
Abbey St Bathans.—3D 132
Abbeystead.—4C 99
Abbeytown.—4C 114
Abbey Village.—3D 92
Abbey Wood.—3F 31
Abbots Bickington.—2D 11
Abbots Bromley.—5E 75
Abbotsbury.—5A 14
Abbotsham.—3A 22
Abbotskerswell.—3E 9
Abbots Langley.—2D 43
Abbots Leigh.—5D 58
Abbotsley.—2B 54
Abbots Morton.—2E 51
Abbots Ripton.—5B 66
Abbot's Salford.—2E 51
Abbotstone.—5D 28
Abbots Worthy.—5C 28
Abbotts Ann.—4B 28
Abcott.—3A 60
Abdon.—2C 60
Abenhall.—1E 39
Aber.—3D 47
(Dyfed)
Aber.—3F 83
(Gwynedd)
Aberaeron.—1D 46
Aberaman.—2D 37
Aberangell.—5H 71
Abererard.—3C 46
Aberarder.—1A 152

Aberargie.—2D 138
Aberarth.—1D 47
Aberavon.—3D 36
Aber-banc.—3C 46
Aberbargoed.—3H 37
Aberbeeg.—2A 38
Aber-Bowlan.—4F 47
Aberbran.—5B 48
Abercanaid.—2G 37
Abercarn.—3A 38
Abercastle.—1B 34
Abercegir.—5H 71
Aberchalder.—3F 151
Aberchirder.—3D 162
Abercorn.—2D 131
Abercraf.—1E 36
Abercregan.—3E 37
Abercrombie.—3H 139
Abercwmboi.—3G 37
Abercych.—3B 46
Abercynon.—3G 37
Aber Cywarch.—4A 72
Aberdalgie.—1C 138
Aberdare.—2F 37
Aberdaron.—3A 70
Aberdaugledd.—4C 34
Aberdeen.—3G 155
Aberdeen (Dyce) Airport.
              —2F 155
Aberdesach.—5D 82
Aberdour.—5D 130
Aberdovey.—1B 58
Aberdulais.—3D 36
Aberdyfi.—1B 58
Aberedw.—3C 48
Abereiddy.—1A 34
Abererch.—2C 70
Aberfan.—2G 37
Aberfeldy.—4F 145
Aberffraw.—4C 82
Aberffrwd.—3B 58
Aberford.—2E 95
Aberfoyle.—3E 137
Abergarw.—4F 37
Abergarwed.—2E 36
Abergavenny.—1B 38

Abergele.—3B 84
Abergiar.—3E 47
Abergorlech.—4E 47
Abergwaun.—1C 34
Abergwesyn.—2A 48
Abergwili.—2H 35
Abergwynfi.—3E 37
Abergynolwyn.—5F 71
Aberhonddu.—5C 48
Aberhosan.—1D 58
Aberkenfig.—4E 37
Aberlady.—2A 132
Aberlemno.—3E 147
Aberllefenni.—5G 71
Abermeurig.—2E 47
Abermule.—1G 59
Abernant.—2G 35
(Dyfed)
Abernant.—2G 37
(Mid Glamorgan)
Abernethy.—2D 138
Abernyte.—5B 146
Aber-oer.—1E 73
Aberporth.—2B 46
Abersoch.—3C 70
Abersychan.—2A 38
Abertawe.—3C 36
Aberteifi.—3A 46
Aberthin.—5G 37
Abertillery.—2A 38
Abertridwr.—4H 37
(Mid Glamorgan)
Abertridwr.—4C 72
(Powys)
Abertysswg.—2H 37
Aberuthven.—2B 138
Aber Village.—5D 48
Aberyscir.—5C 48
Aberystwyth.—2A 58
Abingdon.—3F 41
Abinger Common.—1C 18
Abinger Hammer.—1B 18
Abington.—2B 120
Abington Pigotts.—3C 54
Ab Kettleby.—5E 76
Ab Lench.—2E 51

Ablington.—2C 40
(Gloucestershire)
Ablington.—4G 27
(Wiltshire)
Abney.—5B 88
Aboyne.—4C 154
Abram.—2D 86
Abriachan.—5H 159
Abridge.—1F 31
Abson.—5F 39
Abthorpe.—3D 52
Aby.—5G 91
Acairseid.—8C 172
Acaster Malbis.—5A 102
Acaster Selby.—5A 102
Accott.—2C 22
Accrington.—3E 93
Acha.—3C 140
Achachork.—4D 157
Achahoish.—2F 127
Achaleven.—5D 142
Achallader.—4H 143
Achanalt.—2F 159
Achanamara.—1F 127
Achandunie.—1A 160
Ach'an Todhair.—1E 143
Achany.—3C 166
Achaphubuil.—1E 143
Acharacle.—2A 142
Achargory.—3H 169
Acharn.—4E 145
(nr. Aberfeldy, Tayside)
Acharn.—1B 146
(nr. Clova, Tayside)
Acharole.—3E 171
Achateny.—1G 141
Achavanich.—4D 171
Achdalieu.—1E 143
Achduart.—3E 165
Achentoul.—5A 170
Achfary.—5C 168
Achfrish.—2C 166
Achgarve.—4C 164
Achiemore.—2D 168
(nr. Durness, H'land.)

Achiemore.—3A 170
(nr. Thurso, H'land.)
A'Chill.—3A 148
Achiltibuie.—3E 165
Achina.—2H 169
Achinahuagh.—2F 169
Achinduich.—4C 166
Achininver.—2F 169
Achintee.—4B 158
Achintraid.—5H 157
Achleck.—4F 141
Achlorachan.—3F 159
Achluachrach.—5F 151
Achlyness.—3C 168
Achmelvich.—1A 166
Achmony.—5H 159
Achmore.—5A 158
(nr Stromeferry, H'land)
Achmore.—4E 165
(nr. Ullapool, H'land.)
Achmore.—5F 173
(Western Isles)
Achnacarnin.—5A 168
Achnacarry.—5D 150
Achnaclerach.—2G 159
Achnacloich.—3D 149
Achnaconeran.—2G 151
Achnacroish.—4C 142
Achnafalnich.—1B 136
Achnagarron.—1A 160
Achnaha.—2F 141
Achnahanat.—4C 166
Achnahannet.—1D 153
Achnairn.—2C 166
Achnanellan.—5C 150
Achnasheen.—3D 158
Achnashellach.—4C 158
Achnastank.—5G 161
Achosnich.—2F 141
Achow.—5E 171
Achranich.—4B 142
Achreamie.—2C 170
Achriabhach.—2F 143
Achriesgill.—3C 168
Achrimsdale.—3G 167
Achscrabster.—2C 170

Achtoty.—2G 169
Achurch.—4H 65
Achuvoldrach.—3F 169
Achvaich.—4E 166
Achvarasdal.—2B 170
Achvarre.—5A 166
Ackergill.—3F 171
Ackergillshore.—3F 171
Acklam.—3B 108
(Cleveland)
Acklam.—3C 102
(North Yorkshire)
Ackleton.—3B 62
Acklington.—4G 123
Ackton.—3E 94
Ackworth Moor Top.—4E 95
Acle.—4G 81
Acocks Green.—4F 63
Acol.—4H 33
Acomb.—3C 116
(Northumberland)
Acomb.—4A 102
(North Yorkshire)
Aconbury.—4H 49
Acre.—3E 93
(Lancashire)
Acre.—2G 87
(Manchester)
Acrefair.—1E 73
Acrise.—1F 21
Acton.—2A 74
(Cheshire)
Acton.—5F 85
(Clwyd)
Acton.—5E 15
(Dorset)
Acton.—1C 50
(Hereford & Worcester)
Acton.—2C 30
(London)
Acton.—2A 60
(Shropshire)
Acton.—3C 74
(Staffordshire)
Acton.—3A 56
(Suffolk)
Acton Beauchamp.—2A 50

Acton Bridge.—3H 85
Acton Burnell.—5H 73
Acton Green.—2A 50
Acton Pigott.—5H 73
Acton Round.—3A 62
Acton Scott.—2B 60
Acton Trussell.—1D 62
Acton Turville.—4G 39
Adam's Hill.—5D 62
Adbaston.—5B 74
Adber.—1A 14
Adderbury.—4B 52
Adderley.—4A 74
Adderstone.—1F 123
Addiewell.—3C 130
Addingham.—1A 94
Addington.—5E 53
 (Buckinghamshire)
Addington.—5A 32
 (Kent)
Addington.—4E 31
 (London)
Addinston.—4B 132
Addlestone.—4B 30
Addlethorpe.—1E 79
Adeney.—1B 62
Adfa.—5C 72
Adforton.—3B 60
Adgestone.—5D 16
Adisham.—5G 33
Adlestrop.—5B 52
Adlingfleet.—3A 96
Adlington.—4G 87
 (Cheshire)
Adlington.—1C 86
 (Lancashire)
Admaston.—1A 62
 (Shropshire)
Admaston.—5E 75
 (Staffordshire)
Admington.—3G 51
Adpar.—3C 46
Adsborough.—1F 13
Adstock.—4E 53
Adstone.—2C 52
Adversane.—3B 18
Advie.—5F 161
Adwalton.—3C 94
Adwell.—3H 41
Adwick le Street.—2F 89
Adwick upon Dearne.—2E 89
Adziel.—3G 163
Ae Village.—1G 113
Affleck.—1F 155
Affpuddle.—4D 14
Afon-wen.—3D 84
Afton Bridgend.—3F 119
Agglethorpe.—1D 100
Aglionby.—4F 115
Aigburth.—4A 86
Aike.—1C 96
Aikers.—8D 174
Aiketgate.—5F 115
Aikhead.—5D 114
Aikton.—4D 114
Ailey.—3F 49
Ailsworth.—3A 66
Ainderby Quernhow.—1G 101
Ainderby Steeple.—5G 107
Aingers Green.—3D 56
Ainsdale.—1A 86
Ainsdale-on-Sea.—1A 86
Ainstable.—5G 115
Ainsworth.—1E 87
Ainthorpe.—4F 109
Aintree.—3A 86
Aird.—3F 111
 (Dumfries & Galloway)
Aird.—1G 157
 (Highland)
Aird.—3E 135
 (Strathclyde)
Aird.—3C 172
 (Benbecula, Western I.)

Aird.—4H 173
 (Lewis, Western I.)
Airdens.—4D 166
Airdeny.—1G 135
Aird of Sleat.—3D 149
Airdrie.—3A 130
Aird, The.—3D 156
Aird Tong.—4G 173
Aird Uig.—4C 173
Airedale.—3E 95
Airies.—3E 111
Airmyn.—3H 95
Airntully.—5H 145
Airor.—3F 149
Airth.—1B 130
Airton.—4C 100
Aisby.—3A 90
 (nr. Gainsborough, Lincs.)
Aisby.—4H 77
 (nr. Grantham, Lincs.)
Aish.—3C 8
 (nr. Buckfastleigh, Devon)
Aish.—4E 9
 (nr. Totnes, Devon)
Aisholt.—5B 24
Aiskew.—1F 101
Aislaby.—3B 108
 (Cleveland)
Aislaby.—1C 102
 (nr. Pickering, N. Yorks.)
Aislaby.—4F 109
 (nr. Whitby, N Yorks.)
Aisthorpe.—4B 90
Aith.—2H 175
 (Fetlar, Shetland)
Aith.—6E 175
 (Mainland, Shetland)
Akeld.—2D 122
Akeley.—4E 52
Akenham.—3D 56
Albaston.—2A 8
Alberbury.—4F 73
Albert Town.—3C 34
Albourne.—4D 19
Albrighton.—4G 73
 (nr. Shrewsbury, Shrops.)
Albrighton.—2C 62
 (nr. Telford, Shrops.)
Alburgh.—4E 69
Albury.—5D 54
 (Hertfordshire)
Albury.—1B 18
 (Surrey)
Albyfield.—4G 115
Alby Hill.—2D 81
Alcaig.—3H 159
Alcaston.—2B 60
Alcester.—2E 51
Alciston.—5G 19
Alcombe.—1F 23
Alconbury.—5A 66
Alconbury Weston.—5A 66
Aldborough.—2D 81
 (Norfolk)
Aldborough.—3H 101
 (North Yorkshire)
Aldbourne.—4G 40
Aldbrough.—2E 97
Aldbrough St John.—3F 107
Aldbury.—1C 42
Aldcliffe.—3D 98
Aldclune.—2G 145
Aldeburgh.—2G 57
Aldeby.—3G 69
Aldenham.—1C 30
Alderbury.—1G 15
Aldercar.—3B 76
Alderford.—4D 80
Alderholt.—2G 15
Alderley.—3F 39
Alderley Edge.—5F 87
Aldermaston.—2D 28
Aldermaston Soke.—2E 28
Aldermaston Wharf.—2E 28
Alderminster.—3G 51
Alder Moor.—5G 75

Aldersey Green.—5G 85
Aldershot.—3G 29
Alderton.—4E 51
 (Gloucestershire)
Alderton.—3E 53
 (Northamptonshire)
Alderton.—3G 73
 (Shropshire)
Alderton.—3F 57
 (Suffolk)
Alderton.—4G 39
 (Wiltshire)
Alderton Fields.—4E 51
Alderwasley.—2H 75
Aldfield.—3F 101
Aldford.—5G 85
Aldgate.—2G 65
Aldham.—5B 56
 (Essex)
Aldham.—3C 56
 (Suffolk)
Aldingbourne.—3H 17
Aldingham.—2B 98
Aldington.—3E 51
 (Hereford & Worcester)
Aldington.—2E 21
 (Kent)
Aldochlay.—4C 136
Aldon.—3B 60
Aldoth.—5C 114
Aldreth.—5D 66
Aldridge.—2E 63
Aldringham.—1G 57
Aldsworth.—1C 40
 (Gloucestershire)
Aldsworth.—3F 17
 (West Sussex)
Aldwark.—2G 75
 (Derbyshire)
Aldwark.—3H 101
 (North Yorkshire)
Aldwick.—4H 17
Aldwincle.—4H 65
Aldworth.—4D 36
Alexandria.—1E 129
Aley.—5B 24
Aley Green.—1D 42
Alfardisworthy.—2C 10
Alfington.—4E 12
Alfold.—2B 18
Alfold Bars.—2B 18
Alfold Crossways.—2B 18
Alford.—2C 154
 (Grampian)
Alford.—5G 91
 (Lincolnshire)
Alford.—5B 26
 (Somerset)
Alfreton.—2B 76
Alfrick.—2B 50
Alfrick Pound.—2B 50
Alfriston.—5G 19
Algarkirk.—4B 78
Alhampton.—5B 26
Alkborough.—3A 96
Alkerton.—1C 50
Alkham.—1G 21
Alkington.—2H 73
Alkmonton.—4F 75
Alladale Lodge.—5B 166
Allaleigh.—4E 9
Allanton.—4E 133
 (Borders)
Allanton.—4B 130
 (Strathclyde)
Allaston.—2E 39
Allbrook.—1C 16
All Cannings.—2F 27
Allendale Town.—4B 116
Allen End.—3F 63
Allenheads.—5B 116
Allensford.—4D 117
Allen's Green.—1A 44
Allensmore.—4G 49
Allenton.—4A 76
Aller.—1H 13

Allerby.—1B 104
Allercombe.—4D 12
Allerford.—1F 23
Allerston.—1D 103
Allerthorpe.—5C 102
Allerton.—4B 86
 (Mersyside)
Allerton.—2B 94
 (West Yorkshire)
Allerton Bywater.—3E 94
Allerton Mauleverer.—4H 101
Allesley.—4G 63
Allestree.—4H 75
Allet Common.—2E 5
Allexton.—2F 65
Allgreave.—1D 74
Allhallows.—3C 32
Alligin Shuas.—3H 157
Allimore Green.—1C 62
Allington.—5B 32
 (Kent)
Allington.—3F 77
 (Lincolnshire)
Allington.—5H 27
 (nr. Amesbury, Wilts.)
Allington.—2F 27
 (nr. Devizes, Wilts)
Allithwaite.—2C 98
Allnabad.—4E 169
Alloa.—4A 136
Allonby.—5B 114
Alloway.—3C 118
Allowenshay.—2G 13
All Saints South Elmham.
 —4F 69
Allscott.—3B 62
 (nr. Bridgnorth, Shrops.)
Allscott.—1A 62
 (nr. Wellington, Shrops.)
All Stretton.—1B 60
Allt.—2B 36
Alltami.—4E 85
Alltgobhlach.—5G 127
Alltmawr.—3C 48
Alltnacaillich.—4E 169
Allt na h' Airbhe.—4F 165
Alltour.—5E 150
Alltsigh.—2G 151
Alltwalis.—4D 46
Alltwen.—2D 36
Alltyblacca.—3E 47
Allt-y-goed.—3A 46
Allweston.—2B 14
Almeley.—2F 49
Almeley Wooton.—2F 49
Almer.—4E 15
Almholme.—2F 89
Almington.—4B 74
Alminstone Cross.—1D 10
Almodington.—4G 17
Almondbank.—1C 138
Almondbury.—4B 94
Almondsbury.—4E 39
Alne.—3H 101
Alness.—2A 128
Alnessferry.—2A 160
Alnham.—3D 123
Alnmouth.—3G 123
Alnwick.—3F 123
Alphamstone.—4A 56
Alpheton.—4A 56
Alphington.—4C 12
Alpington.—2E 69
Alport.—1G 75
 (Derbyshire)
Alport.—1H 59
 (Powys)
Alpraham.—5H 85
Alresford.—5C 56
Alrewas.—1F 63
Alsager.—2B 74
Alsagers Bank.—3C 74
Alsop en le Dale.—2F 75
Alston.—5A 116
 (Cumbria)
Alston.—4D 51
 (Gloucestershire)

Alstone.—4D 24
 (Somerset)
Alstonefield.—2F 75
Alston Sutton.—3E 25
Alswear.—3D 22
Altandhu.—2D 165
Altanduin.—1F 167
Altarnun.—1G 7
Altass.—3G 77
Alterwall.—2E 171
Altgaltraig.—2B 128
Altham.—2E 93
Althorne.—1D 32
Althorpe.—5A 96
Altnabreac.—4C 170
Altnacealgach.—2G 165
Altnacraig.—1F 135
Altnafeadh.—3G 143
Altnaharra.—5F 169
Altofts.—3D 94
Alton.—1A 76
 (Derbyshire)
Alton.—5F 29
 (Hampshire)
Alton.—3E 75
 (Staffordshire)
Alton Barnes.—2G 27
Altonhill.—1D 118
Alton Pancras.—3B 14
Alton Priors.—2G 27
Altrincham.—4E 87
Altrua.—4E 151
Alva.—4A 138
Alvanley.—3G 85
Alvaston.—4A 76
Alvechurch.—5E 63
Alvecote.—2G 63
Alvediston.—1E 15
Alveley.—2B 60
Alverdiscott.—3B 22
Alverstoke.—4E 16
Alverstone.—5D 16
Alverthorpe.—3D 94
Alverton.—3C 77
Alvescot.—2D 40
Alveston.—4E 39
 (Avon)
Alveston.—5G 51
 (Warwickshire)
Alvie.—3C 152
Alvingham.—3F 91
Alvington.—2E 39
Alwalton.—3A 66
Alwinton.—4D 122
Alwoodley.—1C 94
Alyth.—4B 146
Amatnatua.—4B 166
Ambaston.—4B 75
Ambergate.—2H 75
Amber Hill.—3B 78
Amberley.—2G 39
 (Gloucestershire)
Amberley.—4B 18
 (West Sussex)
Amble.—4G 123
Amblecote.—4C 62
Ambler Thorn.—3A 94
Ambleside.—4E 105
Ambleston.—2D 34
Ambrosden.—1H 41
Amcotts.—4A 96
America.—5D 66
Amerton.—5D 75
Amesbury.—4G 27
Amhuinnsuidhe.—7C 173
Amisfield Town.—1B 114
Amlwch.—1D 82
Amlwch Port.—1D 82
Ammanford.—1C 36
Amotherby.—2C 102
Ampfield.—1C 16
Ampleforth.—2A 102
Ampleforth College.—2A 102
Ampney Crucis.—2B 40
Ampney St Mary.—2B 40

Ampney St Peter.—2B 40
Amport.—4A 28
Ampthill.—4H 53
Ampton.—5A 68
Amroth.—4E 35
Amulree.—5G 145
Amwell.—1E 43
Anaheilt.—2C 142
Ancaster.—3G 77
Anchor.—2G 59
Anchorsholme.—1A 92
An Coroghon.—3A 148
Ancroft.—5G 133
Ancrum.—2A 122
Ancton.—3H 17
Anderby.—5H 91
Anderby Creek.—5H 91
Anderson.—3D 14
Anderton.—5D 86
Andertons Mill.—1C 86
Andover.—4B 28
Andover Down.—4B 28
Andoversford.—1B 40
Andreas.—2D 110
Andwell.—3E 29
Anelog.—3A 70
Anfield.—3A 86
Angarrack.—3C 4
Angelbank.—3C 60
Angerton.—4D 114
Angle.—4B 34
Angmering.—5B 18
Angmering-on-Sea.—5B 18
Angram.—5B 106
 (nr. Keld, N Yorks.)
Angram.—5A 102
 (nr. York, N Yorks.)
Anick.—3C 116
Ankerbold.—1A 76
Ankerville.—1C 160
Anlaby.—3C 96
Anlaby Park.—3C 96
Anmer.—5G 79
Anmore.—2E 17
Annan.—3C 114
Annaside.—1A 98
Annat.—3A 158
 (Highland)
Annat.—1H 135
 (Stathclyde)
Annathill.—2A 130
Anna Valley.—4B 28
Annbank.—2D 118
Annbank Station.—2D 118
Annesley.—2C 76
Annesley Woodhouse.—2B 76
Annfield Plain.—4E 117
Annscroft.—5G 73
Ansdell.—3A 92
Ansford.—5B 26
Ansley.—5G 63
Anslow.—5G 75
Anslow Gate.—5F 75
Ansteadbrook.—2A 18
Anstey.—4D 54
 (Hertfordshire)
Anstey.—2C 64
 (Leicestershire)
Anston.—5D 130
Anstruther Easter.—3H 139
Anstruther Wester.—3H 139
Ansty.—4A 64
 (Warwickshire)
Ansty.—3D 19
 (West Sussex)
Ansty.—1E 15
 (Wiltshire)
Anthill Common.—2E 17
Anthorn.—4C 114
Antingham.—2E 81
Antony.—4A 8
Antrobus.—5D 86
Anvil Corner.—3D 10
Anwick.—2A 78
Anworth.—4C 112
Apethorpe.—3H 65

Apeton.—1C 62
Apley.—5D 90
Apperknowle.—5D 88
Apperley.—5C 50
Apperley Dene.—4D 116
Appersett.—5B 106
Appleby.—4B 96
Appleby-in-Westmoreland.
          —2H 105
Appleby Magna.—2H 63
Appleby Parva.—2H 63
Applecross.—4G 157
Appledore.—2A 22
  (nr. Bideford, Devon)
Appledore.—2D 12
  (nr. Tiverton, Devon)
Appledore.—3D 20
  (Kent)
Appledore Heath.—2D 20
Appleford.—3G 41
Applegarthtown.—1C 114
Applemore.—3B 16
Appleshaw.—4B 28
Applethwaite.—2D 104
Appleton.—4C 86
  (Cheshire)
Appleton.—2F 41
  (Oxfordshire)
Appleton-le-Moors.—1C 102
Appleton-le Street.—2C 102
Appleton Roebuck.—5A 102
Appleton Thorn.—4D 86
Appleton Wiske.—4G 107
Appletree.—3B 52
Appletreehall.—3H 121
Appletreewick.—3D 100
Apsley.—3G 23
Apsley Bridge.—2C 86
Apse Heath.—4D 16
Apsley End.—4A 54
Apuldram.—3G 17
Arabella.—1C 160
Arbeadie.—4D 154
Arbirlot.—4F 147
Arborfield.—2F 29
Arborfield Cross.—2F 29
Arborfield Garrison.—2F 29
Arbourthorne.—4D 88
Arbroath.—4F 147
Arcan.—3H 159
Archiestown.—4G 161
Arclid Green.—1B 74
Ardachu.—3D 166
Ardalanish.—2A 134
Ardaneaskan.—5H 157
Ardarroch.—5H 157
Ardbeg.—3B 128
  (Bute, S'clyde.)
Ardbeg.—1C 126
  (nr. Dunoon, S'clyde.)
Ardbeg.—5C 126
  (Islay, S'clyde.)
Ardcharnich.—5F 165
Ardchiavaig.—2A 134
Ardchonnell.—2G 135
Ardchrishnish.—1B 134
Ardchronie.—5D 166
Ardchullarie.—2E 137
Ardchyle.—1E 137
Ard-dhubh.—4G 157
Ardd-lin.—4E 73
Ardechive.—4D 150
Ardeley.—5C 54
Ardelve.—1G 149
Arden.—1E 129
Ardendrain.—5H 159
Arden Hall.—5C 108
Ardens Grafton.—2F 51
Ardentinny.—1C 128
Ardeonaig.—5D 144
Ardersier.—3B 160
Ardessie.—5E 165
Ardfern.—3F 135
Ardfin.—3C 126

Ardgartan.—3B 136
Ardgay.—4C 166
Ardgour.—2E 143
Ardhasaig.—7D 173
Ardheslaig.—3G 157
Ardindrean.—5F 165
Ardingly.—3E 19
Ardington.—4F 41
Ardivachar.—4C 172
Ardleigh.—5C 56
Ardler.—4B 146
Ardley.—5C 52
Ardlui.—2C 136
Ardmair.—4F 165
Ardmay.—3B 136
Ardmhor.—8C 172
Ardminish.—5E 127
Ardmolich.—1B 142
Ardmore.—3C 168
  (nr. Kinlochbervie, H'land.)
Ardmore.—5E 166
  (nr. Tain, H'land.)
Ardmore.—4D 172
  (Western Isles)
Ardnacross.—4G 141
Ardnadam.—1C 128
Ardnagrask.—4H 159
Ardnamurach.—4G 149
Ardnarff.—5A 158
Ardnastang.—2C 142
Ardoch.—5H 145
Ardochy House.—3E 150
Ardpatrick.—3F 127
Ardrishaig.—1G 127
Ardroag.—4B 156
Ardroil.—4C 173
Ardross.—1A 160
Ardrossan.—5D 128
Ardshealach.—2A 142
Ardslave.—9D 173
Ardsley.—2D 88
Ardsley East.—3D 94
Ardslignish.—2G 141
Ardtalla.—4C 126
Ardtalnaig.—5E 144
Ardtoe.—1A 142
Arduaine.—2F 135
Ardullie.—2E 159
Ardvasar.—3E 149
Ardveenish.—8C 172
Ardvey.—9C 173
Ardvorlich.—1F 137
Ardvourlie.—6D 173
Ardwell.—5G 111
  (Dumfries & Galloway)
Ardwell.—5A 162
  (Grampian)
Arean.—1A 142
Areley Common.—5C 62
Areley Kings.—5C 62
Arford.—5G 29
Argoed.—3H 37
Argoed Mill.—4E 59
Arinacrinachd.—3G 157
Arinagour.—3D 140
Arisaig.—5E 149
Ariundle.—2C 142
Arivegaig.—2A 142
Arivruaich.—6E 173
Arkendale.—3G 101
Arkesden.—4D 55
Arkholme.—2E 99
Arkle Town.—4D 106
Arkley.—1D 30
Arksey.—2F 89
Arkwright Town.—5E 89
Arlecdon.—3B 104
Arlescote.—3A 52
Arlesey.—4A 54
Arleston.—1A 62
Arley.—4D 86
Arlingham.—1F 39
Arlington.—1C 22
  (Devon)

Arlington.—5G 19
  (East Sussex)
Arlington.—2C 40
  (Gloucestershire)
Arlington Beccott.—1C 22
Armadale.—2H 169
  (Highland)
Armadale.—3C 130
  (Lothian)
Armadale Castle.—3E 149
Armathwaite.—5G 115
Arminghall.—2E 69
Armitage.—1E 63
Armitage Bridge.—4B 94
Armley.—2C 94
Armscote.—5G 51
Arms, The.—3A 68
Armston.—4H 65
Armthorpe.—2G 89
Arncliffe.—2C 100
Arncliffe Cote.—2C 100
Arncroach.—3H 139
Arne.—5E 15
Arnesby.—3D 64
Arnicle.—2B 124
Arnisdale.—2G 149
Arnish.—4E 157
Arniston.—4G 131
Arniston Engine.—3G 131
Arnol.—3F 173
Arnold.—1D 96
  (Humberside)
Arnold.—3C 76
  (Nottinghamshire)
Arnprior.—4F 137
Arnside.—2D 98
Aros Mains.—4G 141
Arpafeelie.—3A 160
Arrad Foot.—1C 98
Arram.—1C 96
Arras.—1B 96
Arrathorne.—5F 107
Arreton.—5D 16
Arrington.—2C 54
Arrochar.—3B 136
Arrow.—2E 51
Arscaig.—2C 166
Artafallie.—4A 160
Arthington.—1C 94
Arthingworth.—4E 65
Arthog.—4F 71
Arthrath.—5G 163
Arthurstone.—4B 146
Arundel.—5B 18
Asby.—2B 104
Ascog.—3C 128
Ascot.—4A 30
Ascott-under-Wychwood.
          —1E 40
Asenby.—2G 101
Asfordby.—1E 64
Asfordby Hill.—1E 64
Asgarby.—1C 78
  (nr. Horncastle, Lincs.)
Asgarby.—3A 78
  (nr. Sleaford Lincs.)
Ash.—5E 9
  (Devon)
Ash.—2D 14
  (Dorset)
Ash.—5G 33
  (nr. Sandwich, Kent)
Ash.—4G 31
  (nr. Swanley, Kent)
Ash.—1H 13
  (Somerset)
Ash.—3G 29
  (Surrey)
Ashampstead.—5G 41
Ashbocking.—2D 57
Ashbourne.—3F 75
Ashbrittle.—3G 23
Ashbrook.—1B 60
Ashburton.—2D 8
Ashbury.—4F 11
  (Devon)

Ashbury.—4D 40
  (Oxfordshire)
Ashby.—5A 96
Ashby by Partney.—1D 78
Ashby cum Fenby.—5E 97
Ashby de la Launde.—2H 77
Ashby de la Zouch.—1A 64
Ashby Folville.—1E 64
Ashby Magna.—3C 64
Ashby Parva.—4C 64
Ashby Puerorum.—5F 91
Ashby St Ledgers.—1C 52
Ashby St Mary.—2F 69
Ashcombe.—2F 9
Ashcott.—5E 25
Ashdon.—3E 55
Ashe.—3D 28
Asheldham.—2F 45
Ashen.—3G 55
Ashendon.—1A 42
Ashey.—5D 16
Ashfield.—3G 137
  (Central)
Ashfield.—2B 16
  (Hampshire)
Ashfield.—5H 49
  (Hereford & Worcester)
Ashfield.—2C 60
  (Cheshire)
Ashfield.—1E 57
  (Suffolk)
Ashfield Green.—5E 69
Ashfold Crossways.—3D 18
Ashford.—2B 22
  (nr. Barnstaple, Devon)
Ashford.—5C 8
  (nr. Kingsbridge, Devon)
Ashford.—2G 15
  (Hampshire)
Ashford.—1E 20
  (Kent)
Ashford.—3B 30
  (Surrey)
Ashford Bowdler.—3C 60
Ashford Carbonel.—3C 60
Ashford Hill.—2D 28
Ashford in the Water.—1F 75
Ashgill.—5A 130
Ashgrove.—2G 161
Ashill.—2D 12
  (Devon)
Ashill.—2A 68
  (Norfolk)
Ashill.—1G 13
  (Somerset)
Ashingdon.—1C 32
Ashington.—1F 117
  (Northumberland)
Ashington.—4C 18
  (West Sussex)
Ashkirk.—2G 121
Ashlett.—3C 16
Ashleworth.—5C 50
Ashley.—1F 55
  (Cambridgeshire)
Ashley.—4E 87
  (Cheshire)
Ashley.—2G 11
  (Devon)
Ashley.—3G 15
  (Dorset)
Ashley.—3H 39
  (Gloucestershire)
Ashley.—4A 16
  (New Milton, Hants)
Ashley.—5B 28
  (nr. Winchester, Hants.)
Ashley.—1H 21
  (Kent)
Ashley.—3E 65
  (Northamptonshire)
Ashley.—4B 74
  (Staffordshire)
Ashley.—2D 26
  (Wiltshire)
Ashley Green.—2C 42

Ashley Heath.—3G 15
Ashley Moor.—4B 60
Ash Magna.—2H 73
Ashmanhaugh.—3F 81
Ashmansworth.—3C 28
Ashmansworthy.—2D 10
Ashmead Green.—3F 39
Ashmill.—4D 11
  (nr. Holsworthy, Devon)
Ash Mill.—3D 23
  (nr. South Molton, Devon)
Ashmore.—2E 15
Ashmore Green.—2D 28
Ashorne.—2H 51
Ashover.—1H 75
Ashow.—5H 63
Ash Parva.—2H 73
Ashperton.—3A 50
Ashprington.—4E 9
Ash Priors.—1E 13
Ashreigney.—2G 11
Ash Street.—3C 56
Ashtead.—5C 30
Ash Thomas.—2D 12
Ashton.—2A 66
  (Cambridgeshire)
Ashton.—4H 85
  (Cheshire)
Ashton.—4D 4
  (Cornwall)
Ashton.—4C 60
  (Hereford & Worcester)
Ashton.—4H 65
  (nr. Oundle, Northants.)
Ashton.—3E 53
  (nr. Roade, Northants.)
Ashton Common.—2D 27
Ashton-in-Makerfield.—3C 86
Ashton Keynes.—3B 40
Ashton under Hill.—4D 51
Ashton-under-Lyne.—3E 87
Ashton upon Mersey.—3E 87
Ashurst.—2B 16
  (Hampshire)
Ashurst.—2G 19
  (Kent)
Ashurst.—2B 86
  (Lancashire)
Ashurst.—4C 18
  (West Sussex)
Ashurstwood.—2F 19
Ash Vale.—3G 29
Ashwater.—4D 11
Ashwell.—4B 54
  (Hertfordshire)
Ashwell.—1F 65
  (Leicestershire)
Ashwellthorpe.—3D 68
Ashwick.—4B 26
Ashwicken.—1G 67
Ashwood.—4C 62
Askam in Furness.—2B 98
Askern.—4H 95
Askernish.—6C 172
Askerswell.—4A 14
Askett.—2B 42
Askham.—2G 105
  (Cumbria)
Askham.—5H 89
  (Nottinghamshire)
Askham Bryan.—5A 102
Askham Richard.—5A 102
Askrigg.—5C 106
Askwith.—1B 94
Aslackby.—4H 77
Aslacton.—3D 68
Aslockton.—3E 77
Aspatria.—5C 114
Aspenden.—5C 54
Asperton.—4B 78
Aspley Guise.—4G 53
Aspley Heath.—4G 53
Aspull.—2D 86
Asselby.—3H 95

Assington.—4B 56
Assington Green.—2G 55
Asterby.—1C 74
Astcote.—2D 52
Asterby.—5E 91
Asterley.—5F 73
Asterton.—4D 40
Asthall.—1D 40
Asthall Leigh.—1E 40
Astle.—4E 167
Astley.—1H 50
  (Hereford & Worcester)
Astley.—2E 87
  (Manchester)
Astley.—4H 73
  (Shropshire)
Astley.—4H 63
  (Warwickshire)
Astley Abbots.—3B 62
Astley Bridge.—1E 87
Astley Cross.—1C 50
Aston.—4A 42
  (Berkshire)
Aston.—3H 85
  (nr. Frodsham, Ches.)
Aston.—3A 74
  (nr. Nantwich, Ches.)
Aston.—4F 85
  (Clwyd)
Aston.—4B 88
  (Derbyshire)
Aston.—4C 60
  (nr. Leominster, Here & Worc.)
Aston.—3B 60
  (nr. Ludlow, Here & Worcs.)
Aston.—5B 54
  (Hertfordshire)
Aston.—2E 41
  (Oxfordshire)
Aston.—3C 62
  (nr. Bridgnorth, Shrops.)
Aston.—2A 62
  (nr. Wellington, Shrops.)
Aston.—3H 73
  (nr. Wem, Shrops.)
Aston.—4B 88
  (South Yorkshire)
Aston.—3B 74
  (Staffordshire)
Aston.—4E 63
  (West Midlands)
Aston Abbotts.—5F 53
Aston Botterell.—4A 62
Aston-by-Stone.—4D 74
Aston Cantlow.—2F 51
Aston Clinton.—1B 42
Aston Crews.—5A 50
Aston Cross.—4D 50
Aston End.—5B 54
Aston Eyre.—3G 73
Aston Fields.—1D 50
Aston Flamville.—3B 64
Aston Ingham.—5A 50
Aston juxta Mondrum.—2A 74
Astonlane.—3A 62
Aston le Walls.—2B 52
Aston Magna.—4F 51
Aston Munslow.—2C 60
Aston on Carrant.—4D 50
Aston on Clun.—2A 60
Aston Pigott.—5F 73
Aston Rogers.—5F 73
Aston Rowant.—3A 42
Aston Sandford.—2A 42
Aston Somerville.—4E 51
Aston Subedge.—3F 51
Aston Tirrold.—4G 41
Aston upon Trent.—5B 76
Aston Upthorpe.—4G 41
Astrop.—4C 52
Astwick.—4B 54
Astwood.—3G 53
Astwood Bank.—1E 51
Aswarby.—4H 77
Aswardby.—5F 91
Atcham.—5H 73

Bangor-is-y-coed.—1F 73
Bangors.—4C 10
Bangor's Green.—2A 86
Bangrove.—5B 68
Banham.—6D 62
Bank.—3A 16
Bankend.—3B 114
Bankfoot.—5H 145
Bankglen.—3F 119
Bankhead.—2F 155
(nr. Aberdeen, Grampian)
Bankhead.—3D 154
(nr. Torphins, Grampian)
Bankhead.—5B 130
(Strathclyde)
Bankland.—1G 13
Bank Newton.—4C 100
Banknock.—2A 130
Banks.—3G 115
(Cumbria)
Banks.—3A 92
(Lancashire)
Bankshill.—1C 114
Bank Street.—1A 50
Bank, The.—2C 74
(Cheshire)
Bank, The.—3A 62
(Shropshire)
Bank Top.—2C 86
Banners Gate.—3E 63
Banningham.—3B 81
Banniskirk.—3D 170
Bannister Green.—5F 55
Bannockburn.—4H 137
Banstead.—5D 30
Bantham.—5C 8
Banton.—2A 130
Banwell.—3D 25
Banyard's Green.—5E 69
Bapchild.—4D 32
Bapton.—5E 27
Baramore.—1A 142
Barassie.—1C 118
Baravullin.—4D 142
Barbaraville.—1B 160
Barber Booth.—4B 88
Barber Green.—1C 98
Barbieston.—3C 118
(nr. Dalrymple, S'clyde.)
Barbieston.—3D 118
(nr. Drongan, S'clyde.)
Barbon.—1F 99
Barbourne.—2C 50
Barbridge.—2A 74
Barbrook.—1D 22
Barby.—5C 64
Barby Nortoft.—5C 64
Barcaldine.—4D 142
Barcheston.—4G 51
Barclose.—4F 19
Barcombe.—4F 19
Barcombe Cross.—4F 19
Barden.—5E 107
Barden Scale.—4D 100
Bardfield End Green.—4F 55
Bardfield Saling.—5F 55
Bardnabeinne.—4E 166
Bardney.—1A 78
Bardon.—1B 64
Bardon Mill.—3A 116
Bardowie.—2G 129
Bardsea.—2C 98
Bardsey.—1D 94
Bardsley.—2G 87
Bardwell.—5B 68
Bare.—3D 98
Bareless.—1C 122
Barewood.—2F 49
Barford.—5G 29
(Hampshire)
Barford.—2D 68
(Norfolk)
Barford.—1G 51
(Warwickshire)
Barford St John.—4B 52
Barford St Martin.—5F 27

Barford St Michael.—4B 52
Barfreston.—5G 33
Bargeddie.—3A 130
Bargoed.—3H 37
Bargrennan.—2A 112
Barham.—5A 66
(Cambridgeshire)
Barham.—5G 33
(Kent)
Barham.—2D 56
(Suffolk)
Barharrow.—4D 112
Bar Hill.—1C 54
Barholm.—1H 65
Barkby.—2D 64
Barkestone-le-Vale.—4E 77
Barkham.—2F 29
Barking.—2F 31
(London)
Barking.—2C 56
(Suffolk)
Barkingside.—2F 31
Barking Tye.—2C 56
Barkisland.—4A 94
Barkston.—3G 77
(Lincolnshire)
Barkston.—2E 95
(North Yorkshire)
Barkway.—4C 54
Barlanark.—3H 129
Barlaston.—4C 74
Barlavington.—2H 17
Barlborough.—5E 89
Barlby.—2G 95
Barlestone.—2B 64
Barley.—4C 54
(Hertfordshire)
Barley.—1F 93
(Lancashire)
Barley Mow.—4F 117
Barleythorpe.—2F 65
Barling.—2D 32
Barlings.—5C 90
Barlow.—5D 88
(Derbyshire)
Barlow.—5D 88
(North Yorkshire)
Barlow.—3E 117
(Tyne & Wear)
Barmby Moor.—5C 102
Barmby on the Marsh.—3G 95
Barmer.—2A 80
Barming Heath.—5B 32
Barmoor.—1E 123
Barmouth.—4F 71
Barmpton.—3G 107
Barmston.—4G 103
Barmulloch.—3H 129
Barnack.—2H 65
Barnacle.—4A 64
Barnard Castle.—3D 106
Barnard Gate.—1F 41
Barnbarroch.—4F 113
Barnburgh.—2E 89
Barnby.—4G 69
Barnby Dun.—2G 89
Barnby in the Willows.—2F 77
Barnby Moor.—4G 89
Barnes.—3D 30
Barnes Street.—1H 19
Barnet.—1D 30
Barnetby le Wold.—5C 96
Barney.—2B 80
Barnham.—5A 68
(Suffolk)
Barnham.—3H 17
(West Sussex)
Barnham Broom.—2C 68
Barnhead.—3F 147
Barnhill.—3F 161
(Grampian)
Barnhill.—5D 147
(Dundee, Tayside)
Barnhill.—1D 138
(Perth, Tayside)
Barnhills.—2E 111

Barningham.—3D 107
(Durham)
Barningham.—5B 68
(Suffolk)
Barnoldby le Beck.—5E 97
Barnoldswick.—1F 93
Barns Green.—3C 18
Barnsley.—2B 40
(Gloucestershire)
Barnsley.—3B 62
(Shropshire)
Barnsley.—2D 88
(South Yorkshire)
Barnstaple.—2B 22
Barnston.—1C 44
(Essex)
Barnston.—2E 85
(Merseyside)
Barnstone.—4E 77
Barnt Green.—5E 63
Barnton.—5D 86
Barnwell.—2D 54
Barnwell All Saints.—4H 65
Barnwell St Andrew.—4H 65
Barnwood.—1G 39
Barons Cross.—2G 49
Barony, The.—5B 174
Barr.—4G 119
(Dumfries & Galloway)
Barr.—5B 118
(Strathclyde)
Barra Airport.—8B 172
Barrachan.—5A 112
Barrahormid.—1F 127
Barrapoll.—4A 140
Barrasford.—2C 116
Barravullin.—3F 135
Barregarrow.—3C 110
Barrhead.—4F 129
Barrhill.—1H 111
Barrington.—3C 54
(Cambridgeshire)
Barrington.—2G 13
(Somerset)
Barripper.—3D 4
Barrmill.—4E 129
Barrock.—1E 171
Barrow.—2E 93
(Lancashire)
Barrow.—1F 65
(Leicestershire)
Barrow.—2A 62
(Shropshire)
Barrow.—5C 26
(Somerset)
Barrow.—1G 55
(Suffolk)
Barroway Drove.—2E 67
Barrow Bridge.—1D 87
Barrow Burn.—3C 122
Barrowby.—4F 77
Barrowcliff.—1F 103
Barrow Common.—2F 25
Barrowden.—2G 65
Barrowford.—2F 93
Barrow Gurney.—2F 25
Barrow Haven.—3C 96
Barrow Hill.—5E 88
Barrow-in-Furness.—2A 98
Barrow Nook.—2B 86
Barrow's Green.—1C 99
(Cumbria)
Barrow's Green.—4C 86
(Merseyside)
Barrowstown.—1D 130
Barrow Street.—5D 26
Barrow upon Humber.—3C 96
Barrow upon Soar.—1C 64
Barrow upon Trent.—5A 76
Barry.—5H 37
(South Glamorgan)
Barry.—5E 147
(Tayside)
Barry Island.—5H 37
Barsby.—1D 64
Barsham.—4F 69

Barston.—5G 63
Bartestree.—3H 49
Barthol Chapel.—5F 163
Bartholomew Green.—5G 55
Barthomley.—2B 74
Bartley.—2B 16
Bartley Green.—4E 63
Bartlow.—3E 55
Barton.—3D 25
(Avon)
Barton.—2D 54
(Cambridgeshire)
Barton.—5G 85
(Cheshire)
Barton.—2F 105
(Cumbria)
Barton.—3F 9
(Devon)
Barton.—5F 51
(Gloucestershire)
Barton.—5D 16
(Isle of Wight)
Barton.—2A 86
(nr. Ormskirk, Lancs.)
Barton.—2C 92
(nr. Preston, Lancs.)
Barton.—4F 107
(North Yorkshire)
Barton.—2G 41
(Oxfordshire)
Barton.—2F 51
(Warwickshire)
Barton Bendish.—2G 67
Barton Gate.—1F 63
Barton Green.—1F 63
Barton Hartshorn.—4D 52
Barton Hill.—3C 102
Barton in Fabis.—4C 76
Barton in the Beans.—2A 64
Barton-le-Clay.—4H 53
Barton-le-Street.—2C 102
Barton-le-Willows.—3C 102
Barton Mills.—5G 67
Barton on Sea.—4H 15
Barton-on-the-Heath.—4G 51
Barton Seagrave.—5F 65
Barton Stacey.—4C 28
Barton St. David.—5F 25
Barton Town.—1C 22
Barton Turf.—3F 81
Barton-under-Needwood.—1F 63
Barton-upon-Humber.—3C 96
Barton Waterside.—3C 96
Barugh.—2D 88
Barugh Green.—2D 88
Barvas.—3F 173
Barway.—5C 67
Barwell.—3B 64
Barwick.—1G 43
(Hertfordshire)
Barwick.—2A 14
(Somerset)
Barwick in Elmet.—2E 94
Baschurch.—3G 73
Bascote.—1B 52
Basford Green.—2D 75
Bashall Eaves.—1D 93
Bashall Town.—1E 93
Bashley.—4H 15
Bash Mill.—3D 22
Basildon.—2B 32
Basing.—3E 29
Basingstoke.—3E 29
Baslow.—5C 88
Bason Bridge.—4D 24
Bassaleg.—4A 38
Bassenden.—5C 132
Bassenthwaite.—1D 104
Bassett.—2C 16
Bassingbourn.—3C 54
Bassingfield.—4D 76
Bassingham.—2G 77
Bassingthorpe.—5G 77
Bassus Green.—5C 54
Basta.—2G 175
Baston.—1A 66

Bastonford.—2C 50
Bastwick.—4G 81
Batchley.—1E 51
Batchworth.—1B 30
Batcombe.—3B 14
(Dorset)
Batcombe.—5B 26
(Somerset)
Bate Heath.—5D 87
Bath.—2C 26
Bathampton.—2C 26
Bathealton.—3G 23
Batheaston.—2C 26
Bathford.—2C 26
Bathgate.—3C 130
Bathley.—2E 77
Bathpool.—2G 7
(Cornwall)
Bathpool.—1F 13
(Somerset)
Bathville.—3C 130
Bathway.—3F 25
Batley.—3C 94
Batsford.—4F 51
Batson.—5D 8
Battersby.—4C 108
Battersea.—3D 31
Battisborough Cross.—5B 8
Battisford.—2C 56
Battisford Tye.—2C 56
Battle.—4B 20
(East Sussex)
Battle.—4C 48
(Powys)
Battleborough.—3D 24
Battledown.—5D 50
Battlefield.—4H 73
Battlesbridge.—1B 32
Battlesden.—5G 53
Battlesea Green.—5E 69
Battleton.—3F 23
Battramsley.—4B 16
Batt's Corner.—4G 29
Bauds of Cullen.—2B 162
Baugh.—4B 140
Baughton.—3C 50
Baughurst.—2D 28
Baulking.—3E 40
Baumber.—5E 91
Baunton.—2B 40
Baverstock.—5F 27
Bawburgh.—2D 68
Bawdeswell.—3C 80
Bawdrip.—5D 24
Bawdsey.—3F 57
Bawdsey Manor.—4F 57
Bawsey.—1F 67
Bawtry.—3G 89
Baxenden.—3E 93
Baxterley.—3G 63
Baxter's Green.—2G 55
Baybridge.—1D 16
(Hampshire)
Baybridge.—5C 116
(Northumberland)
Baycliff.—2B 98
Baydon.—5D 40
Bayford.—2G 43
(Hertfordshire)
Bayford.—1C 14
(Somerset)
Bayhead.—8D 173
(Harris, Western I.)
Bayhead.—2C 172
(North Uist, Western I.)
Bayherivagh.—8C 172
Bayles.—5A 116
Baylham.—2D 56
Baymore.—3D 172
Baynard's Green.—5C 52
Bayston Hill.—5G 73
Baythorn End.—3G 55
Baythorpe.—3B 78
Bayton.—5A 62
Bayton Common.—5B 62
Bayworth.—2G 41

Beach.—5F 39
Beachampton.—4E 53
Beachamwell.—2G 67
Beachley.—3D 38
Beacon.—3E 13
Beacon End.—5B 56
Beacon Hill.—5G 29
Beacon's Bottom.—3A 42
Beadlam.—1B 102
Beadnell.—2G 123
Beaford.—2F 11
Beal.—5G 133
(Northumberland)
Beal.—3F 95
(North Yorkshire)
Bealsmill.—2H 7
Beamhurst.—4E 75
Beaminster.—3H 13
Beamish.—4F 117
Beamond End.—1A 30
Beamsley.—4D 100
Bean.—3G 31
Beanacre.—2E 27
Beanley.—3E 123
Beardwood.—3D 92
Beare Green.—1C 18
Bearley.—1F 51
Bearn Hill.—5G 75
Bearpark.—5F 117
Bearsbridge.—4A 116
Bearsden.—2G 129
Bearsted.—5B 32
Bearstone.—4B 74
Bearwardcote.—4G 75
Bearwood.—4F 15
(Dorset)
Bearwood.—4E 63
(West Midlands)
Beattock.—4C 120
Beauchamp Roding.—1B 44
Beauchief.—4D 88
Beaufort.—1H 37
Beaulieu.—3B 16
Beauly.—4H 159
Beaumaris.—3F 83
Beaumont.—4E 115
(Cumbria)
Beaumont.—5D 56
(Essex)
Beaumont Hill.—3F 107
Beausale.—5G 63
Beauvale.—3B 76
Beaworthy.—4E 11
Beazley End.—5G 55
Bebington.—2F 85
Bebside.—1F 117
Beccles.—3G 69
Becconsall.—3B 92
Beckbury.—3B 62
Beckenham.—4E 31
Beckermet.—4B 104
Beckett End.—3C 67
Beckfoot.—1A 98
(nr. Broughton in Furness, Cum
Beckfoot.—5H 105
(nr. Kendal, Cumbria)
Beckfoot.—4C 104
(nr. Seascale, Cumbria)
Beckfoot.—5B 114
(nr. Silloth, Cumbria)
Beckford.—4D 50
Beckhampton.—2F 27
Beck Hole.—4F 109
Beckingham.—3H 77
(Lincolnshire)
Beckingham.—3H 89
(Nottinghamshire)
Beckington.—3D 26
Beckley.—3C 20
(East Sussex)
Beckley.—4H 15
(Hampshire)

eckley.—1G 41
(Oxfordshire)
eck Row.—5F 67
eck Side.—1C 98
(nr. Cartmel, Cumbria)
eckside.—1F 99
(nr. Sedbergh, Cumbria)
eck Side.—1B 98
(nr. Ulverston, Cumbria)
eckton.—2F 31
eckwithshaw.—4F 101
econtree.—2F 31
edale.—1F 101
edchester.—2D 14
eddau.—4E 37
eddgelert.—1E 71
eddingham.—5F 19
eddington.—4E 31
edfield.—1E 57
edh 3H 53
(Bedfordshire)
edford.—2D 86
(Manchester)
edham.—3B 18
edhampton.—3E 17
edingfield.—1D 57
edingstoke.—3E 69
edlam.—3F 116
edlar's Green.—5E 55
edlington.—1F 117
edlington Station.—1F 117
edling.—2G 37
edminster.—5D 39
edmond.—2D 43
ednall.—1D 62
edrule.—3A 122
edstone.—3A 60
edwas.—4H 37
edwelity.—2H 37
edworth.—4A 64
eeby.—2D 64
eech.—5E 29
(Hampshire)
eech.—4C 74
(Staffordshire)
eechcliffe.—1A 94
eech Hill.—2E 29
eechingstoke.—3F 27
eedon.—5F 41
eeford.—4G 103
eeley.—1G 75
eelsby.—5E 97
eenham.—2D 28
eeny.—4B 10
eer.—5F 13
(Devon)
eer.—5E 25
(Somerset)
eercrocombe.—1G 13
eer Hackett.—2A 14
eesands.—5E 9
eesby.—4G 91
eeson.—5E 9
eeston.—3A 54
(Bedfordshire)
eeston.—5H 85
(Cheshire)
eeston.—4B 80
(Norfolk)
eeston.—4C 76
(Nottinghamshire)
eeston.—2C 94
(West Yorkshire)
eeston Regis.—1D 80
eeswing.—3F 113
eetham.—2D 99
(Cumbria)
eetham.—2F 13
(Somerset)
eetley.—4B 80
eftcote.—1C 62
egan.—4A 38
egbroke.—1F 41
egdale.—2D 66
egelly.—4E 35

Beggar Hill.—2C 44
Beggar's Bush.—4H 59
Beggearn Huish.—2G 23
Beguildy.—3G 59
Beighton.—2F 69
(Norfolk)
Beighton.—4B 89
(South Yorkshire)
Beighton Hill.—2G 75
Beith.—4E 129
Bekesbourne.—5F 33
Belaugh.—4E 81
Belbroughton.—5D 62
Belchalwell.—3C 14
Belchalwell Street.—3D 14
Belchamp Otten.—3A 56
Belchamp St Paul.—3A 55
Belchamp Walter.—3A 56
Belchford.—5E 91
Belfatton.—3H 163
Belford.—1F 123
Belgrano.—3B 84
Belhaven.—2C 132
Belhelvie.—2G 155
Belhinnie.—1B 154
Bellabeg.—2A 154
Bellanoch.—4F 135
Bell Busk.—4C 100
Belleau.—5F 91
Bellehiglash.—5F 161
Bell End.—5D 62
Bellerby.—5E 107
Bellerby Camp.—5D 107
Believer.—2C 8
Belle Vue.—1C 104
(Cumbria)
Belle Vue.—4G 73
(Shropshire)
Bellfield.—1H 119
Belliehill.—2E 147
Bellingdon.—2C 42
Bellingham.—1B 116
Bellmount.—5E 79
Bellochantuy.—2A 124
Bellsbank.—4D 119
Bell's Cross.—2D 56
Bellshill.—1F 123
(Northumberland)
Bellshill.—4A 130
(Strathclyde)
Bellside.—4B 130
Bellspool.—1D 120
Bellsquarry.—3D 130
Bells Yew Green.—2H 19
Bellymore.—1H 111
Belmaduthy.—3A 160
Belmesthorpe.—1H 65
Belmont.—1D 86
(Lancashire)
Belmont.—3C 118
(Strathclyde)
Belmore.—1D 128
Belnacraig.—2A 154
Belnie.—4B 78
Belowda.—3D 6
Belper.—3A 76
Belper Lane End.—3H 75
Belph.—5F 89
Belsay.—2E 117
Belsford.—4D 8
Belsize.—2D 42
Belstead.—3D 56
Belston.—2C 118
Belstone.—4G 11
Belstone Corner.—4G 11
Beltasound.—2N 171
Belthorn.—3E 93
Beltinge.—4F 33
Beltoft.—5A 96
Belton.—2H 89
(Humberside)
Belton.—5B 76
(nr. Shepshed, Leics.)
Belton.—2F 65
(nr. Uppingham, Leics.)

Belton.—4G 77
(Lincolnshire)
Belton.—2G 69
(Norfolk)
Beltring.—1A 20
Belts of Collonach.—4D 154
Belvedere.—3F 31
Belvoir.—4F 77
Bembridge.—5E 17
Bemersyde.—1H 121
Bemerton.—5G 27
Bempton.—2G 103
Benacre.—4H 69
Ben Alder Lodge.—1C 144
Ben Armine Lodge.—2E 166
Benbecula Airport.—3C 172
Benbuie.—5G 119
Benderloch.—5D 142
Bendish.—5A 54
Bendronaig Lodge.—5C 158
Benenden.—2C 20
Benfieldside.—4E 117
Bengate.—3F 81
Bengeworth.—3E 51
Bengrove.—4D 50
Benhall Green.—1F 57
Benholm.—2H 147
Beningbrough.—4A 102
Benington.—5B 54
(Hertfordshire)
Benington.—3C 78
(Lincolnshire)
Benington Sea End.—3D 78
Benllech.—2E 83
Benmore Lodge.—2H 165
Bennacott.—4C 10
Bennah.—1E 9
Bennacarrigan.—3D 124
Bennethead.—2F 105
Benniworth.—4E 91
Benover.—1B 20
Benson.—3H 41
Bent.—1F 147
Benthall.—2G 123
(Northumberland)
Benthall.—2A 62
(Shropshire)
Bentham.—1H 39
Benthoul.—3F 155
Bentlawn.—5F 73
Bentley.—4F 29
(Hampshire)
Bentley.—2C 96
(Humberside)
Bentley.—2F 89
(South Yorkshire)
Bentley.—4D 56
(Suffolk)
Bentley.—3G 63
(Warwickshire)
Bentley.—3D 63
(West Midlands)
Bentley Grove.—4D 56
Bentley Heath.—1D 30
(Hertfordshire)
Bentley Heath.—5F 63
(West Midlands)
Bentpath.—5F 121
Bents.—3C 130
Bentworth.—4E 29
Benvie.—5C 146
Benville Lane.—3A 14
Benwell.—3F 117
Benwick.—3C 66
Beoley.—1E 51
Beoraidbeg.—4E 149
Bepton.—2G 17
Berden.—5D 54
Bere Alston.—3A 8
Bere Ferrers.—3A 8
Berepper.—4F 5
Bere Regis.—4D 14
Bergh Apton.—2F 69
Berinsfield.—3G 41
Berkeley.—3E 39
Berkhamsted.—2C 42

Berkley.—4D 26
Berkswell.—5G 63
Bermondsey.—3E 31
Bernera.—1G 149
Bernice.—4A 136
Bernisdale.—3D 156
Berrick Salome.—3H 41
Berriedale.—1H 167
Berrier.—2F 105
Berriew.—5D 72
Berrington.—4C 60
(Hereford & Worcester)
Berrington.—5G 133
(Northumberland)
Berrington.—5H 73
(Shropshire)
Berrington Green.—4C 60
Berringtonlaw.—5F 133
Berrow.—3D 24
Berrow Green.—2B 50
Berry Cross.—2E 11
Berry Down Cross.—1B 22
Berry Hill.—1D 34
(Dyfed)
Berry Hill.—1D 38
(Gloucestershire)
Berryhillock.—2C 162
Berrynarbor.—1B 22
Berry Pomeroy.—3E 9
Berryscaur.—5D 120
Berry's Green.—5F 31
Bersham.—1F 73
Berthengam.—3D 82
Berwick.—5G 19
Berwick Bassett.—5B 40
Berwick Hill.—2E 117
Berwick St James.—5F 27
Berwick St John.—1E 15
Berwick St Leonard.—5E 27
Berwick-upon-Tweed.—4F 133
Bescaby.—5F 77
Bescar.—1A 86
Besford.—3D 50
Bessacarr.—2G 89
Bessels Leigh.—2F 41
Bessingby.—3G 103
Bessingham.—2D 80
Best Beech Hill.—2H 19
Besthorpe.—3C 68
(Norfolk)
Besthorpe.—1F 77
(Nottinghamshire)
Beswick.—1C 96
Betchworth.—5D 30
Bethania.—4A 58
(Dyfed)
Bethania.—1G 71
(nr. Blaenau Ffestiniog, Gwynedd)
Bethania.—5F 83
(nr. Caernarfon, Gwynedd)
Bethel.—2B 72
(nr. Bala, Gwynedd)
Bethel.—4E 83
(nr. Caernarfon, Gwynedd)
Bethersden.—1D 20
Bethesda.—3D 35
(Dyfed)
Bethesda.—4F 83
(Gwynedd)
Bethlehem.—5F 47
Bethnal Green.—2E 31
Betley.—3B 74
Betsham.—3H 31
Betteshanger.—5H 33
Bettiscombe.—3G 13
Bettisfield.—2G 73
Betton.—4A 74
Betton Strange.—5H 73
Bettws.—3A 38
Bettws Bledrws.—2E 47
Bettws Cedewain.—1G 59
Bettws Evan.—3C 46
Bettws Gwerfil Goch.—1C 72
Bettws Newydd.—2B 38
Bettyhill.—2H 169

Betws.—1C 36
(Dyfed)
Betws.—4E 37
(Mid Glamorgan)
Betws Garmon.—5E 83
Betws-y-Coed.—5G 83
Betws-yn-Rhos.—3B 84
Beulah.—3B 46
(Dyfed)
Beulah.—2B 48
(Powys)
Bevendean.—5E 19
Bevercotes.—5G 89
Beverley.—1C 96
Beverstone.—3G 39
Bewaldeth.—1D 104
Bewcastle.—2G 115
Bewdley.—5B 62
Bewerley.—3E 101
Bewholme.—1D 96
Bexfield.—3C 80
Bexhill.—5B 20
Bexley.—3F 31
Bexleyheath.—3F 31
Bexleyhill.—1H 17
Bexwell.—2F 67
Beyton.—1B 56
Beyton Green.—1B 56
Bibbington.—5A 88
Bibury.—2C 40
Bicester.—5C 52
Bickenhall.—2F 13
Bickenhill.—4F 63
Bicker.—4B 78
Bicker Bar.—4B 78
Bicker Gauntlet.—4B 78
Bickershaw.—2D 86
Bickerstaffe.—2B 86
Bickerton.—5H 85
(Cheshire)
Bickerton.—4D 123
(Northumberland)
Bickerton.—4H 101
(North Yorkshire)
Bickford.—1C 62
Bickington.—2B 22
(nr. Barnstaple, Devon)
Bickington.—2D 9
(nr. Newton Abbot, Devon)
Bickleigh.—3B 8
(nr. Plymouth, Devon)
Bickleigh.—3C 12
(nr. Tiverton, Devon)
Bickleton.—2B 22
Bickley.—4F 31
(London)
Bickley.—5G 109
(North Yorkshire)
Bickley Moss.—1H 73
Bicknacre.—2D 44
Bicknoller.—5B 24
Bicknor.—5C 32
Bickton.—2G 15
Bicton.—4B 60
(Hereford & Worcester)
Bicton.—2H 59
(nr. Bishop's Castle, Shrops.)
Bicton.—4G 73
(nr. Shrewsbury,Shrops.)
Bidborough.—1G 19
Biddenden.—2C 20
Biddenden Green.—1C 20
Biddenham.—2H 53
Biddestone.—5G 39
Biddisham.—3D 25
Biddlesden.—3D 52
Biddlestone.—4D 122
Biddulph.—2C 74
Biddulph Moor.—2D 74
Bideford.—3A 22
Bidford-on-Avon.—2E 51
Bidlake.—3F 11
Bidston.—1E 85
Bielby.—5C 102
Bieldside.—3F 155

Bierley.—5D 16
(Isle of Wight)
Bierley.—2B 94
(West Yorkshire)
Bierton.—1B 42
Bigbury.—5C 8
Bigbury-on-Sea.—5C 8
Bigby.—5C 96
Big Corlae.—5F 119
Biggar.—3A 98
(Cumbria)
Biggar.—1C 120
(Strathclyde)
Biggin.—2F 75
(nr. Hartington, Derbys.)
Biggin.—3G 75
(nr. Hulland, Derbys.)
Biggin.—2F 95
(North Yorkshire)
Biggings.—5C 175
Biggin Hill.—5F 31
Biggleswade.—3A 54
Bighouse.—2A 170
Bighton.—5E 28
Biglands.—4D 114
Bignor.—2H 17
Big Sand.—1G 157
Bigton.—9E 175
Bilberry.—3E 6
Bilborough.—3C 76
Bilbrook.—2C 62
(Staffordshire)
Bilbrook.—1G 23
(Somerset)
Bilbrough.—5A 102
Bilbster.—3E 171
Bilby.—4G 89
Bildershaw.—2F 107
Bildeston.—5B 56
Billericay.—1A 32
Billesdon.—2E 64
Billesley.—2F 51
Billingborough.—4A 78
Billinge.—2C 86
Billingford.—5D 68
(nr. Diss. Norf.)
Billingford.—3C 80
(nr. East Dereham, Norf.)
Billingham.—2B 108
Billinghay.—2A 78
Billingley.—2E 89
Billingshurst.—3B 18
Billingsley.—4B 62
Billington.—5G 53
(Bedfordshire)
Billington.—2E 93
(Lancashire)
Billington.—5C 74
(Staffordshire)
Billockby.—4G 81
Billy Row.—1E 107
Bilsborrow.—1C 92
Bilsby.—5G 91
Bilsham.—3H 17
Bilsington.—2E 21
Bilson Green.—1E 39
Bilsthorpe.—1D 76
Bilsthorpe Moor.—2D 76
Bilston.—3F 131
(Lothian)
Bilston.—3D 62
(West Midlands)
Bilstone.—2A 64
Bilting.—1E 21
Bilton.—2D 96
(Humberside)
Bilton.—3G 123
(Northumberland)
Bilton.—4G 101
(Harrogate, N. Yorks.)
Bilton.—1E 45
(nr. York, N Yorks.)
Bilton.—5B 64
(Warwickshire)
Bilton Banks.—3G 123
Binbrook.—3E 91

Binchester Blocks.—1F 107
Bincombe.—5B 14
Bindal.—5G 167
Binegar.—4B 26
Bines Green.—4C 18
Binfield.—5B 42
Binfield Heath.—5A 42
Bingfield.—2C 116
Bingham.—3E 76
Bingham's Melcombe.—3C 14
Bingley.—2B 94
Bings Heath.—4H 73
Binham.—2B 80
Binley.—3C 28
(Hampshire)
Binley.—5A 64
(West Midlands)
Binnegar.—5D 15
Binniehill.—2B 130
Binsoe.—2F 101
Binstead.—4D 16
Binsted.—4F 29
(Hampshire)
Binsted.—3H 17
(West Sussex)
Binton.—2F 51
Bintree.—3C 80
Binweston.—5F 73
Birch.—1F 45
(Essex)
Birch.—2F 87
(Manchester)
Birchall.—2D 75
Bircham Newton.—4G 79
Bircham Tofts.—4G 79
Birchanger.—5E 55
Birchburn.—3D 124
Birch Cross.—4F 75
Bircher.—4B 60
Birches.—1E 63
Birch Green.—1F 45
Birchgrove.—4H 37
(South Glamorgan)
Birchgrove.—3D 36
(West Glamorgan)
Birch Heath.—4H 85
Birch Hill.—3H 85
Birchington.—4G 33
Birchley Heath.—3G 63
Birchmoor.—2G 63
Birchmoor Green.—4G 53
Birchover.—1G 75
Birch Vale.—4H 87
Birchview.—5F 161
Birch Wood.—2F 13
Bircotes.—3G 89
Birdbrook.—3G 55
Birdham.—3G 17
Birdingbury.—1B 52
Birdlip.—1H 39
Birdsall.—3D 102
Birds Edge.—2C 88
Birds Green.—2B 44
(Essex)
Birdsgreen.—4B 62
(Shropshire)
Birdsmoor Gate.—3G 13
Birdston.—2H 129
Birdwell.—2D 88
Birdwood.—1F 39
Birgham.—1B 122
Birichen.—4E 167
Birkby.—1B 104
(Cumbria)
Birkby.—4G 107
(North Yorkshire)
Birkdale.—1A 86
Birkenhead.—2F 85
Birkenhills.—4E 163
Birkenshaw.—3H 129
(Strathclyde)
Birkenshaw.—3C 94
(West Yorkshire)
Birkhall.—4H 153
Birkhill.—5C 146
Birkholme.—5G 77

Birkin.—3F 95
Birley.—2G 49
Birling.—4A 32
(Kent)
Birling.—4G 123
(Northumberland)
Birling Gap.—5G 19
Birlingham.—3D 50
Birmingham.—4E 63
Birmingham Airport.—4F 63
Birnam.—4H 145
Birse.—4C 154
Birsemore.—4C 154
Birstall.—2C 64
Birstall Smithies.—3C 94
Birstwith.—4F 101
Birthorpe.—4A 78
Birtle.—1F 87
Birtley.—4A 60
(Hereford & Worcester)
Birtley.—2B 116
(Northumberland)
Birtley.—4F 117
(Tyne & Wear)
Birtsmorton.—4C 50
Birts Street.—4B 50
Bisbrooke.—3F 65
Bisham.—4B 42
Bishampton.—2D 51
Bishop Auckland.—2F 107
Bishopbridge.—3C 90
Bishopbriggs.—2H 129
Bishop Burton.—2B 96
Bishopdown.—5G 27
Bishop Middleham.—1G 107
Bishopmill.—2G 161
Bishop Monkton.—3G 101
Bishop Norton.—3B 90
Bishopsbourne.—5F 33
Bishops Cannings.—2F 27
Bishop's Castle.—2A 60
Bishop's Caundle.—2B 14
Bishop's Cleeve.—5D 50
Bishop's Down.—2B 14
Bishop's Fonthill.—5E 27
Bishop's Frome.—2C 28
Bishop's Green.—2C 28
(Berkshire)
Bishop's Green.—1C 44
(Essex)
Bishop's Hull.—1F 13
Bishop's Itchington.—2A 52
Bishop's Lydeard.—1E 13
Bishop's Norton.—5C 50
Bishop's Nympton.—3D 22
Bishop's Offley.—3B 74
Bishop's Stortford.—5D 55
Bishops Sutton.—5E 28
Bishop's Tachbrook.—1H 51
Bishop's Tawton.—2B 22
Bishopsteignton.—2F 9
Bishopstoke.—2C 16
Bishopston.—4B 36
Bishopstone.—1B 42
(Buckinghamshire)
Bishopstone.—5F 19
(East Sussex)
Bishopstone.—3G 49
(Hereford & Worcester)
Bishopstone.—1F 15
(nr. Salisbury, Wilts.)
Bishopstone.—4D 40
(nr. Swindon, Wilts.)
Bishopstrow.—4D 27
Bishop Sutton.—3F 25
Bishop's Waltham.—2D 16
Bishopswood.—2F 13
(Somerset)
Bishop's Wood.—2C 62
(Staffordshire)
Bishopsworth.—2F 25
Bishop Thornton.—3F 101
Bishopthorpe.—5A 102
Bishopton.—5B 112
(Dumfries & Galloway)

Bishopton.—2G 107
(Durham)
Bishopton.—2F 101
(North Yorkshire)
Bishopton.—2F 129
(Strathclyde)
Bishopton.—2F 51
(Warwickshire)
Bishop Wilton.—4C 102
Bishton.—4B 38
(Gwent)
Bishton.—5E 75
(Staffordshire)
Bisley.—2H 39
(Gloucestershire)
Bisley.—5A 30
(Surrey)
Bispham.—1A 92
Bispham Green.—1B 86
Bissoe.—2E 5
Bisterne.—3G 15
Bisterne Close.—3H 15
Bitchfield.—5G 77
Bittadon.—1B 22
Bittaford.—4C 8
Bittering.—4B 80
Bittering Street.—4B 80
Bitterley.—3C 60
Bitterne.—2C 16
Bitteswell.—4C 64
Bitton.—2B 26
Bix.—4A 42
Bixter.—6E 175
Blaby.—3C 64
Blackawton.—4E 9
Black Bank.—4E 67
Black Barn.—5D 78
Blackborough.—3D 12
(Devon)
Blackborough.—1F 67
(Norfolk)
Blackborough End.—1F 67
Black Bourton.—2D 40
Blackboys.—3G 19
Blackbrook.—3H 75
(Derbyshire)
Blackbrook.—3C 86
(Merseyside)
Blackbrook.—4B 74
(Staffordshire)
Blackbrook.—1C 18
(Surrey)
Blackburn.—2F 155
(nr. Aberdeen, Grampian)
Blackburn.—3G 161
(nr. Elgin, Grampian)
Blackburn.—3D 93
(Lancashire)
Blackburn.—3C 130
(Lothian)
Black Callerton.—3E 117
Black Car.—3C 68
Black Clauchrie.—1H 111
Black Corries.—3G 143
Black Crofts.—5D 142
Black Cross.—3D 6
Blackden Heath.—5E 87
Blackditch.—2F 41
Black Dog.—3B 12
(Devon)
Blackdog.—2G 155
(Grampian)
Blackdown.—3G 13
Blackdyke.—4C 114
Blacker Hill.—2D 88
Blackfen.—3F 31
Blackfield.—3C 16
Blackford.—3E 115
(Cumbria)
Blackford.—2C 60
(Shropshire)
Blackford.—4E 25
(nr. Cheddar, Som.)
Blackford.—1B 14
(nr. Wincanton, Som.)

Blackford.—3A 138
(Tayside)
Blackfordby.—1H 63
Blackgang.—5C 16
Blackhall.—2F 131
(Lothian)
Blackhall.—3F 129
(Strathclyde)
Blackhall Colliery.—1B 108
Blackhall Mill.—4E 117
Blackhall Rocks.—1B 108
Blackham.—2F 19
Blackheath.—5C 56
(Essex)
Blackheath.—3E 31
(London)
Blackheath.—5G 69
(Suffolk)
Blackheath.—1B 18
(Surrey)
Blackheath.—4D 63
(West Midlands)
Black Heddon.—2D 117
Blackhill.—4H 163
(Grampian)
Blackhill.—3C 156
(Highland)
Black Hill.—2G 51
(Warwickshire)
Blackhills.—2G 163
(Grampian)
Blackhills.—3D 160
(Highland)
Blackjack.—4B 78
Blackland.—2F 27
Black Lane.—2E 87
Blackleach.—2B 92
Blackley.—2F 87
(Manchester)
Blackley.—4B 94
(North Yorkshire)
Blacklunans.—2A 146
Blackmill.—4F 37
Blackmoor.—5F 29
(Hampshire)
Blackmoor.—2D 87
(Manchester)
Blackmoor Gate.—1C 22
Blackmore.—2C 44
Blackmore End.—4G 55
(Essex)
Blackmore End.—1E 43
(Hertfordshire)
Black Mount.—4G 143
Blackness.—2D 130
Blacknest.—4F 29
Blackney.—4H 13
Blacknoll.—5D 14
Black Notley.—5G 55
Blacko.—1F 93
Black Pill.—3C 36
Blackpool.—5E 9
(Devon)
Blackpool.—2A 92
(Lancashire)
Blackpool Airport.—2A 92
Blackpool Gate.—2G 115
Blackridge.—3B 130
Blackrock.—1A 38
(Gwent)
Blackrock.—3B 126
(Strathclyde)
Blackrod.—1D 86
Blackshaw.—3B 114
Blackshaw Head.—3G 93
Blacksmith's Green.—1D 56
Blacksnape.—3E 93
Blackstone.—4D 18
Black Street.—4H 69
Black Tar.—4C 34
Blackthorn.—1H 41
Blackthorpe.—1B 56
Blacktoft.—3A 96
Blacktop.—3F 155
Black Torrington.—3E 11
Blacktown.—4A 38

Blackwater.—2E 5
(Cornwall)
Blackwater.—3G 29
(Hampshire)
Blackwater.—5D 16
(Isle of Wight)
Blackwater.—2F 13
(Somerset)
Blackwaterfoot.—3C 124
Blackwell.—2B 76
(nr. Alfreton, Derbys.)
Blackwell.—5B 88
(nr. Buxton, Derbys.)
Blackwell.—3F 107
(Durham)
Blackwell.—5D 63
(Hereford & Worcester)
Blackwell.—3G 23
(Somerset)
Blackwell.—3G 51
(Warwickshire)
Blackwood.—1G 113
(Dumfries & Galloway)
Blackwood.—3H 37
(Gwent)
Blackwood.—5A 130
(Strathclyde)
Blackwood Hill.—2D 74
Blacon.—4F 85
Bladnoch.—4B 112
Bladon.—1F 41
Blaenannerch.—3B 46
Blaenau Dolwyddelan.—5F 83
Blaenau Ffestiniog.—1G 71
Blaenavon.—2B 38
Blaenawey.—1A 38
Blaen Celyn.—2C 46
Blaen Clydach.—3F 37
Blaenffos.—4A 46
Blaengarw.—3F 37
Blaen-geuffordd.—2B 58
Blaengwrach.—2E 37
Blaengwynfi.—2E 37
Blaenllechau.—3G 37
Blaenpennal.—4B 58
Blaenplwyf.—3A 58
Blaenporth.—3B 46
Blaenrhondda.—3F 37
Blaenwaun.—2F 35
Blaen-y-coed.—2G 35
Blaen-y-cwm.—1H 37
(Gwent)
Blaen-y-cwm.—3F 37
(Mid Glamorgan)
Blagdon.—3F 25
(Avon)
Blagdon.—3E 9
(Devon)
Blagdon Hill.—2F 13
Blaguegate.—2B 86
Blaich.—1E 143
Blain.—2A 142
Blaina.—2A 38
Blair Atholl.—2F 145
Blair Drummond.—4G 137
Blairgowrie.—4A 8
Blairhall.—5C 138
Blairingone.—4B 138
Blairlogie.—4H 137
Blairmore.—5B 162
(Grampian)
Blairmore.—3B 168
(Highland)
Blairmore.—1C 128
(Strathclyde)
Blairquhanan.—1F 129
Blaisdon.—1F 39
Blakebrook.—5C 62
Blakedown.—5C 62
Blake End.—5G 55
Blakemere.—3F 49
Blakeney.—2E 39
(Gloucestershire)
Blakeney.—1C 80
(Norfolk)

Blakenhall.—3B 74
(Cheshire)
Blakenhall.—3D 62
(West Midlands)
Blakeshall.—4C 62
Blakesley.—2D 52
Blanchland.—4C 116
Blandford Camp.—3E 15
Blandford Forum.—3D 15
Blandford St Mary.—3D 15
Bland Hill.—4F 101
Blandy.—3G 169
Blanefield.—2G 129
Blankney.—1H 77
Blantyre.—4H 129
Blarmachfoldach.—2E 143
Blashaval.—1D 172
Blashford.—3G 15
Blaston.—3F 65
Blatchbridge.—4C 26
Blatherwycke.—3G 65
Blawith.—1B 98
Blaxhall.—2F 57
Blaxton.—2G 89
Blaydon.—3E 117
Bleadney.—4E 25
Bleadon.—3D 24
Blean.—4F 33
Bleanrhondda.—3F 37
Bleasby.—4D 90
(Lincolnshire)
Bleasby.—3E 76
(Nottinghamshire)
Bleasby Moor.—4D 90
Blebocraigs.—2G 139
Bledfa.—4H 59
Bledington.—5G 51
Bledlow.—2A 42
Bledlow Ridge.—3A 42
Blencarn.—1H 105
Blencogo.—5C 114
Blendworth.—2F 17
Blenheim.—2G 41
Blennerhasset.—5C 114
Bletchingdon.—1G 41
Bletchingley.—5E 31
Bletchley.—4F 53
(Buckinghamshire)
Bletchley.—4A 74
(Shropshire)
Bletherston.—2D 34
Bletsoe.—2H 53
Blewbury.—4G 41
Blickling.—3D 81
Blidworth.—2C 76
Blindburn.—3D 122
Blindcrake.—1C 104
Blindley Heath.—1E 19
Blisland.—2F 7
Blissford.—2G 15
Bliss Gate.—5B 62
Blisworth.—2E 53
Blithbury.—5E 75
Blitterlees.—4C 114
Blockley.—4F 51
Blofield.—2F 69
Blofield Heath.—4F 81
Blo' Norton.—5C 68
Bloomfield.—2H 121
Blore.—3F 75
Blount's Green.—4E 75
Bloxham.—4F 51
Bloxholm.—2H 77
Bloxwich.—2D 63
Bloxworth.—4D 15
Blubberhouses.—4F 101
Blue Anchor.—1G 23
(Somerset)
Blue Anchor.—3B 36
(West Glamorgan)
Blue Bell Hill.—4B 32
Blue Row.—1G 45
Bluetown.—5D 32
Blundeston.—3H 69
Blunham.—2A 54
Blunsdon St Andrew.—4C

ntington.—5C 62
ntisham.—5C 66
nts.—3H 7
ston.—3C 74
borough.—3B 90
ford.—5G 69
mhill.—1C 62
mhill Lawn.—1C 62
th.—5E 131
orders)
th.—1G 117
orthumberland)
th.—4G 89
ottinghamshire)
th Bank.—5E 131
h Bridge.—5E 131
thburgh.—5G 69
the.—5B 132
the Bridge.—3D 74
the Marsh.—3D 74
the.—5E 75
ton.—3A 90
rhills.—2H 139
rhunt.—3E 16
rshead.—2G 19
ast Sussex)
r's Head.—2C 86
Manchester)
rs Hill.—2F 41
rstall.—1H 41
sley Cross.—4F 11
th.—1H 159
at of Garten.—2D 152
bing.—4C 32
bington.—3C 62
bingworth.—2B 44
addon.—4F 7
king.—5G 55
king Churchstreet.—5G 55
dam.—4H 163
ddam.—10E 175
rkney)
ddington.—5C 50
edern.—2C 82
elwyddan.—3C 84
enham.—2H 49
ereford & Worcester)
enham.—1G 15
Wiltshire)
ewryd.—1D 82
afari.—3C 84
fford.—3D 82
fuan.—2C 70
ham.—1D 80
iam.—3B 20
icote.—4B 52
ine.—2D 6
innick.—4F 7
le Street Green.—4A 20
min.—3E 7
inant.—3H 83
ney.—3A 68
organ.—4C 82
rane.—3G 7
sham Green.—1F 21
ymoor Heath.—3F 63
allan.—3A 160
brae.—5H 163
end.—1C 118
hall.—3C 130
. Bathgate, Lothian)
hall.—3F 131
r. Loanhead, Lothian)
head.—5A 130
noor.—2A 162
nor Regis.—4H 17
raxie.—2E 154
side.—4B 130
The.—1A 60
n.—3D 162
ue.—1D 112
enie.—5E 151
ortha.—3F 5
ewyan.—3A 4
ddick.—3E 7

Bolam.—2E 107
(Durham)
Bolam.—1D 117
(Northumberland)
Bolberry.—5C 8
Bold Heath.—4C 86
Boldon.—3G 117
Boldon Colliery.—3G 117
Boldre.—4B 16
Boldron.—3D 106
Bole.—4H 89
Bolehall.—2G 63
Bolehill.—2G 75
Bolenowe.—3D 5
Boleside.—1G 121
Bolham.—2C 12
Bolham Water.—2E 13
Bolingey.—4B 6
Bollington.—4E 87
(nr. Lymm, Ches.)
Bollington.—5D 87
(nr. Macclesfield, Ches.)
Bolney.—3D 18
Bolnhurst.—2H 53
Bolshan.—3F 147
Bolsover.—5E 89
Bolsterstone.—3C 88
Bolstone.—4H 49
Boltachan.—4F 145
Boltby.—1H 101
Bolton.—2H 105
(Cumbria)
Bolton.—4C 102
(Humberside)
Bolton.—2B 132
(Lothian)
Bolton.—2E 87
(Manchester)
Bolton.—3F 123
(Northumberland)
Bolton Abbey.—4D 100
Bolton by Bowland.—1E 93
Boltonfelland.—3F 115
Boltongate.—5D 114
Bolton Green.—1C 86
Bolton-le-Sands.—3D 99
Bolton Low Houses.—5D 114
Bolton New Houses.—5D 114
Bolton-on-Swale.—5F 107
Bolton Percy.—5A 102
Bolton Town End.—3D 99
Bolton upon Dearne.—2E 89
Bolton Wood Lane.—5D 114
Bolventor.—2F 7
Bolwing Green.—2C 50
Bomarsund.—1F 117
Bomere Heath.—4G 73
Bonar Bridge.—4D 166
Bonawe Quarries.—5E 143
Bonby.—4C 96
Boncath.—4B 46
Bonchester Bridge.—3H 121
Bonchurch.—5D 16
Bond End.—1F 63
Bondleigh.—3G 11
Bonds.—1B 92
Bonehill.—2D 8
(Devon)
Bonehill.—2F 63
(Staffordshire)
Bo'ness.—1C 130
Boney Hay.—1E 63
Bonham.—5C 26
Bonhill.—2C 129
Bonigate.—2C 62
Bonjedward.—2A 122
Bonkle.—4B 130
Bonnington.—2E 21
(Kent)
Bonnington.—3E 131
(Lothian)
Bonnington.—5E 147
(Tayside)
Bonnybank.—3F 139
Bonnybridge.—1B 130
Bonnykelly.—3F 163

Bonnyrigg.—3G 131
Bonnyton.—5C 146
Bonnytown.—2H 139
Bonsall.—2G 75
Bont.—1B 38
Bontddu.—4F 71
Bont Dolgadfan.—5A 72
Bontgoch.—2B 58
Bonthorpe.—5G 91
Bont-newydd.—3C 84
(Clwyd)
Bontnewydd.—4B 58
(Dyfed)
Bontnewydd.—4D 83
(nr. Caernarfon, Gwynedd)
Bont Newydd.—1G 71
(nr. Ffestiniog, Gwynedd)
Bont-uchel.—5C 84
Bonvilston.—5G 37
Bon-y-maen.—3C 36
Booker.—3B 42
Booley.—3H 73
Boorley Green.—2D 16
Boosbeck.—3D 108
Boot.—4C 104
Booth.—3H 93
Boothby Graffoe.—2G 77
Boothby Pagnell.—4G 77
Booth Green.—4G 87
Boothstown.—2E 87
Boothville.—1E 53
Booth Wood.—1H 87
Bootle.—1A 98
(Cumbria)
Bootle.—3A 86
(Merseyside)
Booton.—3D 80
Booze.—4D 106
Boquhan.—1G 129
Boraston.—3A 62
Borden.—4C 32
(Kent)
Borden.—1G 17
(West Sussex)
Bordlands.—5E 131
Bordley.—3C 100
Bordon.—5G 29
Bordon Camp.—5F 29
Boreham.—2D 44
(Essex)
Boreham.—4D 27
(Wiltshire)
Boreham Street.—4A 20
Borehamwood.—1C 30
Boreland.—5D 120
Boreston.—4D 8
Borestone Brae.—4G 137
Boreton.—5H 73
Borgie.—3G 169
Borgue.—5D 112
(Dumfries & Galloway)
Borgue.—1H 167
(Highland)
Borley.—3A 56
Borley Green.—3A 56
(Essex)
Borley Green.—1B 56
(Suffolk)
Borlum.—1H 151
Bornesketaig.—1C 156
Bornish.—6C 172
Boroughbridge.—3G 101
Borough Green.—5C 32
Borras Head.—5F 85
Borreraig.—3A 156
Borrobol Lodge.—1F 167
Borrodale.—4A 156
Borrowash.—4B 76
Borrowby.—1H 101
(nr. Northallerton, N Yorks.)
Borrowby.—3E 109
(nr. Whitby, N Yorks.)
Borrowdale.—3D 104
Borrowston.—4F 171
(Highland)

Borrowston.—3D 173
(Western Isles)
Borstal.—4B 32
Borth.—2B 58
Borthwick.—4G 131
Borthwick Hall.—4G 131
Borth-y-Gest.—2E 71
Borve.—4D 156
(Highland)
Borve.—8B 172
(Barra, Western I.)
Borve.—3C 172
(Benbecula, Western I.)
Borve.—9B 173
(Berneray, Western I.)
Borve.—4C 173
(Harris, Western I.)
Borwick.—2E 99
Bosbury.—3A 50
Boscastle.—4A 10
Boscombe.—4G 15
(Dorset)
Boscombe.—5H 27
(Wiltshire)
Boscoppa.—4E 7
Bosham.—3G 17
Bosherston.—5C 34
Bosley.—1D 74
Bossall.—3C 102
Bossiney.—1E 7
Bossingham.—1F 21
Bossington.—1E 23
Bosta.—3D 173
Bostock Green.—1A 74
Boston.—3C 78
Boston Spa.—1E 95
Boswarthen.—3B 4
Boswinger.—2G 5
Botallack.—3H 4
Botany Bay.—5D 38
(Avon)
Botany Bay.—1D 31
(London)
Botcheston.—2B 64
Botesdale.—5C 68
Bothal.—1E 117
Bothampstead.—5G 41
Bothamsall.—5G 89
Bothel.—1C 104
Bothenhampton.—4H 13
Bothwell.—4A 130
Botley.—2C 42
(Buckinghamshire)
Botley.—2D 16
(Hampshire)
Botley.—2F 41
(Oxfordshire)
Botloe's Green.—5B 50
Botolph Claydon.—5E 53
Botolphs.—5C 18
Bottacks.—2G 159
Bottesford.—5A 96
(Humberside)
Bottesford.—4F 77
(Leicestershire)
Bottisford.—3G 27
Bottisham.—1E 55
Bottlesford.—1G 27
Bottomcraig.—1F 139
Bottom o' th' Moor.—1D 86
Bottoms.—4A 4
(Cornwall)
Bottoms.—3G 93
(West Yorkshire)
Botton Head.—3F 99
Botusfleming.—3A 8
Botwnnog.—2B 70
Bough Beech.—1F 19
Boughrood.—4D 48
Boughspring.—3D 38
Boughton.—2G 67
(Norfolk)
Boughton.—1E 53
(Northamptonshire)
Boughton.—1D 76
(Nottinghamshire)
Boughton Aluph.—1E 21

Boughton Green.—5B 32
Boughton Lees.—1E 20
Boughton Malherbe.—1C 20
Boughton Monchelsea.—5B 32
Boughton Street.—5E 33
Boughton Under Blean.—5E 32
Boulby.—3D 109
Bouldnor.—5B 16
Bouldon.—2C 60
Boulmer.—3G 123
Boulston.—3C 34
Boultham.—1G 77
Boulton.—4A 76
Boundary.—3G 75
Bounds.—4A 50
Bourn.—2C 54
Bournbrook.—4E 63
Bourne.—5H 77
Bourne End.—3G 53
(nr. Cranfield, Beds.)
Bourne End.—1H 53
(nr. Sharnbrook, Beds.)
Bourne End.—4B 42
(Buckinghamshire)
Bourne End.—2D 42
(Hertfordshire)
Bournemouth.—4F 15
Bournemouth (Hurn) Airport.
—4G 15
Bournes Green.—2D 32
(Essex)
Bournes Green.—2H 39
(Gloucestershire)
Bourne, The.—4G 29
Bournheath.—5D 62
Bournmoor.—4G 117
Bournville.—4E 63
Bourton.—2D 25
(Avon)
Bourton.—5C 26
(Dorset)
Bourton.—4D 40
(Oxfordshire)
Bourton.—1C 60
(Shropshire)
Bourton.—2F 27
(Wiltshire)
Bourton on Dunsmore.—5B 64
Bourton-on-the-Hill.—4F 51
Bourton-on-the-Water.—5F 51
Bousd.—2D 140
Boustead Hill.—4D 114
Bouth.—1C 98
Bouthwaite.—2E 100
Boveney.—3A 30
Boveridge.—2F 15
Boverton.—5F 37
Bovey Tracey.—5B 12
Bovingdon.—2D 42
Bovingdon Green.—4B 42
Bovinger.—2B 44
Bovington Camp.—5D 14
Bow.—3H 11
(Devon)
Bow.—8C 174
(Orkney)
Bowbank.—2C 106
Bow Brickhill.—4G 53
Bowbridge.—2C 39
Bowburn.—1G 107
Bowcombe.—5C 16
Bowd.—5E 12
Bowden.—1H 121
(Borders)
Bowden.—5E 9
(Devon)
Bowden Hill.—2E 27
Bowdon.—4E 87
Bower.—1A 116
Bowerchalke.—1F 15
Bower Hinton.—2H 13
Bowermadden.—2E 171
Bowers.—4C 74
Bowers Gifford.—2B 32
Bowershall.—4C 138
Bowertower.—2E 171

Bowes.—3C 106
Bowgreave.—1B 92
Bowhousebog.—4B 130
Bowithick.—1F 7
Bowland Bridge.—1D 98
Bowlees.—2C 106
Bowley.—2H 49
Bowlhead Green.—2A 18
Bowling.—2F 129
(Strathclyde)
Bowling.—2B 94
(West Yorkshire)
Bowling Bank.—1F 73
Bowlish.—4B 26
Bowmanstead.—5E 104
Bowmore.—4B 126
Bowness-on-Solway.—3D 114
Bowness-on-Windermere.
—5F 105
Bow of Fife.—2F 139
Bowood.—4H 13
Bowriefauld.—4E 147
Bowscale.—1E 105
Bowsden.—5F 133
Bowside Lodge.—2A 170
Bowston.—5F 105
Bow Street.—2B 58
Bowthorpe.—2D 69
Box.—2G 39
(Gloucestershire)
Box.—2D 26
(Wiltshire)
Boxbush.—5A 50
Box End.—3H 53
Boxford.—5F 41
(Berkshire)
Boxford.—3B 56
(Suffolk)
Boxgrove.—3H 17
Boxley.—5B 32
Box's Shop.—3C 10
Boxted.—4B 56
(Essex)
Boxted.—2A 56
(Suffolk)
Boxted Heath.—4B 56
Boxworth.—1C 54
Boxworth End.—1C 54
Boyden End.—2G 55
Boyden Gate.—4G 33
Boylestone.—4F 75
Boylestonfield.—4F 75
Boyndie.—2D 162
(nr. Banff, Grampian)
Boyndie.—2G 163
(nr. Fraserburgh, Grampian)
Boynton.—3G 103
Boys Hill.—2B 14
Boythorpe.—1A 76
Boyton.—4D 10
(Cornwall)
Boyton.—3F 57
(Suffolk)
Boyton.—5E 27
(Wiltshire)
Boyton Cross.—2C 44
Boyton End.—4F 55
(Essex)
Boyton End.—3G 55
(Suffolk)
Bozeat.—2G 53
Braaid.—4C 110
Braal Castle.—2D 170
Brabling Green.—1E 57
Brabourne.—1F 21
Brabourne Lees.—1E 21
Brabster.—2F 171
Bracadale.—5C 156
Braceborough.—1H 65
Bracebridge.—1G 77
Bracebridge Heath.—1G 77
Bracebridge Low Fields.—1G 77
Braceby.—4H 77
Bracewell.—1F 93
Brackenfield.—2A 76
Brackenlands.—5D 114

Brackenthwaite.—5D 114
(Cumbria)
Brackenthwaite.—4F 101
(North Yorkshire)
Brackla.—3C 160
Bracklesham.—4G 17
Brackletter.—5D 150
Brackley.—4C 52
Brackley Hatch.—3D 52
Bracknell.—2G 29
Braco.—3H 137
Bracobrae.—3C 162
Bracon.—2H 89
Bracon Ash.—3D 69
Bracora.—4F 149
Bradbourne.—2G 75
Bradbury.—2G 107
Bradda.—4A 110
Bradden.—3D 52
Bradenham.—3B 42
Bradenstoke.—5A 40
Bradfield.—5H 41
(Berkshire)
Bradfield.—4D 56
(Essex)
Bradfield.—2E 81
(Norfolk)
Bradfield Combust.—2A 56
Bradfield Green.—2A 74
Bradfield Heath.—5D 56
Bradfield St Clare.—2B 56
Bradfield St George.—1B 56
Bradford.—1G 75
(Derbyshire)
Bradford.—3E 11
(Devon)
Bradford.—1F 123
(Northumberland)
Bradford.—2B 94
(West Yorkshire)
Bradford Abbas.—2A 14
Bradford Barton.—2B 12
Bradford Leigh.—2D 26
Bradford-on-Avon.—2D 26
Bradford-on-Tone.—1E 13
Bradford Peverell.—4B 14
Bradiford.—2B 22
Brading.—5E 16
Bradley.—3H 85
(Cheshire)
Bradley.—5F 85
(Clwyd)
Bradley.—1H 105
(Cumbria)
Bradley.—3G 75
(Derbyshire)
Bradley.—3F 39
(Gloucestershire)
Bradley.—4E 29
(Hampshire)
Bradley.—5E 97
(Humberside)
Bradley.—1D 100
(North Yorkshire)
Bradley.—1C 62
(Staffordshire)
Bradley.—3D 62
(West Midlands)
Bradley.—3B 94
(West Yorkshire)
Bradley Cross.—3E 25
Bradley Green.—1H 73
(Cheshire)
Bradley Green.—1D 51
(Hereford & Worcester)
Bradley Green.—5C 24
(Somerset)
Bradley Green.—2G 63
(Warwickshire)
Bradley in the Moors.—3E 75
Bradley Mount.—5G 87
Bradley Stoke.—4E 39
Bradlow.—4B 50
Bradmore.—4C 76
(Nottinghamshire)

Bradmore.—3C 62
(West Midlands)
Bradninch.—3C 12
Bradnop.—2E 75
Bradpole.—4H 13
Bradshaw.—1E 87
Bradstone.—1H 7
Bradwall Green.—1B 74
Bradway.—4D 88
Bradwell.—4F 53
(Buckinghamshire)
Bradwell.—4B 88
(Derbyshire)
Bradwell.—5A 56
(Essex)
Bradwell.—2H 69
(Norfolk)
Bradwell-on-Sea.—2G 45
Bradwell Waterside.—2F 45
Bradworthy.—2D 10
Brae.—5C 164
(Highland)
Brae.—5E 175
(Shetland)
Braeantra.—1H 159
Braefield.—5G 159
Braefindon.—3A 160
Braegrum.—1C 138
Braehead.—4B 112
(Dumfries & Galloway)
Braehead.—1H 119
(nr. Coalburn, S'clyde.)
Braehead.—4C 130
(nr. Forth, S'clyde.)
Braehead.—3F 147
(Tayside)
Braehoulland.—4D 175
Braemar.—4F 153
Braemore.—5C 170
(nr. Dunbeath, H'land.)
Braemore.—1D 158
(nr. Ullapool, H'land.)
Brae of Achnahaird.—2E 165
Brae Roy Lodge.—4F 151
Braeside.—5G 163
(Grampian)
Braeside.—2D 128
(Strathclyde)
Braes of Coul.—3B 146
Braetongue.—3F 169
Braeval.—3E 137
Braevallich.—3G 135
Brafferton.—2F 107
(Durham)
Brafferton.—2H 101
(North Yorkshire)
Brafield-on-the-Green.—2F 53
Bragar.—3E 173
Bragbury End.—5B 54
Bragleenbeg.—1G 135
Braichmelyn.—4F 83
Braides.—4D 98
Braidwood.—5B 130
Braigo.—3A 126
Brailsford.—3G 75
Braintree.—5G 55
Braiseworth.—5D 68
Braishfield.—1B 16
Braithwaite.—2D 104
(Cumbria)
Braithwaite.—4G 95
(South Yorkshire)
Braithwaite.—1H 93
(West Yorkshire)
Braithwell.—3F 89
Brakefield Green.—2C 68
Bramber.—4C 18
Brambledown.—3D 32
Brambridge.—1C 16
Bramcote.—4C 76
(Nottinghamshire)
Bramcote.—4B 64
(Warwickshire)
Bramdean.—1E 16
Bramerton.—2E 69

Bramfield.—1F 43
(Hertfordshire)
Bramfield.—5F 69
(Suffolk)
Bramford.—3D 56
Bramhall.—4F 87
Bramham.—1E 94
Bramhope.—1C 94
Bramley.—3E 29
(Hampshire)
Bramley.—3E 89
(South Yorkshire)
Bramley.—1B 18
(Surrey)
Bramley.—2C 94
(West Yorkshire)
Bramley Green.—3E 29
Bramley Head.—4E 101
Bramley Vale.—1B 76
Bramling.—5G 33
Brampford Speke.—4C 12
Brampton.—5B 66
(Cambridgeshire)
Brampton.—2H 105
(nr. Appleby, Cumbria)
Brampton.—3G 115
(nr. Carlisle, Cumbria)
Brampton.—5A 90
(Lincolnshire)
Brampton.—3E 81
(Norfolk)
Brampton.—2E 88
(South Yorkshire)
Brampton.—4G 69
(Suffolk)
Brampton Abbotts.—5A 50
Brampton Ash.—4E 65
Brampton Bryan.—3A 60
Brampton en le Morthen.—4E 89
Bramshall.—2F 75
Bramshaw.—2A 16
Bramshill.—2F 29
Bramshott.—5G 29
Branault.—2G 141
Brancaster.—3G 79
Brancaster Staithe.—3G 79
Brancepeth.—1F 107
Branch End.—3D 116
Branchill.—3E 161
Branderburgh.—1G 161
Brandesburton.—1D 96
Brandeston.—1E 57
Brand Green.—5B 50
Brandhill.—3B 60
Brandis Corner.—3E 11
Brandish Street.—1F 23
Brandiston.—3D 80
Brandon.—1F 107
(Durham)
Brandon.—3G 77
(Lincolnshire)
Brandon.—3E 123
(Northumberland)
Brandon.—4G 67
(Suffolk)
Brandon.—5B 64
(Warwickshire)
Brandon Bank.—4F 67
Brandon Creek.—3F 67
Brandon Parva.—2C 68
Brandsby.—2A 102
Brandy Wharf.—3C 90
Brane.—4B 4
Bran End.—5F 55
Bransbury.—4C 28
Bransby.—5B 90
Branscombe.—5E 13
Bransford.—2B 50
Bransgore.—4G 15
Bransholme.—2D 96
Bransley.—5A 62
Branston.—5F 77
(Leicestershire)
Branston.—1H 77
(Lincolnshire)

Branston.—5G 75
(Staffordshire)
Branston Booths.—1H 77
Branstone.—5D 16
Bransty.—3A 104
Brant Broughton.—2G 77
Brantham.—4D 56
Branthwaite.—1D 104
(nr. Caldbeck, Cumbria)
Branthwaite.—2B 104
(nr. Workington, Cumbria)
Brantingham.—3B 96
Branton.—3E 123
(Northumberland)
Branton.—2G 89
(South Yorkshire)
Branton Green.—3H 101
Branxholme.—3G 121
Branxton.—1C 122
Brassington.—2G 75
Brasted.—5F 31
Brasted Chart.—5F 31
Bratch, The.—3C 62
Brathens.—4D 154
Bratoft.—1D 78
Brattleby.—4B 90
Bratton.—1A 62
(Shropshire)
Bratton.—3E 27
(Wiltshire)
Bratton Clovelly.—4E 11
Bratton Fleming.—2C 22
Bratton Seymour.—1B 14
Braughing.—5C 54
Braulen Lodge.—5E 159
Braunston.—2F 65
(Leicestershire)
Braunston.—1C 52
(Northamptonshire)
Braunstone.—2C 64
Braunton.—2A 22
Brawby.—2C 102
Brawdy.—2B 34
Brawl.—2A 170
Brawlbin.—3C 170
Bray.—3A 30
Braybrooke.—4E 65
Brayford.—2C 22
Bray Shop.—2H 7
Braystones.—4B 104
Brayton.—2G 95
Bray Wick.—5B 42
Brazacott.—4C 10
Brea.—2D 4
Breach.—3F 17
Breachwood Green.—5A 54
Breaclete.—4D 173
Breaden Heath.—2G 73
Breadsall.—4A 76
Breadstone.—2F 39
Breage.—4D 4
Breakachy.—4G 159
Bream.—2E 39
Breamore.—2G 15
Bream's Meend.—2E 39
Brean.—3C 24
Brearton.—3G 101
Breasclete.—4E 173
Breaston.—4B 76
Brechfa.—4E 47
Brechin.—2F 147
Breckles.—3B 68
Brecon.—5C 48
Bredbury.—3G 87
Brede.—4C 20
Bredenbury.—2A 50
Bredfield.—2C 57
Bredgar.—4C 32
Bredhurst.—4B 32
Bredicot.—2D 50
Bredon.—4D 50
Bredon's Norton.—4D 50
Bredwardine.—3F 49
Breedon on the Hill.—5B 76
Breich.—3C 130
Breightmet.—2E 87

Breighton.—2H 95
Breinton.—4G 49
Breinton Common.—4G 49
Breivig.—4G 173
Breiwick.—7F 175
Brelston Green.—1D 38
Bremhill.—5A 40
Brenachie.—1B 160
Brenchley.—1A 20
Brendon.—1D 22
Brenish.—5B 173
Brent.—2C 30
Brent Eleigh.—3B 56
Brentford.—3C 30
Brentingby.—1E 65
Brent Knoll.—3D 24
Brent Pelham.—4D 54
Brentwood.—1G 31
Brenzett.—3E 20
Brereton.—1E 63
Brereton Cross.—1E 63
Brereton Green.—1B 74
Brereton Heath.—1C 74
Bressingham.—4C 68
Bretby.—5G 75
Bretford.—5B 64
Bretforton.—3E 51
Bretherdale Head.—4G 105
Bretherton.—3B 92
Brettenham.—4B 68
(Norfolk)
Brettenham.—2B 56
(Suffolk)
Bretton.—4F 85
Brevig.—9B 172
Brewer Street.—5E 31
Brewlands Bridge.—2A 146
Brewood.—2E 62
Briantspuddle.—4D 14
Bricket Wood.—2E 43
Brickhampton.—3D 51
Bricklehampton.—3D 51
Bride.—1D 110
Bridekirk.—1C 104
Bridell.—3A 46
Bridestowe.—1B 8
Brideswell.—5C 162
Bridford.—1E 9
Bridfordmills.—1E 9
Bridge.—2D 5
(Cornwall)
Bridge.—5F 33
(Kent)
Bridge End.—2H 53
(Bedfordshire)
Bridge End.—5D 104
(Cumbria)
Bridge End.—4A 78
(Lincolnshire)
Bridgefoot.—2B 104
Bridge Green.—4D 54
Bridgehampton.—1A 14
Bridge Hewick.—2G 101
Bridgehill.—4D 117
Bridgemary.—3D 16
Bridgemont.—4H 87
Bridgend.—3E 105
(Cumbria)
Bridgend.—5B 8
(Devon)
Bridgend.—4C 120
(Dumfries & Galloway)
Bridgend.—2F 139
(Fife)
Bridgend.—5A 162
(nr. Dufftown, Grampian)
Bridgend.—5C 162
(nr. Huntly, Grampian)
Bridgend.—5H 163
(nr. Peterhead, Grampian)
Bridgend.—3F 159
(Highland)
Bridgend.—2D 130
(Lothian)
Bridgend.—5F 37
(Mid Glamorgan)

Bridgend.—4F 135
(Argyll, S'clyde.)
Bridgend.—3B 126
(Islay, S'clyde.)
Bridgend.—4C 144
(nr. Brechin, Tayside)
Bridgend.—4C 146
(nr. Kirriemuir, Tayside)
Bridgend.—1D 138
(Perth, Tayside)
Bridgend of Lintrathen.—...
Bridgeness.—1D 130
Bridge of Alford.—2C 154
Bridge of Allan.—4G 137
Bridge of Avon.—5F 161
Bridge of Awe.—1H 135
Bridge of Balgie.—4C 144
Bridge of Brown.—1F 153
Bridge of Cally.—3A 146
Bridge of Canny.—4D 154
Bridge of Dee.—3E 113
Bridge of Don.—3G 155
Bridge of Dun.—3F 147
Bridge of Dye.—5D 154
Bridge of Earn.—2D 138
Bridge of Ericht.—3E 144
Bridge of Feugh.—4E 154
Bridge of Gairn.—4A 154
Bridge of Gaur.—3C 144
Bridge of Muchalls.—4F
Bridge of Oich.—3F 151
Bridge of Orchy.—5G 143
Bridge of Walls.—6D 175
Bridge of Weir.—3E 129
Bridge Reeve.—2C 11
Bridgerule.—3C 10
Bridge Sollers.—3G 49
Bridge Street.—3A 56
Bridgetown.—3E 9
(Devon)
Bridgetown.—2F 23
(Somerset)
Bridge Town.—2G 51
(Warwickshire)
Bridge Trafford.—3G 85
Bridgeyate.—5E 39
Bridgham.—4B 68
Bridgnorth.—3B 62
Bridgtown.—2D 63
Bridgwater.—5D 24
Bridlington.—3G 103
Bridport.—4H 13
Bridstow.—5H 49
Brierfield.—2F 93
Brierley.—1E 39
(Gloucestershire)
Brierley.—2G 49
(Hereford & Worcester)
Brierley.—4E 94
(South Yorkshire)
Brierley Hill.—4D 62
Brierton.—2B 108
Briery.—2D 104
Briestfield.—4C 94
Brigg.—5C 96
Briggate.—3F 81
Briggswath.—4F 109
Brigham.—1B 104
(Cumbria)
Brigham.—4F 103
(Humberside)
Brighouse.—3B 94
Brighstone.—5C 16
Brightgate.—2G 75
Brighthampton.—2E 41
Brightholmlee.—3C 88
Brightley.—4F 11
Brightling.—3A 20
Brightlingsea.—1G 45
Brighton.—4D 6
(Cornwall)
Brighton.—5E 19
(East Sussex)
Brightons.—2C 130
Brightwalton.—5F 41
Brightwalton Green.—5F

Brunton.—2G 123
(Northumberland)
Brunton.—3H 27
(Wiltshire)
Brushford.—3F 23
Brushford Barton.—3G 11
Bruton.—5B 26
Bryanston.—3D 14
Bryant's Bottom.—3B 42
Brydekirk.—2C 114
Brymbo.—5E 85
(Clwyd)
Brymbo.—3H 83
(Gwynedd)
Brympton.—2A 14
Bryn.—2B 36
(Dyfed)
Bryn.—2C 86
(Manchester)
Bryn.—2H 59
(Shropshire)
Bryn.—3E 36
(West Glamorgan)
Brynamman.—1D 36
Brynberian.—4A 46
Brynbryddan.—3D 36
Bryncae.—4F 37
Bryncethin.—4F 37
Bryncir.—1D 71
Bryn-coch.—3D 36
Bryncroes.—2B 70
Bryncrug.—5F 71
Bryn Du.—3C 82
Bryn Eden.—3G 71
Bryneglwys.—1D 72
(Clwyd)
Bryn Eglwys.—4F 83
(Gwynedd)
Brynford.—3D 84
Bryn Gates.—2C 86
Bryn Golau.—4G 37
Bryngwran.—3C 82
Bryngwyn.—2B 38
(Gwent)
Bryngwyn.—3D 48
(Powys)
Bryn-henllan.—1D 34
Bryohoffnant.—2C 46
Bryn-llwyn.—2C 84
Brynllywarch.—2G 59
Brynmawr.—1H 37
(Gwent)
Bryn-mawr.—2B 70
(Gwynedd)
Brynmenyn.—4F 37
Brynmill.—3C 36
Brynna.—4F 37
Brynrefail.—2D 83
(nr. Amlwch, Gwynedd)
Brynrefail.—4E 83
(nr. Caernarfon, Gwynedd)
Brynsadler.—4G 37
Bryn Saith Marchog.—5C 84
Brynsiencyn.—4D 83
Brynteg.—5F 85
(Clwyd)
Brynteg.—2D 83
(Gwynedd)
Brynygwenyn.—1B 38
Bryn-y-maen.—3H 83
Bualintur.—1C 148
Bubbenhall.—5A 64
Bubwith.—2H 95
Buccleuch.—3F 121
Buchanan Smithy.—1F 129
Buchanhaven.—4H 163
Buchanty.—1B 138
Buchany.—3G 137
Buchley.—2G 129
Buchlyvie.—4E 137
Buckabank.—5E 115
Buckden.—1A 54
(Cambridgeshire)
Buckden.—2C 100
(North Yorkshire)
Buckenham.—2F 69

Buckerell.—3E 13
Buckfast.—3D 8
Buckfastleigh.—3D 8
Buckhaven.—4F 139
Buckholm.—1G 121
Buckholt.—1D 38
Buckhorn Weston.—1C 14
Buckhurst Hill.—1F 31
Buckie.—2B 162
Buckingham.—4D 52
(Buckinghamshire)
Buckland.—5C 8
(Devon)
Buckland.—4E 51
(Gloucestershire)
Buckland.—2H 49
(Hereford & Worcester)
Buckland.—4C 54
(Hertfordshire)
Buckland.—1H 21
(Kent)
Buckland.—3E 41
(Oxfordshire)
Buckland.—5D 30
(Surrey)
Buckland Brewer.—3A 22
Buckland Common.—2C 42
Buckland Dinham.—3C 26
Buckland Filleigh.—3E 11
Buckland in the Moor.—2D 8
Buckland Monachorum.—3A 8
Buckland Newton.—2B 14
Buckland Ripers.—5B 14
Buckland St Mary.—2F 13
Buckland-tout-Saints.—5D 8
Bucklebury.—5G 41
Bucklegate.—4C 78
Buckleigh.—3A 22
Bucklers Hard.—3C 16
Bucklesham.—3E 57
Buckley.—4E 85
Buckley Green.—1F 51
Buckley Hill.—3A 86
Bucklow Hill.—4E 87
Buckminster.—5F 77
Bucknall.—1A 78
(Lincolnshire)
Bucknall.—3D 74
(Staffordshire)
Bucknell.—5C 52
(Oxfordshire)
Bucknell.—3A 60
(Shropshire)
Buckpool.—2B 162
Bucksburn.—3F 163
Buck's Cross.—1D 10
Bucks Green.—2B 18
Bucks Hill.—2D 42
Bucks Horn Oak.—4G 29
Buck's Mills.—1D 10
Buckton.—3A 60
(Hereford & Worcester)
Buckton.—2G 103
(Humberside)
Buckton.—1E 123
(Northumberland)
Buckton Vale.—2G 87
Buckworth.—5A 66
Budby.—1D 76
Bude.—3C 10
Budge's Shop.—4H 7
Budlake.—3C 12
Budle.—1F 123
Budleigh Salterton.—5D 12
Budock Water.—3E 5
Buerton.—3A 74
Buffler's Holt.—4D 52
Bugbrooke.—2D 52
Buglawton.—1C 74
Bugle.—4E 141
Bugthorpe.—4C 102
Buildwas.—2A 62
Builth Road.—2C 48
Builth Wells.—2C 48
Bulbourne.—1C 42

Bulby.—5H 77
Bulcote.—3D 76
Buldoo.—2B 170
Bulford.—4G 27
Bulford Barracks.—4G 27
Bulkeley.—5H 85
Bulkington.—4A 64
(Warwickshire)
Bulkington.—3E 27
(Wiltshire)
Bulkworthy.—2D 11
Bull Bay.—1D 82
Bullbridge.—2A 76
Bullgill.—1B 104
Bull Hill.—4B 16
Bullinghope.—4H 49
Bull's Green.—1F 43
Bullwood.—2C 128
Bulmer.—3A 56
(Essex)
Bulmer.—3B 102
(North Yorkshire)
Bulmer Tye.—4A 56
Buloit.—1G 151
Bulphan.—2H 31
Bulverhythe.—5B 20
Bulwark.—4G 163
Bulwell.—3C 76
Bulwick.—3G 65
Bumble's Green.—2H 43
Bunacaimb.—5E 149
Bunarkaig.—5D 150
Bunavoneadar.—7D 173
Bunbury.—5H 85
Bunchrew.—4B 160
Bundalloch.—1G 149
Bunessan.—1A 134
Bungay.—4F 69
Bunkegivie.—2H 151
Bunker's Hill.—2D 66
(Cambridgeshire)
Bunker's Hill.—2B 78
(Lincolnshire)
Bunker's Hill.—2H 69
(Suffolk)
Bunloif.—1G 151
Bunmhullin.—7D 172
Bunny.—5C 76
Bunoich.—3F 151
Bunree.—2E 143
Bunroy.—5E 151
Buntait.—5F 159
Buntingford.—5C 54
Bunting's Green.—4A 56
Bunwell.—3D 68
Bunwell Street.—3D 68
Burbage.—5H 87
(Derbyshire)
Burbage.—3B 64
(Leicestershire)
Burbage.—2H 27
(Wiltshire)
Burcher.—4A 60
Burchett's Green.—4B 42
Burcombe.—5F 27
Burcot.—3G 41
Burcote.—3B 62
Burcott.—5F 53
(Buckinghamshire)
Burcott.—4F 25
(Somerset)
Burdale.—3D 102
Burdrop.—4A 52
Bures.—4B 56
Burford.—1D 40
(Oxfordshire)
Burford.—4C 60
(Shropshire)
Burf, The.—1C 50
Burgate Great Green.—5C 68
Burgate Little Green.—5C 68
Burgess Hill.—4E 19
Burgh.—2E 57
Burgh by Sands.—4E 115

Burgh Castle.—2G 69
Burghclere.—2C 28
Burghead.—2F 161
Burghfield.—2E 29
Burghfield Common.—2E 29
Burghfield Hill.—2E 29
Burgh Heath.—5D 30
Burghill.—3G 49
Burgh le Marsh.—1E 79
Burgh Muir.—2E 155
Burgh next Aylsham.—3E 81
Burgh on Bain.—4E 91
Burgh St Margaret.—4G 81
Burgh St Peter.—3G 69
Burghwallis.—4F 95
Burgie.—3E 161
Burham.—4B 32
Buriton.—1F 17
Burland.—2A 74
(Cheshire)
Burland.—8E 175
(Shetland)
Burlawn.—2D 6
Burleigh.—5B 42
(Berkshire)
Burleigh.—2G 39
(Gloucestershire)
Burlescombe.—2D 12
Burleston.—4C 14
Burlestone.—5E 9
Burley.—3H 15
(Hampshire)
Burley.—1F 65
(Leicestershire)
Burley.—2C 94
(West Yorkshire)
Burleydam.—3A 74
Burley Gate.—3H 49
Burley in Wharfdale.—1B 94
Burley Street.—3H 15
Burley Woodhead.—1B 94
Burlingjobb.—2E 49
Burlton.—3G 73
Burmantofts.—2D 94
Burmarsh.—2E 21
Burmington.—4G 51
Burn.—3F 95
Burnage.—3F 87
Burnaston.—4G 75
Burnbanks.—3G 105
Burnby.—1A 96
Burncross.—3D 88
Burneside.—5G 105
Burness.—3F 174
Burneston.—1G 101
Burnett.—2B 26
Burnfoot.—3H 121
(Hawick, Borders)
Burnfoot.—3G 121
(nr. Roberton, Borders)
Burnfoot.—3B 138
(Tayside)
Burngreave.—4D 88
Burnham.—2A 30
(Buckinghamshire)
Burnham.—4C 96
(Humberside)
Burnham Deepdale.—1A 80
Burnham Green.—1F 43
Burnham Market.—1A 80
Burnham Norton.—1A 80
Burnham-on-Crouch.—1D 32
Burnham-on-Sea.—4D 24
Burnham Overy Staithe.—1A 80
Burnham Overy Town.—1A 80
Burnham Thorpe.—1A 80
Burnhaven.—4H 163
Burnhead.—5A 120
Burnhervie.—2E 155
Burnhill Green.—2B 62
Burnhope.—5E 117
Burnhouse.—4E 129
Burniston.—5H 109
Burnlee.—2B 88
Burnley.—2F 93
Burnmouth.—3F 133

Burn Naze.—1A 92
Burn of Cambus.—3G 137
Burnopfield.—4E 117
Burnsall.—3D 100
Burnside.—3D 138
(Fife)
Burnside.—2D 130
(Broxburn, Lothian)
Burnside.—2D 130
(nr. Winchburgh, Lothian)
Burnside.—4D 175
(Shetland)
Burnside.—2D 130
(Glasgow, S'clyde.)
Burnside.—3E 119
(nr. New Cumnock, S'clyde.)
Burnside.—3E 147
(Tayside)
Burntcommon.—5B 30
Burntheath.—4G 75
(Derbyshire)
Burnt Heath.—5C 56
(Essex)
Burnt Hill.—5G 41
Burntisland.—5E 139
Burnt Oak.—1D 30
Burnton.—4D 119
Burntstalk.—4G 79
Burntwood.—2E 63
Burntwood Green.—2E 63
Burnt Yates.—3F 101
Burnwynd.—3E 131
Burpham.—5B 30
(Surrey)
Burpham.—5B 18
(West Sussex)
Burradon.—4D 123
(Northumberland)
Burradon.—2F 117
(Tyne & Wear)
Burrafirth.—1H 175
Burras.—3D 5
Burraton.—4A 8
Burravoe.—4G 175
Burrells.—3H 105
Burrelton.—5B 146
Burridge.—3G 13
(nr. Chard, Devon)
Burridge.—2H 11
(nr. Chawleigh, Devon)
Burridge.—2D 16
(Hampshire)
Burrigill.—5E 171
Burrill.—1F 101
Burringham.—5A 96
Burrington.—3E 25
(Avon)
Burrington.—2G 11
(Devon)
Burrington.—3B 60
(Hereford & Worcester)
Burrough End.—2F 55
Burrough Green.—2F 55
Burrough on the Hill.—1E 65
Burrow.—5D 12
(Devon)
Burrow.—1F 23
(Somerset)
Burrow Bridge.—1G 13
Burrowhill.—4A 30
Burry.—3A 36
Burry Green.—3A 36
Burry Port.—2A 36
Burscough.—1B 86
Burscough Bridge.—1B 86
Bursea.—2A 96
Burshill.—1C 96
Bursledon.—3C 16
Burslem.—3C 74
Burstall.—3C 56
Burstock.—3H 13
Burston.—3H 11
(Devon)
Burston.—4D 68
(Norfolk)

Burston.—4D 74
(Staffordshire)
Burstow.—1E 19
Burstwick.—3E 97
Burtersett.—1B 100
Burtholme.—3G 115
Burthorpe.—1G 55
Burthwaite.—5F 115
Burtoft.—4B 78
Burton.—4H 85
(nr. Kelsall, Ches.)
Burton.—3F 85
(nr. Neston, Ches.)
Burton.—5F 85
(Clwyd)
Burton.—2E 99
(Cumbria)
Burton.—4G 15
(nr. Christchurch, Dorset)
Burton.—4B 14
(nr. Dorchester, Dorset)
Burton.—4C 34
(Dyfed)
Burton.—5B 90
(Lincolnshire)
Burton.—1F 123
(Northumberland)
Burton.—4B 24
(Somerset)
Burton.—5G 39
(nr. Chippenham, Wilts.)
Burton.—5D 26
(nr. Warminster, Wilts.)
Burton Agnes.—3G 103
Burton Bradstock.—5H 13
Burton Coggles.—5G 77
Burton Constable.—2D 97
Burton Corner.—3C 78
Burton End.—3F 55
(Cambridgeshire)
Burton End.—5C 55
(Essex)
Burton Fleming.—2F 103
Burton Green.—5F 85
(Clwyd)
Burton Green.—5G 63
(Warwickshire)
Burton Hastings.—4B 64
Burton in Lonsdale.—2F 99
Burton Joyce.—3D 76
Burton Latimer.—5F 65
Burton Lazars.—1E 65
Burton Leonard.—3G 101
Burton on the Wolds.—5C 76
Burton Overy.—3D 64
Burton Pedwardine.—3A 78
Burton Pidsea.—2E 97
Burton Salmon.—3E 95
Burton's Green.—5A 56
Burton Stather.—4A 96
Burton upon Stather.—4A 96
Burton upon Trent.—5G 75
Burton Wolds.—5D 76
Burtonwood.—3C 86
Burwardsley.—5H 85
Burwarton.—4A 62
Burwash.—3A 20
Burwash Common.—3H 19
Burwash Weald.—3A 20
Burwell.—1E 55
(Cambridgeshire)
Burwell.—5F 91
(Lincolnshire)
Burwen.—1D 82
Bury.—4B 86
(Cambridgeshire)
Bury.—1F 87
(Manchester)
Bury.—3F 23
(Somerset)
Bury.—4B 18
(West Sussex)
Bury End.—4H 14
Bury Green.—5D 54
Bury St Edmunds.—1A 56
Burythorpe.—3C 102

Carloway.—3E 173
Carlton.—2G 53
(Bedfordshire)
Carlton.—2F 55
(Cambridgeshire)
Carlton.—2G 107
(Cleveland)
Carlton.—2A 64
(Leicestershire)
Carlton.—1B 102
(nr. Helmsley, N Yorks.)
Carlton.—1D 100
(nr. Middleham, N Yorks.)
Carlton.—3G 95
(nr. Selby, N Yorks.)
Carlton.—3D 76
(Nottinghamshire)
Carlton.—2D 88
(South Yorkshire)
Carlton.—1F 57
(Suffolk)
Carlton.—3D 94
(West Yorkshire)
Carlton Colville.—4H 69
Carlton Curlieu.—3D 64
Carlton Husthwaite.—2H 101
Carlton in Lindrick.—4F 89
Carlton-le-Moorland.—2G 77
Carlton Miniott.—1G 101
Carlton-on-Trent.—1E 77
Carlton Scroop.—3G 77
Carluke.—4B 130
Carmarthen.—2H 35
Carmel.—3D 84
(Clwyd)
Carmel.—1B 36
(Dyfed)
Carmel.—5D 83
(nr. Caernarfon, Gwynedd)
Carmel.—2C 82
(nr. Llanerchymedd, Gwynedd)
Carminish.—9C 173
Carmunnock.—4G 129
Carmyle.—3H 129
Carmyllie.—4E 147
Carnaby.—3G 103
Carnach.—4E 161
(Grampian)
Carnach.—1C 150
(nr. Lochcarron, H'land.)
Carnach.—4E 165
(nr. Ullapool, H'land.)
Carnach.—8E 173
(Western Isles)
Carnachy.—3H 169
Carnain.—3B 126
Carnan.—4D 172
Carnbee.—3H 139
Carnbo.—3C 138
Carn Brea.—2D 5
Carndu.—1G 149
Carne.—3G 5
Carnell.—1D 118
Carnforth.—2D 99
Carn-gorm.—1B 150
Carnhedryn Uchaf.—2B 34
Carnhell Green.—3D 4
Carnie.—3F 155
Carnish.—4C 173
Carnkie.—3E 5
(nr. Falmouth, Corn.)
Carnkie.—3D 5
(nr. Redruth, Corn.)
Carnkief.—4B 6
Carno.—1E 59
Carnock.—5C 138
Carnon Downs.—2E 5
Carnoustie.—5E 147
Carntyne.—3H 129
Carnwath.—5C 130
Carnyorth.—3A 4
Carol Green.—5G 63
Carpalla.—4D 6
Carperby.—1D 100
Carradale.—2C 124

Carragreich.—8D 173
Carrbridge.—1D 152
Carr Cross.—1A 86
Carreglefn.—2C 82
Carrick.—4A 136
Carriden.—1D 130
Carrington.—2C 78
(Lincolnshire)
Carrington.—3G 131
(Lothian)
Carrington.—3E 87
(Manchester)
Carrog.—1D 72
(Clwyd)
Carrog.—1G 71
(Gwynedd)
Carron.—1B 130
(Central)
Carron.—4G 161
(Grampian)
Carronbridge.—5A 120
Carronshore.—1B 130
Carrow Hill.—3C 38
Carr Shield.—5B 116
Carrutherstown.—2C 114
Carr Vale.—1B 76
Carscreugh.—4H 111
Carsegowan.—4B 112
Carse House.—3F 127
Carseriggan.—3A 112
Carshalton.—4D 31
Carsington.—2G 75
Carsluith.—4B 112
Carsphairn.—5E 119
Carstairs.—5C 130
Carstairs Junction.—5C 130
Cartbridge.—5B 30
Carterhaugh.—4D 146
Carter's Clay.—1B 16
Carterton.—2D 40
Carterway Heads.—4D 116
Carthew.—4E 6
Carthorpe.—1G 101
Cartington.—4E 123
Cartland.—5B 130
Cartmel.—2C 98
Cartmel Fell.—1D 98
Cartworth.—2B 88
Carwath.—5E 114
Carway.—2A 36
Carwinley.—2F 115
Cascob.—4H 59
Cas-gwent.—3D 38
Cash Feus.—3E 138
Cashlie.—4B 144
Cashmoor.—2E 15
Casnewydd.—4B 38
Cassington.—1F 41
Cassop.—1A 106
Castell.—4D 84
(Clwyd)
Castell.—4G 83
(Gwynedd)
Castell Hendre.—2D 34
Castell-nedd.—3D 36
Castell-y-bwch.—3A 38
Casterton.—2F 99
Castle.—4F 25
Castle Acre.—4A 80
Castle Ashby.—2F 53
Castlebay.—9B 172
Castle Bolton.—5D 106
Castle Bromwich.—4F 63
Castle Bytham.—1G 65
Castlebythe.—2D 34
Castle Caereinion.—5D 72
Castle Camps.—3F 53
Castle Carrock.—4G 115
Castlecary.—2A 130
(Central)
Castle Cary.—5B 26
(Somerset)

Castle Combe.—5G 39
Castlecraig.—2C 160
Castle Donington.—5B 76
Castle Douglas.—3E 113
Castle Eaton.—3C 40
Castle Eden.—1B 108
Castleford.—3E 95
Castle Frome.—3A 50
Castle Green.—4A 30
(Surrey)
Castle Green.—5G 63
(Warwickshire)
Castle Gresley.—1G 63
Castle Heaton.—5F 133
Castle Hedingham.—4G 55
Castle Hill.—1A 20
(Kent)
Castlehill.—4B 130
(nr. Carluke, S'clyde.)
Castlehill.—2E 129
(Dumbarton, S'clyde.)
Castle Hill.—3D 56
(Suffolk)
Castlehill.—5B 146
(Tayside)
Castle Kennedy.—4G 111
Castle Lachlan.—4H 135
Castlemartin.—5C 34
Castlemilk.—4H 129
Castle Morris.—1C 34
Castlemorton.—4B 50
Castle O'er.—5E 121
Castle Park.—3F 109
Castlerigg.—2D 104
Castle Rising.—3F 79
Castleside.—5D 117
Castlethorpe.—3E 53
Castleton.—4B 88
(Derbyshire)
Castleton.—4F 153
(Braemar, Grampian)
Castleton.—1F 153
(nr. Glenlivet, Grampian)
Castleton.—4A 38
(Gwent)
Castleton.—1F 87
(Manchester)
Castleton.—4D 109
(North Yorkshire)
Castleton.—1G 127
(Strathclyde)
Castleton.—2B 138
(Tayside)
Castletown.—1G 105
(Cumbria)
Castletown.—5A 14
(Dorset)
Castletown.—2D 171
(Highland)
Castletown.—5B 110
(Isle of Man)
Castletown.—5D 74
(Staffordshire)
Castletown.—4G 117
(Tyne & Wear)
Castley.—1C 94
Caston.—3B 68
Castor.—3A 66
Caswell.—4B 36
Catacol.—5H 127
Catbrook.—2D 38
Catchems End.—5B 62
Catchgate.—4E 117
Catcleugh.—4B 122
Catcliffe.—4E 88
Catcott.—5D 25
Catcott Burtle.—4E 25
Caterham.—5E 31
Catfield.—3F 81
Catfield Common.—3G 81
Catford.—3E 31
Catforth.—2B 92
Cathcart.—3G 129
Cathedine.—5D 48
Catherine de Barnes.—4F 63
Catherington.—2E 17

Catherston Leweston.—4G 13
Catherton.—5A 62
Catlodge.—4A 152
Catlowdy.—2F 115
Catmore.—4F 41
Caton.—2D 9
(Devon)
Caton.—3E 99
(Lancashire)
Catrine.—2E 119
Cat's Ash.—3B 38
Catsfield.—4B 20
Catsgore.—1A 14
Catshill.—5D 62
Cattal.—4H 101
Cattawade.—4D 56
Catterall.—1B 92
Catterick.—5F 107
Catterick Bridge.—5F 107
Catterick Garrison.—5E 107
Catterlen.—1F 105
Catterline.—1H 147
Catterton.—5A 102
Catthorpe.—5C 64
Cattistock.—4A 14
Catton.—4E 81
(Norfolk)
Catton.—4B 116
(Northumberland)
Catton.—2G 101
(North Yorkshire)
Catton Hall.—1G 63
Catwick.—1D 96
Catworth.—5H 65
Caudle Green.—1H 39
Caulcott.—5C 52
Cauldhame.—4F 137
Cauldmill.—3H 121
Cauldon.—3E 75
Cauldon Lowe.—3E 75
Cauldwell.—1G 63
Caulkerbush.—4G 113
Caulside.—1F 115
Caunsall.—4C 62
Caunton.—1E 77
Causewayend.—1C 120
Causewayhead.—4G 137
Causey Park.—5F 123
Caute.—2E 11
Cautley.—5H 105
Cavendish.—3A 56
Cavendish Bridge.—5B 76
Cavenham.—1G 55
Caverfield.—5C 52
Caversham.—5A 42
Caversham Heights.—5A 42
Caverswall.—3D 74
Cavil.—2H 95
Cawdor.—4C 160
Cawkwell.—5E 91
Cawood.—2F 95
Cawsand.—4A 8
Cawston.—3D 80
(Norfolk)
Cawston.—5B 63
(Warwickshire)
Cawthorne.—1C 102
(North Yorkshire)
Cawthorne.—2C 88
(South Yorkshire)
Cawthorpe.—5H 77
Cawton.—2B 102
Caxton.—2C 54
Caynham.—3C 60
Caythorpe.—3G 77
(Lincolnshire)
Caythorpe.—3D 76
(Nottinghamshire)
Cayton.—1F 103
Ceannacroc Lodge.—2E 151
Cefn Berain.—4B 84
Cefn-brith.—5B 84
Cefn-bryn-brain.—1D 36
Cefn-bychan.—4D 84
Cefncaeau.—3B 36

Cefn Canol.—2E 73
Cefn Coch.—5C 72
Cefn-coed-y-cymmer.—2G 37
Cefn Cribwr.—4E 37
Cefn-ddwysarn.—2B 72
Cefn Einion.—2H 59
Cefneithin.—1B 36
Cefn Glas.—4E 37
Cefn Goch.—3D 72
Cefngorwydd.—3B 48
Cefn-llwyd.—2B 58
Cefn-mawr.—1E 73
Cefnpennar.—2G 37
Cefn-y-bedd.—5F 85
Cefn-y-coed.—1G 59
Cefn-y-pant.—2E 35
Ceidio Fawr.—2B 70
Cellan.—3F 47
Cellardyke.—3H 139
Cellarhead.—3D 74
Celleron.—2F 105
Cemaes.—1C 82
Cemmaes.—5H 71
Cemmes Road.—5H 71
Cenarth.—3B 46
Cennin.—1D 70
Ceres.—2G 139
Cerist.—2E 59
Cerne Abbas.—3B 14
Cerney Wick.—3B 40
Cerrigceinwen.—3D 82
Cerrigydrudion.—1B 72
Cess.—4G 81
Cessford.—2B 122
Ceunant.—4E 83
Chaceley.—4C 50
Chacewater.—2E 5
Chackmore.—4D 52
Chacombe.—3B 52
Chadderton.—2G 87
Chaddesden.—4A 76
Chaddesden Common.—4A 76
Chaddesley Corbett.—5C 62
Chaddlehanger.—2A 8
Chaddleworth.—5F 41
Chadlington.—5H 51
Chadshunt.—2H 51
Chadstone.—2F 53
Chad Valley.—4E 63
Chadwell.—5E 77
(Leicestershire)
Chadwell.—1B 62
(Shropshire)
Chadwell Heath.—2F 31
Chadwell St Mary.—3H 31
Chadwick End.—5G 63
Chadwick Green.—3C 86
Chaffcombe.—2G 13
Chagford.—1D 8
Chailey.—4E 19
Chainbridge.—2D 66
(Cambridgeshire)
Chain Bridge.—3C 78
(Lincolnshire)
Chainhurst.—1B 20
Chalbury.—3F 15
Chalbury Common.—3F 15
Chaldon.—5E 31
Chaldon Herring.—5C 14
Chale.—5C 16
Chale Green.—5C 16
Chalfont Common.—1B 30
Chalfont St Giles.—1A 30
Chalfont St Peter.—1B 30
Chalford.—2G 39
Chalgrove.—3H 41
Chalk.—3A 32
Chalk End.—1C 44
Chalk Hill.—5F 51
Challaborough.—5C 8
Challacombe.—1C 22
Challoch.—3A 112
Chalton.—2A 54
(nr. Bedford, Beds.)
Chalton.—5H 53
(nr. Luton, Beds.)

Chalton.—2F 17
(Hampshire)
Chalvington.—5G 19
Champany.—2D 130
Chance Inn.—2F 139
Chancery.—3A 58
Chandlers Cross.—4B 50
(Hereford & Worcester)
Chandler's Cross.—1B 30
(Hertfordshire)
Chandlers Ford.—1C 16
Chanlockfoot.—4G 119
Channel's End.—2A 54
Chantry.—4C 26
(Somerset)
Chantry.—3D 56
(Suffolk)
Chapel.—1D 104
(Cumbria)
Chapel.—4E 139
(Fife)
Chapel Allerton.—3E 25
(Somerset)
Chapel Allerton.—2D 94
(West Yorkshire)
Chapel Amble.—2D 6
Chapel Brampton.—1E 53
Chapelbridge.—3B 66
Chapel Chorlton.—4C 74
Chapel Cleeve.—1G 23
Chapel End.—3H 53
Chapel-en-le-Frith.—4A 88
Chapelfield.—2G 147
Chapelgate.—5D 78
Chapel Green.—4G 63
(nr. Coventry, Warwicks.)
Chapel Green.—1B 52
(nr. Southam, Warwicks.)
Chapel Haddlesey.—2F 95
Chapelhall.—3A 130
Chapel Hill.—5H 163
(Grampian)
Chapel Hill.—2D 38
(Gwent)
Chapel Hill.—2B 78
(Lincolnshire)
Chapelhill.—1E 138
(nr. Glencarse, Tayside)
Chapelhill.—5H 145
(nr. Harrietfield, Tayside)
Chapelknowe.—2E 114
Chapel Lawn.—3A 60
Chapel le Dale.—2G 99
Chapel Milton.—4A 88
Chapel of Garioch.—1E 154
Chapel Row.—2D 28
Chapels.—1B 98
Chapel St Leonards.—5H 91
Chapel Stile.—4E 104
Chapelthorpe.—3D 94
Chapelton.—3B 22
(Devon)
Chapelton.—2D 152
(nr. Grantown-on-Spey, H'la...)
Chapelton.—3H 159
(nr. Inverness, H'land.)
Chapelton.—5H 129
(Strathclyde)
Chapelton.—4F 147
(Tayside)
Chapel Town.—4C 6
(Cornwall)
Chapeltown.—1G 153
(Grampian)
Chapeltown.—1E 87
(Lancashire)
Chapeltown.—3D 88
(South Yorkshire)
Chapmanslade.—4D 26
Chapmans Well.—4D 10
Chapmore End.—1G 43
Chappel.—5A 56
Chard.—3G 13
Chard Junction.—3G 13
Chardstock.—3G 13
Charfield.—3F 39

aring.—1D 20	Charnock Green.—1C 86	Chelveston.—1G 53	Chettle.—2E 15	Chilworth.—2C 16 (Hampshire)	Christchurch.—4G 15 (Dorset)
aring Heath.—1D 20	Charnock Richard.—1C 86	Chelvey.—2E 25	Chetton.—3A 62	Chilworth.—1B 18 (Surrey)	Christchurch.—1D 38 (Gloucestershire)
aringworth.—4G 51	Charsfield.—2E 57	Chelwood.—2B 26	Chetwode.—5D 52	Chimney.—2E 41	Christian Malford.—5A 40
arlbury.—1E 41	Chart Corner.—5B 32	Chelwood Common.—3F 19	Chetwynd Aston.—1B 62	Chimney Street.—3G 55	Christleton.—4G 85
arlcombe.—2C 26	Charter Alley.—3D 28	Chelwood Gate.—2F 19	Cheveley.—1F 55	Chineham.—3E 28	Christmas Common.—3A 42
arlecote.—2G 51	Charterhouse.—3E 25	Chelworth.—3A 40	Chevening.—5F 31	Chingford.—1E 31	Christon.—3D 25
arles.—2C 22	Charterville Allotments.—1E 40	Chelworth Lower Green.—3B 40	Chevington.—1G 55	Chinley.—4H 87	Christon Bank.—2G 123
arlesfield.—3C 114	Chartham.—5F 33	Chelworth Upper Green.—3B 40	Chevithorne.—2C 12	Chinnor.—2A 42	Chryston.—2H 129
arleshill.—4G 29	Chartham Hatch.—5F 33	Chelynch.—4B 26	Chew Magna.—2E 25	Chipley.—1E 12	Chuck Hatch.—2F 19
arleston.—3F 129 (Strathclyde)	Chartridge.—2C 42	Cheney Longville.—2B 60	Chew Moor.—2D 86	Chipnall.—4B 232	Chudleigh.—2E 9
arleston.—4C 146 (Tayside)	Chart Sutton.—1C 32	Chenies.—1B 30	Chew Stoke.—2E 25	Chippenham.—1F 55 (Cambridgeshire)	Chudleigh Knighton.—2E 9
arlestown.—4E 7 (Cornwall)	Chart, The.—5F 31	Chepstow.—3D 38	Chewton Keynsham.—2B 26	Chippenham.—5H 39 (Wiltshire)	Chulmleigh.—2G 11
arlestown.—5B 14 (Dorset)	Charvil.—5A 42	Chequerfield.—3E 95	Chewton Mendip.—3F 25	Chipperfield.—2D 42	Chunal.—3H 87
arlestown.—5C 138 (Fife)	Charwelton.—2C 52	Chequers Corner.—2D 67	Chicacott.—4G 11	Chipping.—4C 54 (Hertfordshire)	Church.—3E 93
arlestown.—3G 155 (nr. Aberdeen, Grampian)	Chase Terrace.—1E 63	Cherhill.—5B 40	Chicheley.—3G 53	Chipping.—1D 92 (Lancashire)	Churcham.—1F 39
arlestown.—2H 163 (nr. St Combs, Grampian)	Chasetown.—1E 63	Cherington.—3H 39 (Gloucestershire)	Chichester.—3G 17	Chipping Campden.—4F 51	Church Aston.—1B 62
arlestown.—1H 157 (nr. Gairloch, H'land.)	Chastleton.—5G 51	Cherington.—4G 51 (Warwickshire)	Chickerell.—5B 14	Chipping Hill.—1E 44	Church Brampton.—1E 52
arlestown.—4A 160 (nr. Inverness, H'land.)	Chasty.—3D 10	Cheriton.—3E 12 (nr. Honiton, Devon)	Chickering.—5E 69	Chipping Norton.—5H 51	Church Broughton.—4G 75
arlestown.—2F 87 (Manchester)	Chatburn.—1E 93	Cheriton.—1D 22 (nr. Lynton, Devon)	Chicklade.—5E 27	Chipping Ongar.—2B 44	Church Common.—1F 17
arlestown.—3G 93 (West Yorkshire)	Chatcull.—4B 74	Cheriton.—5C 34 (Dyfed)	Chickward.—2E 49	Chipping Sodbury.—4F 39	Church Crookham.—3G 29
arlestown of Aberlour.—4G 161	Chatham.—4B 32	Cheriton.—1D 16 (Hampshire)	Chiddingfold.—2A 18	Chipping Warden.—3B 52	Churchdown.—5C 50
arles Tye.—2C 56	Chatham Green.—1D 44	Cheriton.—2F 21 (Kent)	Chiddingly.—4G 19	Chipstable.—3G 23	Church Eaton.—1C 62
arlesworth.—3H 87	Chathill.—2F 123	Cheriton.—3A 36 (West Glamorgan)	Chiddingstone.—1F 19	Chipstead.—5G 31 (Kent)	Church End.—5G 53 (nr. Dunstable, Beds.)
arlinch.—5C 24	Chatley.—1C 50	Cheriton Bishop.—4A 12	Chiddingstone Causeway.—1G 19	Chipstead.—5D 31 (Surrey)	Church End.—4A 54 (nr. Stotfold, Beds.)
arlton.—4B 28 (Hampshire)	Chattenden.—3B 32	Cheriton Cross.—4A 12	Chiddingstone Hoath.—1F 19	Chirbury.—1H 59	Church End.—4G 53 (nr. Woburn, Beds.)
arlton.—3E 51 (nr. Evesham, Here & Worcs.)	Chatteris.—4C 66	Cheriton Fitzpaine.—3B 12	Chideock.—4H 13	Chirk.—2E 73	Church End.—2D 55 (Cambridge, Cambs.)
arlton.—5C 62 (nr. Stourport-on-Severn, Here & Worcs.)	Chattisham.—3C 56	Cherrington.—5A 74	Chidgley.—2G 23	Chirmorie.—2H 111	Church End.—4B 66 (nr. Sawtry, Cambs.)
arlton.—5A 54 (Hertfordshire)	Chatton.—2E 123	Cherrybank.—1D 138	Chidham.—3F 17	Chirnside.—4E 133	Church End.—5C 66 (nr. Warboys, Cambs.)
arlton.—3F 31 (London)	Chatwall.—1C 60	Cherry Burton.—1B 96	Chieveley.—5F 41	Chirnsidebridge.—4E 133	Church End.—5C 66 (nr. Willingham, Cambs.)
arlton.—4C 52 (Northamptonshire)	Chaulden.—2D 42	Cherry Green.—5C 54	Chignall St James.—2C 44	Chirton.—3F 27	Church End.—2C 66 (nr. Wisbech, Cambs.)
arlton.—1B 116 (Northumberland)	Chaul End.—5H 53	Cherry Hinton.—2D 55	Chignall Smealy.—1C 44	Chisbridge Cross.—4B 42	Church End.—5G 55 (nr. Braintree, Essex)
arlton.—4F 41 (Oxfordshire)	Chawleigh.—2H 11	Cherry Willingham.—5C 90	Chigwell.—1F 31	Chisbury.—2A 28	Churchend.—5F 55 (nr. Great Dunmow, Essex)
arlton.—4H 73 (Shropshire)	Chawley.—2F 41	Chertsey.—4B 30	Chigwell Row.—1F 31	Chiselborough.—2H 13	Church End.—3E 55 (nr. Saffron Walden, Essex)
arlton.—3B 26 (nr. Radstock, Som.)	Chawston.—2A 54	Cheselbourne.—4C 14	Chilbolton.—5B 28	Chiseldon.—5C 40	Churchend.—1E 32 (nr. Southend, Essex)
arlton.—4B 26 (nr. Shepton Mallet, Som.)	Chawton.—5F 29	Chesham.—2C 42 (Buckinghamshire)	Chilcomb.—1D 16	Chiserley.—3H 93	Church End.—2F 39 (Gloucestershire)
arlton.—2G 17 (West Sussex)	Chaxhill.—1F 39	Chesham.—1F 87 (Manchester)	Chilcombe.—4A 14	Chislehampton.—3G 41	Church End.—3E 29 (Hampshire)
arlton.—4A 40 (nr. Malmesbury, Wilts.)	Cheadle.—4F 87 (Manchester)	Chesham Bois.—1A 30	Chilcompton.—3B 26	Chislehurst.—3F 31	Church End.—4F 103 (Humberside)
arlton.—3G 27 (nr. Pewsey, Wilts.)	Cheadle.—3E 75 (Staffordshire)	Cheshunt.—2G 43	Chilcote.—1G 63	Chislet.—4G 33	Church End.—4B 78 (nr. Donington, Lincs.)
arlton.—1G 15 (nr. Salisbury, Wilts.)	Cheadle Hulme.—4F 87	Chesil.—5A 14	Childer Thornton.—3F 85	Chiswell Green.—2E 43	Church End.—3G 91 (nr. North Somercotes, Lincs.)
arlton.—1E 15 (nr. Shaftesbury, Wilts.)	Cheam.—4D 30	Cheslyn Hay.—2D 63	Child Okeford.—2D 14	Chiswick.—3D 30	Church End.—1E 67 (Norfolk)
arlton Abbots.—5E 51	Cheapside.—4A 30 (Berkshire)	Chessetts Wood.—5F 63	Childrey.—4E 41	Chisworth.—3G 87	Church End.—3G 63 (nr. Coleshill, Warwicks.)
arlton Adam.—1A 14	Cheapside.—3F 51 (Hereford & Worcester)	Chessington.—4C 30	Child's Ercall.—5A 74	Chitcombe.—3C 20	Church End.—3G 63 (nr. Nuneaton, Warwicks.)
arlton Horethorne.—1B 14	Chearsley.—1A 42	Chester.—4G 85	Childswickham.—4E 51	Chithurst.—1G 17	Church End.—5B 40 (Wiltshire)
arlton Kings.—5D 50	Chebsey.—5C 74	Chesterblade.—4B 26	Childwall.—4B 86	Chittering.—1D 55	Church Enstone.—5A 52
arlton Mackrell.—1A 14	Checkendon.—4H 41	Chesterfield.—5D 88 (Derbyshire)	Childwick Green.—1E 43	Chitterley.—3C 12	Church Fenton.—2F 95
arlton Marshall.—2F 15	Checkley.—3B 74 (Cheshire)	Chesterfield.—2F 63 (Staffordshire)	Chilfrome.—4A 14	Chitterne.—4E 27	Church Green.—4E 13
arlton Musgrove.—1C 14	Checkley.—4H 49 (Hereford & Worcester)	Chesterhill.—3G 131	Chilgrove.—2G 17	Chittlehamholt.—3C 22	Church Gresley.—1G 63
arlton-on-Otmoor.—1G 41	Checkley.—4E 75 (Staffordshire)	Chesterhope.—1B 116	Chilham.—5E 33	Chittlehampton.—3C 22	Church Hanborough.—1F 41
arlton on the Hill.—3D 15	Chedburgh.—2G 55	Chester-le-Street.—4F 117	Chilhampton.—5F 27	Chittoe.—2E 27	Church Hill.—1A 74 (Cheshire)
arlwood.—5E 29 (Hampshire)	Cheddar.—3E 25	Chester Moor.—5F 117	Chilla.—3E 11	Chivelstone.—5D 9	Church Hill.—1E 51 (Hereford & Worcester)
arlwood.—1D 18 (Surrey)	Cheddington.—1C 42	Chesters.—3A 122	Chilland.—5D 28	Chivenor.—2B 22	Church Hougham.—1G 21
arminster.—4B 14	Cheddleton.—2D 74	Chesterton.—1D 54 (Cambridge, Cambs.)	Chillaton.—1A 8	Chobham.—4A 30	Church Houses.—5D 108
armouth.—4G 13	Cheddon Fitzpaine.—1F 13	Chesterton.—3A 66 (nr. Peterborough, Cambs.)	Chillenden.—5G 33	Cholderton.—4H 28	Churchill.—3E 25 (Avon)
arndon.—5D 52	Chedglow.—3H 39	Chesterton.—2B 40 (Gloucestershire)	Chillerton.—5C 16	Cholesbury.—2C 42	Churchill.—3F 13 (nr. Axminster, Devon)
arney Bassett.—3E 41	Chedgrave.—3F 69	Chesterton.—5C 52 (Oxfordshire)	Chillesford.—2F 57	Chollerford.—2C 116	Churchill.—1E 23 (nr. Barnstaple, Devon)
	Chedington.—3H 13	Chesterton.—3B 62 (Shropshire)	Chillingham.—2E 123	Chollerton.—2C 116	Churchill.—5C 62 (nr. Kidderminster, Here & Worcs.)
	Chediston.—5F 69	Chesterton.—3C 74 (Staffordshire)	Chillington.—5D 9 (Devon)	Cholsey.—4G 41	
	Chediston Green.—5F 69	Chesterton Green.—2H 51	Chillington.—2G 13 (Somerset)	Cholstrey.—2G 49	
	Chedworth.—1B 40	Chesterwood.—3B 116	Chilmark.—5E 27	Chop Gate.—5C 108	
	Chedzoy.—5D 24	Chestfield.—4F 33	Chilmington Green.—1D 20	Choppington.—1F 117	
	Cheese Bay.—1E 172	Cheston.—4C 8	Chilson.—1E 40	Chopwell.—4E 117	
	Cheeseman's Green.—2E 21	Cheswardine.—5B 74	Chilsworthy.—2A 8 (Cornwall)	Chorley.—5H 85 (Cheshire)	
	Cheetham Hill.—2F 87	Cheswell.—1B 62	Chilsworthy.—3D 10 (Devon)	Chorley.—1C 86 (Lancashire)	
	Cheglinch.—1B 22	Cheswick.—5G 133	Chiltern Green.—1E 43	Chorley.—4A 62 (Shropshire)	
	Cheldon.—2H 11	Cheswick Green.—5F 63	Chilthorne Domer.—2A 14	Chorley.—1E 63 (Staffordshire)	
	Chelford.—5F 87	Chetnole.—3B 14	Chilton.—1H 41 (Buckinghamshire)	Chorleywood.—1B 30	
	Chellaston.—4A 76	Chettiscombe.—2C 12	Chilton.—3B 12 (Devon)	Chorlton.—2B 74	
	Chellington.—2G 53	Chettisham.—4E 67	Chilton.—2F 107 (Durham)	Chorlton cum Hardy.—3F 87	
	Chelmarsh.—4B 62		Chilton.—4F 41 (Oxfordshire)	Chorlton Lane.—1G 73	
	Chelmondiston.—4E 57		Chilton Candover.—4D 28	Choulton.—2A 60	
	Chelmorton.—5B 88		Chilton Cantelo.—1A 14	Chrishall.—4D 54	
	Chelmsford.—2D 44		Chilton Foliat.—4B 40	Christchurch.—3D 67 (Cambridgeshire)	
	Chelsea.—3D 30		Chilton Lane.—1G 107		
	Chelsfield.—4F 31		Chilton Polden.—4D 25		
	Chelsham.—5E 31		Chilton Street.—3G 55		
	Chelston.—1E 13		Chilton Trinity.—5C 24		
	Chelsworth.—3B 56		Chilwell.—4C 76		
	Cheltenham.—5D 50				

Churchill.—2D 50
(nr. Worcester, Here & Worcs.)
Churchill.—5G 51
(Oxfordshire)
Churchingford.—2F 13
Church Knowle.—5E 15
Church Laneham.—5A 90
Church Langton.—3E 64
Church Lawford.—5B 64
Church Lawton.—2C 74
Church Leigh.—4E 75
Church Lench.—2E 51
Church Mayfield.—3F 75
Church Minshull.—1A 74
Church Norton.—4G 17
Churchover.—4C 64
Church Preen.—1C 60
Church Pulverbatch.—5G 73
Churchstanton.—2E 13
Church Stoke.—1H 59
Churchstow.—5D 8
Church Stowe.—2D 52
Church Street.—3B 32
(Kent)
Church Street.—4G 69
(Suffolk)
Church Stretton.—1B 60
Churchthorpe.—3F 91
Churchtown.—5E 115
(Cumbria)
Churchtown.—1G 75
(Derbyshire)
Churchtown.—1C 22
(Devon)
Church Town.—2H 89
(Humberside)
Churchtown.—2D 110
(Isle of Man)
Churchtown.—1B 92
(Lancashire)
Church Town.—1A 64
(Leicestershire)
Churchtown.—1A 86
(Merseyside)
Churchtown.—2H 59
(Shropshire)
Church Village.—4G 37
Church Warsop.—1C 76
Church Wilne.—4B 76
Churnsike Lodge.—2H 115
Churston Ferrers.—4F 9
Churt.—5G 29
Churton.—5G 85
Churwell.—2C 94
Chute Standen.—3B 28
Chwilog.—2D 70
Chyandour.—3B 4
Cilan Uchaf.—3B 70
Cilcain.—4D 84
Cilcennin.—1E 47
Cilfrew.—2D 36
Cilfynydd.—2D 36
Cilgerran.—3A 46
Cilgwyn.—5G 47
(nr. Llandovery, Dyfed)
Cilgwyn.—1D 34
(nr. Newport, Dyfed)
Ciliau Aeron.—2D 47
Cilmaengwyn.—2D 36
Cilmery.—2C 48
Cilrhedyn.—4B 46
Cilsan.—5E 47
Ciltalgarth.—1A 72
Cilybebyll.—2D 36
Cilycwm.—5G 47
Cimla.—3D 36
Cinderford.—1E 39
Cinderhill.—3A 76
Cippenham.—2A 30
Cippyn.—3A 46
Cirencester.—2B 40
City.—1H 59
(Powys)
City.—5F 37
(South Glamorgan)
City Dulas.—2D 82

City of London.—2E 31
City, The.—3A 42
Clabhach.—3C 140
Clachaig.—3F 143
(nr. Kinlochleven, H'land.)
Clachaig.—2E 153
(nr. Nether Bridge, H'land.)
Clachaig.—1C 128
(Strathclyde)
Clachamish.—3C 156
Clachan.—2H 169
(nr. Bettyhill, H'land.)
Clachan.—5E 157
(Raasay, H'land.)
Clachan.—2D 157
(nr. Staffin, H'land.)
Clachan.—1D 156
(nr. Uig, H'land.)
Clachan.—4F 127
(Kintyre, Strathclyde)
Clachan.—4C 142
(Lismore, Strathclyde)
Clachan-a-luib.—2D 172
Clachan of Campsie.—2H 129
Clachan of Glendaruel.—1A 128
Clachan Sands.—1D 172
Clachan-Seil.—2E 135
Clachbreck.—2F 127
Clachnaharry.—4A 160
Clachtoll.—1E 165
Clackmannan.—4B 138
Clackmarras.—3G 161
Clacton-on-Sea.—1H 45
Cladach-carinish.—3D 172
Claddach Illeray.—2C 172
Claddach Kirkibost.—2C 172
Claddach-kyles.—2C 172
Cladich.—1H 135
Cladswell.—2E 51
Claggan.—1F 143
(nr. Fort William, H'land.)
Claggan.—4A 142
(nr. Lochaline, H'land.)
Claigan.—3B 156
Clandown.—1B 22
Clanfield.—2E 17
(Hampshire)
Clanfield.—2D 40
(Oxfordshire)
Clanville.—4B 28
(Hampshire)
Clanville.—5B 26
(Somerset)
Claonaig.—4G 127
Clapgate.—3F 15
(Dorset)
Clapgate.—5D 54
(Hertfordshire)
Clapham.—2H 53
(Bedfordshire)
Clapham.—1E 9
(Devon)
Clapham.—3D 31
(London)
Clapham.—3G 99
(North Yorkshire)
Clapham.—5B 18
(West Sussex)
Clap Hill.—2E 21
Clappers.—4F 83
Clappersgate.—4E 105
Clapton.—3H 13
(nr. Crewkerne, Som.)
Clapton.—3B 26
(nr. Radstock, Som.)
Clapton-in-Gordano.—5C 38
Clapton-on-the-Hill.—1C 40
Clapworthy.—3C 22
Clara Vale.—3E 117
Clarbeston.—2D 34
Clarbeston Road.—2D 34
Clarborough.—4H 89
Clare.—3G 55
Clarebrand.—3E 113
Clarencefield.—3B 114
Clarilaw.—3H 121

Clark's Green.—2C 18
Clark's Hill.—5C 78
Clarkston.—4G 129
Clasheddy.—2G 169
Clashindarroch.—5B 162
Clashmore.—5E 167
(nr. Dornoch, H'land.)
Clashmore.—5A 168
(nr. Stoer, H'land.)
Clashnessie.—5A 168
Clashnoir.—1G 153
Clathick.—1H 137
Clathy.—2B 138
Clatt.—1C 154
Clatter.—1F 59
Clatterford.—5C 16
Clatworthy.—2G 23
Claughton.—3E 99
(nr. Caton, Lancs.)
Claughton.—1C 92
(nr. Garstang, Lancs.)
Claughton.—2F 85
(Merseyside)
Claverdon.—1F 51
Claverham.—2E 25
Clavering.—4D 54
Claverley.—3B 62
Claverton.—2C 26
Clawdd-coch.—5G 37
Clawdd-newydd.—5C 84
Clawson Hill.—5E 77
Clawton.—4D 10
Claxby.—5G 91
(nr. Alford, Lincs.)
Claxby.—3D 90
(nr. Market Rasen, Lincs.)
Claxton.—2F 69
(Norfolk)
Claxton.—3B 102
(North Yorkshire)
Claybrooke Magna.—4B 64
Claybrooke Parva.—4B 64
Clay Common.—4G 69
Clay Coton.—5C 64
Clay Cross.—1A 76
Claydon.—2B 52
(Oxfordshire)
Claydon.—2D 56
(Suffolk)
Clay End.—5C 54
Claygate.—1B 20
(Kent)
Claygate.—4C 30
(Surrey)
Claygate Cross.—5H 31
Clayhall.—4E 16
Clayhanger.—3G 23
(Devon)
Clayhanger.—2E 63
(West Midlands)
Clayhidon.—2E 13
Clay Hill.—5E 39
(Avon)
Clayhill.—3C 20
(East Sussex)
Clayhill.—3B 16
(Hampshire)
Clayholes.—5E 147
Clayhythe.—1E 55
Claylake.—2F 15
(Dorset)
Clay Lake.—5B 78
(Lincolnshire)
Clay Lane Head.—1B 92
Clayock.—3D 170
Claypits.—2F 39
Claypole.—3F 77
Claythorpe.—5G 91
Clayton.—3F 87
(Manchester)
Clayton.—2E 89
(South Yorkshire)
Clayton.—3C 74
(Staffordshire)
Clayton.—4E 19
(West Sussex)

Clayton.—2B 94
(West Yorkshire)
Clayton Green.—3C 92
Clayton-le-Moors.—2E 93
Clayton-le-Woods.—3C 92
Clayton West.—4C 94
Clayworth.—4H 89
Cleadale.—5C 148
Cleadon.—3G 117
Clearbrook.—3B 8
Clearwell.—2D 38
Cleasby.—3F 107
Cleat.—9D 174
(Orkney)
Cleat.—8B 172
(Western Isles)
Cleatlam.—3E 107
Cleator.—3B 104
Cleator Moor.—3B 104
Cleckheaton.—3B 94
Cleedownton.—2C 60
Cleehill.—3C 60
Cleekhimin.—4A 130
Clee St Margaret.—2C 60
Cleestanton.—3C 60
Cleethorpes.—5F 97
Cleeton St Mary.—5A 62
Cleeve.—2E 25
(Avon)
Cleeve.—4H 41
(Oxfordshire)
Cleeve Hill.—5D 51
Cleeve Prior.—1F 51
Clehonger.—4G 49
Cleigh.—1H 135
Cleish.—4C 138
Cleland.—4A 130
Clench Common.—2G 27
Clenchwarton.—5E 79
Clennell.—4D 122
Clent.—5D 62
Cleobury Mortimer.—5A 62
Cleobury North.—4A 62
Clephanton.—3C 160
Clerkhill.—2H 169
Clestrain.—7C 174
Clevancy.—5B 40
Clevedon.—5C 38
Cleveley.—5A 52
Cleveleys.—1A 92
Clevelode.—3C 50
Cleverton.—4A 40
Clewer.—3E 25
Cley next the Sea.—1C 80
Cliasmol.—7C 173
Clibberswick.—1H 175
Cliburn.—2G 105
Cliddesden.—4E 29
Clieves Hills.—2A 86
Cliff.—3G 63
(Warwickshire)
Cliff.—4C 173
(Western Isles)
Cliffburn.—4F 147
Cliffe.—3B 32
(Kent)
Cliffe.—2G 95
(North Yorkshire)
Cliff End.—4C 20
Cliffe Woods.—3B 32
Clifford.—3E 49
(Hereford & Worcester)
Clifford.—1E 95
(West Yorkshire)
Clifford Chambers.—2F 51
Clifford's Mesne.—5A 50
Cliffs End.—4H 33
Clifton.—5D 38
(Avon)
Clifton.—4A 54
(Bedfordshire)
Clifton.—5H 143
(Central)
Clifton.—2G 105
(Cumbria)

Clifton.—3F 75
(Derbyshire)
Clifton.—1B 22
(Devon)
Clifton.—3C 50
(Hereford & Worcester)
Clifton.—2B 92
(Lancashire)
Clifton.—2E 87
(Manchester)
Clifton.—1F 117
(Northumberland)
Clifton.—1B 94
(nr. Harrogate, N'Yorks.)
Clifton.—4A 102
(York, N Yorks.)
Clifton.—4C 76
(Nottinghamshire)
Clifton.—4B 52
(Oxfordshire)
Clifton.—3F 89
(South Yorkshire)
Clifton.—3B 94
(West Yorkshire)
Clifton Campville.—1G 63
Clifton Hampden.—3G 41
Clifton Hill.—1B 50
Clifton Reynes.—2G 53
Clifton upon Dunsmore.—5C 64
Clifton upon Teme.—1B 50
Cliftonville.—3H 33
(Kent)
Cliftonville.—2F 81
(Norfolk)
Clifynydd.—3G 37
Climping.—3H 17
Climpy.—4C 130
Clink.—4C 26
Clint.—4F 101
Clint Green.—4C 80
Clintmains.—1A 122
Clipiau.—4H 71
Clippesby.—4G 81
Clippings Green.—4C 80
Clipsham.—1G 65
Clipston.—4E 64
(Northamptonshire)
Clipston.—4D 76
(Nottinghamshire)
Clipstone.—1D 76
Clitheroe.—1E 93
Clive.—3H 73
Clivocast.—1H 175
Clixby.—5D 96
Clocaenog.—5C 84
Clochan.—2B 162
Clochforbie.—3F 163
Clock Face.—3C 86
Cloddiau.—5E 72
Cloddymoss.—3D 161
Clodock.—5F 49
Cloford.—4C 26
Clola.—4H 163
Clophill.—4H 53
Clopton.—4H 65
Clopton Corner.—2E 57
Clopton Green.—2G 55
Closeburn.—5A 120
Close Clark.—4B 110
Closworth.—3A 14
Clothall.—4B 54
Clotton.—4H 85
Clough.—1G 87
(Manchester)
Clough.—4A 94
(West Yorkshire)
Clough Foot.—3G 93
Cloughton.—5H 109
Cloughton Newlands.—5H 109
Clousta.—6C 174
Clova.—1B 154
(Grampian)
Clova.—1C 146
(Tayside)
Clovelly.—1D 10
Clovenfords.—1G 121

Clovenstone.—2E 155
Clovullin.—2C 143
Clowne.—5E 89
Clows Top.—5B 62
Cloy.—1F 73
Cluanie Inn.—2C 150
Cluanie Lodge.—2C 150
Cluddley.—1A 62
Cluer.—8D 173
Clun.—2A 60
Clunas.—4C 160
Clunbury.—2A 60
Clune.—1B 152
Clunes.—5E 150
Clungunford.—3A 60
Clunie.—4A 146
Clunton.—2A 60
Cluny.—4E 139
Cluny Castle.—4A 152
Clutton.—3B 26
(Avon)
Clutton.—5G 85
(Cheshire)
Clwt-y-bont.—4E 83
Clwydfagwyr.—2G 37
Clydach.—1A 38
(Gwent)
Clydach.—2C 36
(West Glamorgan)
Clydach Vale.—3F 37
Clydebank.—2F 129
Clydey.—4B 46
Clyffe Pypard.—5B 40
Clynder.—1D 128
Clynderwen.—3E 35
Clyne.—2E 36
Clynelish.—3F 167
Clynnog-fawr.—1D 70
Clyro.—3E 48
Clyst Honiton.—4C 12
Clyst Hydon.—3D 12
Clyst St George.—5C 12
Clyst St Lawrence.—4D 12
Clyst St Mary.—4C 12
Clyth.—5E 171
Cnwcau.—3B 46
Cnwch Coch.—3B 58
Coadely.—4G 37
Coad's Green.—2G 7
Coal Aston.—5D 88
Coalbrookdale.—2A 62
Coalbrookvale.—2H 37
Coalburn.—1H 119
Coalburns.—3E 117
Coalcleugh.—5B 116
Coaley.—2F 39
Coalford.—4F 155
Coalhall.—3D 118
Coalhill.—1B 32
Coalis.—9B 172
Coalpit Heath.—4E 39
Coal Pool.—2E 63
Coalport.—2A 62
Coalsnaughton.—4B 138
Coaltown of Balgonie.—4E 13
Coaltown of Wemyss.—4F 13
Coalville.—1B 64
Coalway.—1D 39
Coanwood.—4H 115
Coat.—1H 13
Coatbridge.—3A 130
Coatdyke.—3A 130
Coate.—2F 27
(nr. Devizes, Wilts.)
Coate.—4C 40
(nr. Swindon, Wilts.)
Coates.—2A 40
(Cambridgeshire)
Coates.—2A 40
(Gloucestershire)
Coates.—4B 90
(Lincolnshire)
Coates.—2H 17
(West Sussex)
Coatham.—2C 108
Coatham Mundeville.—2F 10

Cormiston.—1C 120
Cornaigbeg.—4A 140
Cornaigmore.—2D 140
(Coll, S'clyde.)
Cornaigmore.—4A 140
(Tiree, S'clyde.)
Corner Row.—2B 92
Corner, The.—2B 60
Corney.—5C 104
Cornforth.—1G 107
Cornhill.—3C 162
(Grampian)
Cornhill.—4C 166
(Highland)
Cornhill on Tweed.—1C 122
Cornholme.—3G 93
Cornish Hall End.—4F 55
Cornriggs.—5B 116
Cornsay.—5E 117
Cornsay Colliery.—5E 117
Corntown.—3H 159
(Highland)
Corntown.—5F 37
(Mid Glamorgan)
Cornwell.—5G 51
Cornwood.—4C 8
Cornworthy.—4E 9
Corpach.—1E 143
Corpusty.—3D 80
Corra.—3F 113
Corran.—2E 143
(nr. Arnisdale. H'land)
Corran.—3G 149
(nr. Fort William, H'land)
Corrany.—3D 110
Corribeg.—1D 143
Corrie.—5B 128
Corrie Common.—1D 114
Corriecravie.—3D 124
Corriekinloch.—1A 166
Corriemoillie.—2F 159
Corrievorrie.—1B 152
Corrimony.—5F 159
Corringham.—2B 32
(Essex)
Corringham.—3A 90
(Lincolnshire)
Corris.—5G 71
Corris Uchaf.—5G 71
Corrour Shooting Lodge.
—2B 144
Corrybrough.—1C 152
Corrygills.—2E 125
Corry of Ardnagrask.—4H 159
Corsback.—1E 171
(nr. Dunnet, H'land)
Corsback.—2E 171
(nr. Halkirk, H'land)
Corscombe.—3A 14
Corse.—4D 162
Corsehill.—3G 163
Corse Lawn.—4C 50
Corse of Kinnoir.—4C 162
Corsham.—5G 39
Corsley.—4D 26
Corsley Heath.—4D 26
Corsock.—2E 113
Corston.—2B 26
(Avon)
Corston.—4H 39
(Wiltshire)
Corstorphine.—2E 131
Cortachy.—3C 146
Corton.—3H 69
(Suffolk)
Corton.—4E 27
(Wiltshire)
Corton Denham.—1B 14
Corwar House.—1H 111
Corwen.—1C 72
Coryates.—5B 14
Coryton.—1A 8
(Devon)
Coryton.—2B 32
(Essex)
Cosby.—3C 64

Coscote.—4G 41
Coseley.—3D 62
Cosgrove.—3E 53
Cosham.—3E 17
Cosheston.—4D 34
Coskills.—4C 96
Cossall.—3B 76
Cossington.—1D 64
(Leicestershire)
Cossington.—4D 24
(Somerset)
Costa.—5C 174
Costessey.—4D 80
Costock.—5C 76
Coston.—5F 77
(Leicestershire)
Coston.—2C 68
(Norfolk)
Cote.—2E 41
Cotebrook.—4H 85
Cotehill.—4F 115
Cotes.—1D 99
(Cumbria)
Cotes.—5C 76
(Leicestershire)
Cotes.—4C 74
(Staffordshire)
Cotesbach.—4C 64
Cotes Heath.—4C 74
Cotgrave.—4D 76
Cothal.—2F 155
Cotham.—3E 77
Cothelstone.—5B 24
Cotheridge.—2B 50
Cotherstone.—3D 106
Cothill.—3F 41
Cotland.—2D 33
Cotleigh.—3F 13
Cotmanhay.—3B 76
Coton.—2D 54
(Cambridgeshire)
Coton.—5D 64
(Northamptonshire)
Coton.—4C 164
(nr. Gnosall, Staffs.)
Coton.—4D 75
(nr. Stone, Staffs.)
Coton.—2F 63
(nr. Tamworth, Staffs.)
Coton Clanford.—5C 74
Coton Hayes.—4D 75
Coton Hill.—4G 73
Coton in the Clay.—5F 75
Coton in the Elms.—1G 63
Cotonwood.—5C 74
Cott.—3D 9
Cottage End.—4C 28
Cotts.—3A 8
Cottam.—3E 103
(Humberside)
Cottam.—2B 92
(Lancashire)
Cottam.—5A 90
(Nottinghamshire)
Cottartown.—5E 161
Cottarville.—1E 53
Cotterdale.—5B 106
Cottered.—5C 54
Cotterstock.—3H 65
Cottesbrooke.—5E 64
Cottesmore.—1G 65
Cotteylands.—2C 12
Cottingham.—2C 96
(Humberside)
Cottingham.—3F 65
(Northamptonshire)
Cottingley.—2B 94
Cottisford.—4C 52
Cotton.—1C 56
Cotton End.—3H 53
Cot-town.—4F 163
Cotwalton.—4D 74
Couch's Mill.—4F 7
Coughton.—5H 49
(Hereford & Worcester)

Coughton.—1E 51
(Warwickshire)
Coulags.—4B 158
Coulderton.—4A 104
Coulin Lodge.—3C 158
Coull.—3C 154
Coulport.—1D 128
Coulsdon.—5E 31
Coulter.—1C 120
Coultershaw Bridge.—2H 17
Coulting.—4C 24
Coulton.—2B 102
Cound.—5H 73
Coundon.—2F 107
Coundon Grange.—2F 107
Countersett.—1C 100
Countess.—4C 27
Countess Cross.—4A 56
Countesthorpe.—3C 64
Countisbury.—1D 22
Coupar Angus.—4B 146
Coupland.—3A 106
(Cumbria)
Coupland.—1D 122
(Northumberland)
Cour.—5G 127
Courance.—5C 120
Court-at-Street.—2E 21
Courteachan.—4F 149
Courteenhall.—2E 53
Court Henry.—5E 47
Courtsend.—1E 33
Courtway.—5C 24
Cousland.—3G 131
Cousley Wood.—2A 20
Coustoun.—2B 128
Cove.—2D 132
(Borders)
Cove.—2C 12
(Devon)
Cove.—3G 29
(Hampshire)
Cove.—4C 164
(Highland)
Cove.—1D 128
(Strathclyde)
Cove Bay.—3G 155
Covehithe.—4H 69
Coven.—2D 62
Coveney.—4D 67
Covenham St Bartholomew.
—3F 91
Covenham St Mary.—3F 91
Coven Heath.—2D 62
Coventry.—5H 63
Coventry Airport.—5A 64
Coverack.—5E 5
Coverham.—1E 100
Covesea.—1F 161
Covingham.—4C 40
Covington.—5H 65
(Cambridgeshire)
Covington.—1B 120
(Strathclyde)
Cowan Bridge.—2F 99
Cowbar.—2F 107
Cowbeech.—4H 19
Cowbit.—1B 66
Cowbridge.—5F 37
Cowden.—1F 19
Cowdenbeath.—4D 138
Cowdenburn.—4F 131
Cowdenend.—5D 138
Cowen Head.—5F 105
Cowers Lane.—3H 75
Cowes.—4C 16
Cowesby.—1H 101
Cowfold.—3D 18
Cowgate.—5B 114
Cowie.—1B 130
(Central)
Cowie.—5F 155
(Grampian)
Cowley.—4C 12
(Devon)

Cowley.—1A 40
(Gloucestershire)
Cowley.—2B 30
(London)
Cowley.—2G 41
(Oxfordshire)
Cowley.—1C 62
(Staffordshire)
Cowleymoor.—2C 12
Cowling.—1C 86
(Lancashire)
Cowling.—1F 101
(nr. Bedale, N Yorks.)
Cowling.—1G 93
(nr. Glusburn, N Yorks.)
Cowlinge.—5G 55
Cowmes.—4B 94
Cowpe.—3F 93
Cowpen.—1F 117
Cowpen Bewley.—2B 108
Cowplain.—2E 17
Cowshill.—5B 116
Cowslip Green.—2E 25
Cowstrandburn.—4C 138
Cowthorpe.—4H 101
Coxall.—3A 60
Coxbank.—3A 74
Coxbench.—3A 76
Cox Common.—4G 69
Coxford.—3A 80
Coxgreen.—4C 62
(Staffordshire)
Cox Green.—2B 18
(Surrey)
Cox Green.—4G 117
(Tyne & Wear)
Coxheath.—5B 32
Coxhoe.—1G 107
Coxley.—4F 25
Coxwold.—2A 102
Coychurch.—5F 37
Coylton.—3D 118
Coylumbridge.—2D 152
Coynach.—3B 154
Coynachie.—5B 162
Coytrahen.—4E 37
Crabbs Cross.—1E 51
Crabgate.—3C 80
Crab Orchard.—3F 15
Crabrach.—1A 154
(Grampian)
Crabtree.—3D 18
Crabtree Green.—1F 73
Crackaig.—2G 167
Crackenthorpe.—2H 105
Crackington Haven.—4B 10
Crackley.—2C 74
(Staffordshire)
Crackley.—5G 63
(Warwickshire)
Crackleybank.—1B 62
Crackpot.—5C 106
Cracoe.—3C 100
Craddock.—2D 12
Cradley.—3B 50
(Hereford & Worcester)
Cradley.—4D 62
(West Midlands)
Cradoc.—4C 48
Crafthole.—4H 7
Crafton.—1B 42
Cragabus.—5B 126
Crag Foot.—2D 99
Cragg.—3H 93
Craggan.—1E 153
(Highland)
Craggan.—4B 136
(Strathclyde)
Cragganvallie.—5H 159
Craggie.—2F 167
Craggiemore.—5B 160
Craghead.—4F 117
Craibstone.—2F 155
Craichie.—4E 147
Craig.—2D 113
(Dumfries & Galloway)

Craig.—4C 158
(nr. Achnashellach, H'land.)
Craig.—2G 157
(nr. Lower Diabaig, H'land.)
Craig.—5H 157
(nr. Stromeferry, H'land.)
Craiganour Lodge.—3D 144
Craigbrack.—4A 136
Craig-cefn-parc.—2C 36
Craigdallie.—1E 139
Craigdam.—5F 163
Craigdarroch.—3G 159
(Highland)
Craigdarroch.—4F 119
(Strathclyde)
Craigdhu.—4G 159
Craigearn.—2E 154
Craigellachie.—4G 161
Craigend.—1D 138
Craigendoran.—1E 128
Craigenputtock.—1E 113
Craigens.—3E 119
Craigiecat.—4F 155
Craighead.—3H 139
Craighouse.—3D 126
Craigie.—2G 155
(Grampian)
Craigie.—1D 118
(Strathclyde)
Craigie.—4A 146
(nr. Blairgowrie, Tayside)
Craigie.—5D 146
(Dundee, Tayside)
Craigie.—1D 138
(Perth, Tayside)
Craigiehall.—2E 131
Craigielaw.—2A 132
Craiglemine.—5B 112
Craig-llwyn.—3E 73
Craiglockhart.—2F 131
Craig Lodge.—2B 128
Craigmalloch.—5D 119
Craigmaud.—3F 163
Craigmill.—4H 137
Craigmillar.—2F 131
Craigmore.—3C 128
Craigneuk.—1E 131
Craignair.—3F 113
Craignant.—2E 73
Craigneuk.—3A 130
(Airdrie, S'clyde.)
Craigneuk.—4A 130
(Motherwell, S'clyde.)
Craignure.—5B 142
Craigo.—2F 147
Craigrory.—4A 160
Craigrothie.—2F 139
Craigs.—2D 114
Craigsglen.—3E 163
Craigshill.—3D 130
Craigside.—1E 107
Craigs, The.—4B 166
Craigton.—3E 154
(nr. Banchory, Grampian)
Craigton.—3F 155
(nr. Peterculter, Grampian)
Craigton.—4A 160
(Highland)
Craigton.—5E 147
(nr. Carnoustie, Tayside)
Craigton.—3C 146
(nr. Kirriemuir, Tayside)
Craigtown.—3A 170
Craig-y-Duke.—2D 36
Craigyloch.—3B 146
Craig-y-nos.—1E 37
Craik.—4F 121
Crail.—3H 139
Crailing.—2A 122
Crailinghall.—2A 122
Craislound.—3H 89
Crakehall.—2H 101
Crakemarsh.—4E 75
Crambe.—3C 102
Crambeck.—3C 102
Cramlington.—2F 117

Cramond.—2E 131
Cramond Bridge.—2E 131
Cranage.—1B 74
Cranberry.—4C 74
Cranborne.—2F 15
Cranbourne.—3A 30
Cranbrook.—2B 20
Cranbrook Common.—2B 20
Crane Moor.—2D 88
Crane's Corner.—4B 80
Cranfield.—3G 53
Cranford.—3C 30
Cranford St Andrew.—5G 65
Cranford St John.—5G 65
Cranham.—1G 39
(Gloucestershire)
Cranham.—2B 31
(London)
Crank.—3C 86
Cranleigh.—2B 18
Cranley.—5D 68
Cranloch.—3G 161
Cranmer Green.—5C 68
Cranmore.—4B 16
(Isle of Wight)
Cranmore.—2A 66
(Lincolnshire)
Crannach.—3B 162
Crannich.—4G 141
Cranoe.—3E 65
Cransford.—1F 57
Cranshaws.—3C 132
Cranstal.—1D 110
Crantock.—3B 6
Cranwell.—2H 77
Cranwich.—3G 67
Cranworth.—2B 68
Craobhnaclag.—4G 159
Crapstone.—3B 8
Crarae.—4G 135
Crask.—2H 169
Crask Inn.—1C 166
Crask of Aigas.—4G 159
Craster.—3G 123
Cratfield.—5F 69
Crathes.—4E 155
Crathie.—4G 153
(Grampian)
Crathie.—4H 151
(Highland)
Crathorne.—4B 108
Craven Arms.—2B 60
Crawcrook.—3E 117
Crawford.—2B 86
(Lancashire)
Crawford.—2B 120
(Strathclyde)
Crawfordsdyke.—5B 130
Crawfordjohn.—2A 120
Crawick.—3G 119
Crawley.—3F 13
(Devon)
Crawley.—5C 28
(Hampshire)
Crawley.—1F 41
(Oxfordshire)
Crawley.—2D 18
(West Sussex)
Crawley Down.—2E 19
Crawley Side.—5D 116
Crawshawbooth.—3F 93
Crawton.—1H 147
Cray.—2C 100
(North Yorkshire)
Cray.—5A 48
(Powys)
Cray.—2A 146
(Tayside)
Crayford.—3G 31
Crayke.—2A 102
Craymere Beck.—2C 80
Crays Hill.—1B 32
Cray's Pond.—4H 41
Crazies Hill.—4A 42
Creacombe.—2B 12
Creagan.—4D 143

Curbridge.—2D 16
(Hampshire)
Curbridge.—2E 41
(Oxfordshire)
Curdridge.—2D 16
Curdworth.—3F 63
Curland.—2F 13
Curridge.—5F 41
Currie.—3E 131
Curry Mallet.—1G 13
Curry Rivel.—1G 13
Curtisden Green.—1B 20
Curtisknowle.—4D 8
Cury.—4D 5
Cusgarne.—2E 5
Cusop.—3E 49
Cusworth.—2F 89
Cutcombe.—2F 23
Cuthill.—2G 131
Cutiau.—4F 71
Cutlers Green.—4E 55
Cutmadoc.—3E 7
Cutnall Green.—1C 50
Cutsdean.—4E 51
Cutthorpe.—5D 88
Cuttivett.—3H 7
Cuttybridge.—3C 34
Cuttyhill.—3H 163
Cuxham.—3H 41
Cuxton.—4B 32
Cuxwold.—5D 96
Cwm.—3C 84
(Clwyd)
Cwm.—2H 37
(Gwent)
Cwm.—1H 59
(Powys)
Cwmafan.—3D 36
Cwmaman.—3G 37
Cwmann.—3E 47
Cwmbach.—2F 35
(Dyfed)
Cwmbach.—2G 37
(Mid Glamorgan)
Cwmbach.—2C 48
(nr. Builth Wells, Powys)
Cwmbach.—4D 48
(nr. Hay-on-Wye, Powys)
Cwmbelan.—2E 59
Cwmbran.—3A 38
Cwmbrwyno.—2C 58
Cwm Capel.—2A 36
Cwmcarn.—3A 38
Cwmcarvan.—2C 38
Cwm-celyn.—2A 38
Cwm-Cewydd.—4A 72
Cwmcoy.—3B 46
Cwm-Crawnon.—1H 37
Cwm Cych.—4B 46
Cwmdare.—2F 37
Cwmdu.—4F 47
(Dyfed)
Cwmdu.—5D 48
(Powys)
Cwmdu.—3C 36
(West Glamorgan)
Cwmduad.—4C 46
Cwm Dulais.—2C 36
Cwmerfyn.—2D 58
Cwmfelin.—4E 37
Cwmfelin Boeth.—3E 35
Cwmfelinfach.—3H 37
Cwmfelin Mynach.—2F 35
Cwmffrwd.—3E 35
Cwmgiedd.—1D 36
Cwmgors.—1D 36
Cwmgwili.—1B 36
Cwmgwrach.—2E 37
Cwmhiraeth.—4C 46
Cwmifor.—5F 47
Cwmisfael.—1A 36
Cwm-Llinau.—5H 71
Cwmllynfell.—1D 36
Cwm-mawr.—1B 36
Cwmmiles.—2E 35
Cwmorgan.—4B 46

Cwmparc.—3F 37
Cwmpennar.—2G 37
Cwm Plysgog.—3A 46
Cwmrhos.—5D 48
Cwmsychpant.—3D 47
Cwmsyfiog.—2H 37
Cwmsymlog.—2B 58
Cwmtillery.—2A 38
Cwm-twrch Isaf.—2D 36
Cwm-twrch Uchaf.—1D 36
Cwmwysg.—5A 48
Cwm-y-glo.—4E 83
Cwmyoy.—5E 49
Cwmystwyth.—3C 58
Cwrt.—1B 58
Cwrt-newydd.—3D 47
Cwrt-y-Cadno.—3F 47
Cyffylliog.—5C 84
Cymau.—5E 85
Cymmer.—3G 37
(Mid Glamorgan)
Cymmer.—3E 37
(West Glamorgan)
Cyncoed.—4H 37
Cynghordy.—4H 47
(Dyfed)
Cynghordy.—2C 36
(West Glamorgan)
Cynheidre.—2A 36
Cynonville.—3E 37
Cynwyd.—1C 72
Cynwyl Elfed.—2G 35
Cywarch.—4A 72

Dacre.—2F 105
(Cumbria)
Dacre.—3E 101
(North Yorkshire)
Dacre Banks.—3E 101
Daddry Shield.—1B 106
Dadford.—4D 52
Dadlington.—3B 64
Dafen.—2B 36
Daffy Green.—2B 68
Dagdale.—4E 75
Dagenham.—2F 31
Daggons.—2G 15
Daglingworth.—2A 40
Dagnall.—1C 42
Dagtail End.—1E 51
Dailly.—4B 118
Dairsie.—2G 139
Daisy Bank.—3E 63
Daisy Hill.—2D 86
(Manchester)
Daisy Hill.—2B 94
(West Yorkshire)
Dalavich.—2G 135
Dalbeattie.—3F 113
Dalblair.—3F 119
Dalbury.—4G 75
Dalby.—4B 110
Dalby Wolds.—5D 76
Dalchalm.—3G 167
Dalcharn.—3G 169
Dalchork.—2C 166
Dalchreichart.—2E 151
Dalchruin.—2G 137
Dalcross.—4B 160
Dalderby.—1B 78
Dale.—5G 115
(Cumbria)
Dale.—4B 76
(Derbyshire)
Dale.—4B 34
(Dyfed)
Dalebank.—1A 76
Dale Bottom.—2D 104
Dalebrook.—4F 75
Dale Head.—3F 105
Dalehouse.—3E 109
Dalelia.—2E 147
Dalgarven.—5D 128
Dalgety Bay.—5D 138
Dalginross.—1G 137

Dalguise.—4G 145
Dalham.—1G 55
Dalhavaig.—3A 170
Daliburgh.—6C 172
Dalintart.—1F 135
Dalkeith.—3G 131
Dall.—3C 144
Dallas.—3F 161
Dalleagles.—3E 119
Dallinghoo.—2E 57
Dallington.—4A 20
Dallow.—2E 101
Dalmally.—1A 136
Dalmarnock.—3H 129
Dalmellington.—4D 119
Dalmeny.—2E 131
Dalmigavie.—2B 152
Dalmilling.—2C 118
Dalmore.—2A 160
(nr. Alness H'land.)
Dalmore.—3E 166
(nr. Rogart, H'land.)
Dalmore.—3E 173
(Western Isles)
Dalmuir.—2F 129
Dalmunach.—4G 161
Dalnabreck.—2B 142
Dalnacardoch Lodge.—1E 144
Dalnamein Lodge.—2E 145
Dalnaspidal Lodge.—1D 144
Dalnatrat.—3D 142
Dalnavie.—1A 160
Dalnawillan Lodge.—4C 170
Dalness.—3F 143
Dalnessie.—2D 166
Dalqueich.—3C 138
Dalquharn.—5C 118
Dalreavoch.—3E 167
Dalreoch.—2C 138
Dalry.—2F 131
(Lothian)
Dalry.—5D 128
(Strathclyde)
Dalrymple.—3C 118
Dalscote.—2D 52
Dalserf.—4B 130
Dalsmirran.—4A 124
Dalston.—4E 115
Dalswinton.—1G 113
Dalton.—2C 114
(Dumfries & Galloway)
Dalton.—2B 86
(Lancashire)
Dalton.—4C 116
(nr. Hexham, Northmb.)
Dalton.—2E 117
(nr. Ponteland, Northmb.)
Dalton.—4E 107
(nr. Richmond, N Yorks.)
Dalton.—2H 101
(nr. Thirsk, N. Yorks.)
Dalton.—3E 89
(South Yorkshire)
Dalton.—4H 129
(Strathclyde)
Dalton-in-Furness.—2B 98
Dalton-le-Dale.—5H 117
Dalton Magna.—3E 89
Dalton-on-Tees.—4F 107
Dalton Piercy.—1B 108
Daltot.—1F 127
Dalvey.—5F 161
Dalwhinnie.—5A 152
Dalwood.—3F 13
Damerham.—2G 15
Damgate.—2G 69
(nr. Acle, Norf.)
Damgate.—4G 81
(nr. Martham, Norf.)
Dam Green.—4C 68
Danaway.—4C 32
Danbury.—2D 44
Danby.—4E 109
Danby Botton.—4D 109
Danby Wiske.—5G 107
Danderhall.—3G 131

Danebank.—4G 87
Danebridge.—1D 74
Dane End.—5C 54
Danehill.—3F 19
Danesford.—3B 62
Danesmoor.—1B 76
Danestone.—2G 155
Dangerous Corner.—1C 86
Daniel's Water.—1D 20
Dan's Castle.—1E 107
Danshillock.—3E 162
Danzey Green.—1F 51
Dapple Heath.—5E 75
Daren.—1A 38
Daren-felen.—1A 38
Darenth.—3G 31
Daresbury.—4C 86
Darfield.—2F 88
Dargate.—4E 33
Dargill.—2A 138
Darite.—3G 7
Darlaston.—4C 74
(Staffordshire)
Darlaston.—3D 63
(West Midlands)
Darley.—4F 101
Darley Abbey.—4H 75
Darley Bridge.—1G 75
Darley Head.—4E 101
Darlingscott.—3G 51
Darlington.—3F 107
Darliston.—2H 73
Darlton.—5H 89
Darmsden.—2C 56
Darnall.—4D 88
Darnford.—4E 155
Darnick.—1H 121
Darowen.—5H 71
Darra.—4E 163
Darras Hall.—2E 117
Darrcott.—2A 22
Darrington.—4E 95
Darrow Green.—4E 69
Darsham.—5G 69
Dartfield.—3H 163
Dartford.—3G 31
Dartington.—3D 9
Dartmeet.—2C 8
Dartmouth.—4E 9
Darton.—4D 94
Darvel.—1E 119
Darwen.—3D 93
Dassels.—5C 54
Datchet.—3A 30
Datchworth.—1F 43
Datchworth Green.—1F 43
Daubhill.—2E 87
Dauntsey.—4A 40
Dauntsey Green.—4A 40
Dauntsey Lock.—4A 40
Dava.—5E 161
Davenham.—5D 86
Daventry.—1C 52
Davidson's Mains.—2F 131
Davidston.—2B 160
Davidstow.—1F 7
David's Well.—3F 59
Davington.—4E 121
Daviot.—1E 155
(Grampian)
Daviot.—5B 160
(Highland)
Davyhulme.—3E 87
Daw Cross.—4F 101
Dawdon.—5H 117
Dawesgreen.—1D 18
Dawley.—2A 62
Dawlish.—2F 9
Dawlish Warren.—2F 9
Dawn.—3A 84
Daws Heath.—2C 32
Dawshill.—2C 50
Daw's House.—1H 7
Dawsmere.—3D 79
Dayhills.—4D 74
Dayhouse Bank.—5D 62

Daylesford.—5G 51
Daywall.—2E 73
Ddol.—3D 84
Ddol Cownwy.—4C 72
Deadwater.—5A 122
Deaf Hill.—1G 107
Deal.—5H 33
Dean.—2B 104
(Cumbria)
Dean.—3D 8
(nr. Buckfastleigh, Devon)
Dean.—1C 22
(nr. Combe Martin, Devon)
Dean.—1B 22
(nr. Ilfracombe, Devon)
Dean.—1D 22
(nr. Lynton, Devon)
Dean.—2E 15
(Dorset)
Dean.—2D 16
(nr. Bishop's Waltham, Hants.)
Dean.—5C 28
(nr. Winchester, Hants.)
Dean.—4B 26
(Somerset)
Dean Bank.—1F 107
Deanburnhaugh.—3G 121
Deane.—3D 28
Deanich Lodge.—5A 166
Deanland.—2E 15
Deanlane End.—2F 17
Dean Park.—4C 60
Dean Prior.—3D 8
Dean Row.—4H 87
Deans.—3D 130
Deanscales.—2B 104
Deanshanger.—4E 53
Deanston.—3G 137
Dearham.—1B 104
Dearne.—2E 89
Dearne Valley.—5E 95
Debach.—2E 57
Debden.—4E 55
Debden Green.—1F 31
(nr. Loughton, Essex)
Debden Green.—4E 55
(nr. Saffron Walden, Essex)
Debenham.—1D 56
Dechmont.—2D 130
Deddington.—4B 52
Dedham.—4C 56
Dedham Heath.—4C 56
Deebank.—4D 154
Deene.—3G 65
Deenethorpe.—3G 65
Deepcar.—3C 88
Deepcut.—5A 30
Deepdale.—1G 99
(Cumbria)
Deepdale.—4C 96
(Humberside)
Deepdale.—2B 100
(North Yorkshire)
Deeping Gate.—2A 66
Deeping St James.—2A 66
Deeping St Nicholas.—1B 66
Deerhill.—3B 162
Deerhurst.—5C 50
Deerhurst Walton.—5C 50
Deerness.—7E 174
Defford.—3D 50
Defynnog.—5B 48
Deganwy.—3G 83
Deighton.—4G 107
(nr. Northallerton, N Yorks.)
Deighton.—5B 102
(nr. York, N Yorks.)
Deighton.—4B 94
(West Yorkshire)
Deiniolen.—4E 83
Delabole.—1F 7
Delamere.—4H 85
Delfour.—3C 152
Delliefure.—5E 161
Dell, The.—3G 69
Delly End.—1E 41

Delny.—1B 160
Delph.—2G 87
Delves.—5E 117
Delves, The.—3E 63
Delvin End.—4G 55
Dembleby.—4H 77
Demelza.—3D 6
Denaby Main.—3E 89
Denbeath.—4F 139
Denbigh.—4C 84
Denbury.—3E 9
Denby.—3A 76
Denby Common.—3B 76
Denby Dale.—2C 88
Denchworth.—3E 41
Dendron.—2B 98
Deneside.—5H 117
Denford.—5G 65
Dengie.—2F 148
Denham.—2B 30
(Buckinghamshire)
Denham.—1G 55
(nr. Bury St Edmunds, Suff.)
Denham.—5D 69
(nr. Eye Suff.)
Denham Green.—2B 30
Denham Street.—5D 69
Denhead.—2G 139
(Fife)
Denhead.—5G 163
(nr. Ellon, Grampian)
Denhead.—3G 163
(nr. Strichen, Grampian)
Denholm.—3H 121
Denholme.—2A 94
Denholme Clough.—2A 94
Denholme Gate.—2A 94
Denio.—2C 70
Denmead.—2E 17
Dennington.—1E 57
Denny.—1B 130
Denny End.—1D 55
Dennyloanhead.—1B 130
Den of Lindores.—2E 139
Denshaw.—1G 87
Denside.—4F 155
Densole.—1G 21
Denston.—2G 55
Denstone.—3E 75
Denstroude.—4F 33
Dent.—1G 99
Den, The.—4E 129
Denton.—4A 66
(Cambridgeshire)
Denton.—3F 107
(Durham)
Denton.—5F 19
(East Sussex)
Denton.—1E 22
(Kent)
Denton.—4F 77
(Lincolnshire)
Denton.—3G 87
(Manchester)
Denton.—4E 69
(Norfolk)
Denton.—2F 53
(Northamptonshire)
Denton.—1B 94
(North Yorkshire)
Denton.—2G 41
(Oxfordshire)
Denver.—2F 67
Denwick.—3G 123
Deopham.—2C 68
Deopham Green.—3C 68
Depden.—2G 55
Depden Green.—2G 55
Deptford.—3E 31
(London)
Deptford.—5F 27
(Wiltshire)
Derby.—4A 76
Derbyhaven.—5B 110
Derculich.—3F 145
Dereham.—1B 68

Drums of Park.—3C 162
Drumsturdy.—5D 147
Drumtochty Castle.—5E 154
Drumuie.—4D 156
Drumuillie.—1D 152
Drumvaich.—3F 137
Drumwhindle.—5G 163
Drunkendub.—4F 147
Drury.—4E 85
Drury Square.—4B 80
Drybeck.—3H 105
Drybridge.—2B 162
(Grampian)
Drybridge.—1C 118
(Strathclyde)
Drybrook.—1E 39
(Gloucestershire)
Drybrook.—1D 39
(Hereford & Worcester)
Dryburgh.—1H 121
Dry Doddington.—3F 77
Dry Drayton.—1C 54
Drym.—3D 4
Drymen.—1F 129
Drymuir.—4G 163
Drynachan Lodge.—5C 160
Drynie Park.—3H 159
Drynoch.—5D 156
Dry Sandford.—2F 41
Dryslwyn.—5E 47
Dry Street.—2A 32
Dryton.—5H 73
Dubford.—2E 163
Dubiton.—3G 162
Dubton.—3E 147
Duchally.—2A 166
Duck End.—5F 55
Duckington.—5G 85
Ducklington.—2E 41
Duckmanton.—5E 89
Duck Street.—4B 28
Dudbridge.—2G 39
Duddenhoe End.—4D 54
Duddington.—2F 131
Duddingston.—2G 65
Duddleswell.—3F 19
Duddo.—5F 133
Duddon.—4H 85
Duddon Bridge.—1A 98
Dudleston.—2F 73
Dudleston Heath.—2F 73
Dudley.—2F 117
(Tyne & Wear)
Dudley.—3D 62
(West Midlands)
Dudsbury.—4F 15
Dudston.—1H 59
Dudwells.—2C 34
Duffield.—3H 75
Duffryn.—3E 37
Dufftown.—5H 161
Duffus.—2F 161
Dufton.—2H 105
Duggleby.—3D 103
Duirinish.—5G 157
Duisdalemore.—2F 149
Duisky.—1E 143
Dukesfield.—4C 116
Dukestown.—1H 37
Dukinfield.—3G 87
Dulas.—2D 83
Dulcote.—4F 25
Dulford.—3D 12
Dull.—4F 145
Dullatur.—2A 130
Dullingham.—2F 55
Dullingham Ley.—2F 55
Dulnain Bridge.—1D 153
Duloe.—1A 54
(Bedfordshire)
Duloe.—6G 7
(Cornwall)
Dulverton.—3F 23
Dulwich.—3E 31
Dumbarton.—2E 129
Dumbleton.—4E 51

Dumfin.—1E 129
Dumfries.—2G 113
Dumgoyne.—1G 129
Dummer.—4D 28
Dumpford.—1G 17
Dun.—3F 147
Dunagoil.—4B 128
Dunalastair.—3E 144
Dunan.—1D 149
(Highland)
Dunan.—2C 128
(Strathclyde)
Dunball.—4D 24
Dunbar.—2C 132
Dunbeath.—5D 170
Dunbeg.—5C 142
Dunblane.—3G 137
Dunbog.—2E 139
Dunbridge.—1B 16
Duncanston.—1C 154
(Grampian)
Duncanston.—3H 159
(Highland)
Dunchurch.—5B 64
Duncote.—2D 52
Duncow.—1G 113
Duncrievie.—3D 138
Duncton.—2H 17
Dundee.—5D 146
Dundee Airport.—1F 139
Dundon.—5E 25
Dundonald.—1C 118
Dundonnell.—5E 165
Dundraw.—5D 114
Dundreggan.—2F 151
Dundrennan.—5E 113
Dundridge.—2D 16
Dundry.—2F 25
Dunecht.—3E 155
Dunfermline.—5C 138
Dunford Bridge.—2B 88
Dungate.—5D 32
Dunge.—3D 27
Dungeness.—4F 21
Dungworth.—4C 88
Dunham-on-the-Hill.—3G 85
Dunham on Trent.—5A 90
Dunhampton.—1C 50
Dunham Town.—4E 87
Dunham Woodhouses.—4E 87
Dunholme.—5C 90
Dunino.—2H 139
Dunipace.—1B 130
Dunira.—1E 137
Dunkeld.—4H 145
Dunkerton.—3C 26
Dunkeswell.—3E 13
Dunkeswick.—1D 94
Dunkirk.—4F 39
(Avon)
Dunkirk.—5E 33
(Kent)
Dunkirk.—2C 74
(Staffordshire)
Dunkirk.—2E 27
(Wiltshire)
Dunk's Green.—5H 31
Dunlappie.—2F 147
Dunley.—3C 28
(Hampshire)
Dunley.—1B 50
(Hereford & Worcester)
Dunlichity Lodge.—6A 160
Dunlop.—5F 129
Dunmaglass Lodge.—1H 151
Dunmail Raise.—3E 105
Dunmore.—1B 130
(Central)
Dunmore.—4H 159
(Highland)
Dunmore.—3F 127
(Strathclyde)
Dunnet.—1E 171
Dunnichen.—4E 147
Dunning.—2C 138

Dunnington.—4G 103
(Humberside)
Dunnington.—4B 102
(North Yorkshire)
Dunnington.—2E 51
(Warwickshire)
Dunnockshaw.—3F 93
Dunoon.—2C 128
Dunphail.—4E 161
Dunragit.—4G 111
Dunrostan.—1F 127
Duns.—4D 132
Dunsby.—5A 78
Dunscar.—1E 87
Dunscore.—1F 113
Dunscroft.—2G 89
Dunsdale.—3D 108
Dunsden Green.—5A 42
Dunsfold.—2B 18
Dunsford.—1E 9
Dunshelt.—2E 139
Dunshillock.—4G 163
Dunsley.—3F 109
(North Yorkshire)
Dunsley.—4C 62
(Staffordshire)
Dunsmore.—5H 43
Dunsop Bridge.—4F 99
Dunstable.—5H 53
Dunstal.—5F 75
Dunstall.—5F 75
Dunstall Green.—1G 55
Dunstall Hill.—2D 62
Dunstan.—3G 123
Dunster.—1F 23
Duns Tew.—5B 52
Dunston.—1H 77
(Lincolnshire)
Dunston.—2E 69
(Norfolk)
Dunston.—1D 62
(Staffordshire)
Dunston.—3F 117
(Tyne & Wear)
Dunstone.—2D 8
(nr. Ashburton, Devon)
Dunstone.—4B 8
(nr. Plymouth, Devon)
Dunston Heath.—1D 62
Dunsville.—2G 89
Dunswell.—2C 96
Dunsyre.—5D 130
Dunterton.—2F 9
Duntisbourne Abbots.—2A 40
Duntisbourne Leer.—2A 40
Duntish.—3B 14
Duntocher.—2F 129
Dunton.—3B 54
(Bedfordshire)
Dunton.—5F 53
(Buckinghamshire)
Dunton.—2A 80
(Norfolk)
Dunton Bassett.—3C 64
Dunton Green.—5G 31
Dunton Park.—2A 80
Duntulm.—1D 156
Dunure.—3D 118
Dunvant.—3B 36
Dunvegan.—4B 156
Dunwich.—5G 69
Dunwood.—2D 74
Durdar.—4F 115
Durgates.—2H 19
Durham.—5F 117
Durisdeer.—4A 120
Durisdeermill.—4A 120
Durkar.—4D 94
Durleigh.—5C 24
Durley.—2D 16
(Hampshire)
Durley.—2H 27
(Wiltshire)
Durley Street.—2D 16
Durlow Common.—4A 50
Durnamuck.—4E 165

Durness.—2E 168
Durno.—1E 154
Durns Town.—4A 16
Duror Inn.—3D 143
Durran.—3G 135
(nr. Dunblane, H'land.)
Durran.—2D 171
(nr. Thurso, H'land.)
Durrant Green.—2C 20
Durrants.—3F 17
Durrington.—5C 18
(West Sussex)
Durrington.—4G 27
(Wiltshire)
Dursley.—3F 39
Dursley Cross.—5B 50
Durston.—1F 13
Durweston.—3D 14
Duston.—1E 52
Duthil.—1D 152
Dutlas.—3H 59
Duton Hill.—5F 55
Dutson.—1H 7
Dutton.—3H 85
Duxford.—3D 55
(Cambridgeshire)
Duxford.—2E 41
(Oxfordshire)
Dwygyfylchi.—3G 83
Dwyran.—4D 82
Dyce.—2F 155
Dye House.—4C 116
Dyffryn.—2G 35
(nr. Carmarthen, Dyfed)
Dyffryn.—1C 34
(nr. Fishguard, Dyfed)
Dyffryn.—5G 37
(South Glamorgan)
Dyffryn.—3E 37
(West Glamorgan)
Dyffryn Ardudwy.—3E 71
Dyffryn Castell.—2C 58
Dyffryn Ceidrych.—5G 47
Dyffryn Cellwen.—2E 37
Dyke.—1D 10
(Devon)
Dyke.—3D 161
(Grampian)
Dyke.—5A 78
(Lincolnshire)
Dykehead.—4E 137
(Central)
Dykehead.—4B 130
(Strathclyde)
Dykehead.—2C 146
(Tayside)
Dykends.—3B 146
Dykesfield.—4E 114
Dylife.—1D 58
Dymchurch.—3F 21
Dymock.—4A 50
Dyrham.—3F 39
Dysart.—4F 139
Dyserth.—3C 84

Eachwick.—2E 117
Eagland Hill.—1B 92
Eagle.—1F 77
Eagle Barnsdale.—1F 77
Eagle Moor.—1F 77
Eaglescliffe.—3B 108
Eaglesfield.—2B 104
(Cumbria)
Eaglesfield.—2D 114
(Dumfries & Galloway)
Eaglesham.—4G 129
Eaglethorpe.—3H 65
Eagley.—1E 87
Eairy.—4B 110
Eakley Lanes.—2F 53
Eakring.—1D 76
Ealand.—4H 95
Ealing.—2C 30
Eallabus.—3B 126
Eals.—4H 115

Eamont Bridge.—2G 105
Earby.—1G 93
Earcroft.—3D 93
Eardington.—3B 62
Eardisland.—2G 49
Eardisley.—3F 49
Eardiston.—1A 50
(Hereford & Worcester)
Eardiston.—3F 73
(Shropshire)
Earith.—5C 66
Earle.—2D 123
Earlesfield.—4F 77
Earlestown.—3C 86
Earlham.—2D 69
Earlish.—2C 156
Earls Barton.—1F 53
Earls Colne.—5A 56
Earls Common.—2D 50
Earl's Croome.—3C 50
Earlsdon.—5H 63
Earlsferry.—3G 139
Earlsford.—5F 163
Earl's Green.—1C 56
Earlsheaton.—3C 94
Earl Shilton.—3B 64
Earl Soham.—1E 57
Earl Sterndale.—1E 75
Earlston.—1H 121
(Borders)
Earlston.—1D 118
(Strathclyde)
Earl Stonham.—2D 56
Earlstoun.—1D 112
Earlswood.—5F 63
Earlswood Common.—3C 38
Earlyvale.—4F 131
Earnley.—4G 17
Earsary.—9C 172
Earsdon.—2G 117
Earshader.—4D 173
Earsham.—4F 69
Earsham Street.—5E 69
Earswick.—4B 102
Eartham.—3H 17
Earthcott Green.—4E 39
Easby.—4C 108
(nr. Great Ayton, N Yorks.)
Easby.—4E 107
(nr. Richmond, N Yorks.)
Easdale.—2G 135
Easebourne.—1G 17
Easenhall.—5B 64
Eashing.—1A 18
Easington.—1H 41
(Buckinghamshire)
Easington.—3E 109
(Cleveland)
Easington.—5H 117
(Durham)
Easington.—4F 97
(Humberside)
Easington.—1F 123
(Northumberland)
Easington.—4B 52
(Banbury, Oxon)
Easington.—3H 41
(nr. Watlington, Oxon.)
Easington Colliery.—5H 117
Easington Lane.—5G 117
Easingwold.—3A 102
Easole Street.—5G 33
Eassie.—4C 146
East Aberthaw.—5G 37
Eastacombe.—3B 22
Eastacott.—3C 22
East Allington.—5D 8
East Anstey.—3E 23
East Anton.—4B 28
East Appleton.—5F 107
East Ashling.—3G 17
East Aston.—4C 28
East Ayton.—1E 103
East Bagborough.—5B 24
East Barkwith.—4D 90
East Barming.—5B 32

East Barnby.—3F 109
East Barnet.—1D 30
East Barns.—2D 132
East Barsham.—2B 80
East Beach.—4G 17
East Beckham.—2D 80
East Bedfont.—3B 30
East Bennan.—3D 125
East Bergholt.—4C 56
East Bierley.—3B 94
East Bilney.—4B 80
East Blatchington.—5F 19
East Bloxworth.—4D 15
East Boldre.—3B 16
East Bolton.—3F 123
Eastbourne.—3G 107
(Durham)
Eastbourne.—5H 19
(East Sussex)
East Bradenham.—2B 68
East Brent.—3D 24
Eastbridge.—2E 11
(Devon)
East Bridge.—1G 57
(Suffolk)
East Bridgford.—3D 76
East Briscoe.—3C 106
East Brunton.—2F 117
East Buckland.—2C 22
East Budleigh.—5D 12
Eastburn.—1H 93
East Burnham.—2A 30
East Burrafirth.—6E 175
East Burton.—4D 14
Eastbury.—5E 41
(Berkshire)
Eastbury.—1B 30
(Hertfordshire)
East Butsfield.—5E 117
East Butterleigh.—3C 12
East Butterwick.—5A 96
Eastby.—4D 100
East Calder.—3D 131
East Carleton.—2D 68
East Carlton.—4F 65
(Northamptonshire)
East Carlton.—1C 94
(West Yorkshire)
East Chaldon.—5C 14
East Challow.—4E 41
East Charleton.—5D 8
East Chelborough.—3A 14
East Chiltington.—4E 19
East Chinnock.—2H 13
East Chisenbury.—3G 27
Eastchurch.—3D 32
East Clandon.—5B 30
East Claydon.—5E 53
East Clevedon.—5C 38
East Clyne.—3F 167
East Clyth.—5E 171
East Coker.—2A 14
Eastcombe.—2G 39
(Gloucestershire)
East Combe.—5B 24
(Somerset)
East Common.—2G 95
East Compton.—4B 26
East Cornworthy.—4E 9
Eastcote.—2C 30
(London)
Eastcote.—2D 52
(Northamptonshire)
Eastcote.—5F 63
(West Midlands)
Eastcott.—2C 10
(Cornwall)
Eastcott.—3F 27
(Wiltshire)
East Cottingwith.—5C 102
East Coulston.—3E 27
Eastcourt.—2H 27
(nr. Pewsey, Wilts.)
Eastcourt.—3A 40
(nr. Tetbury, Wilts.)
East Cowes.—4D 16

East Cowick.—3G 95
East Cowton.—4G 107
East Cramlington.—2F 117
East Cranmore.—4B 26
East Creech.—5E 15
East Croachy.—1A 152
Eastdean.—5G 19
(East Sussex)
East Dean.—1A 16
(Hampshire)
East Dean.—5A 50
(Hereford & Worcester)
East Dean.—2H 17
(West Sussex)
East Dereham.—4B 80
East Down.—1C 22
East Drayton.—5H 89
East Dundry.—2F 25
East Ella.—3C 96
East End.—5C 38
(Avon)
East End.—5C 66
(Cambridgeshire)
East End.—4E 15
(Dorset)
East End.—4B 16
(nr. Lymington, Hants.)
East End.—2C 28
(nr. Newbury, Hants.)
East End.—5D 54
(Hertfordshire)
East End.—4G 103
(nr. Ulrome, Humberside)
East End.—3E 97
(nr. Withernsea, Humberside)
East End.—3D 32
(nr. Minster, Kent)
East End.—2C 20
(nr. Tenterden, Kent)
East End.—1E 41
(Oxfordshire)
East End.—3F 25
(Somerset)
East End.—4C 56
(Suffolk)
Easter Ardross.—1A 160
Easter Balgedie.—3D 138
Easter Balmoral.—4G 153
Easter Brae.—2A 160
Easter Buckieburn.—1A 130
Easter Bush.—3F 131
Easter Compton.—4D 38
Eastergate.—3H 17
Easterhouse.—3H 129
Easter Howgate.—3F 131
Easter Kinkell.—3H 159
Easter Lednathie.—2C 146
Easter Ord.—3F 155
Easter Orgil.—2D 146
Easter Pencaitland.—3H 131
Easter Quarff.—8F 175
Easter Skeld.—7E 175
Easter Slumbay.—5A 158
Easter Suddie.—3A 160
Easterton.—3F 27
Eastertown.—3D 24
Eastertown ofAuchleuchries.
—5H 163
Easter Tulloch.—1G 147
East Everleigh.—3H 27
East Farleigh.—5B 32
East Farndon.—4E 64
East Ferry.—3A 90
Eastfield.—1F 103
(North Yorkshire)
Eastfield.—3B 130
(nr. Caldercruix, S'clyde)
Eastfield.—2A 130
(nr. Cumbernauld, S'clyde.)
Eastfield.—3H 129
(Glasgow, S'clyde.)
Eastfield.—3B 130
(nr. Harthill, S'clyde.)
Eastfield Hall.—4G 123

East Fortune.—2B 132
East Garforth.—2E 94
East Garston.—5E 41
Eastgate.—1C 106
(Durham)
Eastgate.—3D 80
(Norfolk)
East Ginge.—4F 41
East Gores.—5A 56
East Goscote.—1D 64
East Grafton.—2A 28
East Grimstead.—1H 15
East Grinstead.—2E 19
East Guldeford.—3D 20
East Haddon.—1D 52
East Hagbourne.—4G 41
East Halton.—3D 96
Eastham.—1A 50
(Hereford & Worcester)
East Ham.—2F 31
(London)
Eastham.—2F 85
(Merseyside)
Eastham Ferry.—2F 85
Easthampstead.—2G 29
Easthampton.—4B 60
East Hanney.—3F 41
East Hanningfield.—2D 44
East Hardwick.—4E 95
East Harling.—4B 68
East Harlsey.—5B 108
East Harnham.—1G 15
East Harptree.—3F 25
East Hartford.—2F 117
East Harting.—2G 17
East Hatch.—1E 15
East Hatley.—2B 54
Easthaugh.—4C 80
East Hauxwell.—5E 107
Eastheath.—2G 29
East Heckington.—3A 78
East Hedleyhope.—5E 117
East Hendred.—4F 41
East Heslerton.—2E 103
East Hoathly.—4G 19
East Hogaland.—4E 175
Easthope.—1C 60
Easthorpe.—5B 56
(Essex)
Easthorpe.—4F 77
(Leicestershire)
East Horrington.—4F 25
East Horsley.—5B 30
East Horton.—1E 123
Easthouses.—3G 131
East Howe.—4F 15
East Huntspill.—4D 24
East Hyde.—1E 43
East Ilsley.—4F 41
Eastington.—3H 11
(Devon)
Eastington.—1C 40
(nr. Northleach, Glos.)
Eastington.—2F 39
(nr. Stonehouse, Glos.)
East Keal.—1C 78
East Kennett.—2G 27
East Keswick.—1D 94
East Kilbride.—4H 129
(Strathclyde)
East Kilbride.—7C 172
(Western Isles)
East Kirkby.—1C 78
East Knapton.—2D 103
East Knighton.—5D 14
East Knowstone.—3E 23
East Kyloe.—1E 123
East Lambrook.—2H 13
East Langdon.—1H 21
East Langton.—3E 65
East Langwell.—3E 166
East Lavant.—3G 17
East Lavington.—2H 17

East Layton.—4E 107
Eastleach Martin.—2D 40
Eastleach Turville.—2C 40
East Leake.—5C 76
East Learmouth.—1C 122
Eastleigh.—3A 22
(nr. Bideford, Devon)
East Leigh.—3H 11
(nr. Crediton, Devon)
East Leigh.—4C 8
(nr. Modbury, Devon)
Eastleigh.—2C 16
(Hampshire)
East Lexham.—4A 80
East Lilburn.—2E 123
Eastling.—5D 32
East Linton.—2B 132
East Liss.—1F 17
East Lockinge.—4F 41
East Looe.—4G 7
East Lound.—3H 89
East Lulworth.—5D 14
East Lutton.—3E 103
East Lydford.—5F 25
East Mains.—4D 154
East Malling.—5B 32
East Marden.—2G 17
East Markham.—5H 89
East Marton.—4C 100
East Meon.—1E 17
East Mersea.—1G 45
East Mey.—1F 171
East Midlands Airport.—5B 76
East Molesey.—4C 30
Eastmoor.—2G 67
East Morden.—4E 15
East Morton.—1B 94
East Ness.—2B 102
East Newton.—2E 97
(Humberside)
East Newton.—2B 102
(North Yorkshire)
Eastney.—4E 17
Eastnor.—4B 50
East Norton.—2E 65
East Oakley.—3D 28
Eastoft.—4A 96
East Ogwell.—2E 9
Easton.—4D 114
(nr. Burgh by Sands, Cumbria)
Easton.—2F 115
(nr. Longtown, Cumbria)
Easton.—1D 8
(Devon)
Easton.—5A 14
(Dorset)
Easton.—5D 28
(Hampshire)
Easton.—5G 77
(Lincolnshire)
Easton.—4D 80
(Norfolk)
Easton.—4F 25
(Somerset)
Easton.—2E 57
(Suffolk)
Easton.—5G 39
(Wiltshire)
Easton Grey.—4G 39
Easton-in-Gordano.—5D 38
Easton Maudit.—2F 53
Easton on the Hill.—2H 65
Easton Royal.—2H 27
East Orchard.—2D 14
East Ord.—4F 133
East Panson.—4D 10
East Peckham.—1A 20
East Pennar.—4C 34
East Pennard.—5F 25
East Perry.—1A 54
East Pitcorthie.—3H 139
East Portlemouth.—5D 8
East Prawle.—5D 9
East Preston.—5B 18

East Putford.—2D 10
East Quantoxhead.—4B 24
East Rainton.—5G 117
East Ravendale.—3E 91
East Raynham.—3A 80
Eastrea.—3B 66
East Retford.—4H 89
East Rhidorroch Lodge.—4G 165
Eastriggs.—3D 114
East Rigton.—1D 94
Eastrington.—3H 95
East Rounton.—4B 108
East Row.—3F 109
East Rudham.—3A 80
East Runton.—1D 81
East Ruston.—3F 81
Eastry.—5E 41
East Saltoun.—3A 132
East Shaws.—3D 107
East Shefford.—5E 41
Eastshore.—10F 175
East Sleekburn.—1F 117
East Somerton.—4G 81
East Stockwith.—3H 89
East Stoke.—5D 14
(Dorset)
East Stoke.—3E 77
(Nottinghamshire)
East Stoke.—2H 13
(Somerset)
East Stour.—1C 14
East Stourmouth.—4G 33
East Stowford.—3C 22
East Stratton.—4D 28
East Studdal.—1H 21
East Taphouse.—3F 7
East Thirston.—5F 123
East Tilbury.—3A 32
East Tisted.—5F 29
East Torrington.—4D 90
East Tuddenham.—4C 80
East Tytherley.—1A 16
East Tytherton.—5A 40
East Village.—3B 12
Eastville.—2D 78
East Wall.—1C 60
East Walton.—1G 67
East Week.—4G 11
Eastwell.—5E 77
East Wellow.—1B 16
East Wemyss.—4F 139
East Whitburn.—3C 130
Eastwick.—1H 43
East Williamston.—4D 35
East Winch.—1F 67
East Winterslow.—5H 27
East Wittering.—4F 17
East Witton.—1E 101
Eastwood.—2C 32
(Essex)
Eastwood.—3B 76
(Nottinghamshire)
East Woodburn.—1C 116
Eastwood End.—3D 66
East Woodhay.—2C 28
East Woodlands.—4C 26
East Worldham.—5F 29
East Worlington.—2C 10
East Youlstone.—1A 52
Eathorpe.—4A 52
Eaton.—1C 74
(nr. Congleton, Ches.)
Eaton.—4H 85
(nr. Kelsall, Ches.)
Eaton.—5E 77
(Leicestershire)
Eaton.—4F 79
(nr. Heacham, Norf.)
Eaton.—2E 68
(Norwich, Norf.)
Eaton.—5H 89
(Nottinghamshire)
Eaton.—2F 41
(Oxfordshire)

Eaton.—2A 60
(nr. Bishop's Castle, Shrops.)
Eaton.—1C 60
(nr. Church Stretton, Shrops.)
Eaton Bishop.—4H 49
Eaton Bray.—5C 53
Eaton Constantine.—5H 73
Eaton Green.—5G 53
Eaton Hastings.—3D 40
Eaton Socon.—2A 54
Eaton upon Tern.—5A 74
Eau Brink.—4F 67
Eaves Green.—4G 63
Ebberston.—1D 103
Ebbesbourne Wake.—1E 15
Ebblake.—3G 15
Ebbw Vale.—2H 37
Ebchester.—4E 117
Ebford.—5C 12
Ebley.—2G 39
Ebnal.—1G 73
Ebrington.—3F 51
Ebsworthy Town.—4F 11
Ecchinswell.—3C 28
Ecclefechan.—2C 114
Eccles.—5D 132
(Borders)
Eccles.—4B 32
(Kent)
Eccles.—3E 87
(Manchester)
Ecclesall.—4D 88
Ecclesfield.—3D 88
Eccles Green.—3F 49
Eccleshall.—5C 74
Eccleshill.—2B 94
Ecclesmachan.—2D 130
Eccles on Sea.—3G 81
Eccles Road.—3C 68
Eccleston.—4G 85
(Cheshire)
Eccleston.—1C 86
(Lancashire)
Eccleston.—3B 86
(Merseyside)
Eccup.—1C 94
Echt.—3E 155
Eckford.—2B 122
Eckington.—5E 89
(Derbyshire)
Eckington.—3D 50
(Hereford & Worcester)
Ecton.—1F 53
Edale.—4B 88
Eday Airport.—4E 174
Edburton.—4D 18
Edderside.—5C 114
Edderton.—5E 166
Eddington.—2B 28
Eddleston.—5F 131
Eddlewood.—4A 130
Edenbridge.—1F 19
Edendonich.—1A 136
Edenfield.—1F 87
Edenhall.—1G 105
Edenham.—5H 77
Edensor.—1G 75
Edentaggart.—4C 136
Edenthorpe.—2G 89
Eden Vale.—1B 108
Edern.—2B 70
Edgarley.—5F 25
Edgbaston.—4E 63
Edgcott.—5D 52
(Buckinghamshire)
Edgcott.—2E 23
(Somerset)
Edge.—2D 107
(Durham)
Edge.—2G 39
(Gloucestershire)
Edge.—5F 73
(Shropshire)
Edgebolton.—3H 73
Edge End.—1D 39
Edgefield.—2C 80

Edgefield Street.—2C 80
Edge Green.—5G 85
Edgehead.—3G 131
Edgeley.—1H 73
Edgeside.—2F 87
Edgeworth.—2H 39
Edgiock.—1E 51
Edgmond.—1B 62
Edgmond Marsh.—5B 74
Edgton.—2A 60
Edgware.—1C 30
Edgworth.—1E 87
Edinbane.—3C 156
Edinburgh.—2F 131
Edinburgh Airport.—2E 131
Edingale.—1G 63
Edingley.—2D 76
Edingthorpe.—2F 81
Edington.—5D 25
(Somerset)
Edington.—3E 27
(Wiltshire)
Edington Burtle.—4D 25
Edingworth.—3D 24
Edistone.—1C 10
Edithmead.—4D 24
Edith Weston.—2G 65
Edlesborough.—1C 42
Edlaston.—3F 75
Edlingham.—4F 123
Edlington.—5E 91
Edmondsham.—2F 15
Edmondsley.—5F 117
Edmondthorpe.—1F 65
Edmonstone.—5E 174
Edmonton.—2D 6
(Cornwall)
Edmonton.—1E 31
(London)
Edmundbyers.—4D 116
Ednam.—1B 122
Ednaston.—3G 75
Edney Common.—2C 44
Edrom.—4E 133
Edstaston.—2H 73
Edstone.—1F 51
Edwalton.—4C 76
Edwardstone.—3B 56
Edwardsville.—3G 37
Edwinsford.—4F 47
Edwinstowe.—1D 76
Edworth.—3B 54
Edwyn Ralph.—2A 50
Edzell.—2F 147
Efail-fach.—3D 36
Efail Isaf.—4G 37
Efailnewydd.—2C 70
Efail-rhyd.—3D 72
Efailwen.—2E 35
Efenechtyd.—5D 84
Effingham.—5C 30
Effingham Common.—5C 30
Effirth.—6E 175
Efflinch.—1F 63
Efford.—3B 12
Egbury.—3C 28
Egdon.—5D 50
Egerton.—1D 20
(Kent)
Egerton.—1E 87
(Manchester)
Eggbuckland.—4B 8
Eggesford.—2G 11
Eggington.—5G 53
Egginton.—5G 75
Egglescliffe.—3B 108
Eggleston.—2C 106
Egham.—3B 30
Egleton.—2F 65
Eglingham.—3F 123
Egloshayle.—2E 6
Egloskerry.—1G 7
Eglwysbach.—3H 83
Eglwys-Brewis.—5G 37
Eglwysfach.—1B 58
Eglwyswrw.—4A 46

Egmanton.—1E 77
Egremont.—3B 104
(Cumbria)
Egremont.—1F 85
(Merseyside)
Egton.—4F 109
Egton Bridge.—4F 109
Egypt.—2A 30
Eight Ash Green.—5B 56
Eight Mile Burn.—4E 131
Eignaig.—4B 142
Eilanreach.—2G 149
Eildon.—1H 121
Eileanach Lodge.—2H 159
Eishken.—6F 173
Eisingrug.—2F 71
Elan Village.—4E 59
Elberton.—4D 39
Elbridge.—3H 17
Elburton.—4B 8
Elcho.—1D 138
Elcombe.—4C 40
Elcot.—2B 28
Eldernell.—3C 66
Eldersfield.—4C 50
Elderslie.—3F 129
Elder Street.—4E 55
Eldon.—2F 107
Eldroth.—3G 99
Eldwick.—1B 94
Elerch.—2B 58
Elfhowe.—5F 105
Elford.—1F 123
(Northumberland)
Elford.—1F 63
(Staffordshire)
Elford Closes.—5D 67
Elgin.—2G 161
Elgol.—2D 148
Elham.—1F 21
Elie.—3G 139
Eling.—5G 41
(Berkshire)
Eling.—2B 16
(Hampshire)
Elishader.—2E 157
Elishaw.—5C 122
Elizafield.—2B 114
Elkesley.—5G 89
Elkington.—5D 64
Elkins Green.—2C 44
Elkstone.—1A 40
Ellan.—1C 152
Ellanbeich.—2E 135
Elland.—3B 94
Ellary.—2F 127
Ellastone.—3F 75
Ellbridge.—3A 8
Eliel.—4D 99
Ellemford.—3D 132
Ellenborough.—1B 104
Ellenbrook.—2F 43
Ellenhall.—5C 74
Ellen's Green.—2B 18
Ellerbeck.—5B 108
Ellerburn.—1D 102
Ellerby.—3E 109
Ellerdine.—5A 74
Ellerdine Heath.—5A 74
Ellerhayes.—3C 12
Elleric.—4E 143
Ellerker.—3B 96
Ellerton.—2H 95
(Humberside)
Ellerton.—5F 107
(North Yorkshire)
Ellerton.—5B 74
(Shropshire)
Ellesborough.—2B 42
Ellesmere.—2F 73
Ellesmere Port.—5B 86
Ellingham.—3G 15
(Hampshire)
Ellingham.—3F 69
(Norfolk)

Ellingham.—2F 123
(Northumberland)
Ellingstring.—1E 101
Ellington.—5A 66
(Cambridgeshire)
Ellington.—5G 123
(Northumberland)
Ellington Thorpe.—5A 66
Ellisfield.—4E 29
Ellistown.—1B 64
Ellon.—5G 163
Ellonby.—1F 105
Ellough.—4G 69
Elloughton.—3B 96
Ellwood.—2D 39
Elm.—2D 66
Elmbridge.—1G 39
(Gloucestershire)
Elmbridge.—1D 50
(Hereford & Worcester)
Elmbridge.—2B 18
(Surrey)
Elmdon.—4D 54
(Essex)
Elmdon.—4F 63
(West Midlands)
Elmdon Heath.—4F 63
Elmesthorpe.—3B 64
Elmfield.—4E 16
Elmhurst.—1F 63
Elmley Castle.—3D 51
Elmley Lovett.—1C 50
Elmore.—1F 39
Elmore Back.—1F 39
Elm Park.—2F 31
Elmscott.—1C 10
Elmsett.—3C 56
Elmstead.—5C 56
Elmstead Heath.—5C 56
Elmstead Market.—5C 56
Elmsted.—1F 21
Elmstone.—4G 33
Elmstone Hardwicke.—5D 50
Elmswell.—4E 103
(Humberside)
Elmswell.—1B 56
(Suffolk)
Elmton.—5F 89
Elphin.—2G 165
Elphinstone.—2G 131
Elrick.—3F 155
(nr. Aberdeen, Grampian)
Elrick.—1B 154
(nr. Rhynie, Grampian)
Elrig.—5A 112
Elsdon.—5D 122
Elsecar.—2D 88
Elsenham.—5E 55
Elsfield.—1G 41
Elsham.—4C 96
Elsing.—4C 80
Elslack.—1G 93
Elsrickle.—5D 130
Elstead.—1A 18
Elsted.—2G 17
Elsthorpe.—5H 77
Elstob.—2G 107
Elston.—3A 12
(Devon)
Elston.—2D 92
(Lancashire)
Elston.—5E 77
(Nottinghamshire)
Elston.—4F 27
(Wiltshire)
Elstone.—2G 11
Elstow.—1H 53
Elstree.—1C 30
Elstronwick.—2E 228
Elswick.—2B 92
(Lancashire)
Elswick.—3F 117
(Tyne & Wear)
Elsworth.—1C 54
Elterwater.—4E 105
Eltham.—3F 31

Eltisley.—2B 54
Elton.—3H 65
(Cambridgeshire)
Elton.—3G 85
(Cheshire)
Elton.—3B 108
(Cleveland)
Elton.—1G 75
(Derbyshire)
Elton.—1F 39
(Gloucestershire)
Elton.—3B 60
(Hereford & Worcester)
Elton.—1E 87
(Manchester)
Elton.—4E 77
(Nottinghamshire)
Elton Green.—3G 85
Eltringham.—3D 116
Elvanfoot.—3B 120
Elvaston.—4B 76
Elveden.—5A 68
Elvington.—2A 132
(Kent)
Elvington.—5C 102
(North Yorkshire)
Elwick.—1B 108
(Cleveland)
Elwick.—1F 123
(Northumberland)
Elworth.—1B 74
(Cheshire)
Elworth.—5A 14
(Dorset)
Elworthy.—2G 23
Ely.—4E 67
(Cambridgeshire)
Ely.—5H 37
(South Glamorgan)
Emberton.—3F 53
Embleton.—1C 104
(Cumbria)
Embleton.—2B 108
(Durham)
Embleton.—2G 123
(Northumberland)
Embo.—4F 167
Emborough.—3B 26
Embo Street.—4F 167
Embsay.—4D 100
Emery Down.—3A 16
Emley.—4C 94
Emmbrook.—2G 29
Emmer Green.—5A 42
Emmington.—2A 42
Emneth.—2D 67
Emneth Hungate.—2E 67
Empingham.—2G 65
Empshott.—5F 29
Emsworth.—3F 17
Enaclete.—5D 173
Enborne.—2C 28
Enborne Row.—2C 28
Enchmarsh.—1C 60
Enderby.—3C 64
Endmoor.—1E 99
Endon.—2D 74
Endon Bank.—2D 74
Enfield.—1E 31
Enfield Wash.—1E 31
Enford.—3C 27
Engine Common.—4E 39
Engine, The.—2B 66
Englefield.—5H 41
Englefield Green.—3A 30
Englesea-brook.—2B 74
English Bicknor.—1D 39
Englishcombe.—2C 26
English Frankton.—3G 73
Enham-Alamein.—4B 28
Enmore.—5C 24
Ennerdale Bridge.—3B 104
Enniscaven.—4D 6
Enoch.—4A 120
Enochdhu.—2H 145

Ensay.—4E 141
Ensbury.—4F 15
Ensdon.—4G 73
Ensis.—3B 22
Enson.—5D 74
Enstone.—5A 52
Enterkinfoot.—4A 120
Enville.—4C 62
Eochar.—4C 172
Eoligarry.—8B 172
Eorabus.—1A 134
Eoropie.—1H 173
Epney.—1F 39
Epperstone.—3D 76
Epping.—2A 44
Epping Green.—2H 43
(Essex)
Epping Green.—2F 43
(Hertfordshire)
Epping Upland.—2H 43
Eppleby.—3E 107
Eppleworth.—2C 96
Epsom.—4D 30
Epwell.—3A 52
Epworth.—2H 89
Epworth Turbary.—2H 89
Erbistock.—1F 73
Erbusaig.—1F 149
Erchless Castle.—4G 159
Erdington.—3F 63
Eredine.—3G 135
Eriboll.—3E 169
Ericstane.—3C 120
Eridge Green.—2G 19
Erines.—2G 127
Eriswell.—5G 67
Erith.—3G 31
Erlestoke.—3E 27
Ermine East.—5B 90
Ermine West.—5B 90
Ermington.—4C 8
Ernesettle.—3A 8
Erpingham.—2D 81
Errittwood.—5D 32
Errogie.—1H 151
Errol.—1E 139
Erskine.—2F 129
Ervie.—3F 111
Erwarton.—4E 57
Erwood.—3C 48
Eryholme.—4G 107
Eryrys.—5E 84
Escalls.—4A 4
Escomb.—1E 107
Escrick.—5B 102
Esgair.—2G 35
(nr. Carmarthen, Dyfed)
Esgair.—3F 35
(nr. St. Clears, Dyfed)
Esgairgeiliog.—5G 71
Esh.—5E 117
Esher.—4C 30
Esholt.—1B 94
Eshott.—5G 123
Eshton.—4C 100
Esh Winning.—5E 117
Eskadale.—5G 159
Eskbank.—3G 131
Eskdale Green.—4C 104
Eskdalemuir.—5E 121
Eskham.—3F 91
Esknish.—3B 126
Esk Valley.—4F 109
Eslington Hall.—3E 123
Espley Hall.—5F 123
Esprick.—2B 92
Essendine.—1H 65
Essendon.—2F 43
Essich.—5A 160
Essington.—2D 62
Eston.—3C 108
Estover.—4B 8
Eswick.—6F 175
Etal.—1D 122
Etchilhampton.—2F 27
Etchingham.—3B 20

Etchinghill.—2F 21
(Kent)
Etchinghill.—1E 63
(Staffordshire)
Ethie Haven.—4F 17
Etling Green.—4C 80
Etloe.—2E 39
Eton.—3A 30
Eton Wick.—3A 30
Etteridge.—4A 152
Ettersgill.—2B 106
Ettiley Heath.—1B 74
Ettington.—3G 51
Etton.—2A 66
(Cambridgeshire)
Etton.—1B 96
(Humberside)
Ettrick.—3E 121
Ettrickbridge.—2F 121
Etwall.—4G 75
Eudon Burnell.—4B 62
Eudon George.—4A 62
Euston.—5G 68
Euxton.—1C 86
Evanstown.—4F 37
Evanton.—2A 160
Evedon.—3H 77
Evelix.—4E 167
Evendine.—3B 50
Evenjobb.—4H 59
Evenley.—4C 52
Evenlode.—5G 51
Even Swindon.—4C 40
Evenwood.—2E 107
Evenwood Gate.—2E 107
Everbay.—5F 174
Evercreech.—5B 26
Everdon.—2C 52
Everingham.—1A 96
Everleigh.—3G 27
Everley.—1E 103
Eversholt.—4G 53
Evershot.—3A 14
Eversley.—2F 29
Eversley Cross.—2F 29
Everthorpe.—2B 96
Everton.—2B 54
(Bedfordshire)
Everton.—4A 16
(Hampshire)
Everton.—3A 86
(Merseyside)
Everton.—3G 89
(Nottinghamshire)
Evertown.—2E 115
Evesbatch.—3A 50
Evesham.—3E 51
Evington.—2D 64
Ewden.—3C 88
Ewden Village.—3C 88
Ewdness.—3B 62
Ewell.—4D 30
Ewell Minnis.—1G 21
Ewelme.—3H 41
Ewen.—3B 40
Ewenny.—5F 37
Ewerby.—3A 78
Ewes.—5F 121
Ewesley.—5E 123
Ewhurst.—1B 18
Ewhurst Green.—3B 20
(East Sussex)
Ewhurst Green.—2B 18
(Surrey)
Ewloe.—4E 85
Ewood Bridge.—3E 93
Eworthy.—4E 11
Ewshot.—3G 29
Ewyas Harold.—5F 49
Exbourne.—3G 11
Exbury.—3C 16
Exceat.—5G 19
Exebridge.—3F 23
Exelby.—1F 101
Exeter.—4C 12
Exeter Airport.—4D 12

Exford.—2E 23
Exfords Green.—5G 73
Exhall.—2F 51
Exlade Street.—4H 41
Exminster.—5C 12
Exmouth.—5D 12
Exning.—1F 55
Exton.—5C 12
(Devon)
Exton.—1E 16
(Hampshire)
Exton.—1G 65
(Leicestershire)
Exton.—2F 23
(Somerset)
Exwick.—4C 12
Eyam.—5C 88
Eydon.—2C 52
Eye.—2B 66
(Cambridgeshire)
Eye.—4B 60
(Hereford & Worcester)
Eye.—5D 68
(Suffolk)
Eye Green.—2B 66
Eyemouth.—3F 133
Eyeworth.—3B 54
Eyhorne Street.—5C 32
Eyke.—2F 57
Eynesbury.—2A 54
Eynort.—1B 148
Eynsford.—4G 31
Eynsham.—2F 41
Eype.—4H 13
Eyre.—5E 157
(Rassay, H'land)
Eyre.—3D 156
(Skye, H'land)
Eythorne.—1G 21
Eyton.—1F 73
(Clwyd)
Eyton.—4B 60
(Hereford & Worcester)
Eyton.—2A 60
(nr. Bishop's Castle, Shrops.)
Eyton.—4F 73
(nr. Shrewsbury, Shrops.)
Eyton on Severn.—5H 73
Eyton upon the Weald Moors.
—1A 62

Faccombe.—3B 28
Faceby.—4B 108
Faddiley.—5H 85
Fadmoor.—1B 102
Fagwyr.—2C 36
Faichem.—3E 151
Failfley.—2G 129
Fail.—2D 118
Failand.—5D 38
Failford.—2D 118
Failsworth.—2F 87
Fairbourne.—4F 71
Fairbourne Heath.—5C 32
Fairburn.—3C 95
Fairfield.—5A 88
(Derbyshire)
Fairfield.—5D 62
(nr. Bromsgrove, Here & Worcs.)
Fairfield.—3E 51
(Evesham, Here & Worcs.)
Fairfield.—3D 20
(Kent)
Fairford.—2C 40
Fair Green.—1F 67
Fair Hill.—1G 105
(Cumbria)
Fairhill.—4A 130
(Strathclyde)
Fair Isle Airport.—1A 174
Fairlands.—3A 30
Fairlie.—4D 128
Fairlight.—4C 20
Fairlight Cove.—4C 20

Five Roads.—2A 36
Five Ways.—5G 63
Flack's Green.—1D 44
Flackwell Heath.—4B 42
Fladbury.—3D 51
Fladdabister.—8F 175
Flagg.—1F 75
Flamborough.—2H 103
Flamstead.—1D 43
Flansham.—3H 17
Flasby.—4C 100
Flash.—1E 75
Flashader.—3C 156
Flatt, The.—2C 115
Flaunden.—2D 42
Flawborough.—3E 77
Flawith.—3H 101
Flax Bourton.—2F 25
Flaxby.—4G 101
Flaxholme.—3H 75
Flaxley.—1E 39
Flaxley Green.—1E 63
Flaxpool.—5B 24
Flaxton.—3B 102
Fleckney.—3D 64
Flecknoe.—1C 52
Fledborough.—5A 90
Fleet.—5B 14
 (Dorset)
Fleet.—3G 29
 (nr. Farnborough, Hants.)
Fleet.—3F 17
 (nr. South Hayling, Hants.)
Fleet.—5C 78
 (Lincolnshire)
Fleet Hargate.—5C 78
Fleetville.—2E 43
Fleetwood.—1A 92
Flemingston.—5G 37
Flemington.—4H 129
 (Glasgow, S'clyde.)
Flemington.—5A 130
 (Strathaven, S'clyde.)
Flempton.—1A 56
Flesherin.—4H 173
Fletcher's Green.—5G 31
Fletchertown.—5D 114
Fletching.—3F 19
Fleuchary.—4E 167
Flexbury.—3C 10
Flexford.—1A 18
Flimby.—1B 104
Flimwell.—2B 20
Flint.—3E 85
Flint Mountain.—3E 85
Flinton.—2E 97
Flintsham.—5F 59
Flishinghurst.—2B 20
Flitcham.—5G 79
Flitton.—4H 53
Flitwick.—4H 53
Flixborough.—4A 96
Flixton.—3E 87
 (Manchester)
Flixton.—4F 69
 (Suffolk)
Flockton.—4C 94
Flodaby.—9C 173
Flodden.—1D 122
Flodigarry.—1D 156
Flood's Ferry.—1B 66
Flookburgh.—2C 98
Flordon.—3D 69
Flore.—1D 52
Flotterton.—4D 123
Flowton.—3C 56
Flushing.—3F 5
 (Cornwall)
Flushing.—4H 163
 (Grampian)
Fluxton.—4D 12
Flyford Flavell.—2D 51
Fobbing.—2B 32
Fochabers.—3H 161
Fochriw.—2H 37

Fockerby.—4A 96
Fodderty.—3H 159
Foddington.—1A 14
Foel.—4B 72
Foffarty.—4D 146
Foggathorpe.—2H 95
Foggo.—5D 132
Fogorig.—5D 132
Foindle.—4B 168
Folda.—2A 146
Fole.—4E 75
Foleshill.—4A 64
Foley Park.—5C 62
Folke.—3C 14
Folkestone.—2G 21
Folkingham.—3H 159
Folkington.—5G 19
Folksworth.—4A 66
Folkton.—2F 103
Folla Rule.—5E 163
Follifoot.—4G 101
Folly Cross.—3E 11
Folly Gate.—4F 11
Folly, The.—2C 28
 (Berkshire)
Folly, The.—1E 43
 (Hertfordshire)
Fonthill Gifford.—5E 27
Fontmell Magna.—2D 14
Fontwell.—3H 17
Foodieash.—2F 139
Foolow.—5B 88
Footdee.—3G 155
Footherley.—2F 63
Foots Cray.—3F 31
Forbestown.—2A 154
Forcett.—3E 107
Ford.—2A 42
 (Buckinghamshire)
Ford.—4E 88
 (Derbyshire)
Ford.—3A 22
 (nr. Bideford, Devon)
Ford.—1C 40
 (Hartland, Devon)
Ford.—4C 8
 (nr. Holbeton, Devon)
Ford.—4A 8
 (Plymouth, Devon)
Ford.—5D 9
 (nr. Salcombe, Devon)
Ford.—5E 51
 (Gloucestershire)
Ford.—1D 122
 (Northumberland)
Ford.—4G 73
 (Shropshire)
Ford.—3F 25
 (nr. Wells, Som.)
Ford.—3G 23
 (nr. Wiveliscombe, Som.)
Ford.—2E 75
 (Staffordshire)
Ford.—3F 135
 (Strathclyde)
Ford.—3H 17
 (West Sussex)
Ford.—5G 39
 (nr. Chippenham, Wilts.)
Ford.—5G 27
 (nr. Salisbury, Wilts.)
Ford Barton.—2C 12
Fordcombe.—1G 19
Fordell.—5D 138
Forden.—5E 73
Ford End.—1C 44
Forder Green.—3D 9
Ford Green.—1B 92
Fordham.—5F 67
 (Cambridgeshire)
Fordham.—5B 56
 (Essex)
Fordham.—3F 67
 (Norfolk)
Fordham Heath.—5B 56
Ford Heath.—4G 73

Ford Houses.—2D 62
Fordie.—1G 137
Fordingbridge.—2G 15
Fordington.—5G 91
Fordon.—2F 103
Fordoun.—1G 147
Fordstreet.—5B 56
 (Essex)
Ford Street.—2E 13
 (Somerset)
Fordton.—4B 12
Fordwells.—1E 40
Fordwich.—5F 33
Fordyce.—2C 162
Forebridge.—5D 74
Foremark.—5H 75
Forest.—2B 106
 (Durham)
Forest.—4F 107
 (North Yorkshire)
Forestburn Gate.—5E 123
Foresterseat.—3F 161
Forest Green.—2E 39
 (Gloucestershire)
Forest Green.—1C 18
 (Surrey)
Forest Hall.—4G 105
Forest Head.—4G 115
Forest Hill.—2G 41
Forest Lodge.—1G 145
Forest Mill.—4B 138
Forest Row.—2F 19
Forestside.—2F 17
Forest Town.—1C 76
Forfar.—3D 146
Forgandenny.—2C 138
Forge.—1C 58
Forge Side.—2A 38
Forge, The.—2F 49
Forgewood.—4A 130
Forgie.—3A 162
Forgue.—4D 162
Formby.—2A 86
Forncett End.—3D 68
Forncett St Mary.—3D 68
Forncett St Peter.—3D 68
Forneth.—4H 145
Fornham All Saints.—1A 56
Fornham St Martin.—1A 56
Forres.—3E 161
Forrestfield.—3B 130
Forrest Lodge.—1C 112
Forsbrook.—3D 74
Forse.—5E 171
Forsinard.—4A 170
Forstal, The.—2E 21
Forston.—4B 14
Fort Augustus.—3F 151
Forteviot.—2C 138
Fort George.—3B 160
Forth.—4C 130
Forthampton.—4C 50
Forthay.—3F 39
Fortingall.—4E 145
Fort Matilda.—2D 128
Forton.—4C 28
 (Hampshire)
Forton.—4D 99
 (Lancashire)
Forton.—4G 73
 (Shropshire)
Forton.—3G 13
 (Somerset)
Forton.—5B 74
 (Staffordshire)
Forton Heath.—4G 73
Fortrie.—4D 162
Fortrose.—3B 160
Fortuneswell.—5A 14
Fort William.—1F 143
Forty Green.—1A 30
Forty Hill.—1E 31
Forward Green.—2C 56
Fosbury.—3B 28
Foscot.—5G 51

Fosdyke.—4C 78
Foss.—3E 145
Fossebridge.—1B 40
Foster Street.—2A 44
Foston.—4F 75
 (Derbyshire)
Foston.—3D 64
 (Leicestershire)
Foston.—5F 77
 (Lincolnshire)
Foston.—3B 102
 (North Yorkshire)
Foston-on-the-Wolds.—4F 103
Fotherby.—3F 91
Fothergill.—1B 104
Fotheringhay.—3H 65
Foubister.—7E 174
Foul Anchor.—1D 66
Foulbridge.—5F 115
Foulden.—4F 133
 (Borders)
Foulden.—3G 67
 (Norfolk)
Foul Mile.—4H 19
Foulridge.—1F 93
Foulsham.—3C 80
Fountainhall.—5H 131
Four Alls, The.—4A 74
Four Ashes.—2D 62
 (nr. Cannock, Staffs.)
Four Ashes.—4C 62
 (nr. Kinver, Staffs.)
Four Ashes.—5C 68
 (Suffolk)
Four Crosses.—5C 72
 (nr. Llanerfyl, Powys)
Four Crosses.—4E 73
 (nr. Llanymynech, Powys)
Four Crosses.—2D 62
 (Staffordshire)
Four Elms.—1F 19
Four Forks.—3E 23
Four Gotes.—1D 66
Four Lane End.—2C 88
Four Lane Ends.—1A 92
 (nr. Blackpool, Lancs.)
Four Lane Ends.—4E 99
 (nr. Lancaster, Lancs.)
Four Lanes.—3B 5
Fourlanes End.—2C 74
Four Marks.—3E 17
Four Mile Bridge.—3B 82
Four Oaks.—3C 20
 (East Sussex)
Four Oaks.—5A 50
 (Gloucestershire)
Four Oaks.—4G 63
 (West Midlands)
Four Roads.—4H 35
 (Dyfed)
Four Roads.—5B 110
 (Isle of Man)
Fourstones.—3B 116
Four Throws.—3B 20
Fovant.—1F 15
Foveran.—1G 155
Fowey.—4F 7
Fowlershill.—2G 155
Fowley Common.—3D 86
Fowlis.—5C 146
Fowlis Wester.—1B 138
Fowlmere.—3D 54
Fownhope.—4H 49
Foxcombe Hill.—2F 41
Fox Corner.—5A 30
Foxcote.—1B 40
 (Gloucestershire)
Foxcote.—3C 26
 (Somerset)
Foxdale.—4B 110
Foxearth.—3A 56
Foxfield.—1B 98
Foxham.—5A 40
Fox Hatch.—1G 31
Foxhole.—4D 6
Foxholes.—2F 103

Foxhunt Green.—4G 19
Fox Lane.—3G 29
Foxley.—3C 80
 (Norfolk)
Foxley.—2D 52
 (Northamptonshire)
Foxley.—4G 39
 (Wiltshire)
Foxlydiate.—1E 51
Fox Street.—5C 56
Foxt.—3E 75
Foxton.—3D 54
 (Cambridgeshire)
Foxton.—2E 107
 (Durham)
Foxton.—4E 64
 (Leicestershire)
Foxton.—5B 108
 (North Yorkshire)
Foxup.—2B 100
Foxwist Green.—1A 74
Foxwood.—5A 62
Foy.—5H 49
Foyers.—1G 151
Foynesfield.—3C 160
Fraddam.—3C 4
Fraddon.—4D 6
Fradley.—1F 63
Fradswell.—4D 75
Fraisthorpe.—3G 103
Framfield.—3F 19
Framingham Earl.—2E 69
Framingham Pigot.—2E 69
Framlingham.—1E 57
Frampton.—4B 14
 (Dorset)
Frampton.—4C 78
 (Lincolnshire)
Frampton Cotterell.—4E 39
Frampton Mansell.—2F 39
Frampton on Severn.—2F 39
Frampton West End.—3B 78
Framsden.—2D 57
Framwellgate Moor.—5F 117
Franche.—5C 62
Frandley.—5D 86
Frankby.—2E 85
Frankfort.—3F 81
Frankley.—4D 63
Frank's Bridge.—2D 48
Frankton.—5B 64
Frankwell.—4G 73
Frant.—2G 19
Fraserburgh.—2G 163
Frating Green.—5C 56
Fratton.—3E 17
Freathy.—4H 7
Freckenham.—5F 67
Freckleton.—3B 92
Freeby.—5G 77
Freefolk Priors.—4C 28
Freeland.—1F 41
Freethorpe.—2G 69
Freiston.—3C 78
Fremington.—2B 22
 (Devon)
Fremington.—5D 106
 (North Yorkshire)
Frenchbeer.—1C 8
French Street.—5F 31
Frenich.—3D 136
Frensham.—4G 29
Frenze.—4D 68
Fresgoe.—2B 170
Freshfield.—2A 86
Freshford.—2C 26
Freshwater.—5B 16
Freshwater Bay.—5B 16
Freshwater East.—5D 34
Fressingfield.—5E 69
Freston.—4D 56
Freswick.—2F 171
Fretherne.—2F 39
Frettenham.—4E 81
Freuchie.—3E 139
Freystrop Cross.—3C 34

Friar's Gate.—2F 19
Friar Waddon.—5B 14
Friday Bridge.—2D 66
Friday Street.—5H 19
 (East Sussex)
Friday Street.—1C 18
 (Surrey)
Fridaythorpe.—4D 102
Friden.—1F 75
Friern Barnet.—1D 31
Friesthorpe.—4C 90
Frieston.—3G 77
Frieston Shore.—3C 78
Frieth.—3A 42
Friezeland.—2B 76
Frilford.—3F 41
Frilsham.—5G 41
Frimley.—3G 29
Frimley Green.—3G 29
Frindsbury.—4B 32
Fring.—4G 79
Fringford.—5D 52
Frinsted.—5C 32
Frinton-on-Sea.—5E 57
Friockheim.—4E 147
Friog.—4F 71
Frisby on the Wreake.—1D 64
Friskney.—2D 78
Friskney Eaudyke.—2D 78
Friston.—5G 19
 (East Sussex)
Friston.—1G 57
 (Suffolk)
Fritchley.—2A 76
Fritham.—2H 15
Frith Bank.—3C 78
Frith Common.—1A 50
Frithelstock.—2E 11
Frithelstock Stone.—2E 11
Frithsden.—2D 42
Frithville.—2C 78
Frittenden.—1C 20
Frittiscombe.—5E 9
Fritton.—2G 69
 (nr. Great Yarmouth, Norf.)
Fritton.—3E 69
 (nr. Long Stratton, Norf.)
Fritwell.—5C 52
Frixton.—2F 103
Frizinghall.—2B 94
Frizington.—3B 104
Frobost.—6C 172
Frocester.—2F 39
Frochas.—5D 72
Frodesley.—5H 73
Frodingham.—4A 96
Frodsham.—3H 85
Froggatt.—5C 88
Froghall.—3E 75
Frogham.—2G 15
 (Hampshire)
Frogham.—5G 33
 (Kent)
Frogmore.—5D 8
 (Devon)
Frogmore.—2G 29
 (Hampshire)
Frogmore.—2E 43
 (Hertfordshire)
Frognall.—1A 66
Frogshall.—2E 81
Frogwell.—3H 7
Frolesworth.—3C 64
Frome.—4C 26
Fromefield.—4C 26
Frome St Quintin.—3A 14
Fromes Hill.—3A 50
Fron.—4G 47
 (Dyfed)
Fron.—5E 83
 (nr. Caernarfon, Gwynedd)
Fron.—2C 70
 (nr. Pwllheli, Gwynedd)
Fron.—4F 59
 (nr. Llandrindod Wells, Powys)

Fron.—1G 59
(nr. Newtown, Powys)
Fron.—5E 73
(nr. Welshpool, Powys)
Froncysyllte.—1E 73
Fron Isaf.—1E 73
Fron-goch.—2B 72
Fron-oleu.—2G 71
Frosterley.—1D 106
Froxfield.—4G 53
(Bedfordshire)
Froxfield.—2A 28
(Wiltshire)
Froxfield Green.—1F 17
Fryern Hill.—1C 16
Fryerning.—2C 44
Fryning.—1G 17
Fryton.—2B 102
Fugglestone St Peter.—5G 27
Fulbeck.—2G 77
Fulbourn.—5C 65
Fulbrook.—1D 40
Fulflood.—1C 16
Fulford.—5B 102
(North Yorkshire)
Fulford.—1F 13
(Somerset)
Fulford.—4D 74
(Staffordshire)
Fulham.—3D 30
Fulking.—4D 18
Fuller's Moor.—5G 85
Fuller Street.—1D 44
Fullerton.—5B 28
Fulletby.—5E 91
Full Sutton.—4C 102
Fullwood.—4F 129
Fulmer.—2A 30
Fulmodestone.—2B 80
Fulnetby.—5C 90
Fulney.—5B 78
Fulstow.—3F 91
Fulthorpe.—4G 117
Fulwell.—4G 117
Fulwood.—2C 92
(Lancashire)
Fulwood.—2B 76
(Nottinghamshire)
Fulwood.—1F 13
(Somerset)
Fulwood.—4D 88
(South Yorkshire)
Fundenhall.—3D 68
Funtington.—3F 17
Funtley.—3D 16
Funzie.—2H 175
Furley.—3F 13
Furnace.—1B 58
(nr. Aberystwyth, Dyfed)
Furnace.—2B 36
(Llanelli, Dyfed)
Furnace.—1H 135
(Strathclyde)
Furner's Green.—3F 19
Furness Vale.—4H 87
Furneux Pelham.—5D 54
Furzebrook.—5E 15
Furzehill.—1D 22
Furzley Corner.—2E 17
Furzey Lodge.—3B 16
Fyfield.—2B 44
(Essex)
Fyfield.—2D 40
(Gloucestershire)
Fyfield.—4A 28
(Hampshire)
Fyfield.—3F 41
(Oxfordshire)
Fyfield.—2G 27
(Wiltshire)
Fylingthorpe.—4G 109
Fyvie.—5E 163

Gabrach.—1A 154
(Grampian)
Gabroc Hill.—4F 129
Gadbrook.—1D 18
Gaddesby.—4D 64
Gadgirth.—2D 118
Gaer.—5D 48
Gaerwen.—3D 83
Gagingwell.—5B 52
Gaick Lodge.—5B 152
Gailey.—1D 62
Gainford.—3E 107
Gainsborough.—3A 90
(Lincolnshire)
Gainsborough.—3D 57
(Suffolk)
Gainsford End.—4G 55
Gairletter.—1C 128
Gairloch.—3E 155
(Grampian)
Gairloch.—1H 157
(Highland)
Gairlochy.—5D 150
Gairney Bank.—4D 138
Gairnshiel Lodge.—3G 153
Gaisgill.—4H 105
Gaitsgill.—5E 115
Galashiels.—1G 121
Galgate.—4D 99
Galhampton.—1B 14
Gallatown.—4E 139
Galley Common.—3H 63
Galleyend.—2D 44
Galleywood.—2D 44
Gallin.—4C 144
Gallowfauld.—4D 146
Gallowhill.—2H 129
(Kirkintilloch, S'clyde)
Gallowhill.—2F 129
(Paisley, S'clyde)
Gallowhill.—5A 146
(Tayside)
Gallowhills.—3H 163
Gallows Green.—1D 50
(Hereford & Worcester)
Gallows Green.—3E 75
(Staffordshire)
Gallowstree Common.—4H 41
Galltair.—1G 149
Galmington.—1F 13
Galmisdale.—5C 148
Galmpton.—4E 9
(nr. Paignton, Devon)
Galmpton.—5C 8
(nr. Salcombe, Devon)
Galmpton Warborough.—4E 9
Galphay.—2F 101
Galston.—1D 119
Galton.—5C 14
Galtrigill.—3A 156
Gamblesby.—1H 105
Gamelsby.—4D 114
Gamesley.—3H 87
Gamlingay.—2B 54
Gamlingay Cinques.—2B 54
Gamlingay Great Heath.—2B 54
Gammersgill.—1D 100
Gamrie.—2E 163
Gamston.—5H 89
(nr. East Retford, Notts.)
Gamston.—4D 76
(nr. Nottingham, Notts.)
Ganarew.—1D 38
Ganavan.—5C 142
Ganborough.—5F 51
Gang.—3H 7
Ganllwyd.—4G 73
Gannochy.—1E 147
(nr. Brechin, Tayside)
Gannochy.—1D 138
(Perth, Tayside)
Gansclet.—4F 171
Ganstead.—2D 96
Ganthorpe.—2B 102

Ganton.—2E 103
Garboldisham.—4C 68
Garden City.—4F 85
Gardeners Green.—2G 29
Gardenstown.—2E 163
Garden Village.—3C 88
(South Yorkshire)
Garden Village.—3B 36
(West Glamorgan)
Garden Village.—2E 95
(West Yorkshire)
Garderhouse.—7E 175
Gardham.—1B 96
Gare Hill.—4C 26
Garelochhead.—4B 136
Garenin.—3D 173
Garford.—3F 41
Garforth.—2E 94
Gargrave.—4C 100
Gargunnock.—4G 137
Garlieston.—5B 112
Garlinge Green.—5F 33
Garlogie.—3E 155
Garmelow.—5B 74
Garmond.—3F 163
Garmondsway.—1G 107
Garmony.—4A 142
Garmouth.—2H 161
Garmston.—2A 62
Garn.—2B 70
Garnant.—1C 36
Garndiffaith.—2A 38
Garn Dolbenmaen.—1D 71
Garnett Bridge.—5G 105
Garnfadryn.—2B 70
Garnkirk.—3H 129
Garnlydan.—7H 37
Garnsgate.—5D 78
Garnswllt.—2C 36
Garn-y-erw.—1A 38
Garrabost.—4H 173
Garrafad.—2D 157
Garral Green.—4D 74
Garrallan.—3E 119
Garras.—4E 5
Garreg.—1F 71
Garrigill.—5A 116
Garriston.—5E 107
Garros.—2D 157
Garrow.—4F 145
Garrycloddach.—2D 172
Garrynamonie.—7C 172
Garsdale.—1G 99
Garsdale Head.—5A 106
Garsdon.—4A 40
Garshall Green.—4D 74
Garsington.—2G 41
Garstang.—1B 92
Garston.—4B 86
Garswood.—3C 86
Gartcosh.—3H 129
Garth.—2E 71
(Clwyd)
Garth.—2E 71
(Gwynedd)
Garth.—4C 110
(Isle of Man)
Garth.—3E 37
(Mid Glamorgan)
Garth.—3B 48
(nr. Builth Wmlls, Powys)
Garth.—3H 59
(nr. Knighton, Powys)
Garthamlock.—3H 129
Garthbrengy.—4C 48
Gartheli.—2E 47
Garthmyl.—1G 59
Garthorpe.—4A 96
(Humberside)
Garthorpe.—5F 77
(Leicestershire)
Garth Owen.—1G 59
Garth Penrhyncoch.—2B 58
Garth Place.—4H 37
Garth Row.—5G 105
Gartly.—5C 162
Gartmore.—4E 137

Gartness.—1G 129
(Central)
Gartness.—3A 130
(Strathclyde)
Gartocharn.—1F 129
Garton.—2E 97
Garton-on-the-Wolds.—4E 103
Gartsherrie.—3A 130
Gartymore.—2H 167
Garvald.—2B 132
Garvamore.—4H 151
Garvard.—4A 134
Garvault.—5H 169
Garve.—2F 159
Garvestone.—2C 68
Garvie.—4H 135
Garvock.—2D 128
(Strathclyde)
Garvock.—1G 147
(Tayside)
Garway.—5G 49
Garway Common.—5G 49
Garway Hill.—5G 49
Garwick.—3A 78
Garyvard.—5F 173
Gaskan.—1B 142
Gasper.—5C 26
Gastard.—2D 27
Gasthorpe.—4B 68
Gatcombe.—5C 16
Gateacre.—4B 86
Gatebeck.—1E 99
Gate Burton.—4H 90
Gateforth.—3F 95
Gatehead.—1C 118
Gatehouse.—1A 116
Gatehouse of Fleet.—4D 112
Gatelawbridge.—5B 120
Gateley.—3B 80
Gatenby.—1G 101
Gatesgarth.—3C 104
Gateshead.—3F 117
Gatesheath.—4G 85
Gateside.—3D 138
(Fife)
Gateside.—4E 129
(Strathclyde)
Gateside.—4D 146
(nr. Forfar, Tayside)
Gateside.—4C 146
(nr. Kirriemuir, Tayside)
Gathurst.—2C 86
Gatisfield.—3D 16
Gatley.—4F 87
Gatton.—5D 31
Gattonside.—1H 121
Gatwick Airport.—1D 18
Gaufron.—4F 59
Gaulby.—2D 64
Gaulden Sutton.—4G 85
Gauldry.—1F 139
Gaultree.—2D 67
Gaunt's Common.—3F 15
Gaunt's Earthcott.—4E 39
Gautby.—5D 90
Gavinton.—4D 132
Gawber.—2D 88
Gawcott.—4D 52
Gawsworth.—1C 74
Gawthorpe.—3C 94
Gawthrop.—1F 99
Gawthwaite.—1B 98
Gay Bowers.—2D 44
Gaydon.—2A 52
Gayhurst.—3F 53
Gayle.—1B 100
Gayles.—4E 107
Gay Street.—3B 18
Gayton.—2E 85
(Merseyside)
Gayton.—1G 67
(Norfolk)
Gayton.—2E 52
(Northamptonshire)
Gayton.—5D 75
(Staffordshire)

Gayton le Marsh.—4G 91
Gayton le Wold.—4E 91
Gayton Thorpe.—1G 67
Gaywood.—5F 79
Gazeley.—1G 55
Geanies.—1C 160
Geary.—2B 156
Geddes.—3C 160
Gedding.—2B 56
Geddington.—4F 65
Gedintailor.—5E 157
Gedling.—3D 76
Gedney.—5D 78
Gedney Broadgate.—5D 78
Gedney Drove End.—5D 78
Gedney Dyke.—5D 78
Gedney Hill.—1C 66
Gee Cross.—3E 87
Geeston.—2G 65
Geilston.—2E 129
Geise.—2D 170
Gelder Shiel.—5G 153
Geldeston.—3F 69
Gell.—4A 84
Gelli.—3F 37
Gellifor.—4D 84
Gelligaer.—3H 37
Gellilydan.—2F 71
Gellinudd.—2D 36
Gelly.—3D 35
Gellyburn.—5H 145
Gellywen.—2F 35
Gelston.—3E 113
(Dumfries & Galloway)
Gelston.—3G 77
(Lincolnshire)
Gembling.—4G 103
Geneva.—2D 46
Gentleshaw.—1E 63
Geocrab.—8D 173
George Green.—2A 30
Georgeham.—2A 22
George Nympton.—3D 22
Georgetown.—2H 37
(Gwent)
Georgetown.—3F 129
(Strathclyde)
Georth.—5C 174
Gerdinen.—2C 36
Gerlan.—4F 83
Germansweek.—4E 11
Germoe.—4C 4
Gerrans.—3F 5
Gerrard's Bromley.—4B 74
Gerrard's Cross.—2A 30
Gerston.—3D 170
Geshader.—4D 173
Gestingthorpe.—4A 224
Geuffordd.—4E 72
Gibraltar.—1A 42
(Buckinghamshire)
Gibraltar.—4H 91
(Mablethorpe, Lincs.)
Gibraltar.—2E 79
(nr. Skegness, Lincs.)
Gibraltar.—2D 57
(Suffolk)
Gibsmere.—3E 76
Giddeahall.—5G 39
Gidea Park.—2G 31
Gidleigh.—1C 8
Giffnock.—4G 129
Gifford.—3B 132
Giffordtown.—2E 139
Giggetty.—3G 62
Giggleswick.—3B 100
Gignog.—2B 34
Gilberdyke.—3A 96
Gilbert's End.—3C 50
Gilbert's Green.—5F 63
Gilchriston.—3A 132
Gilcrux.—1C 104
Gildersome.—3C 94
Gildingwells.—4F 89
Gilesgate Moor.—5F 117
Gileston.—5G 37

Gilfach.—3H 37
Gilfach Goch.—4F 37
Gilfachrheda.—7D 46
Gill.—2F 105
Gillamoor.—5D 109
Gillan.—4E 5
Gillar's Green.—3B 86
Gillen.—3B 156
Gilling East.—2B 102
Gillingham.—1D 14
(Dorset)
Gillingham.—4B 32
(Kent)
Gillingham.—3G 69
(Norfolk)
Gilling West.—4E 107
Gillock.—3E 171
Gillow Heath.—2C 74
Gills.—1F 171
Gill's Green.—2B 20
Gilmanscleuch.—2F 121
Gilmerton.—3F 131
(Lothian)
Gilmerton.—1A 138
(Tayside)
Gilmonby.—3C 106
Gilmorton.—4C 64
Gilsland.—3H 115
Gilsland Spa.—3H 115
Gilson.—3F 63
Gilston.—4H 131
Giltbrook.—3B 76
Gilwern.—1A 38
Gimingham.—2E 81
Gipping.—1C 56
Gipsey Bridge.—3B 78
Gipton.—2D 94
Girdle Toll.—5E 129
Girlsta.—6F 175
Girsby.—4G 107
Girthon.—4D 112
Girton.—1D 54
(Cambridgeshire)
Girton.—1F 77
(Nottinghamshire)
Girvan.—5A 118
Gisburn.—1F 93
Gisla.—5D 173
Gisleham.—4H 69
Gislingham.—5C 68
Gissing.—4D 68
Gittisham.—4E 13
Gladestry.—2E 49
Gladsmuir.—2A 132
Glaichbea.—5H 159
Glais.—2D 36
Glaisdale.—4E 109
Glame.—4E 157
Glamis.—4C 146
Glanaber Terrace.—1G 71
Glanaman.—1C 36
Glan-Conwy.—5H 83
Glandford.—1C 80
Glan Duar.—3E 47
Glandwr.—2E 35
(Dyfed)
Glandwr.—2A 38
(Gwent)
Glan-Dwyfach.—1D 71
Glandyfi.—1B 58
Glangrwyne.—1A 38
Glanmule.—1G 59
Glanrhyd.—3A 46
(nr. Cardigan, Dyfed)
Glan-rhyd.—4A 46
(nr. Crymmych, Dyfed)
Glan-rhyd.—2B 36
(Powys)
Glanton.—3E 123
Glanton Pike.—3E 123
Glanvilles Wootton.—3B 14
Glan-y-don.—3D 84
Glan-y-nant.—2E 59
Glan-yr-afon.—1C 72
(nr. Bala, Gwynedd)

Glan-yr-afon.—2F 83
(nr. Bangor, Gwynedd)
Glan-yr-afon.—5C 72
(Powys)
Glan-y-wern.—2F 71
Glapthorn.—3H 65
Glapwell.—1B 76
Glas Aird.—4B 134
Glas-allt-Shiel.—5G 153
Glasbury.—4D 48
Glascoed.—3B 84
(Clwyd)
Glascoed.—2B 38
(Gwent)
Glascote.—2G 63
Glascwm.—2D 48
Glasfryn.—5B 84
Glasgow.—3G 129
Glasgow Airport.—3F 129
Glashvin.—2D 156
Glasinfryn.—4E 83
Glasnacardoch.—4E 149
Glasnakille.—2D 148
Glaspwll.—1C 58
Glassburn.—5F 159
Glassenbury.—2B 20
Glasserton.—5B 112
Glassford.—5A 130
Glasshouse.—5B 50
Glasshouses.—3E 101
Glasson.—3D 114
(Cumbria)
Glasson.—4D 98
(Lancashire)
Glassonby.—1G 105
Glasterlaw.—3E 147
Glaston.—2F 65
Glastonbury.—5F 25
Glatton.—4A 66
Glazebrook.—3D 87
Glazebury.—3D 86
Glazeley.—4B 62
Gleadless.—4D 88
Gleadsmoss.—1C 74
Gleaston.—2B 98
Glecknabae.—3B 128
Gledrid.—2E 73
Gleiniant.—1E 59
Glemsford.—3A 56
Glen.—4C 112
Glenalmond.—1B 138
Glenancross.—4E 149
Glen Auldyn.—2D 110
Glenbarr.—2A 124
Glenbeg.—2G 141
Glen Bernisdale.—4D 156
Glenbervie.—5E 155
Glenbog.—3A 130
Glenborrodale.—2A 142
Glenbranter.—4A 136
Glenbreck.—2C 120
Glenbrein Lodge.—2G 151
Glenbrittle.—1C 148
Glenbuchat Lodge.—2H 153
Glenbuck.—2G 119
Glenburn.—3F 129
Glencalvie Lodge.—5B 166
Glencaple.—3G 113
Glencarron Lodge.—3C 158
Glencarse.—1D 138
Glencassley Castle.—3B 166
Glencat.—4C 154
Glencoe.—3F 143
Glen Cottage.—5E 149
Glencraig.—4D 138
Glendavon.—3B 138
Glendoebeg.—3G 151
Glendoick.—1E 138
Glenduckie.—2E 139
Gleneagles.—3B 138
Glenegedale.—4B 126
Glenegedale Lots.—4B 126
Glenelg.—2G 149
Glenernie.—4E 161
Glenesslin.—1F 113
Glenfarg.—2D 138

Glenfarquhar Lodge.—5E 155
Glenferness Mains.—4D 160
Glenfeshie Lodge.—4C 152
Glenfiddich Lodge.—5H 161
Glenfield.—2C 64
Glenfinnan.—5B 150
Glenfintaig Lodge.—5E 151
Glenfoot.—2D 138
Glenfyne Lodge.—2B 136
Glengap.—4D 112
Glengarnock.—4E 128
Glengolly.—2D 170
Glengorm Castle.—3F 141
Glengrasco.—4D 156
Glenhead Farm.—2B 146
Glenholm.—1D 120
Glen House.—1E 121
Glenhurich.—2C 142
Glenkerry.—3E 121
Glenkiln.—2F 113
Glenkindie.—2B 154
Glenkirk.—2C 120
Glenlean.—1B 128
Glenlee.—1D 112
Glenleraig.—5B 168
Glenlichorn.—2G 137
Glenlivet.—1F 153
Glenlochar.—3E 113
Glenlochsie Lodge.—1H 145
Glenluce.—4G 111
Glenmarksie.—3F 159
Glenmassan.—1B 128
Glenmavis.—3A 130
Glenmaye.—4B 110
Glenmazeran Lodge.—1B 152
Glenmidge.—1F 113
Glen Mona.—3D 110
Glenmore.—2G 141
(nr. Glenborrodale, H'land.)
Glenmore.—3D 153
(nr. Kingussie, H'land.)
Glenmore.—4D 156
(Skye, H'land.)
Glenmoy.—2D 146
Glen of Coachford.—4B 162
Glenogil.—2D 146
Glen Parva.—3C 64
Glenprosen Village.—2C 146
Glenree.—3D 124
Glenridding.—3E 105
Glenrisdell.—4G 127
Glenrosa.—2E 125
Glenrothes.—3E 139
Glensanda.—4C 142
Glensaugh.—1F 147
Glenshee.—1A 146
Glenside.—6F 173
Glensluain.—4H 135
Glenstockadale.—3F 111
Glenstriven.—2B 128
Glen Tanar House.—4B 154
Glentham.—3C 90
Glen Tolsta.—3F 171
Glenton.—1D 154
Glentress.—1E 121
Glentromie Lodge.—4B 152
Glentrool Lodge.—1B 112
Glentrool Village.—2A 112
Glentruim House.—4A 152
Glentworth.—4B 90
Glenuig.—1A 142
Glen Village.—2B 130
Glen Vine.—4C 110
Glenwhilly.—2G 111
Glenzierfoot.—2E 115
Glespin.—2H 119
Gletness.—6F 173
Glewstone.—5H 49
Glidden.—2E 17
Glinton.—2A 66
Glooston.—3E 65
Glossop.—3H 87
Gloster Hill.—4G 123
Gloucester.—1G 39
Gloup.—1G 175
Glusburn.—1H 93

Glutt Lodge.—5B 170
Glutton Bridge.—1E 75
Gluvian.—3D 6
Glympton.—5B 52
Glyn.—3A 84
Glynarthen.—3C 46
Glynbrochan.—2C 58
Glyn Ceiriog.—2E 72
Glyncoch.—3G 37
Glyncorrwg.—3E 37
Glynde.—5F 19
Glyndebourne.—4F 19
Glyngollyo.—2D 170
Glyndyfrdwy.—1D 72
Glynllan.—4F 37
Glyn-neath.—2E 37
Glynogwr.—4F 37
Glyntaff.—4G 37
Glyntawe.—1E 37
Glynteg.—4C 46
Gnosall.—5C 74
Gnosall Heath.—5C 74
Goadby.—3E 65
Goadby Marwood.—5E 77
Goatacre.—5B 40
Goathill.—2B 14
Goathland.—4F 109
Goathurst.—5C 24
Goathurst Common.—5F 31
Goat Lees.—1E 20
Gobernuisgach Lodge.—4E 169
Gobernuisgeach.—5B 170
Gobowen.—2F 73
Godalming.—1A 18
Goddard's Corner.—1E 57
Goddard's Green.—2C 20
(nr. Benenden, Kent)
Goddard's Green.—2B 20
(nr. Cranbrook, Kent)
Goddard's Green.—3D 19
(West Sussex)
Godford Cross.—3E 13
Godleybrook.—5D 75
Godmanchester.—5B 66
Godmanstone.—4B 14
Godmersham.—5E 33
Godolphin Cross.—3D 4
Godre'r-graig.—2D 36
Godshill.—2G 15
(Hampshire)
Godshill.—5D 16
(Isle of Wight)
Godstone.—4E 75
(Staffordshire)
Godstone.—5E 31
(Surrey)
Godwell.—4C 8
Goetre.—2B 38
Goff's Oak.—2G 43
Gogar.—2E 131
Goginan.—2B 58
Golan.—1E 71
Golant.—4F 7
Golberdon.—2H 7
Golborne.—3D 86
Golcar.—4A 94
Goldcliff.—4B 38
Golden Cross.—4G 19
Golden Green.—1H 19
Golden Grove.—1B 36
(Dyfed)
Golden Grove.—4G 109
(North Yorkshire)
Goldenhill.—2C 74
Golden Pot.—4F 29
Golden Valley.—5D 50
Golders Green.—2D 30
Goldhanger.—2F 45
Gold Hill.—3E 67
Golding.—5H 73
Goldington.—7H 73
Goldsborough.—4G 101
(nr. Harrogate, N Yorks.)
Goldsborough.—3F 109
(nr. Whitby, N Yorks.)
Goldsithney.—3C 4

Goldstone.—4G 33
(Kent)
Goldstone.—5B 74
(Shropshire)
Goldthorpe.—2E 89
Goldworthy.—1D 11
Golfa.—3D 72
Gollanfield.—3C 160
Gollinglith Foot.—1E 101
Golsoncott.—2G 23
Golspie.—4F 167
Gomeldon.—5G 27
Gomersal.—3C 94
Gometra House.—4E 141
Gomshall.—1B 18
Gonalston.—3D 76
Gonerby Hill Foot.—4G 77
Gonnabarn.—4D 6
Good Easter.—1C 44
Gooderstone.—2G 67
Goodleigh.—2C 22
Goodmanham.—1A 96
Goodmayes.—2F 31
Goodnestone.—5G 33
(nr. Aylesham, Kent)
Goodnestone.—4E 33
(nr. Faversham, Kent)
Goodrich.—1D 38
Goodrington.—4E 9
Goodshaw.—3F 93
Goodshaw Fold.—3F 93
Goodstone.—2D 9
Goodwick.—1C 34
Goodworth Clatford.—4B 28
Goole.—3H 95
Goom's Hill.—2E 51
Goonbell.—2E 5
Goonhavern.—4B 6
Goonvrea.—2E 5
Goose Green.—4F 39
(Avon)
Goose Green.—1E 99
(Cumbria)
Gooseham.—2C 10
Goosewells.—4B 8
Goosey.—3E 41
Goosnargh.—2C 92
Goostrey.—5E 87
Gorcott Hill.—1E 51
Gordon.—5C 132
Gordonbush.—3F 167
Gordonstown.—3C 162
(nr. Cornhill, Grampian)
Gordonstown.—5E 162
(nr. Fyvie, Grampian)
Gorebridge.—3G 131
Gorefield.—1D 66
Gores.—3G 27
Gorgie.—2F 131
Goring.—4H 41
Goring-by-Sea.—5C 18
Goring Heath.—5H 41
Gorleston-on-Sea.—2H 69
Gornalwood.—3D 62
Gorran Churchtown.—2G 5
Gorran Haven.—2H 5
Gors.—3B 58
Gorsedd.—3D 84
Gorseinon.—3B 36
Gorseness.—6D 174
Gorseybank.—2G 75
Gorsgoch.—2D 47
Gorslas.—1B 36
Gorsley.—5A 50
Gorsley Common.—5A 50
Gorstan.—2F 159
Gorstella.—4F 83
Gorsty Common.—4G 49
Gorsty Hill.—5E 75
Gortantaoid.—2B 126
Gorteneorn.—2A 142
Gortenfern.—2A 142
Gorton.—3F 87
Gosbeck.—2D 56
Gosberton.—4B 78
Gosberton Clough.—5A 78

Goseley Dale.—5H 75
Gosfield.—5G 55
Gosford.—1G 41
Gosforth.—4B 104
(Cumbria)
Gosforth.—3F 117
(Tyne & Wear)
Gosmore.—5A 54
Gosport.—4E 16
Gossabrough.—3G 175
Gossington.—2F 39
Gossops Green.—2D 18
Goswick.—5G 133
Gotham.—4C 76
Gotherington.—5D 50
Gott.—4B 140
Goudhurst.—2B 20
Goulceby.—5E 91
Gourdon.—1H 147
Gourock.—2D 128
Govan.—3G 129
Govanhill.—3G 129
Goverton.—2E 76
Goveton.—5D 8
Govig.—7C 173
Govilon.—1A 38
Gowanhill.—2H 163
Gowdall.—3G 95
Gowerton.—3B 36
Gowkhall.—5C 138
Gowthorpe.—4C 102
Goxhill.—3D 96
(nr. Barton-upon-Humber,
Humberside)
Goxhill.—1D 97
(nr. Hornsea, Humberside)
Goxhill Haven.—3D 96
Goytre.—4D 36
Graby.—5H 77
Graffham.—2H 17
Grafham.—1A 54
(Cambridgeshire)
Grafham.—1B 18
(Surrey)
Grafton.—4D 51
(nr. Evesham, Here & Worcs.)
Grafton.—4G 49
(nr. Hereford, Here & Worcs.)
Grafton.—4C 60
(nr. Leominster, Here & Worcs.)
Grafton.—3H 101
(North Yorkshire)
Grafton.—2D 40
(Oxfordshire)
Grafton.—4G 73
(Shropshire)
Grafton Flyford.—2D 50
Grafton Regis.—3E 53
Grafton Underwood.—4G 65
Grafty Green.—1C 20
Graianrhyd.—5E 84
Graig.—3C 84
(Clwyd)
Graig.—4H 35
(Dyfed)
Graig.—3H 83
(Gwynedd)
Graig-fechan.—5D 84
Graig Penllyn.—5F 37
Graig Trewyddfa.—3C 36
Grain.—3C 32
Grainsby.—3E 91
Grainthorpe.—3F 91
Grainthorpe Fen.—3F 91
Grampound.—2G 5
Grampound Road.—4D 6
Gramsdale.—3D 172
Granborough.—5E 53
Granby.—4E 77
Grandborough.—1B 52
Grandpont.—2G 41
Grandtully.—3G 145
Grange.—3D 104
(Cumbria)
Grange.—3B 60
(Hereford & Worcester)

Grange.—2E 85
(Merseyside)
Grange.—5C 108
(North Yorkshire)
Grange.—1D 118
(Strathclyde)
Grange.—1E 139
(Tayside)
Grange Crossroads.—3B 162
Grange Hill.—1F 31
Grangemill.—2G 75
Grange Moor.—4C 94
Grangemouth.—1C 130
Grange of Lindores.—2E 139
Grange-over-Sands.—2D 98
Grangepans.—1D 130
Grangetown.—2C 108
(Cleveland)
Grangetown.—5H 37
(South Glamorgan)
Grangetown.—4H 117
(Tyne & Wear)
Grange Villa.—4F 117
Granish.—2C 152
Gransmoor.—4G 103
Granston.—1B 34
Grantchester.—2D 54
Grantham.—4G 77
Grantley.—3F 101
Grantlodge.—2E 154
Granton.—2F 131
Grantown-on-Spey.—1E 153
Grantshouse.—3E 132
Grappan.—2E 9
Grappenhall.—4D 86
Grasby.—5C 96
Grasmere.—4E 105
Grasscroft.—2G 87
Grassendale.—4A 86
Grassgarth.—5E 115
Grassholme.—2C 106
Grassington.—3D 100
Grassmoor.—3B 86
Grassthorpe.—1E 77
Grateley.—4A 28
Gratton.—2D 11
(Devon)
Gratton.—2D 74
(Staffordshire)
Gratwich.—4E 75
Graveley.—5B 54
(Cambridgeshire)
Graveley.—5B 54
(Hertfordshire)
Gravelhill.—4G 73
Gravel Hole.—2G 87
Gravelly Hill.—3F 63
Graveney.—4E 33
Gravesend.—3H 32
Gravir.—6F 173
Grayingham.—3B 90
Grayrigg.—5G 105
Grays.—3H 31
Grayshott.—5G 29
Grayson Green.—2A 104
Grayswood.—2A 18
Graythorp.—2C 108
Grazeley.—2E 29
Grealin.—2E 157
Grean.—8B 172
Greasbrough.—3E 88
Greasby.—2E 85
Great Abington.—3E 55
Great Addington.—5G 65
Great Alne.—2F 51
Great Altcar.—2A 86
Great Amwell.—1G 43
Great Asby.—3H 105
Great Ashfield.—1B 56
Great Ayton.—3C 108
Great Baddow.—2D 44
Great Badminton.—4G 39
Great Bardfield.—4F 55
Great Barford.—2A 54
Great Barr.—3E 63
Great Barrington.—1D 40

Great Barrow.—4G 85
Great Barton.—1A 56
Great Barugh.—2C 102
Great Bavington.—1C 116
Great Bealings.—3E 57
Great Bedwyn.—2A 28
Great Bentley.—5D 56
Great Billing.—1F 53
Great Bircham.—4G 79
Great Blakenham.—2D 56
Great Blencow—1F 105
Great Bolas.—5A 74
Great Bookham.—5C 30
Great Bosullow.—3B 4
Great Bourton.—3B 52
Great Bowden.—4E 65
Great Bradley.—2F 55
Great Braxted.—1E 45
Great Bricett.—2C 56
Great Brickhill.—4G 53
Great Bridgeford.—5C 74
Great Brington.—1D 52
Great Bromley.—5C 56
Great Broughton.—1B 104
(Cumbria)
Great Broughton.—4C 108
(North Yorkshire)
Great Budworth.—5D 86
Great Burdon.—3G 107
Great Burstead.—1A 32
Great Busby.—4C 108
Great Canfield.—1B 44
Great Carlton.—4G 91
Great Casterton.—2H 65
Great Chalfield.—2D 26
Great Chart.—1D 20
Great Chatwell.—1B 62
Great Chesterford.—3E 55
Great Cheverell.—3E 27
Great Chilton.—1F 107
Great Chishill.—4D 54
Great Clacton.—1H 45
Great Cliff.—4D 94
Great Clifton.—2B 94
Great Coates.—4E 97
Great Comberton.—3D 50
Great Corby.—4F 115
Great Cornard.—3A 56
Great Cowden.—1E 97
Great Coxwell.—3D 40
Great Crakehall.—1F 101
Great Cransley.—5F 65
Great Cressingham.—2A 68
Great Crosby.—3A 86
Great Cubley.—4F 75
Great Dalby.—1E 65
Great Doddington.—1F 53
Great Doward.—1D 38
Great Driffield.—4F 103
Great Dunham.—4A 80
Great Dunmow—5F 55
Great Durnford.—5G 27
Great Easton.—5F 55
(Essex)
Great Easton.—3F 65
(Leicestershire)
Great Eccleston.—1B 92
Great Edstone.—1C 102
Great Ellingham.—3C 68
Great Elm.—4C 26
Great Eppleton.—5G 117
Great Eversden.—2C 54
Great Fencote.—5F 107
Great Finborough.—2C 56
Greatford.—1H 65
Great Fransham.—4A 80
Great Gaddesden.—1D 42
Greatgate.—3E 75
Great Gidding.—4A 66
Great Givendale.—4D 102
Great Glemham.—1F 57
Great Glen.—3D 64
Great Gonerby.—4F 77
Great Gransden.—2B 54
Great Green.—4E 69
(Norfolk)

Great Green.—2B 56
(nr. Lavenham, Suff.)
Great Green.—5D 68
(nr. Palgrave, Suff.)
Great Habton.—2C 102
Great Hale.—3A 78
Great Hallingbury.—1B 44
Greatham.—2B 108
(Cleveland)
Greatham.—5F 29
(Hampshire)
Greatham.—4B 18
(West Sussex)
Great Harrowden.—5F 65
Great Harwood.—2E 93
Great Haseley.—2H 41
Great Hatfield.—1D 97
Great Haywood.—5D 75
Great Heath.—4H 63
Great Heck.—1G 91
Great Henny.—4A 56
Great Hinton.—3E 27
Great Hockham.—3B 68
Great Holland.—5E 57
Great Horkesley.—4B 56
Great Hormead.—5D 54
Great Horton.—2B 94
Great Horwood.—4E 53
Great Houghton.—2E 53
(Northamptonshire)
Great Houghton.—2E 89
(South Yorkshire)
Great Hucklow.—5B 88
Great Kelk.—1E 103
Great Kendale.—3F 103
Great Kimble.—2B 42
Great Kingshill.—3B 42
Great Langton.—5F 107
Great Leighs.—1D 44
Great Limber.—5D 96
Great Linford.—3F 53
Great Livermere.—5A 68
Great Longstone.—5C 88
Great Lumley.—5F 117
Great Lyth.—5G 73
Great Malvern.—3B 50
Great Maplestead.—4A 56
Great Marton.—2A 92
Great Massingham.—5G 79
Great Melton.—2D 68
Great Milton.—2E 93
(Lancashire)
Great Milton.—2H 41
(Oxfordshire)
Great Missenden.—2B 42
Great Mongeham.—5H 33
Great Moulton.—3D 68
Great Munden.—5C 54
Great Musgrave.—3A 106
Great Ness.—4F 73
Great Oak.—2B 38
Great Oakley.—5D 57
(Essex)
Great Oakley.—4F 65
(Northamptonshire)
Great Offley.—5A 54
Great Ormside.—3A 106
Great Orton.—4E 115
Great Ouseburn.—3H 101
Great Oxenden.—4E 65
Great Oxney Green.—2C 44
Great Parndon.—2H 43
Great Paxton.—1B 54
Great Plumpton.—2A 92
Great Plumstead.—2E 69
Great Ponton.—4G 77
Great Potheridge.—2F 11
Great Preston.—3E 94
Great Raveley.—4B 54
Great Rissington.—1C 40
Great Rollright.—4H 51
Great Roxbourton.—2C 34
Great Ryburgh.—3B 80
Great Ryle.—3F 123
Great Ryton.—5G 73
Great Saling.—5G 55

Great Salkeld.—1G 105
Great Sampford.—4F 55
Great Sankey.—4C 86
Great Saredon.—2D 62
Great Saxham.—1G 55
Great Shefford.—5E 41
Great Shelford.—2D 54
Great Shoddesden.—4A 28
Great Smeaton.—4G 107
Great Snoring.—2B 80
Great Somerford.—4A 40
Great Stainton.—2G 107
Great Stambridge.—1C 32
Great Staughton.—1A 54
Great Steeping.—1D 78
Great Stonar.—5H 33
Greatstone-on-Sea.—3E 21
Great Strickland.—2G 105
Great Stukeley.—5B 66
Great Sturton.—5E 91
Great Sutton.—3F 85
(Cheshire)
Great Sutton.—2C 60
(Shropshire)
Great Swinburne.—2C 116
Great Tarpots.—2B 32
Great Tew.—5A 52
Great Tey.—5A 56
Great Thorness.—4C 16
Great Thurlow.—2F 55
Great Torr.—5C 8
Great Torrington.—2E 11
Great Tosson.—4E 123
Great Totham North.—1E 45
Great Totham South.—1E 45
Great Tows.—3E 91
Great Urswick.—2B 98
Great Wakering.—2D 32
Great Waldingfield.—3B 56
Great Walsingham.—2B 80
Great Waltham.—1C 44
Great Warley.—1G 31
Great Washbourne.—4D 51
Great Welnetham.—2A 56
Great Wenham.—4C 56
Great Whittington.—2D 116
Great Wigborough.—1F 45
Great Wilbraham.—2E 55
Great Wilne.—4B 76
Great Wishford.—5F 27
Great Witchingham.—1D 68
Great Witcombe.—1H 39
Great Witley.—1B 50
Great Wolford.—4G 51
Greatworth.—3C 52
Great Wratting.—3F 55
Great Wymondley.—5B 54
Great Wyrley.—2D 63
Great Wytheford.—4H 73
Great Yarmouth.—2H 69
Great Yeldham.—4G 55
Grebby.—1D 78
Greeba Castle.—3C 110
Greenbank.—1G 175
Green Bottom.—2E 5
Greenburn.—3C 130
Greencroft.—4E 117
Greencroft Hall.—5E 117
Greendikes.—2E 123
Greendown.—3F 25
Green End.—3H 53
(Bedfordshire)
Green End.—4A 66
(Cambridgeshire)
Green End.—4C 54
(nr. Buntingford, Herts.)
Green End.—5C 54
(nr. Stevenage, Herts.)
Green End.—4F 109
(North Yorkshire)
Green End.—4G 63
(Warwickshire)
Greenfield.—4H 53
(Bedfordshire)
Greenfield.—3D 84
(Clwyd)

Greenfield.—2G 87
(Manchester)
Greenfield.—3A 42
(Oxfordshire)
Greenfield.—4B 136
(Strathclyde)
Greenfoot.—3A 130
Greenford.—2C 30
Greengairs.—2A 130
Greengate.—4C 80
Greengill.—1C 104
Greenhalgh.—2B 92
Greenham.—2C 28
(Berkshire)
Greenham.—3H 13
(Dorset)
Greenham.—3G 23
(Somerset)
Green Hammerton.—4H 101
Greenhaugh.—1A 116
Greenhead.—3H 115
Green Heath.—1D 63
Greenhill.—2B 130
(Central)
Greenhill.—2C 114
(Dumfries & Galloway)
Greenhill.—5C 62
(Hereford & Worcester)
Greenhill.—4F 33
(Kent)
Greenhill.—4D 88
(South Yorkshire)
Greenhills.—4E 129
Greenhithe.—3G 31
Greenholm.—1E 119
Greenholme.—4G 105
Greenhow Hill.—3E 100
Greenigo.—7D 174
Greenland.—2E 171
Greenland Mains.—2E 171
Greenlands.—1E 51
Green Lane.—1E 51
(Hereford & Worcester)
Green Lane.—5A 74
(Shropshire)
Greenlaw.—5D 132
Greenlea.—2B 114
Greenloaning.—3H 137
Greenmount.—1E 87
Greenock.—2D 128
Greenodd.—1C 98
Green Ore.—3F 25
Greenrow.—4C 114
Greens.—4E 163
Greensgate.—4C 80
Greenside.—3E 117
Greensidehill.—3D 123
Greens Norton.—3D 52
Greenstead Green.—5A 56
Greensted Green.—2B 44
Green Street.—1C 30
(Hertfordshire)
Green Street.—5D 69
(Suffolk)
Green Street Green.—3G 31
(Kent)
Green Street Green.—4F 31
(London)
Greenstreet Green.—3C 56
(Suffolk)
Greenwich.—3E 31
Greet.—4E 51
Greete.—3C 60
Greetham.—1G 65
(Leicestershire)

Greetham.—5F 91
(Lincolnshire)
Greetland.—3A 94
Gregson Lane.—3C 92
Greinton.—5E 25
Grenaby.—4B 110
Grendon.—1F 53
(Northamptonshire)
Grendon.—3G 63
(Warwickshire)
Grendon Common.—3G 63
Grendon Green.—2H 49
Grendon Underwood.—5D 52
Grenitote.—1D 172
Grenofen.—2A 8
Grenoside.—3D 88
Gresford.—5F 85
Gresham.—2D 80
Greshornish.—3C 156
Gress.—3G 173
Gressenhall.—4B 80
Gressingham.—2E 99
Greta Bridge.—3D 107
Gretna.—3E 114
Gretna Green.—3E 114
Gretton.—4E 51
(Gloucestershire)
Gretton.—3G 65
(Northamptonshire)
Gretton.—1C 60
(Shropshire)
Grewelthorpe.—2F 101
Greygarth.—2E 101
Grey Green.—2H 89
Greylake.—5D 25
Greysouthen.—2B 104
Greystoke.—1F 105
Greystone.—4E 147
Greystones.—4D 88
Greywell.—3F 29
Grianan.—4G 173
Gribthorpe.—2H 95
Gribun.—5F 141
Gridley Corner.—4D 10
Griff.—4A 64
Griffithstown.—3A 38
Grigghall.—5F 105
Grigg's Green.—5G 29
Grimbister.—6C 174
Grimeford Village.—1D 86
Grimethorpe.—2E 88
Griminish.—3C 172
(Benbecula, Western I.)
Griminish.—1C 172
(North Uist, Western I.)
Grimister.—2F 175
Grimley.—1C 50
Grimoldby.—4F 91
Grimpo.—3F 73
Grimsargh.—2C 92
Grimsby.—5E 97
Grimscote.—2D 52
Grimscott.—3C 10
Grimshader.—5G 173
Grimshaw.—3E 93
Grimshaw Green.—1B 86
Grimsthorpe.—5H 77
Grimston.—2E 97
(Humberside)
Grimston.—5D 76
(Leicestershire)
Grimston.—5G 79
(Norfolk)
Grimston.—4B 102
(North Yorkshire)
Grimstone.—4B 14
Grimstone End.—1B 56
Grinacombe Moor.—4E 11
Grindale.—2G 103
Grindhill.—4E 11
Grindiscol.—8F 175
Grindle.—2B 62
Grindleford.—5C 88
Grindleton.—1E 93
Grindley.—5E 75
Grindley Brook.—1H 73

Grindlow.—5B 88
Grindon.—5F 133
(Northumberland)
Grindon.—2E 75
(Staffordshire)
Gringley on the Hill.—3H 89
Grinsdale.—4E 115
Grinshill.—3H 73
Grinton.—5D 106
Grishipoll.—3C 140
Grisling Common.—3F 19
Gristhorpe.—1F 103
Griston.—3B 68
Gritley.—7E 174
Grittenham.—4B 40
Grittleton.—4G 39
Grizebeck.—1B 98
Grizedale.—5C 100
Grobister.—5F 174
Groby.—2C 64
Groes.—4C 84
(Clwyd)
Groes.—4D 36
(West Glamorgan)
Groes-faen.—4G 37
Groesffordd.—2B 70
(Gwynedd)
Groesffordd.—5C 48
(Powys)
Groesllwyd.—4E 72
Groeslon.—5D 82
Groes-wen.—4H 37
Grogarry.—5C 172
Grogport.—5G 127
Gromford.—2F 57
Gronant.—2C 84
Groombridge.—2G 19
Grosebay.—8D 173
Grosmont.—5G 49
(Gwent)
Grosmont.—4F 109
(North Yorkshire)
Groton.—3B 56
Grove.—5A 14
(Dorset)
Grove.—4G 33
(Kent)
Grove.—5H 89
(Nottinghamshire)
Grove.—3F 41
(Oxfordshire)
Grovehill.—2C 96
Grove Park.—3F 31
Grovesend.—2B 36
Grove, The.—2C 113
(Dumfries & Galloway)
Grove, The.—3C 50
(Hereford & Worcester)
Grub Street.—5B 74
Grudie.—2F 159
Gruids.—3C 166
Gruinard House.—4D 164
Gruinart.—3A 126
Grulinbeg.—3A 126
Gruline.—4G 141
Grummore.—5G 169
Grunasound.—8E 175
Grundisburgh.—2E 57
Gruting.—7D 175
Grutness.—10F 175
Gualachulain.—4F 143
Gualin House.—3D 168
Guardbridge.—2G 139
Guarlford.—3C 50
Guay.—4H 145
Gubblecote.—1C 42
Guestling Green.—4C 20
Guestling Thorn.—4C 20
Guestwick.—3C 80
Guestwick Green.—3C 80
Guide.—3E 93
Guide Post.—1F 117
Guilden Down.—2A 60
Guilden Morden.—3B 54
Guildford.—1A 18
Guildtown.—5A 146

Headley Heath.—5E 63
Headley Park.—2F 25
Head of Muir.—1B 130
Headon.—5H 89
Heads Nook.—4F 115
Heage.—2A 76
Healaugh.—5D 106
Heald Green.—4F 87
Heale.—1C 22
Healey.—1F 87
(Manchester)
Healey.—4D 116
(Northumberland)
Healey.—1E 101
(North Yorkshire)
Healeyfield.—5D 116
Healey Hall.—4D 116
Healing.—4E 97
Heamoor.—3B 4
Heanish.—4B 140
Heanor.—3B 76
Heanton Punchardon.—2B 22
Heapham.—5H 89
Heartsease.—4G 59
Heasley Mill.—2D 22
Heast.—2E 149
Heath.—1B 76
Heath and Reach.—5G 53
Heathcote.—1F 75
Heath Cross.—4H 11
Heathencote.—3E 52
Heath End.—2D 28
(Hampshire)
Heath End.—5A 76
(Leicestershire)
Heath End.—2E 63
(West Midlands)
Heather.—1A 64
Heatherfield.—4D 157
(Cumbria)
Heathfield.—5C 114
(Cumbria)
Heathfield.—2E 9
(Devon)
Heathfield.—3G 19
(East Sussex)
Heathfield.—1E 13
(Somerset)
Heathfield.—3E 128
(Strathclyde)
Heath Green.—5E 63
Heathhall.—2G 113
Heath Hayes.—1E 63
Heath Hill.—1B 62
Heath House.—4E 25
Heathrow Airport.—3B 30
Heathstock.—3F 13
Heath, The.—3D 81
(nr. Aylesham, Norf.)
Heath, The.—3B 80
(Fakenham, Norf.)
Heath, The.—4E 75
(Staffordshire)
Heath, The.—4D 56
(nr. Ipswich, Suff.)
Heath, The.—3B 56
(nr. Sudbury, Suff.)
Heathton.—2E 62
Heathtop.—4G 75
Heath Town.—3D 62
Heatley.—4E 87
(Cheshire)
Heatley.—5E 75
(Staffordshire)
Heaton.—3D 98
(Lancashire)
Heaton.—1D 74
(Staffordshire)
Heaton.—3F 117
(Tyne & Wear)
Heaton.—2B 94
(West Yorkshire)
Heaton Moor.—3F 87
Heaton's Bridge.—1B 86
Heaverham.—5G 31
Heavitree.—4C 12

Hebburn.—3G 117
Hebden.—3D 100
Hebden Bridge.—3G 93
Hebden Green.—1A 74
Hebing End.—5C 54
Hebron.—2E 35
(Dyfed)
Hebron.—1E 117
(Northumberland)
Heck.—1B 114
Heckdyke.—3H 89
Heckfield.—2F 29
Heckfield Green.—5D 69
Heckfordbridge.—5B 56
Heckington.—3A 78
Heckmondwike.—3C 94
Heddington.—2E 27
Heddon.—3C 22
Heddon-on-the-Wall.—3E 117
Hedenham.—3F 69
Hedge End.—2C 16
Hedgerley.—2A 30
Hedging.—1G 13
Hedley on the Hill.—4D 117
Hednesford.—1E 63
Hedon.—3D 97
Hegdon Hill.—2H 49
Heighington.—2F 107
(Durham)
Heighington.—1H 77
(Lincolnshire)
Heightington.—3B 62
Heights of Brae.—2H 159
Heights of Fodderty.—2H 159
Heights of Kinlochewe.—2C 158
Heiton.—1B 122
Hele.—2D 8
(nr. Ashburton, Devon)
Hele.—3C 12
(nr. Exeter, Devon)
Hele.—4D 10
(nr. Holsworthy, Devon)
Hele.—1B 22
(nr. Ilfracombe, Devon)
Hele.—3F 9
(Torquay, Devon)
Helensburgh.—1D 128
Helford.—4E 5
Helford Passage.—4E 5
Helhoughton.—3A 80
Helions Bumpstead.—3F 55
Helland.—2E 7
(Cornwall)
Helland.—1G 13
(Somerset)
Hellesdon.—4E 81
Hellesveor.—2C 4
Hellidon.—2C 52
Hellifield.—4B 100
Hellingly.—4G 19
Hellington.—2F 69
Helmdon.—3C 52
Helmingham.—2D 57
Helmington Row.—1E 107
Helmsdale.—2H 167
Helmshore.—3E 93
Helmsley.—1B 102
Helperby.—3H 101
Helperthorpe.—2E 103
Helpringham.—3A 78
Helpston.—2A 66
Helsby.—3G 85
Helsey.—5H 91
Helston.—4D 4
Helstone.—1E 7
Helton.—2G 105
Helwith.—4D 106
Helwith Bridge.—3B 100
Hemblington.—4F 81
Hemel Hempstead.—2D 42
Hemerdon.—4B 8
Hemingbrough.—2G 95
Hemingby.—5E 91
Hemingfield.—2D 88
Hemingford Abbots.—5B 66
Hemingford Grey.—5B 66

Hemingstone.—2D 56
Hemington.—5B 76
(Leicestershire)
Hemington.—4H 65
(Northamptonshire)
Hemington.—3C 26
(Somerset)
Hemley.—3E 57
Hemlington.—3C 108
Hempholme.—4F 103
Hempnall.—3E 69
Hempnall Green.—3E 69
Hempriggs.—4F 171
Hemp's Green.—5B 56
Hempstead.—4F 55
(Essex)
Hempstead.—4B 32
(Kent)
Hempstead.—2D 80
(nr. Holt, Norf.)
Hempstead.—3G 81
(nr. Stalham, Norf.)
Hempton.—4E 39
(Avon)
Hempton.—3B 80
(Norfolk)
Hempton.—4B 52
(Oxfordshire)
Hemsby.—4G 81
Hemswell.—3B 90
Hemsworth.—3E 15
(Dorset)
Hemsworth.—4E 95
(West Yorkshire)
Hem, The.—2B 62
Hemyock.—2E 13
Henallt.—2H 35
Henbury.—5D 38
(Avon)
Henbury.—5F 87
(Cheshire)
Hendomen.—1H 59
Hendon.—2D 30
(London)
Hendon.—4H 117
(Tyne & Wear)
Hendra.—4D 6
Hendre.—4F 37
Hendreforgan.—4F 37
Hendre, The.—1C 38
Hendy.—2B 36
Heneglwys.—3D 82
Hen-feddau.—4B 46
Henfield.—5E 39
(Avon)
Henfield.—4D 18
(West Sussex)
Henford.—4D 10
Hengoed.—3H 37
(Mid Glamorgan)
Hengoed.—2E 73
(Shropshire)
Hengrave.—1A 56
Henham.—5E 55
Heniarth.—5D 72
Henlands.—1F 13
Henley.—3B 14
(Dorset)
Henley.—2B 60
(nr. Church Stretton, Shrops.)
Henley.—3C 60
(nr. Ludlow, Shrops.)
Henley.—5E 25
(Somerset)
Henley.—2D 56
(Suffolk)
Henley.—1G 17
(West Sussex)
Henley-in-Arden.—1F 51
Henley-on-Thames.—4A 42
Henley's Down.—4B 20
Henley Street.—4A 32
Henllan.—4C 84
(Clwyd)
Henllan.—3C 46
(Dyfed)

Henllan.—5E 49
(Gwent)
Henllan Amgoed.—2E 35
Henllys.—3A 38
Henlow.—4A 54
Hennock.—1E 9
Henny Street.—4A 56
Henryd.—3G 83
Henry's Moat.—2D 34
Hensall.—3F 95
Henshaw.—3A 116
Hensingham.—3A 104
Henstead.—4G 69
Hensting.—1C 16
Henstridge.—2C 14
Henstridge Ash.—1C 14
Henstridge Bowden.—1B 14
Henstridge Marsh.—1C 14
Henton.—2A 42
(Oxfordshire)
Henton.—4E 25
(Somerset)
Henwood.—2G 7
Heogan.—7F 175
Heol Senni.—5B 48
Heol-y-Cyw.—4F 37
Hepburn.—2E 123
Hepple.—4D 122
Hepscott.—1F 117
Heptonstall.—3G 93
Hepworth.—5B 68
(Suffolk)
Hepworth.—2B 88
(West Yorkshire)
Herbrandston.—4B 34
Hereford.—4H 49
Heribusta.—1D 156
Heriot.—4H 131
Hermiston.—4B 102
Hermitage.—5G 41
(Berkshire)
Hermitage.—5H 121
(Borders)
Hermitage.—3B 14
(Dorset)
Hermitage.—3F 17
(West Sussex)
Hermon.—4B 46
(nr. Crymmych, Dyfed)
Hermon.—5F 47
(nr. Llandeilo, Dyfed)
Hermon.—4C 82
(Gwynedd)
Herne.—4F 33
Herne Bay.—4E 33
Herne Common.—4F 33
Herne Pound.—5A 32
Herner.—3B 22
Hernhill.—4E 33
Herodsfoot.—3G 7
Heronden.—5G 33
Herongate.—1H 31
Heronsford.—1G 111
Heronsgate.—1B 30
Heron's Ghyll.—3F 19
Herra.—2H 175
Herriard.—4F 29
Herringfleet.—3G 69
Herringswell.—1G 55
Herrington.—4G 117
Hersden.—4G 33
Hersham.—3C 10
(Cornwall)
Hersham.—4C 30
(Surrey)
Herstmonceux.—4H 19
Herston.—5F 15
(Dorset)
Herston.—8D 174
(Orkney)
Hertford.—1G 43
Hertford Heath.—1G 43
Hertingfordbury.—1G 43
Hesketh.—3B 92
Hesketh Bank.—3B 92
Hesketh Lane.—1D 92
Hesket Newmarket.—1E 105

Heskin Green.—1C 86
Hesleden.—1B 108
Hesleyside.—1B 116
Heslington.—4B 102
Hessay.—4A 102
Hessenford.—4H 7
Hessett.—1B 56
Hessilhead.—4F 129
Hessle.—3C 96
Hestaford.—6D 175
Hest Bank.—3D 98
Hester's Way.—5D 50
Heston.—3C 30
Hestwall.—6B 174
Heswall.—2E 85
Hethe.—5C 52
Hethelpit Cross.—5B 50
Hethersett.—2D 68
Hethersgill.—3F 115
Hetherside.—3F 115
Hethpool.—2C 122
Hett.—1F 107
Hetton.—4C 100
Hetton-le-Hole.—5G 117
Hetton Steads.—1E 123
Heugh.—2D 117
Heugh-head.—2A 154
Heveningham.—5F 69
Hever.—1F 19
Heversham.—1D 99
Hevingham.—3D 81
Hewas Water.—2G 5
Hewelsfield.—2D 38
Hewish.—2D 25
(Avon)
Hewish.—3H 13
(Somerset)
Heworth.—4B 102
Hexham.—3C 116
Hextable.—3G 31
Hexton.—4A 54
Hexworthy.—2C 8
Heybridge.—1H 31
(nr. Brentwood, Essex)
Heybridge.—2E 45
(nr. Maldon, Essex)
Heybrook Bay.—5A 8
Heydon.—3D 54
(Cambridgeshire)
Heydon.—3D 80
(Norfolk)
Heydour.—4H 77
Heylipoll.—4A 140
Heyop.—3H 59
Heysham.—3D 98
Heyshott.—2G 17
Heytesbury.—4E 27
Heythrop.—5A 52
Heywood.—1F 87
(Manchester)
Heywood.—3D 26
(Wiltshire)
Hibaldstow.—5B 96
Hickleton.—2E 89
Hickling.—3G 81
(Norfolk)
Hickling.—5D 76
(Nottinghamshire)
Hickling Green.—3G 81
Hickling Heath.—3G 81
Hickstead.—3D 18
Hidcote Bartrim.—3F 51
Hidcote Boyce.—3F 51
Higford.—2B 62
High Ackworth.—4E 95
Higham.—2A 76
(Derbyshire)
Higham.—3B 32
(Kent)
Higham.—2F 93
(Lancashire)
Higham.—2D 88
(South Yorkshire)
Higham.—4C 56
(nr. Ipswich, Suff.)

Higham.—1G 55
(nr. Newmarket, Suff.)
Higham Dykes.—2E 117
Higham Ferrers.—1G 53
Higham Gobion.—4A 54
Higham on the Hill.—3A 64
Highampton.—3F 11
Higham Wood.—1H 19
High Angerton.—1D 117
High Auldgirth.—1G 113
High Bankhill.—5G 115
High Banton.—1A 130
High Barnet.—1D 30
High Beech.—1F 31
High Bentham.—3F 99
High Bickington.—3C 22
High Birkwith.—2B 100
High Blantyre.—4H 129
High Bonnybridge.—2B 130
High Borrans.—4F 105
High Borve.—2G 173
High Bradfield.—3C 88
High Bray.—2C 22
High Brooms.—1G 19
Highbridge.—5D 150
(Highland)
Highbridge.—4D 24
(Somerset)
Highbrook.—2E 19
High Brooms.—1G 19
High Bullen.—3B 22
Highburton.—4B 94
Highbury.—4B 26
High Buston.—4G 123
High Callerton.—2E 117
High Carlinghill.—4H 105
High Catton.—4C 102
High Church.—1E 117
Highclere.—2C 28
Highcliffe.—4H 15
High Cogges.—2E 41
High Common.—2B 68
High Coniscliffe.—3F 107
High Crosby.—4F 115
High Cross.—1F 17
(Hampshire)
High Cross.—1G 43
(Hertfordshire)
High Cross Bank.—1G 63
High Easter.—1C 44
High Eggborough.—3F 95
High Ellington.—1E 101
Higher Alham.—4B 26
Higher Ansty.—3C 14
Higher Ashton.—1E 9
Higher Ballam.—2A 92
Higher Bockhampton.—4C 14(?)
High Ercall.—4H 73
Higher Dinting.—3H 87
Higher End.—2C 86
Higher Gabwell.—3F 132(?)
Higher Heysham.—3D 98
Higher Hurdsfield.—5G 87
Higher Kingcombe.—4A 14
Higher Kinnerton.—4F 85
Higher Onn.—1C 62
Higher Penwortham.—3C 92
Higher Porthpean.—4E 7
Higher Poynton.—4G 87
Higher Shotton.—4F 85
Higher Shurlach.—5D 87
Higher Tale.—3D 12
Highertown.—2F 5
(Cornwall)
Higher Town.—1B 4
(Isles of Scilly)
Higher Town.—1F 23
(Somerset)
Higher Walton.—4C 86
(Cheshire)
Higher Walton.—3C 92
(Lancashire)
Higher Whatcombe.—3D 14
Higher Wheelton.—3D 92
Higher Whiteleigh.—4C 10

er Whitley.—4D 86
er Wincham.—5D 87
er Wych.—1G 73
h Etherley.—2E 107
n Ferry.—3C 78
nfield.—2H 95
(umberside)
nfield.—4E 128
(trathclyde)
nfield.—4E 117
(yne & Wear)
nfields.—2C 54
(ambridgeshire)
n Garrett.—5C 55
gate.—2D 31
(ondon)
gate.—1G 59
(owys)
gate.—4E 129
(trathclyde)
n Grange.—1E 107
(umbria)
n Green.—4F 105
(umbria)
n Green.—3C 50
(ereford & Worcester)
n Green.—2D 68
(orfolk)
n Green.—4B 62
(hropshire)
n Green.—3D 88
(outh Yorkshire)
n Green.—4B 94
(West Yorkshire)
ngreen Manor.—5C 122
(Suffolk)
n Halden.—2C 20
n Halstow.—3B 32
n Ham.—5E 25
n Harrington.—2B 104
n Haswell.—5G 117
n Hatton.—5A 74
n Hawsker.—4G 109
n Hesket.—5F 115
n Hesleden.—1B 108
n Hoyland.—4C 94
n Hunsley.—2B 96
n Hurstwood.—3F 19
n Hutton.—3C 102
n Ireby.—1D 104
n Keil.—5A 124
n Kelling.—2D 80
n Kilburn.—2A 102
n Killerby.—1F 103
n Knipe.—3G 105
n Lands.—2E 107
nlands, The.—4A 62
nlane.—1C 74
(heshire)
nlane.—4E 88
(erbyshire)
n Lane.—1A 50
(ereford & Worcester)
n Lane.—4G 87
(Manchester)
n Lanes.—2G 5
n Laver.—2B 44
nlaws.—5C 114
leadon.—5B 50
n Legh.—4E 87
leigh.—4G 17
n Leven.—3B 108
aley.—4B 62
n Littleton.—3B 26
n Longthwaite.—5D 114
n Lorton.—2C 104
n Marishes.—2D 102
n Marnham.—5A 90
n Melton.—3F 89
n Mickley.—3D 117
moor.—5D 114
(umbria)
n Moor.—1C 86
(ancashire)
moor.—4A 42
(xfordshire)

Highmoor Hill.—4C 38
High Mowthorpe.—3D 103
Highnam.—5B 50
High Newport.—4G 117
High Newton.—1D 98
High Newton-by-the-Sea.
—2G 123
High Nibthwaite.—1B 98
High Offley.—5B 74
High Ongar.—2B 44
High Orchard.—1G 39
High Park.—1A 86
High Pennyvenie.—4E 119
High Portling.—4F 133
High Roding.—1C 44
High Row.—1E 105
High Salvington.—5C 18
High Scales.—5C 114
High Seaton.—1B 104
High Shaw.—5B 106
High Side.—1D 104
High Spen.—4E 117
Highsted.—4D 32
High Stoop.—5E 117
High Street.—4D 6
(Cornwall)
High Street.—2G 57
(nr. Aldeburgh, Suff.)
High Street.—4F 69
(nr. Bungay, Suff.)
High Street.—5G 69
(nr. Yoxford, Suff.)
Highstreet Green.—4G 55
(Essex)
High Street Green.—2C 56
(Suffolk)
Highstreet Green.—2A 18
(Surrey)
Hightae.—2B 114
High Throston.—1B 108
Hightown.—1C 74
(Cheshire)
Hightown.—2A 86
(Merseyside)
High Town.—1D 63
(Staffordshire)
Hightown Green.—2B 56
High Toynton.—1B 78
High Trewhitt.—4E 123
High Valleyfield.—5C 138
Highway.—3G 49
Highweek.—2E 9
High Westwood.—4E 117
Highwood.—1A 50
(Hereford & Worcester)
Highwood.—4E 75
(Staffordshire)
High Worsall.—4G 107
Highworth.—3D 40
High Wray.—5E 105
High Wych.—1A 44
High Wycombe.—3B 42
Hilborough.—2A 68
Hilcott.—3G 27
Hildenborough.—1G 19
Hildersham.—1E 55
Hilderstone.—4D 74
Hilderthorpe.—3G 103
Hilfield.—3B 14
Hilgay.—3F 67
Hill.—3E 39
(Avon)
Hill.—3D 51
(Hereford & Worcester)
Hill.—1B 52
(Warwickshire)
Hillam.—3F 95
Hillbeck.—3A 106
Hillberry.—4C 110
Hillborough.—4G 33
Hillbourne.—4F 15
Hillbrae.—4D 162
(nr. Aberchirder, Grampian)
Hillbrae.—1E 155
(nr. Inverurie, Grampian)

Hillbrae.—5F 163
(nr. Methlick, Grampian)
Hill Brow.—1F 17
Hillbutts.—3E 15
Hillclifflane.—3G 75
Hill Deverill.—2D 26
Hill Dyke.—3D 26
Hill End.—1D 106
(Durham)
Hillend.—5D 138
(nr. Inverkeithing, Fife)
Hill End.—4C 138
(nr. Saline, Fife)
Hill End.—4D 100
(North Yorkshire)
Hillend.—3C 62
(Shropshire)
Hillend.—3B 130
(Strathclyde)
Hillend.—3A 36
(West Glamorgan)
Hillersland.—1D 38
Hillerton.—4H 11
Hillesden.—5D 52
Hillesley.—4F 39
Hillfarance.—1E 13
Hill Furze.—3D 51
Hill Gate.—5G 49
Hillgreen.—5F 41
(Berkshire)
Hill Green.—4D 55
(Essex)
Hillhead.—4F 9
(Devon)
Hill Head.—3D 16
(Hampshire)
Hillhead.—3D 118
(Strathclyde)
Hilliard's Cross.—1F 63
Hilliclay.—2D 170
Hillingdon.—2B 30
Hillington.—5G 79
(Norfolk)
Hillington.—3G 129
(Strathclyde)
Hillmorton.—5C 64
Hill of Beath.—4D 138
Hill of Fearn.—1C 160
Hill of Fiddes.—1G 155
Hill of Keillor.—4B 146
Hill of Overbrae.—2F 163
Hill Ridware.—1E 63
Hill Row.—5D 66
Hillsborough.—3D 88
Hillside.—3D 8
(Devon)
Hillside.—4G 155
(Grampian)
Hillside.—3F 29
(Hampshire)
Hillside.—1B 50
(Hereford & Worcester)
Hillside.—1A 86
(Merseyside)
Hillside.—5C 174
(Orkney)
Hillside.—5F 175
(Shetland)
Hillside.—4A 62
(Shropshire)
Hillside.—2G 147
(Tayside)
Hill Side.—4B 94
(West Yorkshire)
Hill Somersal.—4F 75
Hills Town.—1B 76
Hillstreet.—2B 16
Hillswick.—4D 175
Hill, The.—1A 98
Hill Top.—2C 106
(nr. Barnard Castle, Durham)
Hill Top.—5F 117
(nr. Durham, Durham)
Hill Top.—4E 117
(nr. Stanley, Durham)

Hill Top.—3C 16
(Hampshire)
Hill View.—4E 15
Hill Wootton.—1H 51
Hillyland.—1C 138
Hilmarton.—5B 40
Hilperton.—3D 26
Hilperton Marsh.—3D 26
Hilsea.—3E 17
Hilston.—2E 97
Hiltingbury.—1C 16
Hilton.—1B 54
(Cambridgeshire)
Hilton.—4G 75
(Cheshire)
Hilton.—3B 108
(Cleveland)
Hilton.—2A 106
(Cumbria)
Hilton.—3C 14
(Dorset)
Hilton.—2E 107
(Durham)
Hilton.—5E 167
(Highland)
Hilton.—3B 62
(Shropshire)
Hilton.—2C 63
(Staffordshire)
Hilton of Cadboll.—1C 160
Himbleton.—2D 50
Himley.—3C 62
Hincaster.—1E 99
Hinchcliffe Mill.—2B 88
Hinchwick.—4F 51
Hinckley.—3B 64
Hinderclay.—5C 68
Hinderwell.—3E 109
Hindford.—2F 73
Hindhead.—5G 29
Hindley.—2D 86
(Manchester)
Hindley.—4D 116
(Northumberland)
Hindley Green.—2D 86
Hindlip.—2C 50
Hindolveston.—3C 80
Hindon.—5E 27
Hindringham.—2B 80
Hingham.—2C 68
Hinksford.—4C 62
Hinstock.—5A 74
Hintlesham.—3C 56
Hinton.—5F 39
(Avon)
Hinton.—4H 15
(Hampshire)
Hinton.—4F 49
(Hereford & Worcester)
Hinton.—2C 52
(Northamptonshire)
Hinton.—5G 73
(Shropshire)
Hinton Ampner.—1D 16
Hinton Blewett.—3F 25
Hinton Charterhouse.—3C 26
Hinton-in-the-Hedges.—4C 52
Hinton Marsh.—1D 16
Hinton Martell.—3F 15
Hinton on the Green.—3E 51
Hinton Parva.—4D 40
Hinton St George.—2H 13
Hinton St Mary.—2C 14
Hinton Waldrist.—3E 41
Hints.—5A 62
(Shropshire)
Hints.—2F 63
(Staffordshire)
Hinwick.—1G 53
Hinxhill.—1E 21
Hinxton.—3D 55
Hinxworth.—3B 54
Hipley.—2E 16
Hipperholme.—3B 94
Hipsburn.—3G 123
Hipswell.—5E 107

Hiraeth.—2E 35
Hirn.—3E 155
Hirnant.—3C 72
Hirst.—1F 117
Hirst Courtney.—3G 95
Hirst Head.—1F 117
Hirwaen.—4D 80
Hirwaun.—2F 37
Hiscott.—3B 22
Histon.—1D 54
Hitcham.—2B 56
Hitchin.—5A 54
Hittisleigh Barton.—4H 11
Hittisleigh Cross.—4H 11
Hive.—2A 96
Hixon.—5E 75
Hoaden.—5G 33
Hoar Cross.—5F 75
Hoarwithy.—5H 49
Hoath.—4G 33
Hobarris.—3A 60
Hobbles Green.—2G 55
Hobbs Cross.—1F 31
Hobkirk.—3H 121
Hobson.—4E 117
Hoby.—1D 64
Hockering.—4C 80
Hockering Heath.—4C 80
Hockerton.—2E 76
Hockley.—1C 32
(Essex)
Hockley.—2G 63
(Staffordshire)
Hockley.—5G 63
(West Midlands)
Hockley Heath.—5F 63
Hockliffe.—5G 53
Hockwold cum Wilton.—4G 67
Hockworthy.—2D 12
Hoddesdon.—2G 43
Hoddlesden.—3E 93
Hoddomcross.—2C 114
Hodgeston.—5D 34
Hodley.—1G 59
Hodnet.—5A 74
Hodsoll Street.—4H 31
Hodson.—4C 40
Hodthorpe.—5F 89
Hoe.—4B 80
Hoe Beg.—1E 172
Hoe Gate.—2E 17
Hoff.—3H 105
Hoffleet Stow.—4B 78
Hogben's Hill.—5E 33
Hoggard's Green.—2A 56
Hoggeston.—5F 53
Hoggrill's End.—3G 63
Hoghton.—3D 92
Hoghton Bottoms.—3D 92
Hognaston.—2G 75
Hogsthorpe.—5H 91
Hogstock.—3E 15

Holbeach.—5C 78
Holbeach Bank.—5C 78
Holbeach Clough.—5C 78
Holbeach Drove.—1C 66
Holbeach Hurn.—5C 78
Holbeach St Johns.—1C 66
Holbeach St Marks.—4C 78
Holbeach St Matthew.—4D 78
Holbeck.—5C 89
(Nottinghamshire)
Holbeck.—2C 94
(West Yorkshire)
Holberrow Green.—2E 51
Holbeton.—4C 8
Holborn.—2E 31
Holbrook.—3A 76
(Derbyshire)
Holbrook.—4E 89
(South Yorkshire)
Holbrook.—4D 56
(Suffolk)
Holburn.—1E 123
Holbury.—3C 16

Holcombe.—2F 9
(Devon)
Holcombe.—1E 87
(Manchester)
Holcombe.—4B 26
(Somerset)
Holcombe Cross.—1E 87
Holcombe Rogus.—2D 12
Holcot.—1E 53
Holden.—1E 93
Holdenby.—1D 52
Holder's Green.—5F 55
Holdgate.—2C 60
Holdingham.—3H 77
Holditch.—3G 13
Holemoor.—3E 11
Hole Street.—4C 18
Holford.—4B 24
Holker.—2C 98
Holkham.—1A 80
Hollacombe.—3D 11
Holland.—2D 174
Holland Fen.—3B 78
Holland Lees.—2C 86
Holland-on-Sea.—1H 45
Holland Park.—2E 63
Hollandstoun.—2G 174
Hollesley.—3F 57
Hollinfare.—3D 87
Hollingbourne.—5C 32
Hollingbury.—5E 19
Hollingdon.—5F 53
Hollingrove.—3A 20
Hollington.—4B 20
(East Sussex)
Hollington.—4E 75
(Staffordshire)
Hollington Grove.—4G 75
Hollingworth.—3H 87
Hollins.—5D 88
(Derbyshire)
Hollins.—2F 87
(Manchester)
Hollinsclough.—1E 75
Hollinswood.—2A 62
Hollinthorpe.—2D 94
Hollinwood.—2G 87
(Manchester)
Hollinwood.—2H 73
(Shropshire)
Hollocombe.—2G 11
Holloway.—2H 75
Hollow Court.—2D 51
Hollowell.—5D 64
Hollow Meadows.—4C 88
Hollows.—2E 115
Hollybush.—2H 37
(Gwent)
Hollybush.—4B 50
(Hereford & Worcester)
Hollybush.—3C 118
(Strathclyde)
Holly End.—2D 67
Holly Hill.—4E 107
Hollyhurst.—1H 73
Hollym.—3F 97
Hollywood.—5E 63
(Hereford & Worcester)
Hollywood.—4D 74
(Staffordshire)
Holm.—4G 173
Holmacott.—3B 22
Holmbridge.—2B 88
Holmbury St Mary.—1C 18
Holmbush.—4E 7
Holmcroft.—5D 74
Holme.—4A 66
(Cambridgeshire)
Holme.—2E 99
(Cumbria)
Holme.—5B 96
(Humberside)
Holme.—1G 101
(North Yorkshire)

Holme.—2F 77
(Nottinghamshire)
Holme.—2B 88
(West Yorkshire)
Holmebridge.—5D 15
Holme Chapel.—3F 93
Holme Hale.—2A 68
Holme Lacy.—4H 49
Holme Lane.—4D 76
Holme Marsh.—2F 49
Holmend.—4C 120
Holme next the Sea.—3G 79
Holme on the Wolds.—1B 96
Holme Pierrepont.—4D 76
Holmer.—3H 49
Holmer Green.—1A 30
Holmes.—1B 86
Holme St Cuthbert.—5C 114
Holmes Chapel.—1B 74
Holmesfield.—5D 88
Holmeswood.—1B 86
Holme upon Spalding Moor.
—2A 96
Holmewood.—1B 76
Holmfirth.—2B 88
Holmhead.—2E 119
Holmisdale.—4A 156
Holm of Drumlanrig.—5H 119
Holmpton.—3F 97
Holmrook.—5B 104
Holmsey Green.—5F 67
Holmside.—5F 117
Holmwrangle.—5G 115
Holne.—3D 8
Holsworthy.—3D 10
Holsworthy Beacon.—3D 10
Holt.—5G 85
(Clwyd)
Holt.—3F 15
(Dorset)
Holt.—1C 50
(Hereford & Worcester)
Holt.—2C 80
(Norfolk)
Holt.—2D 26
(Wiltshire)
Holtby.—4B 102
Holt End.—5E 29
(Hampshire)
Holt End.—1E 51
(Hereford & Worcester)
Holt Fleet.—1C 50
Holt Green.—2A 86
Holt Heath.—3F 15
(Dorset)
Holt Heath.—1C 50
(Hereford & Worcester)
Holton.—2H 41
(Oxfordshire)
Holton.—1B 14
(Somerset)
Holton.—5F 69
(Suffolk)
Holton cum Beckering.—4D 90
Holton Heath.—4E 15
Holton le Clay.—5E 97
Holton le Moor.—3C 90
Holton St Mary.—4C 56
Holt Pound.—4G 29
Holtsmere End.—1D 43
Holtye.—2F 19
Holwell.—2C 14
(Dorset)
Holwell.—4A 54
(Hertfordshire)
Holwell.—5E 77
(Leicestershire)
Holwell.—2D 40
(Oxfordshire)
Holwell.—4C 26
(Somerset)
Holwick.—2C 106
Holworth.—5C 14
Holybourne.—4F 29
Holy Cross.—5D 62
Holyfield.—2G 43

Holyhead.—2B 82
Holy Island.—5H 133
Holymoorside.—1H 75
Holyport.—5B 42
Holystone.—4D 122
Holytown.—3A 130
Holywell.—5C 66
(Cambridgeshire)
Holywell.—3D 84
(Clwyd)
Holywell.—4B 6
(Cornwall)
Holywell.—3A 14
(Dorset)
Holywell.—3F 39
(Gloucestershire)
Holywell.—2G 117
(Northumberland)
Holywell.—1F 51
(Warwickshire)
Holywell Green.—4A 94
Holywell Lake.—1E 12
Holywell Row.—5G 67
Holywood.—1G 113
Homer.—2A 62
Homer Green.—2A 86
Homersfield.—4E 69
Hom Green.—5H 49
Homington.—1G 15
Honeyborough.—4C 34
Honeybourne.—3F 51
Honeychurch.—3G 11
Honey Hill.—4F 33
Honeymead.—2D 23
Honey Street.—2G 27
Honey Tye.—4B 56
Honiley.—5G 63
Honing.—3F 81
Honingham.—4D 80
Honington.—3G 77
(Lincolnshire)
Honington.—5B 68
(Suffolk)
Honington.—3G 51
(Warwickshire)
Honiton.—3E 13
Honley.—4B 94
Honnington.—1B 62
Hoo.—2E 57
Hoobrook.—5C 62
Hood Green.—2D 88
Hooe.—4B 8
(Devon)
Hooe.—5A 20
(East Sussex)
Hooe Common.—4A 20
Hoo Hatch.—4G 29
Hoohill.—1A 92
Hook.—3D 66
(Cambridgeshire)
Hook.—3C 34
(Dyfed)
Hook.—3F 29
(nr. Basingstoke, Hants.)
Hook.—3D 16
(nr. Fareham, Hants.)
Hook.—3H 95
(Humberside)
Hook.—4C 30
(London)
Hook.—4B 40
(Wiltshire)
Hook-a-Gate.—5G 73
Hook Bank.—3C 50
Hooke.—3A 14
Hooker Gate.—4E 117
Hookgate.—4B 74
Hook Green.—2A 20
(nr. Lamberhurst, Kent)
Hook Green.—3H 31
(nr. Longfield, Kent)
Hook Green.—4H 31
(nr. Meopham, Kent)
Hook Norton.—4A 52
Hook's Cross.—5B 54
Hook Street.—3E 39

Hookway.—4B 12
Hookwood.—1D 18
Hoole.—4G 85
Hooley.—5D 31
Hooley Bridge.—1F 87
Hooley Brow.—1F 87
Hoo St Werburgh.—3B 32
Hooton.—3F 85
Hooton Levitt.—3F 89
Hooton Pagnell.—2F 17
Hooton Roberts.—3E 89
Hope.—5F 85
(Clwyd)
Hope.—4B 88
(Derbyshire)
Hope.—2E 169
(Highland)
Hope.—5E 73
(Powys)
Hope.—5F 73
(Shropshire)
Hope.—2F 75
(Staffordshire)
Hope Bagot.—3C 60
Hope Bowdler.—1B 60
Hopedale.—2F 75
Hope Green.—4G 87
Hopeman.—2F 161
Hope Mansell.—1E 39
Hopesay.—2A 60
Hope's Green.—2B 32
Hopetown.—3D 94
Hope under Dinmore.—2H 49
Hopley's Green.—2F 49
Hopperton.—4H 101
Hop Pole.—1A 66
Hoppyland Hall.—1D 107
Hopstone.—3B 62
Hopton.—2G 75
(Derbyshire)
Hopton.—1H 59
(Powys)
Hopton.—3F 73
(nr. Oswestry, Shrops.)
Hopton.—3H 73
(nr. Wem, Shrops.)
Hopton.—5D 74
(Staffordshire)
Hopton.—5B 68
(Suffolk)
Hopton Cangeford.—2C 60
Hopton Castle.—3A 60
Hoptonheath.—3A 60
(Shropshire)
Hopton Heath.—5D 74
(Staffordshire)
Hopton on Sea.—2H 69
Hopton Wafers.—5A 62
Hopwas.—2F 63
Hopwood.—5E 63
Horam.—4G 19
Horbling.—4A 78
Horbury.—4C 94
Horcott.—2C 40
Horden.—5H 117
Horderley.—2B 60
Hordle.—4A 16
Hordley.—2F 73
Horeb.—5E 47
(nr. Brechfa, Dyfed)
Horeb.—3C 46
(nr. Llandyssul, Dyfed)
Horeb.—2B 36
(nr. Llanelli, Dyfed)
Horgabost.—8C 173
Horham.—5E 69
Horkesley Heath.—5B 56
Horkstow.—4E 97
Horley.—3B 52
(Oxfordshire)
Horley.—1D 19
(Surrey)
Hornblotton Green.—5F 25
Hornby.—3E 99
(Lancashire)

Hornby.—4G 107
(nr. Appleton Wiske, N Yorks)
Hornby.—5F 107
(nr. Catterick Garrison, N Yorks)
Horncastle.—1B 78
Hornchurch.—2G 31
Horncliffe.—5F 133
Horndean.—5E 133
(Borders)
Horndean.—2F 17
(Hampshire)
Horndon.—1B 8
Horndon on the Hill.—2A 32
Horne.—1E 19
Horner.—1E 23
Horning.—4F 81
Horninghold.—1F 65
Horninglow.—5G 75
Horningsea.—1D 55
Horningsham.—4D 26
Horningtoft.—3B 80
Hornsby.—4G 115
Hornsbygate.—4G 115
Horns Corner.—3B 20
Horns Cross.—1D 11
Hornsea.—1E 97
Hornsea Burton.—1E 97
Hornsey.—2D 31
Hornton.—3A 52
Horpit.—4D 40
Horrabridge.—3B 8
Horringer.—1A 56
Horringford.—5D 16
Horrocks Fold.—1E 87
Horrocksford.—1E 93
Horsbrugh Ford.—1E 121
Horsebridge.—2A 8
(Devon)
Horsebridge.—5B 28
(Hampshire)
Horse Bridge.—2D 74
(Staffordshire)
Horsebrook.—1C 62
Horsecastle.—2E 25
Horsehay.—2A 62
Horseheath.—3F 55
Horsehouse.—1D 100
Horsell.—5A 30
Horseman's Green.—1G 73
Horsenden.—2A 42
Horseway.—4D 66
Horsey.—3G 81
(Norfolk)
Horsey.—5D 24
(Somerset)
Horsford.—4D 81
Horsforth.—2C 94
Horsham.—2B 50
(Hereford & Worcester)
Horsham.—2C 18
(West Sussex)
Horsham St Faith.—4E 81
Horsington.—1A 78
(Lincolnshire)
Horsington.—1C 14
(Somerset)
Horsley.—3A 76
(Derbyshire)
Horsley.—3G 39
(Gloucestershire)
Horsley.—3D 117
(nr. Prudhoe, Northmb.)
Horsley.—5C 122
(nr. Rochester, Northmb.)
Horsley Cross.—5D 56
Horsleycross Street.—5D 56
Horsleyhill.—3H 121
Horsleyhope.—5D 116
Horsley Woodhouse.—3A 76
Horsmonden.—1B 20
Horspath.—2G 41
Horstead.—4E 81
Horsted Keynes.—3E 19
Horton.—4F 39
(Avon)

Horton.—3B 30
(Berkshire)
Horton.—1C 42
(Buckinghamshire)
Horton.—3F 15
(Dorset)
Horton.—4B 100
(Lancashire)
Horton.—2F 53
(Northamptonshire)
Horton.—1A 62
(nr. Telford, Shrops.)
Horton.—2G 73
(nr. Wem, Shrops.)
Horton.—2G 13
(Somerset)
Horton.—2D 74
(Staffordshire)
Horton.—4A 36
(West Glamorgan)
Horton.—2F 27
(Wiltshire)
Horton Cross.—2G 13
Horton-cum-Studley.—1G 41
Horton Green.—1G 73
Horton Heath.—2C 16
Horton in Ribblesdale.—2B 100
Horton Kirby.—4G 31
Horwich.—1D 86
Horwich End.—4H 87
Horwood.—3B 22
Hoscar.—1B 86
Hose.—5E 77
Hosh.—1A 138
Hosta.—1C 172
Hoswick.—9F 175
Hotham.—2A 96
Hothfield.—1D 20
Hoton.—5C 76
Houbie.—2H 175
Hough.—2B 74
(nr. Crewe, Ches.)
Hough.—5F 87
(nr. Wilmslow, Ches.)
Hough.—4A 140
(Strathclyde)
Hougham.—3F 77
Hougharry.—1C 172
Hough Green.—4B 86
Hough-on-the-Hill.—3G 77
Houghton.—5B 66
(Cambridgeshire)
Houghton.—4F 115
(Cumbria)
Houghton.—4C 34
(Dyfed)
Houghton.—5B 28
(Hampshire)
Houghton.—3E 117
(Northumberland)
Houghton.—4B 18
(West Sussex)
Houghton Bank.—2F 107
Houghton Conquest.—3H 53
Houghton Green.—2D 20
Houghton-le-Side.—2F 107
Houghton-le-Spring.—5G 117
Houghton on the Hill.—2D 64
Houghton Regis.—5H 53
Houghton St Giles.—2B 80
Houlsyke.—4E 109
Hound.—3C 16
Hound Green.—3F 29
Houndslow.—5C 132
Houndsmoor.—1E 13
Houndwood.—3E 133
Hounsdown.—2B 16
Hounslow Green.—1C 44
Housay.—4H 175
Househill.—3C 160
Housetter.—3E 175
Houss.—8E 175
Houston.—3F 129
Housty.—5D 170
Hove.—5D 19
Hoveringham.—3D 76

Hoveton.—4F 81
Hovingham.—2B 102
How.—4G 115
Howbeg.—5C 172
How Caple.—4A 50
Howden.—3H 95
Howden le Wear.—1E 107
Howe.—1D 98
(Cumbria)
Howe.—2F 171
(Highland)
Howe.—3E 69
(Norfolk)
Howe Green.—2D 44
(nr. Chelmsford, Essex)
Howegreen.—2E 45
(nr. Maldon, Essex)
Howell.—3A 78
How End.—3A 53
Howe of Teuchar.—4E 163
Howes.—3C 114
Howe Street.—1C 44
(nr. Chelmsford, Essex)
Howe Street.—4F 55
(nr. Finchingfield, Essex)
Howe, The.—5A 110
Howey.—2C 48
Howgate.—4F 131
Howgill.—1F 93
(Lancashire)
Howgill.—4D 100
(North Yorkshire)
How Green.—1F 19
(Kent)
How Green.—4H 63
(Warwickshire)
How Hill.—1F 69
Howick.—3G 123
Howle.—2D 107
(Durham)
Howle.—5A 74
(Shropshire)
Howle Hill.—5A 50
Howleigh.—2F 13
Howlett End.—4E 55
Howley.—4D 86
(Cheshire)
Howley.—3F 13
(Somerset)
Howmore.—5C 172
Hownam.—3B 122
Howsham.—5C 96
(Humberside)
Howsham.—3C 102
(North Yorkshire)
Howtel.—1C 122
Howt Green.—4C 32
Howton.—5G 49
Hoxne.—5D 69
Hoylake.—2E 84
Hoyland.—2D 88
Hoyland Swaine.—2C 88
Hoyle.—2H 17
Hubberholme.—2C 100
Hubberston.—4B 34
Hubbert's Bridge.—3B 78
Huby.—1C 94
(nr. Harrogate, N Yorks.)
Huby.—3A 102
(nr. York, N Yorks.)
Huccaby.—2C 8
Hucclecote.—1G 39
Hucking.—5C 32
Hucknall.—3C 76
Huddersfield.—4B 94
Huddington.—2D 50
Huddlesford.—2F 63
Hudswell.—4E 107
Huggate.—4D 103
Hugglescote.—1B 64
Hughenden Valley.—3B 42
Hughley.—1C 60
Hughton.—4G 159
Hugh Town.—1B 4
Hugus.—2E 5
Huish.—2G 27

Isle of Whithorn.—5B 112
Isleornsay.—2F 149
Islesteps.—2G 113
Isleworth.—3C 30
Isley Walton.—5B 76
Islington.—2E 31
(London)
Islington.—5B 74
(Shropshire)
Islip.—1G 41
(Oxfordshire)
Islip.—5G 65
(Warwickshire)
Isliving.—5B 113
Islwyn.—3A 38
Istead Rise.—4H 31
Itchen.—2C 16
Itchen Abbas.—5D 28
Itchen Stoke.—5D 28
Itchingfield.—3C 18
Itchington.—4E 39
Itlaw.—3D 162
Itteringham.—2D 80
Itteringham Common.—3D 80
Itton.—4G 11
Itton Common.—3C 38
Ivegill.—5F 115
Ivelet.—5C 104
Iver Heath.—2B 30
Iveston.—4E 117
Ivetsey Bank.—1C 62
Ivinghoe.—1C 42
Ivinghoe Aston.—1C 42
Ivington.—2G 49
Ivington Green.—2G 49
Ivybridge.—4C 8
Ivychurch.—3E 21
Ivy Hatch.—5G 31
Ivy Todd.—2A 68
Iwade.—4D 32
Iwerne Courtney.—2D 14
Iwerne Minster.—2D 14
Ixworth.—5B 68
Ixworth Thorpe.—5B 68

Jackfield.—2A 62
Jack Hill.—4E 101
Jacksdale.—2B 76
Jackton.—4G 129
Jacobstow.—4B 10
Jacobstowe.—3F 11
Jacobswell.—5B 30
Jameston.—5D 34
Jamestown.—5F 121
(Dumfries & Galloway)
Jamestown.—5D 138
(Fife)
Jamestown.—3G 159
(Highland)
Jamestown.—1E 129
(Strathclyde)
Janetstown.—2C 170
(nr. Thurso, H'land.)
Janetstown.—3F 171
(nr. Wick, H'land.)
Jarrow.—3G 117
Jarvis Brook.—3G 19
Jasper's Green.—5G 55
Jaywick.—1H 45
Jedburgh.—2A 122
Jeffreyston.—4D 35
Jellieston.—3D 118
Jemimaville.—2B 158
Jenkins Park.—3F 151
Jersey Marine.—3D 36
Jesmond.—3F 117
Jevington.—5G 19
Jingle Street.—1C 38
Jockey End.—1D 42
Jodrell Bank.—5E 87
Johnby.—1F 105
John O'Gaunts.—3D 94
John o'Groats.—1F 171
John's Cross.—3B 20
Johnshaven.—2G 147

Johnson's Street.—4F 81
Johnston.—3C 34
Johnstone.—3F 129
Johnstonebridge.—5C 120
Johnstown.—1F 73
(Clwyd)
Johnstown.—3G 35
(Dyfed)
Joppa.—2G 131
(Lothian)
Joppa.—3D 118
(Strathclyde)
Jordan Green.—3C 80
Jordans.—1A 30
Jordanston.—1C 34
Jump.—2D 88
Jumpers Common.—4G 15
Juniper Green.—3E 131
Jurby East.—2C 110
Jurby West.—2C 110

Kaber.—3A 106
Kaimend.—5C 130
Kaimes.—3F 131
Kaimrig End.—5D 131
Kallin.—3D 172
Kalnakill.—3F 157
Kames.—2F 119
(nr. Muirkirk, S'clyde.)
Kames.—2A 128
(nr. Rothesay, S'clyde.)
Kea.—2F 5
Keadby.—4A 96
Keal Cotes.—1C 78
Kearsley.—2E 87
Kearsney.—1G 21
Kearstwick.—1F 99
Kearton.—5C 106
Kearvaig.—1C 168
Keasden.—3G 99
Keason.—3H 7
Keckwick.—4C 86
Keddington.—4F 91
Keddington Corner.—4F 91
Kedington.—3G 55
Kedleston.—3H 75
Kedlock Feus.—2F 139
Keelby.—5D 96
Keele.—3C 74
Keeley Green.—3H 53
Keeston.—3C 34
Keevil.—3E 27
Kegworth.—5B 76
Kehelland.—2D 4
Keig.—2D 154
Keighley.—1A 94
Keilarsbrae.—4A 138
Keillmore.—1E 127
Keillor.—4B 146
Keillour.—1B 138
Keiloch.—4F 153
Keils.—3D 126
Keinton Mandeville.—5F 25
Keir Mill.—5A 120
Keirsleywell Row.—4A 116
Keisby.—5H 77
Keisley.—2A 106
Keiss.—2F 171
Keith.—3B 162
Keith Inch.—4H 163
Kelbrook.—1G 93
Kelby.—3H 77
Keld.—3G 105
(Cumbria)
Keld.—4B 106
(North Yorkshire)
Keldholme.—1C 102
Kelfield.—5A 96
(Humberside)
Kelfield.—2F 95
(North Yorkshire)
Kelham.—2E 77
Kellacott.—1A 8
Kellan.—4G 141

Kellas.—3F 161
(Grampian)
Kellas.—5D 146
(Tayside)
Kellaton.—5E 9
Kelleth.—4H 105
Kelling.—1C 80
Kellingley.—3F 95
Kellington.—3F 95
Kelloe.—1G 107
Kelloholm.—3G 119
Kells.—3A 104
Kelly.—1H 7
Kelly Bray.—2H 7
Kelmarsh.—5E 65
Kelmscot.—3D 40
Kelsale.—1F 57
Kelsall.—4H 85
Kelshall.—4C 54
Kelsick.—4C 114
Kelso.—1B 122
Kelstedge.—1H 75
Kelstern.—3E 91
Kelsterton.—3E 85
Kelston.—2C 26
Keltneyburn.—4E 145
Kelton.—2G 113
Kelton Hill.—4E 113
Kelty.—4D 138
Kelvedon.—1E 45
Kelvedon Hatch.—1G 31
Kelvinside.—3G 129
Kelynack.—3A 4
Kemback.—2G 139
Kemberton.—2B 62
Kemble.—3A 40
Kemerton.—4D 50
Kemeys Commander.—2B 38
Kemnay.—2E 155
Kempley.—5A 50
Kempley Green.—5A 50
Kempsey.—3C 50
Kempsford.—3C 40
Kemps Green.—5F 156
Kempshott.—3E 28
Kempston.—3H 53
Kempston Hardwick.—3H 53
Kempton.—2A 60
Kemp Town.—5E 19
Kemsing.—5G 31
Kemsley.—4D 32
Kenardington.—2D 20
Kenchester.—3G 49
Kencot.—2D 40
Kendal.—5G 105
Kenderchurch.—5E 39
Kendray.—2D 88
Kenfig.—4E 36
Kenfig Hill.—4E 37
Kengharair.—4F 141
Kenidjack.—3A 4
Kenilworth.—5G 63
Kenknock.—5B 144
Kenley.—5E 31
(London)
Kenley.—5H 73
(Shropshire)
Kenmore.—3G 157
(Highland)
Kenmore.—4E 145
(Tayside)
Kenn.—2E 25
(Avon)
Kenn.—5C 12
(Devon)
Kennacraig.—3G 127
Kennavay.—8E 173
Kenneggy Downs.—4C 4
Kennerleigh.—3B 12
Kennet.—4B 138
Kennethmont.—1C 154
Kennett.—1F 55
Kennford.—5C 12
Kenninghall.—4C 68
Kennington.—1E 21
(Kent)

Kennington.—2G 41
(Oxfordshire)
Kennoway.—3F 139
Kennyhill.—5F 67
Kennythorpe.—3C 102
Kenovay.—4A 140
Kensaleyre.—3D 156
Kensington.—3D 30
Kenstone.—3H 73
Kensworth.—1D 42
Kensworth Common.—1D 42
Kentallen.—3E 143
Kentchurch.—5G 49
Kentford.—1G 55
Kent InternationalAirport.
—4H 33
Kentisbeare.—3D 12
Kentisbury.—1C 22
Kentisbury Ford.—1C 22
Kentmere.—4F 105
Kenton.—5C 12
(Devon)
Kenton.—2C 30
(London)
Kenton.—1D 57
(Suffolk)
Kenton Bank Foot.—3F 117
Kentra.—2A 142
Kentrigg.—5G 105
Kents Bank.—2C 98
Kent's Green.—5B 50
Kent's Oak.—4B 16
Kent Street.—4B 20
(East Sussex)
Kent Street.—5A 32
(Kent)
Kent Street.—3D 18
(West Sussex)
Kenwick.—2G 73
Kenwyn.—2F 5
Kenyon.—3D 86
Keoldale.—2D 168
Keose.—5F 173
Keose Glebe.—5F 173
Keppoch.—1B 150
Kepwick.—5B 106
Keresley.—4H 63
Kerital.—4C 110
Kerne Bridge.—1D 39
Kerridge.—5G 87
Kerris.—4B 4
Kerrow.—5F 159
Kerry.—2G 59
Kerrycroy.—3C 128
Kerry's Gate.—4F 49
Kersall.—1E 76
Kersbrook.—5D 12
Kerse.—4E 69
Kersey.—3B 56
Kershader.—5F 173
Kershopefoot.—1F 115
Kersoe.—4D 51
Kerswell.—3D 12
Kerswell Green.—3C 50
Kesgrave.—3E 57
Kessingland.—4H 69
Kessingland Beach.—4H 69
Kestle.—2C 5
Kestle Mill.—4C 6
Keston.—4F 31
Keswick.—2D 104
(Cumbria)
Keswick.—2F 81
(nr. North Walsham, Norf.)
Keswick.—2E 69
(nr. Norwich, Norf.)
Ketsby.—5F 91
Kettering.—5F 65
Ketteringham.—2D 68
Kettins.—5B 146
Kettlebaston.—2B 56
Kettlebridge.—3F 139
Kettlebrook.—2G 63
Kettleburgh.—1E 57
Kettleholm.—2C 114
Kettleness.—3F 109

Kettleshulme.—5G 87
Kettlesing.—4F 101
Kettlesing Bottom.—4F 101
Kettlestone.—2B 80
Kettlethorpe.—5A 90
Kettletoft.—4F 174
Kettlewell.—2C 100
Ketton.—2G 65
Kew.—3C 30
Kewaigue.—4C 110
Kewstoke.—2D 24
Kexbrough.—2D 88
Kexby.—4A 90
(Lincolnshire)
Kexby.—4C 102
(North Yorkshire)
Keyford.—4C 26
Key Green.—1C 74
(Cheshire)
Key Green.—4F 109
(North Yorkshire)
Keyham.—2D 64
Keyhaven.—4B 16
Keyhead.—3H 163
Keyingham.—3E 97
Keymer.—4E 19
Keynsham.—2B 26
Keysoe.—1H 53
Keysoe Row.—1H 53
Key's Toft.—2D 79
Keyston.—5H 65
Key Street.—4C 32
Keyworth.—4D 76
Kibblesworth.—4F 117
Kibworth Beauchamp.—3D 64
Kibworth Harcourt.—3D 64
Kidbrooke.—3F 31
Kidburngill.—2B 104
Kiddemore Green.—2C 62
Kidderminster.—5C 62
Kiddington.—5B 52
Kidd's Moor.—2D 68
Kidlington.—1F 41
Kidmore End.—5H 41
Kidnall.—1G 73
Kidsgrove.—2C 74
Kidstones.—1C 100
Kidwelly.—4H 35
Kiel Crofts.—5D 142
Kielder.—5A 122
Kiells.—3C 126
Kilalauy.—4C 172
Kilbagie.—4B 138
Kilbarchan.—3F 129
Kilbeg.—3E 149
Kilberry.—3F 127
Kilbirnie.—4E 128
Kilbride.—1D 149
(Highland)
Kilbride.—1F 135
(Strathclyde)
Kilburn.—3A 76
(Derbyshire)
Kilburn.—2D 30
(London)
Kilburn.—2A 102
(North Yorkshire)
Kilby.—3D 64
Kilcadzow.—5B 130
Kilchattan.—4C 128
(Bute, S'clyde.)
Kilchattan.—4A 134
(Colonsay, S'clyde.)
Kilchenzie.—3A 124
Kilcheran.—5C 142
Kilchiaran.—3A 126
Kilchoan.—4F 149
(nr. Inverie, H'land.)
Kilchoan.—2F 141
(nr. Tobermory, H'land.)
Kilchoman.—3A 126
Kilchrenan.—1H 135
Kilconquhar.—3G 139
Kilcot.—5A 50
Kilcoy.—3H 159

Kilcreggan.—1D 128
Kildale.—4C 108
Kildary.—1B 160
Kildermorie Lodge.—1H 15[?]
Kildonan.—4F 111
(Dumfries & Galloway)
Kildonan.—1G 167
(nr. Helmsdale, H'land.)
Kildonan.—3C 156
(Skye, H'land.)
Kildonan.—3E 125
(Strathclyde)
Kildonan.—6C 172
(Western Isles)
Kildonnan.—5C 148
Kildrummy.—2B 154
Kildwick.—1H 93
Kilfillan.—4H 111
Kilfinan.—2H 127
Kilfinnan.—4E 151
Kilgetty.—4E 35
Kilgour.—3E 138
Kilgrammie.—4B 118
Kilham.—3F 103
(Humberside)
Kilham.—1C 122
(Northumberland)
Kilkenneth.—4A 140
Kilkhampton.—2C 10
Killamarsh.—4E 89
Killay.—3C 36
Killean.—5E 127
Killearn.—1G 129
Killellan.—4A 124
Killen.—3A 160
Killerby.—3E 107
Killichonan.—3C 144
Killichronan.—4G 141
Killicrankie.—2G 145
Killilan.—5B 158
Killimster.—3F 171
Killin.—5C 144
Killinghall.—4F 101
Killinghurst.—2A 18
Killington.—1F 99
Killingworth.—2F 117
Killin Lodge.—3H 151
Killinochonoch.—4F 135
Killochyett.—5A 132
Killundine.—4G 141
Kilmacolm.—3E 129
Kilmahog.—3F 137
Kilmahumaig.—4E 135
Kilmalieu.—3C 142
Kilmaluag.—1D 156
Kilmany.—1F 139
Kilmarie.—2D 148
Kilmarnock.—1D 118
Kilmaron.—2F 139
Kilmartin.—4F 135
Kilmaurs.—5F 129
Kilmelford.—2F 135
Kilmeny.—3B 126
Kilmersdon.—3B 26
Kilmeston.—1D 16
Kilmichael Glassary.—4F 1
Kilmichael of Inverlussa.
—1[?]
Kilmington.—4F 13
(Devon)
Kilmington.—5C 26
(Wiltshire)
Kilmoluag.—4A 140
Kilmorack.—4G 159
Kilmore.—3E 149
(Highland)
Kilmore.—1F 135
(Strathclyde)
Kilmory.—1G 141
(nr. Kilchoan, H'land.)
Kilmory.—3B 148
(Rhum, H'land.)
Kilmory.—3D 124
(Arran, S'clyde.)
Kilmory.—2F 127
(Knapdale, S'clyde.)

Kingledores.—2D 120
King o' Muirs.—4A 138
Kingoodie.—1F 139
King's Acre.—3G 49
Kingsand.—4A 8
Kingsash.—2B 42
Kingsbarns.—2H 139
Kingsbridge.—5D 8
(Devon)
Kingsbridge.—2F 23
(Somerset)
Kings Bromley.—1F 63
Kingsburgh.—3C 156
Kingsbury.—2C 30
(London)
Kingsbury.—3G 63
(Warwickshire)
Kingsbury Episcopi.—1H 13
Kings Caple.—5H 49
Kingscavil.—2D 130
Kingsclere.—3D 28
King's Cliffe.—3H 65
Kingscote.—2F 11
Kingscote.—3G 39
Kingscott.—2F 11
Kings Coughton.—2E 51
Kingscross.—3E 125
Kingsdon.—1A 14
Kingsdown.—1H 21
(Kent)
Kingsdown.—2D 26
(nr. Bath, Wilts.)
Kingsdown.—4C 40
(Swindon, Wilts.)
Kingseat.—4D 138
Kingsey.—2A 42
Kingsfold.—2C 18
Kingsford.—4C 62
(Hereford & Worcester)
Kingsford.—5F 129
(Strathclyde)
Kingsforth.—4C 96
Kingsgate.—3H 33
Kings Green.—4B 50
Kingshall Street.—1B 56
King's Heath.—4E 63
Kingsholm.—1G 39
Kingshouse.—1E 137
(Central)
Kingshouse.—3G 143
(Highland)
Kingshurst.—4F 63
Kingskerswell.—3E 9
Kingskettle.—3F 139
Kingsland.—2B 82
(Gwynedd)
Kingsland.—4B 60
(Hereford & Worcester)
Kings Langley.—2D 42
Kingsley.—3H 85
(Cheshire)
Kingsley.—5F 29
(Hampshire)
Kingsley.—3F 75
(Staffordshire)
Kingsley Green.—5G 29
Kingsley Holt.—3E 75
King's Lynn.—1F 67
King's Meaburn.—2H 105
Kings Moss.—2C 86
Kings Muir.—1E 121
(Borders)
Kingsmuir.—3H 139
(Fife)
Kingsmuir.—4D 147
(Tayside)
King's Newnham.—5B 64
Kings Newton.—5A 76
Kingsnorth.—2E 20
King's Norton.—2D 64
(Leicestershire)
King's Norton.—5E 63
(West Midlands)
King's Nympton.—2G 11
Kings Pyon.—2G 49
Kings Ripton.—5B 66

King's Somborne.—5B 28
King's Stag.—2C 14
King's Stanley.—2G 39
King's Sutton.—4B 52
Kingstanding.—3E 63
Kingsteignton.—3E 9
Kingsteps.—3D 160
King Sterndale.—4H 49
King's Thorn.—4H 49
Kingsthorpe.—1E 53
Kingston.—2C 54
(Cambridgeshire)
Kingston.—5C 8
(Devon)
Kingston.—3C 14
(nr, Sturminster Newton, Dorset)
Kingston.—5E 15
(nr Swanage, Dorset)
Kingston.—2H 161
(Grampian)
Kingston.—3G 15
(Hampshire)
Kingston.—5C 16
(Isle of Wight)
Kingston.—5F 33
(Kent)
Kingston.—1B 132
(Lothian)
Kingston.—5B 18
(West Sussex)
Kingston Bagpuize.—3F 41
Kingston Blount.—3A 42
Kingston by Sea.—5D 18
Kingston Deverill.—5D 26
Kingstone.—4G 49
(Hereford & Worcester)
Kingstone.—2G 13
(Somerset)
Kingstone.—5E 75
(Staffordshire)
Kingston Lisle.—4E 40
Kingston near Lewes.—5E 19
Kingston on Soar.—5C 76
Kingston Russell.—4A 14
Kingston St Mary.—1F 13
Kingston Seymour.—2E 25
Kingston Stert.—2A 42
Kingston upon Hull.—3C 96
Kingston upon Thames.—4C 30
King's Walden.—5A 54
Kingswear.—4E 9
Kingswells.—3F 155
Kingswinford.—4C 62
Kingswood.—5E 39
(Avon)
Kingswood.—1H 41
(Buckinghamshire)
Kingswood.—3F 39
(Gloucestershire)
Kingswood.—5C 32
(Kent)
Kingswood.—5E 73
(Powys)
Kingswood.—5B 24
(Somerset)
Kingswood.—5D 30
(Surrey)
Kingswood.—5H 145
(Tayside)
Kingswood.—5F 63
(Warwickshire)
Kingswood Common.—2E 49
(Hereford & Worcs.)
Kingswood Common.—2C 62
(Staffordshire)
Kings Worthy.—5C 28
Kingthorpe.—5D 90
Kington.—3E 39
(Avon)
Kington.—2E 49
(nr. Hereford, Here & Worcs.)
Kington.—2D 51
(nr. Worcester, Here & Worcs.)
Kington Langley.—5H 39
Kington Magna.—1C 14
Kington St Michael.—5H 39

Kingussie.—3B 152
Kingweston.—5F 25
Kinharrachie.—5G 163
Kinhrive.—1A 160
Kinkell Bridge.—2B 138
Kinknockie.—4H 163
Kinkry Hill.—2G 115
Kinlet.—4B 62
Kinloch.—4C 148
(Rhum, H'land.)
Kinloch.—3A 142
(nr. Lochaline, H'land.)
Kinloch.—5C 168
(Loch More, H'land.)
Kinloch.—4A 146
(Tayside)
Kinlochard.—3D 136
Kinlochbervie.—3C 168
Kinlochewe.—2C 158
Kinloch Hourn.—3B 150
Kinloch Laggan.—5H 151
Kinlochleven.—2F 143
Kinloch Lodge.—3F 169
Kinlochmoidart.—1B 142
Kinlochmore.—2F 143
Kinloch Rannoch.—3D 144
Kinlochspelve.—1D 134
Kinloid.—5E 149
Kinloss.—2E 161
Kinmel Bay.—2B 84
Kinmuck.—2F 155
Kinnadie.—4G 163
Kinnaird.—1E 139
Kinneff.—1H 147
Kinnelhead.—4C 120
Kinnell.—3F 147
Kinnerley.—3F 73
Kinnernie.—2E 154
Kinnersley.—3F 49
(nr. Kington, Here & Worcs.)
Kinnersley.—3C 50
(nr. Pershore, Here & Worcs.)
Kinnerton.—4H 59
(Powys)
Kinnerton.—1A 60
(Shropshire)
Kinnesswood.—3D 138
Kinninvie.—2D 106
Kinnordy.—3C 146
Kinoulton.—4D 76
Kinross.—3D 138
Kinrossie.—5A 146
Kinsbourne Green.—1E 43
Kinsey Heath.—3A 74
Kinsham.—4A 60
(nr. Leominster, Here & Worcs.)
Kinsham.—4D 50
(nr. Tewkesbury, Here & Worcs.)
Kinsley.—4E 94
Kinson.—4F 15
Kintarvie.—6E 173
Kintbury.—2B 28
Kintessack.—2E 161
Kintillo.—2D 138
Kinton.—3B 60
(Hereford & Worcester)
Kinton.—4F 73
(Shropshire)
Kintore.—2E 155
Kintour.—4C 126
Kintra.—1A 134
Kintraw.—3F 135
Kinveachy.—2D 152
Kinver.—4C 62
Kinwarton.—2F 51
Kippax.—2E 94
Kippen.—4F 137
Kippford.—4F 113
Kipping's Cross.—2H 19
Kirbister.—7C 174
Kirby Bedon.—2E 69
Kirby Bellars.—1E 64
Kirby Cane.—3F 69
Kirby Cross.—5E 57
Kirby Fields.—2C 64

Kirby Grindalyth.—3E 103
Kirby Hill.—4E 107
(nr. Richmond, N Yorks.)
Kirby Hill.—3G 101
(nr. Ripon, N Yorks.)
Kirby Knowle.—1H 101
Kirby le Soken.—5E 57
Kirby Misperton.—2C 102
Kirby Muxloe.—2C 64
Kirby Row.—3F 69
Kirby Sigston.—5B 108
Kirby Underdale.—4D 102
Kirby Wiske.—1G 101
Kirdford.—3B 18
Kirivick.—3D 173
Kirk.—3E 171
Kirkabister.—6G 175
Kirkandrews.—5D 112
Kirkandrews-on-Eden.—4E 115
Kirkapol.—4B 140
Kirkbampton.—4E 114
Kirkbean.—4G 113
Kirk Bramwith.—4G 95
Kirkbride.—4D 114
Kirkbridge.—5F 107
Kirkbuddo.—4E 147
Kirkburn.—4E 103
Kirkburton.—4B 94
Kirkby.—3C 90
(Lincolnshire)
Kirkby.—3B 86
(Merseyside)
Kirkby.—4C 108
(North Yorkshire)
Kirkby Fenside.—1C 78
Kirkby Fleetham.—5F 107
Kirkby Green.—2H 77
Kirkby in Ashfield.—2C 76
Kirkby la Thorpe.—3H 77
Kirkby Lonsdale.—2F 99
Kirkby Malham.—3G 100
Kirkby Mallory.—2B 64
Kirkby Malzeard.—2F 101
Kirkby Mills.—1C 102
Kirkbymoorside.—1B 102
Kirkby on Bain.—1B 78
Kirkby Overblow.—1D 94
Kirkby Stephen.—4A 106
Kirkby Thore.—2H 105
Kirkby Underwood.—5H 77
Kirkby Wharfe.—5A 102
Kirkcaldy.—4E 139
Kirkcambeck.—3G 115
Kirkcolm.—3F 111
Kirkconnel.—3G 119
Kirkconnell.—3G 113
Kirkcowan.—3A 112
Kirkcudbright.—4D 113
Kirkdale.—3A 86
Kirk Deighton.—4G 101
Kirk Ella.—3C 96
Kirkfield.—4A 130
Kirkfieldbank.—5B 130
Kirkforthar Feus.—3E 139
Kirkgunzeon.—3F 113
Kirk Hallam.—3B 76
Kirkham.—2B 92
(Lancashire)
Kirkham.—3C 102
(North Yorkshire)
Kirkhamgate.—3C 94
Kirk Hammerton.—4H 101
Kirkharle.—1D 116
Kirkheaton.—2D 116
(Northumberland)
Kirkheaton.—4B 94
(West Yorkshire)
Kirkhill.—4H 159
Kirkhope.—4B 120
Kirkhouse.—1F 121
Kirkibost.—2D 148
(Highland)
Kirkibost.—4D 173
(Western Isles)
Kirkinch.—4C 146
Kirkinner.—4B 112

Kirkintilloch.—2H 129
Kirk Ireton.—2G 75
Kirkland.—3B 104
(nr. Cleator Moor, Cumbria)
Kirkland.—1H 105
(nr. Penrith, Cumbria)
Kirkland.—5D 114
(nr. Wigton, Cumbria)
Kirkland.—3G 119
(nr. Kirkconnel, Dum & Gall.)
Kirkland.—5H 119
(nr. Moniaive, Dum & Gall.)
Kirkland Guards.—5C 114
Kirk Langley.—4G 75
Kirklauchline.—4F 111
Kirkleatham.—2C 108
Kirklevington.—4B 108
Kirkley.—3H 69
Kirklington.—1G 101
(North Yorkshire)
Kirklington.—2D 76
(Nottinghamshire)
Kirklinton.—3F 115
Kirkliston.—2E 131
Kirkmabreck.—4B 112
Kirkmaiden.—5G 111
Kirk Merrington.—1F 107
Kirk Michael.—2C 110
(Isle of Man)
Kirkmichael.—4C 118
(Strathclyde)
Kirkmichael.—2H 145
(Tayside)
Kirkmuirhill.—5A 130
Kirknewton.—3E 131
(Lothian)
Kirknewton.—1D 122
(Northumberland)
Kirkney.—5C 162
Kirk of Shotts.—3B 130
Kirkoswald.—5G 115
(Cumbria)
Kirkoswald.—4B 118
(Strathclyde)
Kirkpatrick.—5B 120
Kirkpatrick Durham.—2E 113
Kirkpatrick-Fleming.—2D 114
Kirk Sandall.—2G 89
Kirksanton.—1A 98
Kirk Smeaton.—4F 95
Kirkstall.—2C 94
Kirkstead.—1A 78
Kirkstile.—5F 121
Kirkstyle.—1F 171
Kirkthorpe.—3D 94
Kirkton.—3H 121
(Borders)
Kirkton.—1G 113
(Dumfries & Galloway)
Kirkton.—1F 139
(Fife)
Kirkton.—2D 154
(nr. Alford, Grampian)
Kirkton.—1D 154
(nr. Insch, Grampian)
Kirkton.—4F 163
(nr. Turriff, Grampian)
Kirkton.—4E 167
(nr. Golspie, H'land.)
Kirkton.—4B 158
(Loch Carron, H'land.)
Kirkton.—2B 120
(Strathclyde)
Kirkton.—4D 146
(nr. Forfar, Tayside)
Kirkton.—5B 154
(nr. Tarfside, Tayside)
Kirktonhill.—2E 129
Kirkton Manor.—1E 120
Kirkton of Airlie.—3C 146
Kirkton of Auchterhouse.
—5C 146
Kirkton of Bourtie.—1F 155
Kirkton of Burris.—4E 155
Kirkton of Collace.—5A 146
Kirkton of Craig.—3G 147

Kirkton of Culsalmond.—5D 162
Kirkton of Glenbuchat.—2A 154
Kirkton of Glenisla.—2B 146
Kirkton of Kingoldrum.—3C 146
Kirkton of Largo.—3G 139
Kirkton of Lethendy.—4A 146
Kirkton of Logie Buchan.
  —1G 155
Kirkton of Maryculter.—4F 155
Kirkton of Menmuir.—2E 147
Kirkton of Monikie.—5E 147
Kirkton of Oyne.—1D 154
Kirkton of Rayne.—1E 154
Kirkton of Skene.—3F 155
Kirkton of Tealing.—5D 146
Kirktown.—2G 163
  (nr. Fraserburgh, Grampian)
Kirktown.—3H 163
  (nr. Peterhead, Grampian)
Kirktown of Alvah.—2D 162
Kirktown of Auchterless.
  —4E 162
Kirktown of Deskford.—2C 162
Kirktown of Fetteresso.—5F 155
Kirktown of Mortlach.—5H 161
Kirktown of Slains.—1H 155
Kirkurd.—5E 131
Kirkwall.—6D 174
Kirkwall Airport.—7D 174
Kirkwhelpington.—1C 116
Kirk Yetholm.—2C 122
Kirmington.—4D 96
Kirmond le Mire.—3D 91
Kirn.—2C 128
Kirriemuir.—3C 146
Kirstead Green.—3E 69
Kirtlebridge.—2D 114
Kirtleton.—1D 114
Kirtling.—2F 55
Kirtling Green.—2F 55
Kirtlington.—1F 41
Kirtomy.—2H 169
Kirton.—1G 149
  (Highland)
Kirton.—4C 78
  (Lincolnshire)
Kirton.—1D 76
  (Nottinghamshire)
Kirton.—4E 57
  (Suffolk)
Kirton End.—3B 78
Kirton Holme.—3B 78
Kirton in Lindsey.—3B 90
Kishorn.—4H 157
Kislingbury.—2D 52
Kites Hardwick.—1B 52
Kittisford.—3G 23
Kittle.—4B 36
Kittybrewster.—3G 155
Kitwood.—5E 29
Kivernoll.—4G 49
Kiveton Park.—4E 89
Knaith.—4A 90
Knaith Park.—4A 90
Knap Corner.—1D 14
Knaphill.—5A 184
Knapp.—1C 16
  (Hampshire)
Knapp.—1G 13
  (Somerset)
Knapp.—5B 146
  (Tayside)
Knapton.—2F 81
  (Norfolk)
Knapton Green.—2G 49
Knapwell.—1C 54
Knaresborough.—4G 101
Knarsdale.—4H 115
Knatts Valley.—4G 31
Knaven.—4F 163
Knayton.—1H 101
Knebworth.—5B 54
Knedlington.—3H 95
Kneep.—4C 173
Kneesall.—1E 76
Kneesworth.—3C 54

Kneeton.—3E 76
Knelston.—4A 36
Knenhall.—4D 74
Knightacott.—2C 22
Knightcote.—2A 52
Knightcott.—3D 25
Knightley.—5C 74
Knightley Dale.—5C 74
Knightlow Hill.—5B 64
Knighton.—5B 8
  (Devon)
Knighton.—2B 14
  (Dorset)
Knighton.—2E 51
  (Hereford & Worcester)
Knighton.—2D 64
  (Leicestershire)
Knighton.—3H 59
  (Powys)
Knighton.—4B 24
  (Somerset)
Knighton.—5B 74
  (nr. Adbaston, Staffs.)
Knighton.—3B 74
  (nr. Ashley Heath, Staffs.)
Knighton.—5D 40
  (Wiltshire)
Knighton Common.—5A 62
Knight's End.—3D 66
Knightswood.—3G 129
Knightwick.—2B 50
Knill.—4H 59
Knipton.—4F 77
Knitsley.—5E 117
Kniveton.—2G 75
Knock.—2H 105
  (Cumbria)
Knock.—3C 162
  (Grampian)
Knock.—5G 141
  (Strathclyde)
Knock.—4G 173
  (Western Isles)
Knockally.—5D 170
  (Highland)
Knockan.—2G 165
  (Highland)
Knockan.—1B 134
  (Strathclyde)
Knockandhu.—1G 153
Knockando.—4F 161
Knockarthur.—3E 167
Knockbain.—3A 160
Knockbreck.—2B 156
Knockdee.—2D 170
Knockdolian.—1G 111
Knockdon.—3C 118
Knockdown.—3D 34
Knockenbaird.—1D 154
Knockenkelly.—3E 125
Knockentiber.—1C 118
Knockfarrel.—3H 159
Knockglass.—2C 170
Knockholt.—5F 31
Knockholt Pound.—5F 31
Knockie Lodge.—2G 151
Knockin.—3F 73
Knockinlaw.—1D 118
Knockinnon.—5D 171
Knockintorran.—2C 172
Knockrome.—2D 126
Knocksharry.—3B 110
Knockvennie.—2E 113
Knodishall.—1G 57
Knole.—1H 13
Knollbury.—4C 38
Knolls Green.—5F 87
Knolton.—2F 73
Knook.—4E 27
Knossington.—2F 65
Knott.—3C 156
Knott End-on-Sea.—1A 92
Knotting.—1H 53
Knotting Green.—1H 53
Knottingley.—3F 95
Knotts.—2F 105
Knotty Ash.—3B 86

Knotty Green.—1A 30
Knowbury.—3C 60
Knowe.—2A 112
Knowefield.—4F 115
Knowehead.—5F 119
Knowesgate.—1C 116
Knoweside.—3B 118
Knowle.—5E 39
  (Avon)
Knowle.—2A 22
  (nr. Braunton, Devon)
Knowle.—5D 12
  (nr. Budleigh Salterton, Devon)
Knowle.—3A 12
  (nr. Crediton, Devon)
Knowle.—3C 60
  (Shropshire)
Knowle.—5F 63
  (West Midlands)
Knowle Green.—2D 92
Knowle St Giles.—2G 13
Knowl Hill.—5B 42
Knowlton.—5G 33
Knowsley.—3B 86
Knowsley Hall.—3B 86
Knowsley IndustrialEstate.
  —3B 86
Knowstone.—3E 23
Knucklas.—3H 59
Knuston.—1G 53
Knutsford.—5E 87
Knypersley.—2C 74
Krumlin.—4A 94
Kuggar.—5E 5
Kyleakin.—1F 149
Kyle of Lochalsh.—1F 149
Kylerhea.—1F 149
Kylesku.—5C 168
Kylesmorar.—4G 149
Kyles Scalpay.—8E 173
Kyles Stockinish.—8D 173
Kylestrome.—5C 168
Kymin.—1D 38
Kynaston.—4A 50
  (Hereford & Worcester)
Kynaston.—4F 73
  (Shropshire)
Kynnersley.—1A 62
Kyre Green.—1A 50
Kyre Park.—1A 50
Kyrewood.—1A 50
Kyrle.—3G 23

Labost.—3E 173
Laceby.—5E 97
Lacey Green.—2B 42
Lach Dennis.—5E 87
Lache.—4F 85
Lackalee.—8D 173
Lackford.—5G 67
Lacock.—2E 27
Ladbroke.—2B 52
Laddingford.—1A 20
Lade Bank.—2C 78
Ladock.—4C 6
Ladybank.—2F 139
Ladycross.—1H 7
Lady Green.—2A 86
Lady Hall.—1A 98
Ladykirk.—5E 133
Ladysford.—2G 163
Ladywood.—1C 50
  (Hereford & Worcester)
Ladywood.—4E 63
  (West Midlands)
Laga.—2A 142
Lagavulin.—5C 126
Lagg.—3D 124
  (Arran, S'clyde.)
Lagg.—2D 127
  (Jura, S'clyde.)
Laggan.—5H 161
  (Grampian)
Laggan.—4E 151
  (nr. Fort Augustus, H'land.)

Laggan.—4A 152
  (nr. Newtonmore, H'land.)
Laggan.—4A 126
  (Strathclyde)
Lagganlia.—3C 152
Laglingarten.—3A 136
Lagness.—3G 17
Laid.—3E 168
Laide.—4D 164
Laigh Fenwick.—5F 129
Laindon.—2A 32
Lairg.—3C 166
Lairg Muir.—3C 166
Laithes.—1F 105
Laithkirk.—2C 106
Lake.—2B 22
  (Devon)
Lake.—4E 15
  (Dorset)
Lake.—5D 16
  (Isle of Wight)
Lake.—5G 27
  (Wiltshire)
Lakenham.—2E 69
Lakenheath.—4G 67
Lakesend.—3E 67
Lake Side.—1C 98
Laleham.—4B 30
Laleston.—5E 37
Lamancha.—4F 131
Lamarsh.—4A 56
Lamas.—3E 81
Lamb Corner.—4C 56
Lambden.—5D 132
Lamberhead Green.—2C 86
Lamberhurst.—2A 20
Lamberhurst Quarter.—2A 20
Lamberton.—4F 133
Lambeth.—3E 31
Lambfell Moar.—3B 110
Lambhill.—3G 129
Lambley.—4H 115
  (Northumberland)
Lambley.—3D 76
  (Nottinghamshire)
Lambourn.—5E 41
Lambourne End.—1F 31
Lambourn Woodlands.—5E 41
Lambrook.—1F 13
Lambs Green.—4E 15
  (Dorset)
Lambs Green.—2D 18
  (West Sussex)
Lambston.—3C 34
Lamellion.—3G 7
Lamerton.—2A 8
Lamesley.—4F 117
Laminess.—4F 174
Lamington.—1B 160
  (Highland)
Lamington.—1B 120
  (Strathclyde)
Lamlash.—2E 125
Lamonby.—1F 105
Lamorick.—3E 7
Lamorna.—4B 4
Lamorran.—2F 5
Lampeter.—3E 47
Lampeter Velfrey.—3E 35
Lamphey.—4D 34
Lamplugh.—2B 104
Lamport.—5E 65
Lamyatt.—5B 26
Lana.—4D 10
  (nr. Ashwater, Devon)
Lana.—3D 10
  (nr. Holsworthy, Devon)
Lanark.—5B 130
Lanarth.—4E 5
Lanbether.—5G 37
Lancaster.—3D 98
Lanchester.—5E 117
Lancing.—5C 18
Landbeach.—1D 54
Landcross.—3A 22
Landerberry.—3E 155

Landewednack.—5E 5
Landford.—2C 16
Land Gate.—2C 86
Landhallow.—5D 171
Landimore.—3A 36
Landkey Newland.—2B 22
Landkey Town.—2B 22
Landore.—3C 36
Landport.—3E 17
Landrake.—3H 7
Landscove.—3D 8
Landshipping.—3D 34
Landulph.—3A 8
Landywood.—2D 63
Lane.—3C 6
Laneast.—1G 7
Lane Bottom.—2F 93
Lane End.—3B 42
  (Buckinghamshire)
Lane End.—5C 104
  (Cumbria)
Lane End.—1D 16
  (Hampshire)
Lane End.—5E 17
  (Isle of Wight)
Lane End.—4D 26
  (Wiltshire)
Lane Ends.—4G 75
  (Derbyshire)
Lane Ends.—1E 107
  (Durham)
Lane Ends.—4G 99
  (Lancashire)
Laneham.—3E 76
Lanehead.—5B 116
  (Durham)
Lane Head.—3D 86
  (Manchester)
Lane Head.—1A 116
  (Northumberland)
Lane Head.—2B 88
  (West Yorkshire)
Lane Heads.—2B 92
Lanercost.—3G 115
Laneshaw Bridge.—1G 93
Laney Green.—2D 62
Langal.—2B 142
Langar.—4E 76
Langass.—2D 172
Langbank.—2E 129
Langbar.—4D 100
Langburnshiels.—4H 121
Langcliffe.—3B 100
Langdale End.—5G 109
Langdon.—4C 10
  (nr. Bude, Corn.)
Langdon.—1H 7
  (nr. Launceston, Corn.)
Langdon Beck.—1B 106
Langdon Hills.—2A 32
Langdown.—3C 16
Langdyke.—3F 139
Langenhoe.—1G 45
Langford.—3A 54
  (Bedfordshire)
Langford.—3D 12
  (Devon)
Langford.—2E 45
  (Essex)
Langford.—2F 77
  (Nottinghamshire)
Langford.—2D 40
  (Oxfordshire)
Langford Budville.—1E 12
Langham.—1C 14
  (Dorset)
Langham.—4C 56
  (Essex)
Langham.—1F 65
  (Leicestershire)
Langham.—1C 80
  (Norfolk)
Langham.—1B 56
  (Suffolk)
Langho.—2E 93
Langholm.—1E 115

Langland.—4C 36
Langleeford.—2D 122
Langley.—3B 30
  (Berkshire)
Langley.—5G 87
  (Cheshire)
Langley.—3B 76
  (Derbyshire)
Langley.—4D 54
  (Essex)
Langley.—5E 51
  (Gloucestershire)
Langley.—3C 16
  (Hampshire)
Langley.—5B 54
  (Hertfordshire)
Langley.—5C 32
  (Kent)
Langley.—2F 87
  (Manchester)
Langley.—3B 116
  (Northumberland)
Langley.—3G 23
  (Somerset)
Langley.—1F 51
  (Warwickshire)
Langley Burrell.—5H 39
Langleybury.—2D 43
Langley Common.—4G 75
Langley Green.—4G 75
  (Derbyshire)
Langley Green.—2F 69
  (Norfolk)
Langley Green.—1F 51
  (Warwickshire)
Langley Green.—2D 18
  (West Sussex)
Langley Heath.—5C 32
Langley Marsh.—3G 23
Langley Moor.—5F 117
Langley Park.—5F 117
  (Durham)
Langleypark.—2F 147
  (Tayside)
Langley Street.—2F 69
Langney.—5H 19
Langold.—4F 89
Langore.—1H 7
Langport.—1H 13
Langrick.—3B 78
Langridge.—2C 26
Langridgeford.—3B 22
Langrigg.—5C 114
Langrish.—1F 17
Langriville.—3B 78
Langsett.—2C 88
Langshaw.—1H 121
Langstone.—3F 17
Langthorne.—5F 107
Langthorpe.—3G 101
Langthwaite.—4D 106
Langtoft.—3F 103
  (Humberside)
Langtoft.—1A 66
  (Lincolnshire)
Langton.—3E 107
  (Durham)
Langton.—1B 78
  (nr. Horncastle, Lincs.)
Langton.—5F 91
  (nr. Spilsby, Lincs.)
Langton.—3C 102
  (North Yorkshire)
Langton by Wragby.—5D 90
Langton Green.—2B 19
Langton Herring.—5B 14
Langton Long Blandford.—3D
Langton Matravers.—5E 15
Langtree.—2E 11
Langwathby.—1G 105
Langwith.—1C 76
Langworth.—5C 90
Lanivet.—3E 7
Lanjeth.—4D 6
Lank.—2E 7
Lanlivery.—4E 7

Lime Kiln Nook.—5E 115
Limekilns.—5C 138
Limerigg.—2B 130
Limestone Brae.—5A 116
Lime Street.—4C 50
Limington.—1A 14
Limpenhoe.—2F 69
Limpley Stoke.—2C 26
Limpsfield.—5F 31
Linburn.—3E 131
Linby.—2C 76
Linchmere.—5G 29
Includen.—2G 113
Lincoln.—5D 98
Lincomb.—1C 50
Lindale.—1D 98
Lindal in Furness.—2B 98
Lindean.—1G 121
Linden.—1G 39
Lindfield.—3E 19
Lindford.—5G 29
Lindores.—2E 139
Lindridge.—1A 50
Lindsell.—5F 55
Lindsey.—3B 56
Lindsey Tye.—3B 56
Linford.—3A 32
(Essex)
Linford.—3G 15
(Hampshire)
Lingague.—4B 110
Lingarabay.—9C 173
Lingdale.—3D 108
Lingen.—4A 60
Lingfield.—1E 19
Ling, The.—3F 69
Lingwood.—2F 69
Lingyclose Head.—4E 115
Liniclate.—4C 172
Linicro.—2C 156
Linique.—4C 172
Linkend.—4C 50
Linkenholt.—3B 28
Linkinhorne.—2H 7
Linklater.—9D 174
Linktown.—4E 139
Linkwood.—2G 161
Linley.—1A 60
(nr. Bishop's Castle, Shrops.)
Linley.—3A 62
(nr. Bridgenorth, Shrops.)
Linley Green.—2A 50
Linlithgow.—2D 130
Linlithgow Bridge.—2C 130
Linneraineach.—3F 165
Linshader.—4E 173
Linshiels.—4C 122
Linsidemore.—4C 166
Linslade.—5G 53
Linstead Parva.—5F 69
Linstock.—4F 115
Linthwaite.—4B 94
Lintlaw.—4E 131
Lintmill.—2C 162
Linton.—2B 122
(Borders)
Linton.—3E 55
(Cambridgeshire)
Linton.—1G 63
(Derbyshire)
Linton.—5A 50
(Hereford & Worcester)
Linton.—1B 20
(Kent)
Linton.—3C 100
(North Yorkshire)
Linton.—1D 94
(West Yorkshire)
Linton Colliery.—5G 123
Linton Hill.—5A 50
Linton-on-Ouse.—3H 101
Lintzgarth.—5C 116
Linwood.—3G 15
(Hampshire)
Linwood.—4D 90
(Lincolnshire)

Linwood.—3F 129
(Strathclyde)
Lionel.—1H 173
Liphook.—5G 29
Lipley.—4B 74
Lipyeate.—3B 26
Liquo.—4B 130
Liscard.—1F 85
Liscombe.—2E 23
Liskeard.—3G 7
Lisle Court.—4B 16
Liss.—1F 17
Lisset.—4G 103
Liss Forest.—1F 17
Lissington.—4D 90
Liston.—3A 56
Lisvane.—4H 37
Liswerry.—4B 38
Litcham.—4A 80
Litchard.—4F 37
Litchborough.—2D 52
Litchfield.—3C 28
Litherland.—3A 86
Litlington.—3C 54
(Cambridgeshire)
Litlington.—5B 19
(East Sussex)
Litterty.—3E 163
Little Abington.—3E 55
Little Addington.—5G 65
Little Airmyn.—3H 95
Little Alne.—1F 51
Little Ardo.—5F 163
Little Asby.—4H 105
Little Aston.—3C 68
Little Ayton.—3C 108
Little Baddow.—2D 44
Little Badminton.—4G 39
Little Ballinluig.—3G 145
Little Bampton.—4D 114
Little Bardfield.—4F 55
Little Barford.—2A 54
Little Barningham.—2D 80
Little Barrington.—1D 40
Little Barrow.—3G 85
Little Barugh.—2C 102
Little Bavington.—2C 116
Little Bealings.—3E 57
Little Bedwyn.—2A 28
Little Bentley.—5D 56
Little Berkhamsted.—2F 43
Little Billing.—1F 53
Little Billington.—5G 53
Little Birch.—4H 49
Little Bispham.—1A 92
Little Blakenham.—1E 18
Little Blencow.—1F 105
Little Bognor.—3B 18
Little Bolas.—5A 74
Little Bookham.—5C 30
Littleborough.—1G 87
(Manchester)
Littleborough.—4A 90
(Nottinghamshire)
Littlebourne.—5G 33
Little Bourton.—3B 52
Little Bowden.—4E 65
Little Bradley.—2F 55
Little Brampton.—2A 60
Little Brechin.—2E 147
Littlebredy.—5A 14
Little Brickhill.—4G 53
Little Bridgeford.—5C 74
Little Brington.—1D 52
Little Bromley.—5C 56
Little Broughton.—1B 104
Little Budworth.—4H 85
Little Burstead.—1A 32
Little Burton.—1D 96
Littlebury.—4E 55
Littlebury Green.—4D 55
Little Bytham.—1H 65
Little Canfield.—5E 55
Little Canford.—4F 15
Little Carlton.—4F 91
(Lincolnshire)

Little Carlton.—2E 77
(Nottinghamshire)
Little Casterton.—2H 65
Little Catwick.—1D 96
Little Catworth.—5A 66
Little Cawthorpe.—4F 91
Little Chalfont.—1A 30
Little Chart.—1D 20
Little Chesterford.—3E 55
Little Cheverell.—3E 27
Little Chishill.—4D 54
Little Clacton.—1H 45
Little Clanfield.—2D 40
Little Clifton.—2B 104
Little Clinterty.—2F 155
Little Coates.—5E 97
Little Comberton.—3D 50
Little Common.—5B 20
Little Compton.—4G 51
Little Cornard.—4B 56
Littlecote.—5F 53
Littlecott.—3G 27
Little Coxwell.—3D 40
Little Crakehall.—5F 107
Little Crawley.—3G 53
Little Creich.—5D 166
Little Cressingham.—3A 68
Little Crosby.—2A 86
Little Crosthwaite.—2D 104
Little Cubley.—4F 75
Little Dalby.—1E 65
Little Dawley.—2A 62
Littledean.—1E 39
Little Dens.—4H 163
Little Dewchurch.—4H 49
Little Ditton.—2F 55
Little Down.—3B 28
Little Drayton.—4A 74
Little Driffield.—4F 103
Little Dunham.—4A 80
Little Dunkeld.—4H 145
Little Dunmow.—5F 55
Little Easton.—5F 55
Little Eaton.—3A 76
Little Ellingham.—3C 68
Little Elm.—4C 26
Little End.—2B 44
Little Everdon.—2C 52
Little Eversden.—2C 54
Little Fakenham.—5B 68
Little Faringdon.—2D 40
Little Fencote.—5F 107
Little Fenton.—2F 95
Littleferry.—4F 167
Little Fransham.—4B 80
Little Gaddesden.—1C 42
Little Garway.—5G 49
Little Gidding.—4A 66
Little Glemham.—2F 57
Little Glenshee.—5G 145
Little Gransden.—2B 54
Little Green.—1G 73
Little Grimsby.—3F 91
Little Habton.—2C 102
Little Hadham.—5D 54
Little Hale.—3A 78
Little Hallingbury.—1A 44
Littleham.—3A 22
(nr. Bideford, Devon)
Littleham.—5D 12
(nr. Exmouth, Devon)
Little Hampden.—2B 42
Littlehampton.—5B 18
Little Haresfield.—2G 39
Little Harrowden.—5F 65
Little Haseley.—2H 41
Little Hatfield.—1D 96
Little Hautbois.—3E 81
Little Haven.—3B 34
Little Hay.—2F 63
Little Hayfield.—4H 87
Little Haywood.—5E 75
Little Heath.—4H 63
Little Heck.—3F 95
Littlehempston.—3E 9
Little Hereford.—4C 60

Little Horkesley.—4B 56
Little Hormead.—5D 54
Little Horsted.—4F 19
Little Horton.—2B 94
Little Horwood.—4E 53
Little Houghton.—2F 53
(Northamptonshire)
Little Houghton.—4G 93
(South Yorkshire)
Little Hucklow.—5B 88
Little Hulton.—2E 87
Little Ingestre.—5D 75
Little Irchester.—1G 53
Little Kelk.—3F 103
Little Kimble.—2B 42
Little Kineton.—2H 51
Little Kingshill.—3B 42
Little Langdale.—4E 104
Little Langford.—2F 17
Little Laver.—2B 44
Little Leigh.—5D 86
Little Leighs.—1D 44
Little Leven.—1D 96
Little Lever.—2E 87
Little Linford.—3F 53
Little London.—1H 41
(Buckinghamshire)
Little London.—4G 19
(East Sussex)
Little London.—4B 28
(nr. Andover, Hants.)
Little London.—3E 28
(nr. Basingstoke, Hants.)
Little London.—5D 78
(nr. Long Sutton, Lincs.)
Little London.—5B 78
(Spalding, Lincs.)
Little London.—2E 81
(nr. North Walsham, Norf.)
Little London.—3G 67
(nr. Northwold, Norf.)
Little London.—2D 80
(nr. Saxthorpe, Norf.)
Little London.—3F 67
(nr. Southery, Norf.)
Little London.—2F 59
(Powys)
Little Longstone.—5B 88
Little Malvern.—3B 50
Little Maplestead.—4A 56
Little Marcle.—4A 50
Little Marlow.—4B 42
Little Massingham.—5G 79
Little Melton.—2D 68
Littlemill.—4H 153
(Grampian)
Little Mill.—2B 38
(Gwent)
Littlemill.—3D 160
(Highland)
Littlemill.—3G 123
(Northumberland)
Littlemill.—3D 118
(Strathclyde)
Little Milton.—2H 41
Little Missenden.—1A 30
Littlemoor.—1A 76
(Derbyshire)
Littlemoor.—5B 14
(Dorset)
Littlemore.—2G 41
Little Mountain.—4E 85
Little Musgrave.—3A 106
Little Ness.—4G 73
Little Neston.—3E 85
Little Newcastle.—2C 34
Little Newsham.—3E 107
Little Oakley.—5E 57
(Essex)
Little Oakley.—4F 65
(Northamptonshire)
Little Onn.—1C 62
Little Ormside.—3A 106

Little Orton.—4E 115
(Cumbria)
Little Orton.—2H 63
(Leicestershire)
Little Ouse.—4F 67
Little Ouseburn.—3H 101
Littleover.—4H 75
Little Packington.—4G 63
Little Paxton.—1A 54
Little Petherick.—2D 6
Little Plumpton.—2A 92
Little Plumstead.—4F 81
Little Ponton.—4G 77
Littleport.—4E 67
Little Posbrook.—3D 16
Little Potheridge.—2F 11
Little Preston.—2C 52
Little Raveley.—5B 66
Little Reynoldson.—4A 36
Little Ribston.—4G 101
Little Rissington.—1C 40
Little Rogart.—3E 167
Little Rollright.—4G 51
Little Ryburgh.—3B 80
Little Ryle.—3E 123
Little Ryton.—5G 73
Little Salkeld.—1G 105
Little Sampford.—4F 55
Little Sandhurst.—2C 29
Little Saredon.—2D 62
Little Saxham.—5G 65
Little Scatwell.—3F 159
Little Shelford.—2D 54
Little Shoddesden.—4A 28
Little Singleton.—2A 92
Little Smeaton.—4F 95
Little Snoring.—2B 80
Little Sodbury.—4F 39
Little Somborne.—5B 28
Little Somerford.—4A 40
Little Soudley.—5B 74
Little Sowarne.—2A 50
Little Stainforth.—3B 100
Little Stainton.—2G 107
Little Stanney.—3G 85
Little Staughton.—1A 54
Little Steeping.—1D 78
Littlester.—4G 175
Little Stoke.—4D 74
Littlestone-on-Sea.—3E 21
Little Stonham.—1D 56
Little Street.—4E 67
Little Stretton.—2D 64
(Leicestershire)
Little Stretton.—1B 60
(Shropshire)
Little Strickland.—3G 105
Little Stukeley.—5B 66
Little Sugnall.—4C 74
Little Sutton.—3F 85
Little Swinburne.—2C 116
Little Tew.—5A 52
Little Tey.—5A 56
Little Thetford.—5E 67
Little Thirkleby.—2H 101
Little Thornton.—1A 92
Littlethorpe.—3C 64
(Leicestershire)
Littlethorpe.—3G 101
(North Yorkshire)
Little Thorpe.—3B 94
(West Yorkshire)
Little Thurlow.—2F 55
Little Thurrock.—3H 31
Littleton.—4G 85
(Cheshire)
Littleton.—5C 28
(Hampshire)
Littleton.—5E 25
(Somerset)
Littleton.—1A 18
(nr. Guildford, Surrey)
Littleton.—4B 30
(nr. Shepperton, Surrey)
Littleton Drew.—4G 39
Littleton-on-Severn.—3D 39

Littleton Pannell.—3E 27
Little Torboll.—4E 167
Little Torrington.—2E 11
Little Totham.—1E 45
Little Town.—3D 104
(Cumbria)
Littletown.—5G 117
(Durham)
Littletown.—5E 167
(Highland)
Little Town.—2D 92
(Lancashire)
Little Twycross.—2H 63
Little Urswick.—2B 98
Little Wakering.—2D 32
Little Walden.—3E 55
Little Waldingfield.—3B 56
Little Walsingham.—2B 80
Little Waltham.—1D 44
Little Warley.—1H 31
Little Washbourne.—4D 51
Little Weighton.—2B 96
Little Welnetham.—1A 56
Little Wenham.—4C 56
Little Wenlock.—2A 62
Little Whittingham Green.
—5E
Littlewick Green.—5B 42
Little Wilbraham.—2E 55
Littlewindsor.—3H 13
Little Wisbeach.—4A 78
Little Witcombe.—1H 39
Little Witley.—1B 50
Little Wittenham.—3G 41
Little Wolford.—4G 51
Littleworth.—3H 53
(Bedfordshire)
Littleworth.—4F 51
(Gloucestershire)
Littleworth.—1D 51
(nr. Redditch, Here & Worcs)
Littleworth.—2C 50
(nr. Worcester, Here & Worcs)
Littleworth.—3E 40
(Oxfordshire)
Littleworth.—1E 63
(nr. Cannock, Staffs.)
Littleworth.—5B 74
(nr. Eccleshall, Staffs.)
Littleworth.—5D 74
(Stafford, Staffs.)
Littleworth.—3C 18
(West Sussex)
Little Wymington.—1G 53
Little Wymondley.—5B 54
Little Wyrley.—2E 63
Little Yeldham.—4G 55
Littley Green.—1C 44
Litton.—5B 88
(Derbyshire)
Litton.—2C 100
(North Yorkshire)
Litton.—3F 25
(Somerset)
Litton Cheney.—4A 14
Liverpool.—3A 86
Liverpool Airport.—4B 86
Liversedge.—3B 94
Liverton.—3E 109
(Cleveland)
Liverton.—2E 9
(Devon)
Liverton Mines.—3E 109
Livingston.—3D 130
Livingston Village.—3D 130
Lixwm.—3D 84
Lizard.—5E 5
Llaingoch.—2B 82
Llaithddu.—2F 59
Llampha.—5F 37
Llan.—5A 72
Llanaber.—4F 71
Llanaelhaearn.—1C 70
Llanafan.—3B 58
Llanafan-fawr.—2B 48
Llanafan-fechan.—2B 48

Lochore.—4D 138
Lochportain.—1E 172
Lochranza.—4H 127
Lochside.—2G 147
(Grampian)
Lochside.—5A 170
(nr. Achentoul, H'land.)
Lochside.—3C 160
(nr. Nairn, H'land.)
Lochskipport.—5D 172
Lochslin.—5F 167
Lochstack Lodge.—4C 168
Lochton.—4E 155
Lochty.—3H 139
Lochuisge.—3B 142
Lochussie.—3G 159
Lochwinnoch.—4E 129
Lochyside.—1F 143
Lockengate.—3E 7
Lockerbie.—1C 114
Lockeridge.—2G 27
Lockerley.—1A 16
Lockhills.—5G 115
Locking.—3D 24
Lockington.—1B 96
(Humberside)
Lockington.—5B 76
(Leicestershire)
Lockleywood.—5A 74
Locksgreen.—4C 16
Lock's Heath.—3D 16
Lockton.—1D 102
Loddington.—2E 65
(Leicestershire)
Loddington.—5F 65
(Northamptonshire)
Loddiswell.—5D 8
Loddon.—3F 69
Lode.—1E 55
Loders.—4H 13
Lodsworth.—1H 17
Lofthouse.—2E 100
(North Yorkshire)
Lofthouse.—3D 94
(West Yorkshire)
Lofthouse Gate.—3D 94
Loftus.—3E 109
Logan.—2E 119
Loganlea.—3C 130
Logaston.—2F 49
Loggerheads.—4B 74
Loggie.—4F 165
Logie.—1G 139
(Fife)
Logie.—3E 161
(Grampian)
Logie.—2F 147
(Tayside)
Logie Coldstone.—3B 154
Logie Pert.—2F 147
Logierait.—3G 145
Login.—2E 35
Lolworth.—1C 54
Lonbain.—3F 157
Londesborough.—1A 96
London.—2E 31
London Apprentice.—4E 6
London City Airport.—2F 31
London Colney.—2E 43
Londonderry.—1G 101
London (Gatwick) Airport.
—1D 18
London (Heathrow)Airport.
—3B 30
London (Stansted)Airport.
—5E 25
Londonthorpe.—4G 77
Londubh.—5C 164
Lone.—4D 168
Lonemore.—5E 167
(nr. Dornoch, H'land.)
Lonemore.—1G 157
(nr. Gairloch, H'land.)
Long Ashton.—5D 38
Long Bank.—5B 62
Longbar.—4E 129

Long Bennington.—3F 77
Longbenton.—3F 117
Longborough.—5F 51
Long Bredy.—4A 14
Longbridge.—1G 51
(Warwickshire)
Longbridge.—5E 63
(West Midlands)
Longbridge Deverill.—4D 26
Long Buckby.—1D 52
Long Buckby Wharf.—1D 52
Longburgh.—4E 114
Longburton.—2B 14
Long Clawson.—5E 76
Longcliffe.—2G 75
Long Common.—2D 16
Long Compton.—5C 74
(Staffordshire)
Long Compton.—4G 51
(Warwickshire)
Longcot.—3D 40
Long Crendon.—2H 41
Long Crichel.—2E 15
Longcroft.—2A 130
(Central)
Longcroft.—4D 114
(Cumbria)
Longcross.—4A 30
Longdale.—4H 105
Longdales.—5G 115
Longden.—5G 73
Longden Common.—5G 73
Long Ditton.—4C 30
Longdon.—4C 50
(Hereford & Worcester)
Longdon.—1E 63
(Staffordshire)
Longdon Green.—1E 63
Longdon on Tern.—1A 62
Longdown.—4B 12
Longdowns.—3E 5
Long Drax.—3G 95
Long Duckmanton.—5E 89
Long Eaton.—4B 76
Longfield.—4H 31
Longfield Hill.—4H 31
Longford.—4G 75
(Derbyshire)
Longford.—5C 50
(Gloucestershire)
Longford.—3B 30
(London)
Longford.—4A 74
(nr. Market Drayton, Shrops.)
Longford.—1B 62
(nr. Newport, Shrops.)
Longford.—4H 63
(West Midlands)
Longforgan.—1F 139
Longformacus.—4C 132
Longframlington.—4F 123
Long Gardens.—4A 56
Long Green.—3G 85
(Cheshire)
Long Green.—4C 50
(Hereford & Worcester)
Longham.—4F 15
(Dorset)
Longham.—4B 80
(Norfolk)
Long Hanborough.—1F 41
Longhedge.—4D 26
Long Hermiston.—2E 131
Longhill.—3H 163
Longhirst.—1F 117
Longhope.—1E 39
Longhorsley.—5F 123
Longhoughton.—3G 123
Long Itchington.—1B 52
Longlands.—1D 104
Longlane.—5G 41
(Berkshire)
Longlane.—4G 75
(Derbyshire)
Long Lane.—1A 62
(Shropshire)

Long Lawford.—5B 64
Long Lease.—4G 109
Longley Green.—2B 50
Long Load.—1H 13
Longmanhill.—2E 163
Long Marston.—1B 42
(Hertfordshire)
Long Marston.—4A 102
(North Yorkshire)
Long Marston.—3F 51
(Warwickshire)
Long Marton.—2H 105
Long Meadow.—1E 55
Long Meadowend.—2B 60
Long Melford.—3A 56
Longmoor Camp.—5F 29
Longmorn.—3G 161
Longmoss.—5F 87
Long Newnton.—3H 39
Longnewton.—2H 121
(Borders)
Long Newton.—3G 107
(Cleveland)
Longney.—1F 39
Longniddry.—2H 131
Longnor.—5G 73
(Shropshire)
Longnor.—1E 75
(nr. Leek, Staffs.)
Longnor.—1C 62
(nr. Stafford, Staffs.)
Longparish.—4C 28
Longpark.—3F 115
Long Preston.—4B 100
Longridge.—2D 92
(Lancashire)
Longridge.—3C 130
(Lothian)
Longridge.—1D 62
(Staffordshire)
Longriggend.—2B 130
Long Riston.—1D 96
Long Rock.—3C 4
Longsdon.—2D 74
Longshaw.—2C 86
(Manchester)
Longshaw.—3E 75
(Staffordshire)
Longside.—4H 163
Longslow.—4A 74
Longstanton.—1C 54
Longstock.—5B 28
Longstone.—2C 54
Long Stratton.—3D 69
Long Street.—3E 53
(Buckinghamshire)
Longstreet.—3G 27
(Wiltshire)
Long Sutton.—4F 29
(Hampshire)
Long Sutton.—5D 78
(Lincolnshire)
Long Sutton.—1H 13
(Somerset)
Longthorpe.—3A 66
Long Thurlow.—1C 56
Longthwaite.—2F 105
Longton.—3B 92
(Lancashire)
Longton.—3D 74
(Staffordshire)
Long Sutton.—3E 115
(Cumbria)
Longtown.—5F 49
(Hereford & Worcester)
Longville in the Dale.—1C 60
Long Waste.—1A 62
Long Whatton.—5B 76
Longwick.—2A 42
Long Wittenham.—3G 41
Longwitton.—1D 117
Longworth.—3E 41
Longyester.—3B 132
Lonmore.—4B 156
Looe.—4G 7
Loose.—5B 32

Loosegate.—5C 78
Loosley Row.—2B 42
Lootcherbrae.—3D 162
Lopcombe Corner.—5H 27
Lopen.—2H 13
Loppington.—3G 73
Lorbottle.—4E 123
Lorbottle Hall.—4E 123
Lordington.—3F 17
Loscoe.—3B 76
Loscombe.—4H 13
Lossiemouth.—1G 161
Lossit.—4A 126
Lostock Gralam.—5D 87
Lostock Green.—5D 87
Lostock Junction.—2D 86
Lostwithiel.—4F 7
Lothbeg.—2G 167
Lothersdale.—1G 93
Lothianbridge.—3G 131
Lothianburn.—3F 131
Lothmore.—2G 167
Lottisham.—5F 25
Loudwater.—1A 30
Loughborough.—1C 64
Loughor.—3B 36
Loughton.—4F 53
(Buckinghamshire)
Loughton.—1F 31
(Essex)
Loughton.—4A 62
(Shropshire)
Lound.—1H 65
(Lincolnshire)
Lound.—4G 89
(Nottinghamshire)
Lound.—3H 69
(Suffolk)
Lound, The.—5G 105
Lount.—1A 64
Louth.—4F 91
Love Clough.—3F 93
Lovedean.—2E 17
Lover.—1H 15
Loversall.—3F 89
Loves Green.—2C 44
Loveston.—4D 35
Lovington.—5F 25
Low Ackworth.—4E 95
Low Angerton.—1D 117
Low Ardwell.—5F 111
Lowbands.—4B 50
Low Baring.—5E 109
Low Barlings.—5C 90
Low Bell End.—5E 109
Low Bentham.—3F 99
Low Bradfield.—3C 88
Low Bradley.—1H 93
Low Braithwaite.—5F 115
Low Brunton.—2C 116
Low Burnham.—2H 89
Lowca.—2A 104
Low Catton.—4C 102
Low Coniscliffe.—3F 107
Low Coylton.—3D 118
Low Crosby.—4F 115
Low Dalby.—1D 102
Lowdham.—3D 76
Low Dinsdale.—3G 107
Lowe.—2G 73
Low Eggborough.—3F 95
Low Ellington.—1F 101
Lower Amble.—2D 6
Lower Ansty.—3C 14
Lower Arboll.—5F 167
Lower Arncott.—1H 41
Lower Ashton.—1E 9
Lower Assendon.—4A 42
Lower Auchenreath.—2A 162
Lower Badcall.—4B 168
Lower Ballam.—2A 92
Lower Barvas.—2F 173
Lower Basildon.—5H 41
Lower Bayble.—4H 173
Lower Beeding.—3D 18
Lower Benefield.—4G 65

Lower Bentley.—1D 51
Lower Beobridge.—3B 62
Lower Boddington.—2B 52
Lower Bordean.—1E 17
Lower Brailes.—4H 51
Lower Breakish.—1E 149
Lower Broadheath.—2C 50
Lower Brynamman.—1D 36
Lower Bullingham.—4H 49
Lower Bullington.—4C 28
Lower Burgate.—2G 15
Lower Cam.—2F 39
Lower Catesby.—2C 52
Lower Chapel.—4C 48
Lower Chicksgrove.—5E 27
Lower Chute.—3B 28
Lower Clopton.—2F 51
Lower Crossings.—4H 87
Lower Cumberworth.—2C 88
Lower Darwen.—3D 93
Lower Dean.—1H 53
Lower Diabaig.—2G 157
Lower Dicker.—4G 19
Lower Dounreay.—2B 170
Lower Down.—2A 60
Lower Drift.—4B 4
Lower Dunsforth.—3H 101
Lower East Carleton.—2D 69
Lower Egleton.—3A 50
Lower Ellastone.—3F 75
Lower Elsted.—1G 17
Lower End.—1F 53
Lower Everleigh.—3G 27
Lower Failand.—5D 38
Lower Faintree.—4A 62
Lower Farringdon.—5F 29
Lower Foxdale.—4B 110
Lower Froyle.—4F 29
Lower Gabwell.—3F 9
Lower Gledfield.—4C 166
Lower Godney.—4E 25
Lower Gravenhurst.—4A 54
Lower Green.—4D 54
(Essex)
Lower Green.—2B 80
(Norfolk)
Lower Green.—2D 62
(Staffordshire)
Lower Halstow.—4C 32
Lower Hardres.—5F 33
Lower Hardwick.—2G 49
Lower Hartshay.—2A 76
Lower Hawthwaite.—1B 98
Lower Hayton.—2C 60
Lower Hergest.—2E 49
Lower Heyford.—5B 52
Lower Heysham.—3D 98
Lower Higham.—3B 32
Lower Holbrook.—4D 57
Lower Hordley.—3F 73
Lower Horncroft.—4B 18
Lower Horsebridge.—4G 19
Lower Kilcott.—4F 39
Lower Killeyan.—5A 126
Lower Kingcombe.—4A 14
Lower Kingswood.—5D 30
Lower Kinnerton.—4F 85
Lower Langford.—2E 25
Lower Largo.—3G 139
Lower Layham.—3C 56
Lower Ledwyche.—3C 60
Lower Leigh.—4E 75
Lower Lemington.—4G 51
Lower Lenie.—1H 151
Lower Ley.—1F 39
Lower Llanfadog.—4E 59
Lower Lode.—4C 50
Lower Loxhore.—2C 22
Lower Loxley.—4E 75
Lower Lydbrook.—1D 39
Lower Lye.—4B 60
Lower Machen.—4A 38
Lower Maes-coed.—4F 49
Lower Meend.—2D 38
Lower Milovaig.—3A 156
Lower Moor.—3D 51

Lower Morton.—3E 39
Lower Mountain.—5F 85
Lower Nash.—4D 34
Lower Nazeing.—2G 43
Lower Nyland.—1C 14
Lower Oakfield.—4D 138
Lower Ollach.—5E 157
Lower Penarth.—5H 37
Lower Penn.—3C 62
Lower Pennington.—4B 16
Lower Peover.—5E 87
Lower Pitkerrie.—1C 160
Lower Place.—1G 87
Lower Quinton.—3F 51
Lower Rainham.—4C 32
Lower Raydon.—4C 56
Lower Seagry.—4A 40
Lower Shelton.—3G 53
Lower Shiplake.—5A 42
Lower Shuckburgh.—1B 52
Lower Sketty.—3C 36
Lower Slaughter.—5F 51
Lower Soudley.—1E 39
Lower Stanton St Quintin.
—4H
Lower Stoke.—3C 32
Lower Stonnall.—2E 63
Lower Stow Bedon.—3B 68
Lower Street.—2E 81
Lower Strensham.—3D 50
Lower Sundon.—5H 53
Lower Swanwick.—3C 16
Lower Swell.—5F 51
Lower Tale.—3D 12
Lower Tean.—4E 75
Lower Thurlton.—3G 69
Lower Thurvaston.—4G 75
Lowertown.—4D 4
(Cornwall)
Lower Town.—2D 8
(Devon)
Lower Town.—1C 34
(Dyfed)
Lower Town.—3A 50
(Hereford & Worcester)
Lower Town.—1B 4
(Isles of Scilly)
Lower Tysoe.—3H 51
Lower Upham.—2D 16
Lower Upnor.—3B 32
Lower Vexford.—5B 24
Lower Walton.—4D 86
Lower Wear.—5C 12
Lower Weare.—3E 25
Lower Welson.—2E 49
Lower Whatcombe.—3D 14
Lower Whitley.—5D 86
Lower Wield.—4E 29
Lower Winchendon.—1A 42
Lower Woodend.—4B 42
Lower Woodford.—5G 27
Lower Wych.—1G 73
Lower Wyche.—3B 50
Lower Yelland.—2A 22
Lowesby.—2E 64
Lowestoft.—3H 69
Loweswater.—2C 104
Low Etherley.—2E 107
Lowfield Heath.—1D 18
Lowford.—2C 16
Low Fulney.—5B 78
Low Gate.—3C 116
Lowgill.—5H 105
(Cumbria)
Lowgill.—3F 99
(Lancashire)
Low Grantley.—2C 101
Low Green.—4F 101
Low Habberley.—5C 62
Low Ham.—1H 13
Low Hameringham.—1C 78
Low Hawsker.—4G 109
Low Hesket.—5F 115
Low Hesleyhurst.—5E 123
Low Hutton.—3C 102

222 G.B. Handy

thyr Vale.—3G 37
ton.—2F 11
evon)
ton.—4D 30
ondon)
ton.—3B 68
orfolk)
ton.—1G 41
xfordshire)
shaw.—2A 12
sing.—1E 45
singham.—5A 96
combe.—4D 12
field.—4E 69
herell.—3A 8
heringham.—1H 77
hill.—4F 139
hill.—1F 139
hley.—3D 94
hley Junction.—3D 94
hick.—5F 163
hven.—1C 138
hwold.—3G 67
hwold Hythe.—3G 67
tingham.—4F 69
ton.—2E 81
ragissey.—2H 5
borough.—2E 89
v.—1E 171
ysey Hampton.—3C 40
l.—1G 157
vaig.—4C 173
hael.—2C 110
haelchurch.—5H 49
haelchurch Escley.—4F 49
haelchurch-on-Arrow.
　　　　　—2E 49
haelston-le-Pit.—5H 37
haelston-y-Vedw.—4A 38
haelstow.—2E 7
helcombe.—3C 8
heldever.—5D 28
helmersh.—1B 16
kfield.—1D 56
klebring.—3F 89
kleby.—3F 109
klefield Green.—1B 30
kleham.—5C 30
kleover.—4H 75
klethwaite.—4D 114
umbria)
klethwaite.—1B 94
West Yorkshire)
kleton.—2C 16
kirham)
kleton.—3F 51
loucestershire)
kletown.—3D 94
kle Trafford.—4G 85
kley.—2F 101
kley Green.—2A 56
kley Square.—3D 117
Arlaw.—2G 163
bea.—3D 174
Beltie.—3D 154
Calder.—3D 131
Clyth.—5E 171
dle Ascendon.—4A 42
dle Aston.—3D 40
dle Barton.—5B 52
dlebie.—2D 114
dle Chinnock.—2H 13
dle Claydon.—5E 52
dlecliff.—2E 89
dlecot.—1D 8
dle Drums.—3E 147
dle Essie.—3H 163
dleham.—1E 101
dle Handley.—5B 68
dle Harling.—4B 68
dlehope.—2B 60
dle Littleton.—3E 51
dle Maes-coed.—4F 49
dlemarsh.—3B 14
dle Marwood.—2B 22

Middle Mayfield.—3F 75
Middlemuir.—4F 163
(nr. New Deer, Grampian)
Middlemuir.—3G 163
(nr. Strichen, Grampian)
Middlequarter.—1D 172
Middle Rainton.—5G 117
Middle Rasen.—4C 90
Middlesbrough.—3B 108
Middlesceugh.—5E 115
Middleshaw.—1E 99
Middlesmoor.—2D 100
Middles, The.—5H 117
Middlestone.—1F 107
Middlestone Moor.—1F 107
Middle Stoughton.—4E 25
Middlestown.—4C 94
Middle Street.—2F 39
Middle Taphouse.—3F 7
Middleton.—1C 108
(Cleveland)
Middleton.—1F 99
(Cumbria)
Middleton.—1F 75
(nr. Bakewell, Derbys.)
Middleton.—2G 75
(nr. Wirksworth, Derbys)
Middleton.—4A 56
(Essex)
Middleton.—4C 28
(Hampshire)
Middleton.—4C 60
(Hereford & Worcester)
Middleton.—5B 16
(Isle of Wight)
Middleton.—4D 98
(Lancashire)
Middleton.—4G 131
(Lothian)
Middleton.—2F 87
(Manchester)
Middleton.—1F 67
(Norfolk)
Middleton.—3F 65
(Northamptonshire)
Middleton.—1F 123
(nr. Belford, Northmb.)
Middleton.—1D 116
(nr. Morpeth, Northmb.)
Middleton.—1C 102
(North Yorkshire)
Middleton.—3C 60
(nr. Ludlow, Shrops.)
Middleton.—3F 73
(nr. Oswestry, Shrops.)
Middleton.—4A 140
(Strathclyde)
Middleton.—1G 57
(Suffolk)
Middleton.—3D 138
(nr. Kinross, Tayside)
Middleton.—4E 147
(nr. Letham, Tayside)
Middleton.—3F 63
(Warwickshire)
Middleton.—4A 36
(West Glamorgan)
Middleton.—1B 94
(nr. Ilkley, W, Yorks.)
Middleton.—3D 94
(nr. Leeds, W Yorks.)
Middleton Cheney.—3C 52
Middleton Green.—4D 75
Middleton Hall.—4G 131
(Lothian)
Middleton Hall.—2D 123
(Northumberland)
Middleton in Teesdale.—2C 106
Middleton One Row.—3G 107
Middleton-on-Leven.—4B 108
Middleton-on-Sea.—3H 17
Middleton-on-the.—4C 60
Middleton-on-the Hill.—4C 60
Middleton-on-the-Wolds.
　　　　　—1B 96
Middleton Priors.—3A 62

Middleton Quernhow.—2G 101
Middleton St George.—3G 107
Middleton Scriven.—4A 62
Middleton Stoney.—5C 52
Middleton Tyas.—4F 107
Middletown.—4A 104
(Cumbria)
Middle Town.—1B 4
(Isles of Scilly)
Middletown.—4F 73
(Powys)
Middle Tysoe.—3H 51
Middle Wallop.—5A 28
Middlewich.—1B 74
Middle Winterslow.—5H 27
Middlewood.—2G 7
(Cornwall)
Middlewood.—3D 88
(South Yorkshire)
Middle Woodford.—5G 27
Middlewood Green.—1C 56
Middleyard.—2G 39
Middlezoy.—5D 24
Middridge.—2F 107
Midfield.—2F 169
Midford.—2C 26
Midge Hall.—3C 92
Midgeholm.—4H 115
Midgham.—2D 28
Midgley.—3H 93
(nr. Halifax, W Yorks.)
Midgley.—4C 94
(nr. Horbury, W Yorks.)
Midhopestones.—3C 88
Midhurst.—1G 17
Mid Kirkton.—4C 128
Mid Lambrook.—2H 13
Midland.—7C 174
Mid Lavant.—3G 17
Midlem.—2H 121
Midney.—1H 13
Mid Sannox.—5B 128
Midsomer Norton.—3B 26
Mid Thundergay.—5G 127
Midton.—2D 128
Midtown.—5C 164
(nr. Poolewe, H'land.)
Midtown.—2F 169
(nr. Tongue, H'land.)
Midville.—2C 78
Midway.—5H 75
Mid Yell.—2G 175
Migdale.—4D 166
Migvie.—3B 154
Milarrochy.—4B 130
Milber.—4B 80
Milborne Port.—2B 14
Milborne St Andrew.—4D 14
Milborne Wick.—1B 14
Milbourne.—2E 117
(Northumberland)
Milbourne.—4H 39
(Wiltshire)
Milburn.—2H 105
Milbury Heath.—3E 39
Milby.—3H 101
Milcombe.—4B 52
Milden.—3B 56
Mildenhall.—5G 67
(Suffolk)
Mildenhall.—2H 27
(Wiltshire)
Milebrook.—3A 60
Milebush.—1B 20
Mile End.—4F 67
(Cambridgeshire)
Mile End.—5B 56
(Essex)
Mileham.—4B 80
Mile Oak.—5D 18
Miles Green.—5C 74
Miles Hope.—4C 60
Milesmark.—5C 138
Mile Town.—3D 32
Milfield.—1D 122
Milford.—3A 76
(Derbyshire)

Milford.—1C 10
(Devon)
Milford.—1F 59
(Powys)
Milford.—5D 74
(Staffordshire)
Milford.—1A 18
(Surrey)
Milford Haven.—4C 34
Milford on Sea.—4A 16
Milkwall.—2D 39
Milkwell.—1E 15
Milland.—1G 17
Milland Marsh.—1G 17
Millbank.—2D 170
(Highland)
Mill Bank.—3H 93
(West Yorkshire)
Millbeck.—2D 104
Millbounds.—4E 174
Millbreck.—4H 163
Millbridge.—4G 29
Millbrook.—4H 53
(Bedfordshire)
Millbrook.—4A 8
(Cornwall)
Millbrook.—2B 16
(Hampshire)
Millbrook.—3C 87
(Manchester)
Mill Common.—4G 69
Mill Corner.—3C 20
Mildale.—2F 75
Millden Lodge.—1E 147
Milldens.—3E 147
Millearn.—2B 138
Mill End.—4A 42
(Buckinghamshire)
Mill End.—2F 55
(Cambridgeshire)
Millend.—3F 39
(nr. Dursley, Glos.)
Mill End.—1C 40
(nr. Northleach, Glos.)
Mill End.—4C 54
(Hertfordshire)
Millerhill.—3G 131
Miller's Dale.—5B 88
Millers Green.—2G 75
Millerston.—3H 129
Millfield.—2A 66
(Cambridgeshire)
Millfield.—4B 154
(Grampian)
Millgate.—1F 87
Mill Green.—2C 44
(Essex)
Mill Green.—4D 68
(Norfolk)
Mill Green.—5A 74
(Shropshire)
Mill Green.—5E 75
(Staffordshire)
Mill Green.—3E 57
(Suffolk)
Millhalf.—3E 49
Millhall.—4G 129
Millhayes.—3F 13
(nr. Honiton, Devon)
Millhayes.—2E 13
(nr. Wellington, Devon)
Millhead.—2D 99
Millheugh.—4A 130
Mill Hill.—3D 92
(Lancashire)
Mill Hill.—1D 30
(London)
Millholme.—5G 105
Millhouse.—2A 128
Millhousebridge.—1C 114
Millhouses.—4D 88
Millikenpark.—3F 129
Millington.—4D 102
Millington Green.—3G 75
Mill Knowe.—3B 124
Mill Lane.—3F 29

Millmeece.—4C 74
Mill of Craigievar.—2C 154
Mill of Fintray.—2F 155
Mill of Haldane.—1F 129
Millom.—1A 98
Millow.—3B 54
Mill Place.—5B 96
Millpool.—2F 7
Millport.—4C 128
Mill Side.—1D 98
Mill Street.—4C 80
(nr. Lyng, Norf.)
Mill Street.—4C 80
(nr. Swanton Morley, Norf.)
Mill Street.—5C 68
(Suffolk)
Millthorpe.—5D 88
(Derbyshire)
Millthorpe.—4A 78
(Lincolnshire)
Millthrop.—5H 105
Milltimber.—3F 155
Milltown.—4F 7
(Cornwall)
Milltown.—1A 76
(Derbyshire)
Milltown.—2B 22
(Devon)
Milltown.—2E 115
(Dumfries & Galloway)
Milltown.—3G 153
(nr. Corgarff, Grampian)
Milltown.—4C 162
(nr. Huntly, Grampian)
Milltown.—3B 154
(nr. Lumsden, Grampian)
Milltown.—3F 159
(Highland)
Milltown of Aberdalgie.—1C 138
Milltown of Auchindoun.
　　　　　—4A 162
Milltown of Campfield.—3D 154
Milltown of Edinvillie.—4G 161
Milltown of Towie.—2B 154
Milnacraig.—3B 146
Milnathort.—3D 138
Milngavie.—2G 129
Milnholm.—1A 130
Milnrow.—1G 87
Milnthorpe.—1D 99
(Cumbria)
Milnthorpe.—4D 94
(West Yorkshire)
Milson.—5A 62
Milstead.—5D 32
Milston.—4G 27
Milthorpe.—3C 52
Milton.—2D 24
(Avon)
Milton.—1D 55
(Cambridgeshire)
Milton.—3E 137
(nr. Aberfoyle, Central)
Milton.—4D 136
(nr. Drymen, Central)
Milton.—3G 115
(Cumbria)
Milton.—5H 75
(Derbyshire)
Milton.—2F 113
(nr. Crocketford, Dum & Gall.)
Milton.—1F 113
(nr. Dunscore, Dum & Gall.)
Milton.—4H 111
(nr. Glenluce, Dum & Gall.)
Milton.—4D 34
(Dyfed)
Milton.—2C 162
(nr. Cullen, Grampian)
Milton.—2F 153
(nr. Tomintoul, Grampian)
Milton.—3E 17
(Hampshire)
Milton.—4G 157
(nr. Applecross, H'land.)

Milton.—5G 159
(nr. Drumnadrochit, H'land.)
Milton.—1B 160
(nr. Invergordon, H'land.)
Milton.—4H 159
(nr. Inverness, H'land.)
Milton.—3F 171
(nr. Wick, H'land.)
Milton.—5H 89
(Nottinghamshire)
Milton.—4B 52
(nr. Banbury, Oxon.)
Milton.—3F 41
(nr. Didcot, Oxon.)
Milton.—1H 13
(Somerset)
Milton.—2D 74
(Staffordshire)
Milton.—2D 118
(nr. Ayr, S'clyde.)
Milton.—2F 129
(nr. Dumbarton, S'clyde.)
Milton.—3G 129
(Glasgow, S'clyde.)
Milton.—3A 146
(nr. Blairgowrie, Tayside)
Milton.—4C 146
(nr. Dundee, Tayside)
Milton.—6C 172
(Western Isles)
Milton Abbas.—3D 14
Milton Abbot.—2A 8
Milton Auchlossan.—3C 154
Milton Bridge.—3F 131
Milton Bryan.—4G 53
Milton Clevedon.—5B 26
Milton Coldwells.—5G 163
Milton Combe.—3A 8
Milton Damerel.—2D 11
Miltonduff.—2F 161
Milton End.—2C 40
Milton Ernest.—2H 53
Milton Green.—5G 85
Milton Hill.—2F 9
(Devon)
Milton Hill.—3F 41
(Oxfordshire)
Milton Keynes.—3F 53
Milton Keynes Village.—4F 53
Milton Lilbourne.—2C 27
Milton Malsor.—2E 53
Milton Morenish.—5D 144
Milton of Auchinhove.—3C 154
Milton of Balgonie.—3F 139
Milton of Campsie.—2H 129
Milton of Cultoquhey.—1A 138
Milton of Cushnie.—2C 154
Milton of Finavon.—3D 147
Milton of Gollanfield.—3B 160
Milton of Lesmore.—1B 154
Milton of Tullich.—4A 154
Milton on Stour.—1C 14
Milton Regis.—4C 32
Milton Street.—5G 19
Milton-under-Wychwood.
　　　　　—1D 40
Milverton.—1E 12
(Somerset)
Milverton.—1H 51
(Warwickshire)
Milwich.—4D 74
Mimbridge.—4A 30
Minard.—4G 135
Minchington.—2E 15
Minchinhampton.—2G 39
Mindrum.—1C 122
Minehead.—1F 23
Minera.—5E 85
Minety.—3B 40
Minffordd.—2E 71
Mingarry.—2G 141
Mingarrypark.—2A 142
Mingary.—6C 172
Miningsby.—1C 78
Minions.—2G 7
Minishant.—3C 118

Minllyn.—4A 72
Minnigaff.—3B 112
Minorca.—3D 110
Minskip.—3G 101
Minstead.—2A 16
Minsted.—1G 17
Minster.—4H 33
(nr. Ramsgate, Kent)
Minster.—3D 32
(nr. Sheerness, Kent)
Minsteracres.—4D 116
Minsterley.—5F 73
Minster Lovell.—1E 40
Minsterworth.—1F 39
Minterne Magna.—3B 14
Minterne Parva.—3B 14
Minting.—5D 91
Mintlaw.—1H 163
Minto.—2H 121
Minton.—1B 60
Minwear.—3D 34
Minworth.—3F 63
Mirehouse.—3A 104
Mireland.—2F 171
Mirfield.—4C 94
Miserden.—2H 39
Miskin.—4G 37
Misson.—3G 89
Misterton.—4C 64
(Leicestershire)
Misterton.—3H 89
(Nottinghamshire)
Misterton.—3H 13
(Somerset)
Mistley.—4D 56
Mistley Heath.—4D 56
Mitcham.—4D 32
Mitcheldean.—1E 39
Mitchell.—4C 6
(Devon)
Mitchel Troy.—1C 38
Mitcheltroy Common.—2C 38
Mitford.—1E 117
Mithian.—4B 6
Mitton.—1C 62
Mitton of Barras.—1H 147
Mixbury.—4D 52
Mixenden.—3A 94
Mixon.—2E 75
Moat.—2F 115
Moats Tye.—2C 56
Mobberley.—5E 87
(Cheshire)
Mobberley.—3E 75
(Staffordshire)
Moccas.—3F 49
Mochdre.—3H 83
(Clwyd)
Mochdre.—2F 59
(Powys)
Mochrum.—5A 112
Mockbeggar.—3G 15
Mockerkin.—2B 104
Modbury.—4C 8
Moddershall.—4F 75
Modsarie.—2G 169
Moelfre.—3D 72
(Clwyd)
Moelfre.—2E 83
(Gwynedd)
Moffat.—4C 120
Mogerhanger.—3A 54
Mogworthy.—2B 12
Moira.—1H 63
Molash.—5E 33
Mol-chalch.—2C 148
Mold.—4E 85
Molehill Green.—5E 55
Molescroft.—1C 96
Molesden.—1E 117
Molesworth.—5H 65
Moll.—5E 157
Molland.—3E 23
Mollington.—3F 85
(Cheshire)
Mollington.—3B 52
(Oxfordshire)

Mollinsburn.—2A 130
Monachty.—1E 47
Monachylemore.—2D 137
Monar Lodge.—4E 158
Monaughty.—4H 59
Monewden.—2E 57
Moneydie.—1C 138
Moneyrow Green.—5B 42
Moniaive.—5G 119
Monifieth.—5D 147
Monikie.—5D 147
Monimail.—2E 139
Monington.—3A 46
Monk Bretton.—2D 88
Monken Hadley.—1D 30
Monk Fryston.—3F 95
Monk Hesleden.—1B 108
Monkhide.—3A 50
Monkhill.—4E 115
Monkhopton.—3A 62
Monkland.—2G 49
Monkleigh.—3A 22
Monknash.—5F 37
Monkokehampton.—3F 11
Monkseaton.—2G 117
Monks Eleigh.—3B 56
Monk's Gate.—3D 18
Monk's Heath.—5F 87
Monkshill.—4E 163
Monksilver.—2G 23
Monks Kirby.—4B 64
Monk Soham.—1E 57
Monk Soham Green.—1E 57
Monks Risborough.—2B 42
Monksthorpe.—1D 78
Monk Street.—5F 55
Monkswood.—2B 38
Monkton.—3E 13
(Devon)
Monkton.—4C 34
(Dyfed)
Monkton.—4G 33
(Kent)
Monkton.—2C 118
(Strathclyde)
Monkton.—3G 117
(Tyne & Wear)
Monkton Combe.—2C 26
Monkton Deverill.—5D 26
Monkton Farleigh.—2D 26
Monkton Heathfield.—1F 13
Monktonhill.—2C 118
Monkton Up Wimborne.—2F 15
Monkton Wyld.—4G 13
Monkwearmouth.—4G 117
Monkwood.—5E 29
Monmarsh.—3H 49
Monmouth.—1D 38
Monnington on Wye.—3F 49
Monorbier Newton.—5D 34
Monorowen.—1C 34
Monreith.—5A 112
Montacute.—2H 13
Montford.—4G 73
Montford Bridge.—4G 73
Montgarrie.—2C 154
Montgarswood.—2E 119
Montgomery.—1H 59
Montgreenan.—5E 129
Montrave.—3F 139
Montrose.—3G 147
Monxton.—4B 28
Monyash.—4F 75
Monymusk.—2D 154
Monzie.—1A 138
Moodiesburn.—2H 129
Moon's Green.—3C 20
Moonzie.—2F 139
Moor Allerton.—2D 94
Moorbath.—4H 13
Moorby.—1B 78
Moorcot.—2F 49
Moor Crichel.—2E 15
Moor Cross.—4C 8
Moordown.—4F 15

Moore.—4C 86
Moorend.—2D 114
(Dumfries & Galloway)
Moorend.—2F 39
(nr. Dursley, Glos.)
Moorend.—1G 39
(nr. Gloucester, Glos.)
Moor End.—2A 96
(Humberside)
Moorends.—4G 95
Moorgate.—3E 89
Moorgreen.—2C 16
(Hampshire)
Moorgreen.—3B 76
(Nottinghamshire)
Moorhaigh.—1C 76
Moorhall.—5D 88
Moorhampton.—3F 49
Moorhouse.—4E 115
(nr. Carlisle, Cumbria)
Moorhouse.—4D 114
(nr. Wigton, Cumbria)
Moorhouse.—1E 77
(Nottinghamshire)
Moorhouse.—5F 31
(Surrey)
Moorhouses.—2B 78
Moorland.—5D 24
Moorlinch.—5D 25
Moor Monkton.—4A 102
Moor Nook.—2D 92
Moor of Granary.—3E 161
Moor Row.—3B 104
(nr. Whitehaven, Cumbria)
Moor Row.—5D 114
(nr. Wigton, Cumbria)
Moorsholm.—3D 109
Moorside.—2C 14
(Dorset)
Moorside.—2G 87
(Manchester)
Moor, The.—3B 20
Moortown.—4D 10
(Devon)
Moortown.—3G 15
(Hampshire)
Moortown.—5C 16
(Isle of Wight)
Moortown.—3C 90
(Lincolnshire)
Moortown.—1A 62
(Shropshire)
Moortown.—2C 94
(West Yorkshire)
Morangie.—5E 167
Morar.—4E 149
Morborne.—3A 66
Morchard Bishop.—3A 12
Morcombelake.—4G 13
Morcott.—2G 65
Morda.—3E 73
Morden.—4E 15
(Dorset)
Morden.—4D 30
(London)
Mordiford.—4H 49
Mordon.—2C 107
More.—1A 60
Morebath.—3F 23
Morebattle.—2B 122
Morecambe.—3D 98
Morefield.—4F 165
Morehouse, The.—1C 60
Moreleigh.—4D 8
Morenish.—5C 144
Moresby.—2A 104
Moresby Parks.—3A 104
Morestead.—1D 16
Moreton.—5C 14
(Dorset)
Moreton.—2B 44
(Essex)
Moreton.—4C 60
(Hereford & Worcester)

Moreton.—1E 85
(Merseyside)
Moreton.—2H 41
(Oxfordshire)
Moreton.—1B 62
(Staffordshire)
Moreton Corbet.—3H 73
Moretonhampstead.—1D 8
Moreton-in-Marsh.—4G 51
Moreton Jeffries.—3A 50
Moreton Mill.—3H 73
Moreton Morrell.—2H 51
Moreton on Lugg.—3H 49
Moreton Pinkney.—3C 52
Moreton Say.—4A 74
Moreton Valence.—2F 39
Morfa.—2C 46
Morfa Bach.—3G 35
Morfa Bychan.—2E 71
Morfa Glas.—2E 37
Morfa Nefyn.—1B 70
Morganstown.—4H 37
Morgan's Vale.—1G 15
Morham.—2B 132
Moriah.—3B 58
Morland.—2G 105
Morley.—4F 87
(Cheshire)
Morley.—3A 76
(Derbyshire)
Morley.—2E 107
(Durham)
Morley.—3C 94
(West Yorkshire)
Morley St Botolph.—3C 68
Morningside.—2F 131
(Lothian)
Morningside.—4B 130
(Strathclyde)
Morningthorpe.—3E 69
Morpeth.—1F 117
Morrey.—1F 63
Morridge Side.—2E 75
Morridge Top.—1E 75
Morrington.—1F 113
Morris Green.—4G 55
Morriston.—3C 36
Morston.—1C 80
Mortehoe.—1A 22
Morthen.—4E 89
Mortimer Common.—2E 29
Mortimer's Cross.—4B 60
Mortimer West End.—2E 29
Mortomley.—3D 88
Morton.—3E 39
(Avon)
Morton.—1F 105
(nr. Calthwaite, Cumbria)
Morton.—4E 115
(Carlisle, Cumbria)
Morton.—1B 76
(Derbyshire)
Morton.—5H 77
(nr. Bourne, Lincs.)
Morton.—3A 90
(Gainsborough, Lincs.)
Morton.—1F 77
(nr. Lincoln, Lincs.)
Morton.—4D 80
(Norfolk)
Morton.—2E 77
(Nottinghamshire)
Morton.—3E 73
(Shropshire)
Morton Bagot.—1F 51
Morton-on-Swale.—5G 107
Morton Tinmouth.—2E 107
Morvah.—3B 4
Morval.—4G 7
Morvich.—3E 167
(nr. Golspie, H'land.)
Morvich.—1B 150
(nr. Shiel Bridge, H'land.)
Morvil.—1D 34
Morville.—3A 62
Morwenstow.—2C 10

Morwick Hall.—4G 123
Mosbrough.—4H 87
Moscow.—5F 129
Mose.—2A 62
Mosedale.—1E 105
Moseley.—2C 50
(Hereford & Worcester)
Moseley.—4E 63
(Birmingham, W Midlands)
Moseley.—2D 62
(nr. Wolverhampton,
W. Midlands)
Moss.—5F 85
(Clwyd)
Moss.—2A 142
(Highland)
Moss.—4F 95
(South Yorkshire)
Moss.—4A 140
(Strathclyde)
Mossat.—2B 154
Moss Bank.—3C 86
(Merseyside)
Mossbank.—4F 175
(Shetland)
Mossbrow.—4E 87
Mossburnford.—3A 122
Mossdale.—2D 112
Mossedge.—3F 236
Mossend.—3A 130
Mossgate.—4D 74
Moss Lane.—5C 87
Mossley.—1C 74
(Cheshire)
Mossley.—2G 87
(Manchester)
Mossley Hill.—4A 86
Moss of Barmuckity.—2G 161
Mosspark.—3G 129
Mosspaul.—5G 121
Moss Side.—4C 114
(Cumbria)
Moss-side.—3G 163
(Grampian)
Moss-side.—3C 160
(Highland)
Moss Side.—2A 92
(Lancashire)
Moss Side.—3F 87
(Manchester)
Moss Side.—2A 86
(Merseyside)
Mosstodloch.—3H 161
Mosswood.—4D 116
Mossy Lea.—1C 86
Mosterton.—3H 13
Moston.—3H 73
Moston Green.—1B 74
Mostyn.—2D 84
Motcombe.—1D 14
Mothecombe.—5C 8
Motherby.—2F 105
Motherwell.—4A 130
Mottingham.—3F 31
Mottisfont.—1B 16
Mottistone.—5C 16
Mottram in Longdendale.
—3G 87
Mottram St Andrew.—5F 87
Mott's Mill.—2G 19
Mouldsworth.—3H 85
Moulin.—3G 145
Moulsecombe.—5E 19
Moulsford.—4G 41
Moulsoe.—3G 53
Moulton.—1A 74
(Cheshire)
Moulton.—5C 78
(Lincolnshire)
Moulton.—1E 53
(Northamptonshire)
Moulton.—4F 107
(North Yorkshire)
Moulton.—5H 37
(South Glamorgan)
Moulton.—1F 55
(Suffolk)

Moulton Chapel.—1B 66
Moulton Eaugate.—1B 66
Moulton St Mary.—2F 69
Moulton Seas End.—5C 78
Mount.—3F 7
(nr. Bodmin, Corn.)
Mount.—4B 6
(nr. Newquay, Corn.)
Mountain Ash.—3G 37
Mountain Cross.—5E 131
Mountain Water.—2C 34
Mount Ambrose.—2E 5
Mountbenger.—2F 121
Mountblairy.—3D 162
Mountblow.—2F 129
Mount Bures.—4B 56
Mountfield.—3B 20
Mountgerald.—2H 159
Mount Hawke.—2E 5
Mount High.—2A 160
Mountjoy.—3C 6
Mount Lothian.—4F 131
Mountnessing.—1H 31
Mounton.—3D 38
Mount Pleasant.—4D 52
(Buckinghamshire)
Mount Pleasant.—2C 74
(Cheshire)
Mount Pleasant.—3H 75
(Derbyshire)
Mount Pleasant.—4F 19
(East Sussex)
Mount Pleasant.—2E 139
(Fife)
Mount Pleasant.—4A 16
(Hampshire)
Mount Pleasant.—3B 68
(Norfolk)
Mountsorrel.—1C 64
Mountstuart.—4C 128
Mousehole.—4B 4
Mouswald.—2B 114
Mow Cop.—2C 74
Mowden.—3F 107
Mowhaugh.—2C 122
Mowmacre Hill.—2C 64
Mowsley.—4D 64
Moy.—5B 160
Moylgrove.—3A 46
Moy Lodge.—5G 151
Muasdale.—5E 127
Muchalls.—4F 155
Much Birch.—4H 49
Much Cowarne.—3A 50
Much Dewchurch.—4G 49
Muchelney.—1H 13
Muchelney Ham.—1H 13
Much Hadham.—1H 43
Much Hoole.—3B 92
Muchlarnick.—4G 7
Much Marcle.—4A 50
Muchrachd.—5E 159
Much Wenlock.—3A 62
Mucking.—2A 32
Muckingford.—3A 32
Muckleford.—4B 14
Mucklestone.—4B 74
Muckleton.—2A 80
(Norfolk)
Muckleton.—3H 73
(Shropshire)
Muckley.—3A 62
Muckley Corner.—2E 63
Muckton.—4F 91
Mudale.—5F 169
Muddiford.—2B 22
Mudeford.—4G 15
Mudford.—2A 14
Mudgley.—4E 25
Mugdock.—2G 129
Mugeary.—5D 152
Mugginton.—3G 75
Muggintonlane End.—3G 75
Muggleswick.—5D 116
Mugswell.—5D 30
Muie.—3D 166

uirden.—3E 162
uirdrum.—5E 147
uiredge.—1E 139
uirend.—4G 129
uirhead.—3E 139
(Fife)
uirhead.—3H 129
(Strathclyde)
uirhead.—5C 146
(Tayside)
uirhouses.—1D 130
uirkirk.—2F 119
uir of Alford.—2C 154
uir of Fairburn.—3G 159
uir of Fowlis.—2C 154
uir of Ord.—3H 159
uir of Tarradale.—3H 159
uirtack.—5G 163
uirton.—2B 160
(Highland)
uirton.—1D 138
(Tayside)
uirton of Ardblair.—4A 146
uuker.—5C 106
ulbarton.—2D 69
ulben.—3A 162
ulcliff.—1B 22
ullacott.—1B 22
ullion.—5D 5
umbles, The.—4C 36
umby.—5H 91
underfield Row.—2A 50
underfield Stocks.—2A 50
undesley.—2F 81
undford.—3A 68
undham.—3F 69
undon.—2E 45
unerigie.—3E 151
uness.—1H 175
ungasdale.—4D 164
ungrisdale.—1E 105
unlochy.—3A 160
unsley.—3A 50
unslow.—2C 60
urchington.—1C 8
urcot.—3E 51
urcott.—1G 41
urieston.—3D 130
urkle.—2D 170
urlaggan.—4C 150
urra.—7B 174
urrayfield.—2F 131
urray, The.—4H 129
urrell Green.—3F 29
urroes.—5D 146
urrow.—2C 66
ursley.—5F 53
urthly.—5H 145
urton.—2A 106
(Cumbria)
urton.—5G 117
(Durham)
urton.—5F 133
(Northumberland)
urton.—4B 102
(North Yorkshire)
urton.—4B 36
(West Glamorgan)
usbury.—4F 13
uscoates.—1B 102
uscott.—1D 52
usselburgh.—2G 131
uston.—4F 77
(Leicestershire)
uston.—2F 103
(North Yorkshire)
ustow Green.—5C 62
uswell Hill.—2D 31
utford.—4G 69
uthill.—2A 138
uttershaw.—3D 12
uxton.—1B 62

Mybster.—3D 170
Myddfai.—4G 47
Myddle.—3G 73
Mydroilyn.—2D 46
Mylor Bridge.—3F 5
Mynachlog-ddu.—1A 46
Mynydd-bach.—3C 38
Mynydd Isa.—4E 85
Mynyddislwyn.—3H 37
Mynydd-y-Briw.—3D 72
Mynyddygarreg.—4H 35
Mynytho.—2C 70
Myrebird.—4E 155
Myrelandhorn.—3E 171
Mytchett.—3G 29
Mythe, The.—4C 50
Mytholmroyd.—3H 93
Myton-on-Swale.—3H 101
Mytton.—4G 73

Naast.—5C 164
Naburn.—5A 102
Nackington.—2B 138
Nacton.—3E 57
Nadford.—2E 13
Nafferton.—4F 103
Nailbridge.—1E 39
Nailsbourne.—1F 13
Nailsea.—5C 38
Nailstone.—2B 64
Nailsworth.—3G 39
Nairn.—3C 160
Naisberry.—1B 108
Nalderswood.—1D 18
Nancegollan.—3D 4
Nancledra.—3B 4
Nangreaves.—1F 89
Nannerch.—4D 84
Nanpantan.—1C 64
Nanpean.—4D 6
Nanstallon.—3E 7
Nant-ddu.—1G 37
Nanternis.—2C 46
Nantgaredig.—5D 47
Nantgarw.—4H 37
Nant-glas.—4E 59
Nantglyn.—4C 84
Nantgwyn.—3E 59
Nantlle.—5E 83
Nantmawr.—3E 73
Nantmel.—4F 59
Nantmor.—1F 71
Nant Peris.—5F 83
Nantwich.—2A 74
Nantybai.—3G 47
Nant-y-Derry.—2B 38
Nant-y-dugoed.—4B 72
Nant-y-felin.—3F 83
Nantyffyllon.—3C 37
Nantyglo.—1H 37
Nant-y-meichiaid.—4D 72
Nant-y-moel.—3F 37
Nant-y-Pandy.—3F 83
Naphill.—3B 42
Nappa.—4B 100
Napton on the Hill.—1B 52
Narberth.—3E 35
Narberth Bridge.—3E 35
Narborough.—3C 64
(Leicestershire)
Narborough.—1G 67
(Norfolk)
Narkurs.—4H 7
Narth, The.—2D 38
Narthwaite.—5A 106
Nasareth.—1D 70
Naseby.—5D 64
Nash.—4E 53
(Buckinghamshire)
Nash.—4B 38
(Gwent)
Nash.—4A 60
(Hereford & Worcester)

Nash.—5G 33
(Kent)
Nash.—5A 62
(Shropshire)
Nash Lee.—2B 42
Nassington.—3H 65
Nasty.—5C 54
Natcott.—1C 10
Nateby.—4A 106
(Cumbria)
Nateby.—1B 92
(Lancashire)
Nately Scures.—3E 29
National ExhibitionCentre.
—4F 63
Natland.—1E 99
Naughton.—3C 56
Naunton.—5F 51
(Gloucestershire)
Naunton.—2A 22
(Hereford & Worcester)
Naunton Beauchamp.—2D 50
Navenby.—2C 77
Navestock.—1G 31
Navestock Side.—1G 31
Navidale.—2H 167
Nawton.—1B 102
Nayland.—4B 56
Nazeing.—2H 43
Neacroft.—4G 15
Neal's Green.—4H 63
Neap House.—4A 96
Near Cotton.—3E 75
Near Sawrey.—5E 105
Neasden.—2D 30
Neasham.—3G 107
Neath.—3D 36
Neath Abbey.—3D 36
Neatishead.—3F 81
Neaton.—2B 68
Nebo.—1E 47
(Dyfed)
Nebo.—1D 82
(nr. Amlwch, Gwynedd)
Nebo.—5D 83
(nr. Caernarfon, Gwynedd)
Nebo.—5H 83
(nr. Llanrwst, Gwynedd)
Necton.—2A 68
Nedd.—5B 168
Nedderton.—1F 117
Nedging.—3B 56
Nedging Tye.—3C 56
Needham.—4E 69
Needham Market.—2C 56
Needham Street.—1G 55
Needingworth.—5D 66
Needwood.—5F 75
Neen Savage.—5A 62
Neen Sollars.—5A 62
Neenton.—4A 62
Nefyn.—1C 70
Neilston.—4F 129
Neithrop.—3B 52
Nelly Andrews Green.—5E 73
Nelson.—2F 93
(Lancashire)
Nelson.—3H 37
(Mid Glamorgan)
Nelson Village.—2F 117
Nemphlar.—5B 130
Nempnett Thrubwell.—2F 25
Nenthall.—5A 116
Nenthead.—5A 116
Nenthorn.—1A 122
Nercwys.—4E 85
Nereabolls.—4A 126
Nerston.—4H 129
Nesbit.—1D 123
Nesfield.—1A 94
Ness.—3E 85
Nesscliffe.—4F 73
Neston.—3E 85
(Cheshire)
Neston.—2D 26
(Wiltshire)

Netchwood.—3A 62
Nethanfoot.—5B 130
Nether Alderley.—5F 87
Netheravon.—4G 27
Nether Blainslie.—5B 132
Netherbrae.—3G 163
Netherbrough.—6C 174
Nether Broughton.—5D 76
Netherburn.—5B 130
Nether Burrow.—2F 99
Netherbury.—4H 13
Netherby.—2E 115
Nether Careston.—3E 147
Nether Cerne.—4B 14
Nether Compton.—2A 14
Nethercote.—5F 51
(Gloucestershire)
Nethercote.—1C 52
(Warwickshire)
Nethercott.—2A 22
(Devon)
Nethercott.—5B 52
(Oxfordshire)
Nether Dallachy.—2A 162
Nether Durdie.—1E 138
Nether End.—5C 88
(Derbyshire)
Netherend.—2D 39
(Gloucestershire)
Nether Exe.—3C 12
Netherfield.—4B 20
(East Sussex)
Netherfield.—3D 76
(Nottinghamshire)
Nethergate.—3H 89
(Humberside)
Nethergate.—3C 80
(Norfolk)
Netherhampton.—1G 15
Nether Handley.—5E 88
Nether Haugh.—3E 88
Nether Heage.—2A 76
Nether Heyford.—2D 52
Netherhouses.—1B 98
Nether Howcleugh.—3C 120
Nether Kellet.—3E 99
Nether Kinmundy.—4H 163
Netherland Green.—4F 75
Nether Langwith.—5F 89
Netherlaw.—5E 113
Netherley.—4F 155
Nethermill.—1B 114
Nethermills.—3C 162
Nether Moor.—1A 76
Nether Padley.—5C 88
Netherplace.—4G 129
Nether Poppleton.—4A 102
Netherseal.—1G 63
Nether Silton.—5B 108
Nether Stowey.—5B 24
Nether Street.—1B 44
(Essex)
Netherstreet.—2E 27
(Wiltshire)
Netherthird.—3E 119
Netherthong.—2B 88
Netherton.—2G 129
(Central)
Netherton.—1B 104
(Cumbria)
Netherton.—2E 9
(Devon)
Netherton.—3B 28
(Hampshire)
Netherton.—3D 51
(nr. Evesham, Here & Worcs.)
Netherton.—5H 49
(nr. Hereford, Here & Worcs.)
Netherton.—2A 86
(Merseyside)
Netherton.—4D 123
(Northumberland)
Netherton.—4B 62
(Shropshire)
Netherton.—4A 130
(Strathclyde)

Netherton.—3A 146
(nr. Blairgowrie, Tayside)
Netherton.—3E 147
(nr. Brechin, Tayside)
Netherton.—4D 62
(West Midlands)
Netherton.—4C 94
(nr. Horbury, W Yorks.)
Netherton.—4B 94
(nr. Huddersfield, W Yorks.)
Netherton Colliery.—1F 117
Nethertown.—4A 104
(Cumbria)
Nethertown.—1F 171
(Highland)
Nethertown.—1F 63
(Staffordshire)
Nether Urquhart.—2E 138
Nether Wallop.—5B 28
Nether Wasdale.—4C 104
Nether Welton.—5E 115
Nether Whitacre.—3G 63
Netherwitton.—5E 123
Nether Worton.—4B 52
Nethy Bridge.—1E 153
Netley.—5G 73
Netley Abbey.—3C 16
Netley Marsh.—2B 16
Nettlebed.—4H 41
Nettlebridge.—4B 26
Nettlecombe.—4A 14
(Dorset)
Nettlecombe.—5D 16
(Isle of Wight)
Nettleden.—1D 42
Nettleham.—5C 90
Nettlestead.—5A 32
Nettlestead Green.—5A 32
Nettlestone.—4E 16
Nettlesworth.—5F 117
Nettleton.—5D 96
(Lincolnshire)
Nettleton.—5G 39
(Wiltshire)
Netton.—5B 8
(Devon)
Netton.—5G 27
(Wiltshire)
Neuadd.—5F 47
(Dyfed)
Neuadd.—5C 72
(Powys)
Neuk, The.—4E 155
Nevay.—4C 146
Nevendon.—1B 32
Nevern.—3A 46
(nr. Aberaeron, Dyfed)
New Abbey.—3G 113
New Aberdour.—2F 163
New Addington.—4E 31
Newall.—1B 94
New Alresford.—5D 28
New Alyth.—4B 146
Newark.—2B 66
(Cambridgeshire)
Newark.—3G 174
(Orkney)
Newark-on-Trent.—2F 77
New Arley.—4G 63
Newarthill.—4A 130
New Ash Green.—4H 31
New Balderton.—2F 77
New Barn.—4H 31
New Barnetby.—4C 96
Newbattle.—3G 131
New Bewick.—2E 123
Newbiggin.—2H 105
(nr. Appleby, Cumbria)
New Biggin.—3B 98
(nr. Barrow-in-Furness, Cumbria)
Newbiggin.—5G 115
(nr. Cumrew, Cumbria)
Newbiggin.—2F 105
(nr. Penrith, Cumbria)
Newbiggin.—5B 104
(nr. Seascale, Cumbria)

Newbiggin.—5E 117
(nr. Consett, Durham)
Newbiggin.—2C 106
(nr. Middleton-in-Teesdale, Durham)
Newbiggin.—5C 116
(Northumberland)
Newbiggin.—5C 106
(nr. Askrigg, N Yorks.)
Newbiggin.—1G 103
(nr. Filey, N Yorks.)
Newbiggin.—1C 100
(nr. Thoralby, N Yorks.)
Newbiggin-by-the-Sea.—1G 117
Newbigging.—2E 131
(Lothian)
Newbigging.—5D 130
(Strathclyde)
Newbigging.—5D 146
(nr. Balgray, Tayside)
Newbigging.—5D 147
(nr. Monikie, Tayside)
Newbigging.—4B 146
(nr. Newtyle, Tayside)
Newbiggin on Lune.—4A 106
New Blyth.—3F 163
Newbold.—5D 88
(Derbyshire)
Newbold.—1B 64
(Leicestershire)
Newbold on Avon.—5B 64
Newbold on Stour.—3G 51
Newbold Pacey.—2G 51
Newbold Verdon.—2B 64
New Bolingbroke.—2C 78
Newborough.—2B 66
(Cambridgeshire)
Newborough.—4D 82
(Gwynedd)
Newborough.—5F 75
(Staffordshire)
Newbottle.—4C 52
(Northamptonshire)
Newbottle.—4G 117
(Tyne & Wear)
New Boultham.—5B 90
Newbourn.—3E 57
New Brancepeth.—5F 117
Newbridge.—1E 73
(Clwyd)
Newbridge.—3B 4
(Cornwall)
New Bridge.—2G 113
(Dumfries & Galloway)
Newbridge.—2E 47
(nr. Aberaeron, Dyfed)
Newbridge.—1C 34
(nr. Fishguard Dyfed)
Newbridge.—3A 38
(Gwent)
Newbridge.—2A 16
(Hampshire)
Newbridge.—5C 16
(Isle of Wight)
Newbridge.—2E 131
(Lothian)
Newbridge.—1D 102
(North Yorkshire)
Newbridge Green.—4C 50
Newbridge-on-Usk.—3B 38
Newbridge on Wye.—2C 48
New Brighton.—4E 85
(Clwyd)
New Brighton.—3F 17
(Hampshire)
New Brighton.—1F 85
(Merseyside)
New Brinsley.—2B 76
Newbrough.—3B 116
New Broughton.—5F 85
New Buckenham.—3C 68
Newbuildings.—3A 12
Newburgh.—2E 139
(Fife)
Newburgh.—1G 155
(Grampian)

Newburgh.—1B 86 (Lancashire)
Newburgh Priory.—2A 102
Newburn.—3E 117
Newbury.—2C 28 (Berkshire)
Newbury.—4D 26 (Wiltshire)
Newby.—2G 105 (Cumbria)
Newby.—2G 99 (nr. Ingleton, N Yorks.)
Newby.—1F 103 (nr. Scarborough, N Yorks.)
Newby.—3C 108 (nr. Stokesley, N Yorks.)
Newby Bridge.—1C 98
Newby Cote.—2G 99
Newby East.—4F 115
Newby Head.—2G 105
Newby West.—4E 115
Newby Wiske.—1G 101
Newcastle.—1C 38 (Gwent)
Newcastle.—5E 37 (Mid Glamorgan)
Newcastle.—2H 59 (Shropshire)
Newcastle Airport.—2E 117
Newcastle Emlyn.—3C 46
Newcastleton.—1F 115
Newcastle-under-Lyme.—3C 74
Newcastle upon Tyne.—3F 117
Newchapel.—4B 46 (Dyfed)
Newchapel.—2E 59 (Powys)
Newchapel.—2C 74 (Staffordshire)
Newchapel.—1E 19 (Surrey)
Newchurch.—2G 35 (Dyfed)
Newchurch.—3C 38 (Gwent)
Newchurch.—2F 49 (Hereford & Worcester)
Newchurch.—5D 16 (Isle of Wight)
Newchurch.—2E 21 (Kent)
Newchurch.—2F 93 (nr. Nelson, Lancs.)
Newchurch.—3F 93 (nr. Rawtenstall, Lancs.)
Newchurch.—2E 48 (Powys)
Newchurch.—5F 75 (Staffordshire)
New Clipstone.—1C 76
New Costessey.—4D 81
Newcott.—3F 13
New Cowper.—5C 114
New Craighall.—2G 131
New Crofton.—4D 94
New Cross.—3B 58
New Cumnock.—3F 119
New Deer.—4F 163
New Denham.—2B 30
Newdigate.—1C 18
New Duston.—1E 52
New Earswick.—4B 102
New Edlington.—3F 89
New Elgin.—2G 161
New Ellerby.—2D 96
Newell Green.—5B 42
New Eltham.—3F 31
New End.—2E 51 (Hereford & Worcester)
New End.—1F 51 (Warwickshire)
Newenden.—3C 20
New England.—2A 66 (Cambridgeshire)
New England.—3G 55 (Essex)

Newent.—5B 50
New Farnley.—2C 94
New Ferry.—2F 85
Newfield.—4F 117 (nr Chester-le-Street, Durham)
Newfield.—1F 107 (nr. Willington, Durham)
Newfound.—3D 28
New Fryston.—3F 95
Newgale.—2B 34
New Galloway.—2D 112
Newgate.—1C 80
Newgate Street.—2G 43
New Greens.—2E 43
New Grimsby.—1A 4
New Hadley.—1A 62
New Hainford.—4E 81
Newhall.—3A 74 (Cheshire)
Newhall.—5G 75 (Derbyshire)
Newham.—2F 31 (London)
Newham.—2F 123 (Northumberland)
New Hartley.—2G 117
Newhaven.—1F 75 (Derbyshire)
Newhaven.—5F 19 (East Sussex)
Newhaven.—2F 131 (Lothian)
New Haw.—4B 30
New Hedges.—4E 35
New Herrington.—4G 117
Newhey.—1G 87
New Holkham.—2A 80
New Holland.—3C 96
Newholm.—3F 109
New Horton Grange.—2E 117
New Houghton.—1B 76 (Derbyshire)
New Houghton.—5G 79 (Norfolk)
Newhouse.—3A 130
New Houses.—2B 100
New Hutton.—5G 105
New Hythe.—5B 32
Newick.—3F 19
Newington.—2F 21 (nr Folkestone, Kent)
Newington.—4C 32 (nr. Sittingbourne, Kent)
Newington.—2F 131 (Lothian)
Newington.—3G 89 (Nottinghamshire)
Newington.—3H 41 (Oxfordshire)
Newington Bagpath.—3G 39
New Inn.—4D 46 (Dyfed)
New Inn.—2C 38 (nr. Devauden, Gwent)
New Inn.—3B 38 (nr. Pontypool, Gwent)
New Inn.—2B 100 (North Yorkshire)
New Invention.—3H 59
New Kelso.—4B 158
New Lanark.—5B 130
Newland.—2D 38 (Gloucestershire)
Newland.—3B 90 (Hereford & Worcester)
Newland.—2C 96 (Humberside)
Newland.—3G 95 (North Yorkshire)
Newland.—2E 23 (Somerset)
Newlandrig.—3G 131
Newlands.—1E 105 (Cumbria)
Newlands.—2C 32 (Essex)

Newlands.—2A 162 (Grampian)
Newlands.—4B 160 (Highland)
Newlands.—4D 117 (Northumberland)
Newlands.—1C 76 (Nottinghamshire)
Newlands.—5E 75 (Staffordshire)
Newlands of Geise.—2C 170
New Lane.—1B 86
New Lane End.—3D 86
New Langholm.—1E 115
New Leake.—2D 78
New Leeds.—3G 163
New Longton.—3C 92
New Luce.—3G 111
Newlyn.—4B 4
Newlyn East.—4C 6
Newmachar.—2F 155
Newmains.—4B 130
New Mains of Ury.—5F 155
Newman's Green.—3A 56
Newmarket.—1F 55 (Suffolk)
Newmarket.—4G 173 (Western Isles)
New Marske.—2D 108
New Marton.—2F 73
New Micklefield.—2E 95
Newmill.—3G 121 (Borders)
New Mill.—3B 4 (Cornwall)
Newmill.—3B 162 (nr. Keith, Grampian)
New Mill.—4E 162 (nr. Turriff, Grampian)
New Mill.—1C 42 (Hertfordshire)
New Mill.—2B 88 (West Yorkshire)
New Mill.—4G 27 (Wiltshire)
Newmillerdam.—4D 94
New Mills.—4D 6 (Cornwall)
New Mills.—4H 87 (Derbyshire)
Newmills.—5C 138 (Fife)
New Mills.—2D 38 (Gwent)
Newmills.—2A 160 (Highland)
New Mills.—1G 101 (Powys)
Newmilns.—5A 146
New Milton.—4H 15
New Mistley.—4D 56
New Moat.—2D 34
Newmore.—3H 159 (nr. Dingwall, H'land.)
Newmore.—1A 160 (nr. Invergordon, H'land.)
Newnham.—2D 54 (Cambridgeshire)
Newnham.—1E 39 (Gloucestershire)
Newnham.—3F 29 (Hampshire)
Newnham.—4B 54 (Hertfordshire)
Newnham.—5D 32 (Kent)
Newnham.—2C 52 (Northamptonshire)
Newnham.—1F 51 (Warwickshire)
Newnham Bridge.—1A 50
New Ollerton.—1D 76
New Oscott.—3E 63
Newpark.—2G 139 (Fife)

New Park.—4F 101 (North Yorkshire)
New Pitsligo.—3F 163
New Polzeath.—2D 6
Newport.—1H 7 (Cornwall)
Newport.—2B 22 (Devon)
Newport.—1D 34 (Dyfed)
Newport.—4E 55 (Essex)
Newport.—3E 39 (Gloucestershire)
Newport.—4B 38 (Gwent)
Newport.—1H 167 (Highland)
Newport.—2A 96 (Humberside)
Newport.—5C 16 (Isle of Wight)
Newport.—4H 81 (Norfolk)
Newport.—1B 62 (Shropshire)
Newport.—1G 13 (Somerset)
Newport-on-Tay.—1G 139
Newport Pagnell.—3F 53
Newpound Common.—3B 18
New Prestwick.—2C 118
Newquay.—3C 6 (Cornwall)
New Quay.—1C 46 (Dyfed)
New Rackheath.—4E 81
New Radnor.—4H 59
New Rent.—1F 105
New Ridley.—4D 116
New Romney.—3E 21
New Rossington.—3G 89
New Row.—3C 58 (Dyfed)
New Row.—3D 108 (North Yorkshire)
New Sauchie.—4A 138
Newsbank.—1C 74
New Scone.—1D 138
Newseat.—5E 162
Newsham.—3E 107 (Durham)
Newsham.—2C 92 (Lancashire)
Newsham.—2C 117 (Northumberland)
Newsham.—1G 101 (North Yorkshire)
New Sharlston.—3D 94
New Shawbost.—3E 173
Newsholme.—3H 95 (Humberside)
Newsholme.—4B 100 (Lancashire)
New Shoreston.—1F 123
New Springs.—2D 86
Newstead.—1H 121 (Borders)
Newstead.—2C 76 (Nottinghamshire)
New Stevenston.—4A 130
New Street.—2F 49
Newstreet Lane.—4A 74
New Swanage.—5F 15
New Swannington.—1B 64
Newthorpe.—2E 95 (North Yorkshire)
Newthorpe.—3B 76 (Nottinghamshire)
New Tolsta.—3H 173
Newton.—2A 122 (Borders)
Newton.—3D 54 (nr. Cambridge, Cambs.)
Newton.—1D 66 (nr. Wisbech, Cambs.)

Newton.—4G 85 (Chester, Ches.)
Newton.—5H 85 (nr. Taitenhall, Ches.)
Newton.—2B 98 (Cumbria)
Newton.—2B 76 (Derbyshire)
Newton.—2D 114 (nr. Annan, Dum & Gall.)
Newton.—5D 120 (nr. Moffat, Dum & Gall.)
Newton.—2F 161 (Grampian)
Newton.—4F 49 (nr. Ewyas Harold, Here & Worcs.)
Newton.—2H 49 (nr. Leominster, Here & Worcs.)
Newton.—2B 160 (nr. Cromarty, H'land.)
Newton.—4B 160 (nr. Inverness, H'land.)
Newton.—5C 168 (nr. Kylestrome, H'land.)
Newton.—4F 171 (nr. Wick, H'land.)
Newton.—2A 92 (nr. Blackpool, Lancs.)
Newton.—2G 99 (nr. Carnforth, Lancs.)
Newton.—4F 93 (nr. Clitheroe, Lancs.)
Newton.—2B 92 (nr. Kirkham, Lancs.)
Newton.—4H 77 (Lincolnshire)
Newton.—2D 131 (Lothian)
Newton.—3G 87 (Manchester)
Newton.—2E 85 (Merseyside)
Newton.—5E 37 (Mid. Glamorgan)
Newton.—4A 80 (Norfolk)
Newton.—4F 65 (Northamptonshire)
Newton.—3D 116 (Northumberland)
Newton.—3D 76 (Nottinghamshire)
Newton.—3B 62 (nr. Bridgnorth, Shrops.)
Newton.—2G 73 (nr. Wem, Shrops.)
Newton.—5B 24 (Somerset)
Newton.—5E 75 (Staffordshire)
Newton.—3H 129 (nr. Glasgow, S'clyde.)
Newton.—1B 120 (nr. Lanark, S'clyde.)
Newton.—4H 135 (nr. Strachur, S'clyde.)
Newton.—3B 56 (Suffolk)
Newton.—5C 64 (Warwickshire)
Newton.—4C 36 (West Glamorgan)
Newton.—1H 15 (Wiltshire)
Newton Abbot.—2E 9
Newton Arlosh.—4D 114
Newton Aycliffe.—2F 107
Newton Bewley.—2B 108
Newton Blossomville.—2G 53
Newton Bromswold.—1H 53
Newton Burgoland.—2A 64
Newton by Toft.—4C 90
Newton Ferrers.—5B 8
Newtonferry.—1D 172
Newton Flotman.—3E 69

Newtongarry Croft.—5C 162
Newtongrange.—3G 131
Newton Green.—3D 38 (Durham)
Newton Hall.—5F 117 (Durham)
Newton Hall.—3D 116 (Northumberland)
Newton Harcourt.—3D 64
Newton Heath.—2F 87
Newtonhill.—4G 155 (Grampian)
Newtonhill.—4H 159 (Highland)
Newton Hill.—3D 94 (West Yorkshire)
Newton Ketton.—2G 107
Newton Kyme.—1E 95
Newton-le-Willows.—3C 86 (Merseyside)
Newton-le-Willows.—1F 101 (North Yorkshire)
Newton Longville.—4F 53
Newton Mearns.—4G 129
Newtonmore.—4B 152
Newton Morrell.—4F 107
Newton Mulgrave.—3E 109
Newton of Ardtoe.—1A 142
Newton of Balcanquhal.—2D 138
Newton of Falkland.—3E 139
Newton of Pitcairns.—2C 138
Newton on Ayr.—2C 118
Newton-on-Ouse.—4A 102
Newton-on-Rawcliffe.—5F 109
Newton on the Hill.—3G 73
Newton-on-the-Moor.—4F 123
Newton on Trent.—5A 90
Newton Poppleford.—5D 12
Newton Purcell.—4D 52
Newton Regis.—2G 63
Newton Reigny.—1F 105
Newton Rigg.—1F 105
Newton St Cyres.—4B 12
Newton St Faith.—4E 81
Newton St Loe.—2C 26
Newton St Petrock.—2E 11
Newton Solney.—5G 75
Newton Stacey.—4C 28
Newton Stewart.—3B 112
Newton Toney.—4H 27
Newton Tracey.—3B 22
Newton under Roseberry.—3C 10
Newton upon Derwent.—5C 10
Newton Valence.—5F 29
New Town.—5H 53 (Bedfordshire)
Newtown.—1H 53 (Cambridgeshire)
Newtown.—1C 130 (Central)
Newtown.—3A 74 (Cheshire)
Newtown.—4E 5 (nr. Helston, Corn.)
Newtown.—2G 7 (nr. Launceston, Corn.)
Newtown.—5C 114 (nr. Aspatria, Cumbria)
Newtown.—1A 98 (Bootle, Cumbria)
Newtown.—3G 115 (nr. Brampton, Cumbria)
Newtown.—2G 105 (nr. Penrith, Cumbria)
Newtown.—5B 114 (nr. Silloth, Cumbria)
Newtown.—4G 87 (Derbyshire)
Newtown.—3D 22 (Devon)
Newtown.—3H 13 (nr. Beaminster, Dorset)
Newtown.—4F 15 (Poole, Dorset)

Patchole.—1C 22
Patchway.—4E 39
Pateley Bridge.—3E 101
Pathe.—5D 25
Pathhead.—4E 139
(Fife)
Pathhead.—2G 147
(Grampian)
Pathhead.—3G 131
(Lothian)
Pathhead.—3F 119
(Strathclyde)
Pathlow.—2F 51
Path of Condie.—2C 138
Pathstruie.—2C 138
Patmore Heath.—5D 54
Patna.—3D 110
Patney.—3F 27
Patrick.—3B 110
Patrick Brompton.—5F 107
Patrington.—3F 97
Patrington Haven.—3F 97
Patrixbourne.—5F 33
Patterdale.—3E 101
Pattiesmuir.—5C 138
Pattingham.—3C 62
Pattishall.—2D 52
Pattiswick.—5A 56
Paul.—4B 4
Paulerspury.—3E 53
Paull.—3D 96
Paulton.—3B 26
Pauperhaugh.—5F 123
Pave Lane.—1B 62
Pavenham.—2G 53
Pawlett.—4D 24
Pawston.—1C 122
Paxford.—4F 51
Paxton.—4F 133
Payhembury.—3D 12
Paythorne.—4B 100
Peacehaven.—5F 19
Peak Dale.—5A 88
Peak Forest.—5B 88
Peak Hill.—1B 66
Peakirk.—2A 66
Peanmeanach.—5F 149
Pearsie.—3C 146
Peasedown St John.—3C 26
Peaseland Green.—4C 80
Peasemore.—5F 41
Peasenhall.—1F 57
Pease Pottage.—2D 18
Peaslake.—1B 18
Peasley Cross.—3C 86
Peasmarsh.—3C 20
(East Sussex)
Peasmarsh.—1A 18
(Surrey)
Peaston.—3H 131
Peaston Bank.—3H 131
Peathill.—2G 163
Peat Inn.—3G 139
Peatling Magna.—3C 64
Peatling Parva.—4C 64
Peaton.—2C 60
(Shropshire)
Peaton.—1D 128
(Strathclyde)
Peats Corner.—1D 57
Pebmarsh.—4A 56
Pebworth.—3F 51
Pecket Well.—5G 93
Peckforton.—5H 85
Peckham Bush.—1A 20
Peckleton.—2B 64
Pedair-ffordd.—3D 72
Pedlinge.—2F 21
Pedmore.—4D 62
Pedwell.—5E 25
Peebles.—5F 131
Peel.—1G 121
(Borders)
Peel.—3B 110
(Isle of Man)
Peel Common.—3D 16

Peening Quarter.—3C 20
Pegg's Green.—1B 64
Pegsdon.—4A 54
Pegswood.—1F 117
Peinchorran.—5E 157
Peinlich.—3D 156
Pelaw.—3F 117
Pelcomb.—3C 34
Pelcomb Bridge.—3C 34
Peldon.—1F 45
Pelsall.—2C 63
Pelton.—4F 117
Pelutho.—5C 114
Pelynt.—4G 7
Pemberton.—2B 36
Pembrey.—4H 35
Pembridge.—2F 49
Pembroke.—4C 34
Pembroke Dock.—4C 34
Pembroke Ferry.—4C 34
Pembury.—1H 19
Penallt.—2D 38
Penally.—5E 35
Penare.—2G 5
Penarth.—5H 37
Pen-bont Rhydybeddau.—2B 58
Penbryn.—2B 46
Pen-cae.—2D 46
Pencaenewydd.—1D 70
Pencaerau.—3D 36
Pencarnisiog.—3C 82
Pencarreg.—3E 47
Pencarrow.—1F 7
Pencelli.—5C 48
Pen-clawdd.—3B 36
Pencoed.—4F 37
Pencombe.—2D 50
Pencraig.—5H 49
(Hereford & Worcester)
Pencraig.—3C 72
(Powys)
Pendeen.—3A 4
Penderyn.—2F 37
Pendine.—4F 35
Pendlebury.—2E 87
Pendleton.—2E 93
(Lancashire)
Pendleton.—3F 87
(Manchester)
Pendock.—4B 50
Pendoggett.—2E 7
Pendomer.—2A 14
Pendoylan.—5G 37
Pendre.—4F 37
Penegoes.—5G 71
Penelewey.—2F 37
Pen-ffordd.—2D 35
(Gwent)
Pengam.—3H 37
(Gwent)
Pengam.—5A 38
(South Glamorgan)
Penge.—3E 31
Pengelly.—1E 7
Pengenffordd.—4D 48
Pengorffwysfa.—1D 82
Pengover Green.—3G 7
Pengwern.—3C 84
Penhale.—5D 5
(nr. Mullion, Corn.)
Penhale.—4B 6
(nr. Newquay, Corn.)
Penhale.—4D 6
(nr. St Austell, Corn.)
Penhallow.—4B 6
Penhalurick.—3E 5
Penhelig.—1B 58
Penhill.—4C 40
Penhow.—3C 38
Penhurst.—4A 20
Peniarth.—5F 71
Penicuik.—3F 131
Peniel.—2H 35
Penifiler.—4D 157
Peninver.—3B 124
Penisarwaun.—4E 83

Penistone.—2C 88
Penketh.—4C 86
Penkill.—5B 118
Penkridge.—1D 62
Penley.—2G 73
Penllech.—2B 70
Penllergaer.—3C 36
Pen-llyn.—2C 82
(Gwynedd)
Penllyn.—5F 37
(South Glamorgan)
Penmachno.—5G 83
Penmaen.—4B 36
Penmaenmawr.—3G 83
Penmaenpool.—4F 71
Penmaen-rhos.—3A 84
Penmark.—5G 37
Penmon.—2F 83
Penmorfa.—1E 71
Penmynydd.—3E 83
Penn.—1A 30
(Buckinghamshire)
Penn.—4G 13
(Dorset)
Penn.—3C 62
(West Midlands)
Pennal.—5G 71
Pennan.—2F 163
Pennant.—2C 72
(Clwyd)
Pennant.—1E 47
(Dyfed)
Pennant.—3B 72
(Gwynedd)
Pennant.—1D 58
(Powys)
Pennant Melangell.—3C 72
Pennard.—4B 36
Pennerley.—1A 60
Pennington.—2B 98
(Cumbria)
Pennington.—4B 16
(Hampshire)
Pennington.—3D 86
(Manchester)
Pennorth.—5D 48
Penn Street.—1A 30
Pennsylvania.—5F 39
(Avon)
Pennsylvania.—4C 12
(Devon)
Penny Bridge.—1C 98
Pennycross.—4A 8
Pennygate.—3F 81
Pennyghael.—1C 134
Penny Hill.—5C 78
Pennymoor.—2B 12
Pennyvenie.—4D 119
Pennywell.—4G 117
Penparc.—3B 46
Penparcau.—2A 58
Penperlleni.—2B 38
Penpillick.—4E 7
Penpoll.—4F 7
(nr. Fowey, Corn.)
Penpoll.—3F 5
(nr. Truro, Corn.)
Penponds.—3D 4
Penpont.—2E 7
(Cornwall)
Penpont.—5H 119
(Dumfries & Galloway)
Penpont.—5B 48
(Powys)
Penprysg.—4F 37
Penquit.—4C 8
Penrherber.—4B 46
Penrhiw.—3B 46
Penrhiwceiber.—3G 37
Pen Rhiwfawr.—1D 36
Penrhiwllan.—1F 47
Penrhiwpal.—3C 46
Penrhos.—1C 38
(Gwent)

Penrhos.—2B 82
(nr. Holyhead, Gwynedd)
Penrhos.—2C 70
(nr. Pwllheli, Gwynedd)
Penrhos.—2F 49
(Hereford & Worcester)
Penrhos.—1E 36
(Powys)
Penrhos-garnedd.—3E 83
Penrhyd Side.—2H 83
Penrhyn.—1C 82
Penrhyn Bay.—2H 83
Penrhyncoch.—2B 58
Penrhyndeudraeth.—2F 71
Penrice.—4A 36
Penrieth.—4B 46
Penrioch.—5G 127
Penrith.—1G 105
Penrose.—2C 6
Penruddock.—2F 105
Penryn.—3E 5
Pensarn.—3H 35
(Dyfed)
Pen-sarn.—3E 71
(Gwynedd)
Pensax.—1B 50
Pensby.—2E 85
Penselwood.—5C 26
Pensford.—2B 26
Pensham.—3D 50
Penshaw.—4G 117
Penshurst.—1G 19
Pensilva.—3G 7
Pensnett.—4D 62
Penston.—2H 131
Penstone.—3A 12
Pentewan.—2H 5
Pentir.—4E 83
Pentire.—3B 6
Pentlepoir.—4E 35
Pentlow.—3H 55
Pentney.—1G 67
Penton Mewsey.—4B 28
Pentraeth.—3E 83
Pentre.—4C 84
(nr. Denbigh, Clwyd)
Pentre.—2D 72
(nr. Llanarmon Dyffryn Ceiriog,
Clwyd)
Pentre.—1E 73
(nr. Rhosllanerchrugog, Clwyd)
Pentre.—3F 37
(Mid Glamorgan)
Pentre.—1H 59
(nr. Church Stoke, Powys)
Pentre.—2G 59
(nr. Kerry, Powys)
Pentre.—2F 59
(nr. Mochdre, Powys)
Pentre.—4F 73
(Shropshire)
Pentrebach.—3E 47
(nr. Lampeter, Dyfed)
Pentrebach.—4H 47
(nr.Llandovery, Dyfed)
Pentrebach.—3F 37
(Mid Glamorgan)
Pentre-bach.—4B 48
(Powys)
Pentrebach.—2C 36
(West Glamorgan)
Pentrebeirdd.—4D 72
Pentre Berw.—3D 82
Pentre-cagal.—3C 46
Pentre-celyn.—5D 84
Pentre-clawdd.—2E 73
Pentreclwydau.—2E 37
Pentre-cwrt.—4C 46
Pentre Dolau-Honddu.—3B 48
Pentre-du.—5G 83
Pentre-dwr.—3C 36
Pentrefelin.—5E 47
(Dyfed)
Pentrefelin.—2E 71
(nr. Criccieth, Gwynedd)
Pentrefelin.—3H 83
(nr. Llandudno, Gwynedd)

Pentrefoelas.—5A 84
Pentre-galar.—4A 46
Pentregat.—2C 46
Pentre-Gwenlais.—1C 36
Pentre Gwynfryn.—3E 71
Pentre Halkyn.—3E 84
Pentre Hodrey.—3A 60
Pentre Llifior.—1E 59
Pentrellwyn.—2E 83
Pentre-llwyn-llwyd.—2B 48
Pentre-llyn-cymmer.—5B 84
Pentre Meyrick.—5F 37
Pentre-piod.—2A 72
Pentre-poeth.—4A 38
Pentre'r-felin.—3F 47
(Dyfed)
Pentre'r-felin.—4B 48
(Powys)
Pentre-tafarn-y-fedw.—4H 83
Pentre ty gwyn.—4H 47
Pentre-uchaf.—2C 70
Pentrich.—2A 76
Pentridge.—2F 15
Pentwyn.—4A 38
(nr. Cardiff, Gwent)
Pen-twyn.—2A 38
(nr. Llanhilleth, Gwent)
Pentwyn.—2H 37
(Mid Glamorgan)
Pentyrch.—4H 37
Penuwch.—4A 58
Penwithick.—4E 7
Penwyllt.—1E 37
Penybanc.—1C 36
(nr. Ammanford, Dyfed)
Pen-y-banc.—5F 47
(nr. Llandeilo, Dyfed)
Pen-y-bont.—3E 72
(Clwyd)
Penybont.—4G 59
(Powys)
Penybontfawr.—3C 72
Pen-y-bryn.—1E 73
(Clwyd)
Pen-y-bryn.—3A 46
(Dyfed)
Penycae.—1E 73
(Clwyd)
Pen-y-cae.—1E 37
(Powys)
Pen-y-cae-mawr.—3C 38
Penycaerau.—3A 70
Pen-y-cefn.—3D 84
Pen-y-clawdd.—2C 38
Pen-y-coedcae.—4G 37
Pencwm.—2B 34
Pen-y-darren.—2G 37
Pen-y-fai.—4E 37
Penyffordd.—4F 85
Penyffridd.—5E 83
Pen-y-garn.—2B 58
(Dyfed)
Pen-y-garn.—2D 38
(Gwent)
Pen-y-garnedd.—3E 83
(Gwynedd)
Penygarnedd.—3D 72
(Powys)
Pen-y-graig.—2B 70
(Gwynedd)
Pen-y-graig.—3F 37
(Mid Glamorgan)
Pen-y-groes.—1B 36
(nr. Ammanford, Dyfed)
Penygroes.—4A 46
(nr. Crymmych, Dyfed)
Penygroes.—5D 82
(Gwynedd)
Penymynydd.—4F 85
Pen-yr-heol.—1C 38
(Gwent)
Penyrheol.—4H 37
(Mid Glamorgan)
Penyrheol.—3B 36
(West Glamorgan)
Pen-yr-Heolgerrig.—2G 37

Penysarn.—1D 82
Pen-y-Stryt.—5D 84
Penywaun.—2F 37
Penzance.—4B 4
Penzance Heliport.—3B 4
Peopleton.—2D 50
Peover Heath.—5E 87
Peper Harow.—1A 18
Peplow.—5A 74
Pepper Arden.—4F 107
Perceton.—5C 129
Percyhorner.—2G 163
Periton.—1F 23
Perkins Beach.—5F 73
Perkinsville.—4F 117
Perlethorpe.—5G 89
Perranarworthal.—3E 5
Perranporth.—4B 6
Perranuthnoe.—4C 4
Perranwell Station.—3E 5
Perranzabuloe.—4B 6
Perrott's Brook.—2B 40
Perry.—3E 63
Perry Barr.—3E 63
Perry Crofts.—2G 63
Perry Green.—4A 56
(Essex)
Perry Green.—1H 43
(Hertfordshire)
Perry Green.—4A 40
(Wiltshire)
Perry Street.—3H 31
(Kent)
Perry Street.—3G 13
(Somerset)
Pershall.—5C 74
Pershore.—3D 50
Pertenhall.—1H 53
Perth.—1D 138
Perthy.—2F 73
Perton.—3C 62
Pertwood.—5D 27
Peterborough.—1A 66
Peterburn.—5B 164
Peterchurch.—4F 49
Peterculter.—3F 155
Peterhead.—4H 163
Peterlee.—5H 117
Petersfield.—1F 17
Petersfinger.—1G 15
Peter's Green.—1E 43
Peters Marland.—2E 11
Peterstone Wentlooge.—4A 38
Peterston-super-Ely.—5G 37
Peterstow.—5H 49
Peter Tavy.—2B 8
Petham.—5F 33
Petherwin Gate.—1G 7
Petrockstowe.—3F 11
Petsoe End.—3F 53
Pett.—4C 20
Pettaugh.—2D 56
Petteridge.—1A 20
Petterril Gremn.—5F 115
Pettinain.—5C 130
Pettistree.—2E 57
Petton.—3G 23
(Devon)
Petton.—3G 73
(Shropshire)
Petts Wood.—4F 31
Pettycur.—5E 139
Pettywell.—3C 80
Petworth.—1H 17
Pevensey.—5H 19
Pevensey Bay.—5A 20
Pewsey.—2G 27
Pheasant's Hill.—4A 42
Philadelphia.—4G 117
Philham.—1C 10
Philiphaugh.—2G 121
Philipstoun.—2D 130
Phillack.—3D 4
Philleigh.—3F 5
Phocle Green.—5A 50
Phoenix Green.—3F 29

232 G.B. Handy

Pibsbury.—1H 13
Pibwrlwyd.—3H 35
Pica.—2B 104
Piccadilly.—3G 63
Piccadilly Corner.—4E 69
Piccotts End.—2D 42
Pickering.—1C 102
Picket Piece.—4B 28
Picket Post.—3G 15
Pickford.—4G 63
Pickhill.—1G 101
Picklenash.—5B 50
Picklescott.—1B 60
Pickletillem.—1G 139
Pickmere.—5D 87
Pickstock.—5B 74
Pickwell.—1A 22
(Devon)
Pickwell.—1E 65
(Leicestershire)
Pickworth.—1G 65
(Leicestershire)
Pickworth.—4H 77
(Lincolnshire)
Picton.—3G 85
(Cheshire)
Picton.—2D 84
(Clwyd)
Picton.—4B 108
(North Yorkshire)
Picton Ferry.—3F 35
Piddinghoe.—5F 19
Piddington.—3B 42
(Buckinghamshire)
Piddington.—2F 53
(Northamptonshire)
Piddington.—1H 41
(Oxfordshire)
Piddlehinton.—4C 14
Piddletrenthide.—4C 14
Pidley.—5C 66
Pidney.—3C 14
Pie Corner.—1A 50
Piercebridge.—1F 107
Pierowall.—3D 174
Pigdon.—1E 117
Pightley.—5C 24
Pikehall.—2F 75
Pikeshill.—3A 16
Pilford.—3F 15
Pilgrims Hatch.—1G 31
Pilham.—3A 90
Pill.—5D 38
(Avon)
Pill.—4C 34
(Dyfed)
Pillaton.—3H 7
(Cornwall)
Pillaton.—1D 62
(Staffordshire)
Pillerton Hersey.—3H 51
Pillerton Priors.—3G 51
Pilleth.—4H 59
Pilley.—4B 16
(Hampshire)
Pilley.—2D 88
(South Yorkshire)
Pillgwenlly.—4B 38
Pilling.—1B 92
Pilling Lane.—1A 92
Pillowell.—2E 39
Pill, The.—4C 38
Pillwell.—2C 14
Pilning.—4D 38
Pilsbury.—1F 75
Pilsdon.—4H 13
Pilsgate.—2H 65
Pilsley.—5C 88
(nr. Bakewell, Derbys.)
Pilsley.—1B 76
(nr. Clay Cross, Derbys.)
Pilson Green.—4F 81
Piltdown.—3F 19
Pilton.—2G 65
(Leicestershire)

Pilton.—2F 131
(Lothian)
Pilton.—4H 65
(Northamptonshire)
Pilton.—4F 25
(Somerset)
Pilton Green.—4A 36
Pimperne.—3E 15
Pinchbeck.—5B 78
Pinchbeck Bars.—5A 78
Pinchbeck West.—5B 78
Pinfold.—1A 86
Pinford End.—2A 56
Pinged.—4H 35
Pinhoe.—4C 12
Pinkerton.—2D 132
Pinkneys Green.—4B 42
Pinley.—5A 64
Pinley Green.—1G 51
Pin Mill.—4E 57
Pinmore.—5B 118
Pinn.—5E 12
Pinner.—2C 30
Pins Green.—3C 50
Pinsley Green.—1H 73
Pinvin.—3D 50
Pinwherry.—1G 111
Pinxton.—2B 76
Pipe and Lyde.—3H 49
Pipe Gate.—3B 74
Pipehill.—4E 73
Piperhill.—3C 160
Pipe Ridware.—1E 63
Pipers Pool.—1G 7
Pipewell.—4E 65
Pippacott.—2B 22
Pipton.—4D 48
Pirbright.—5A 30
Pirnmill.—5G 127
Pirton.—3C 50
(Hereford & Worcester)
Pirton.—4A 54
(Hertfordshire)
Pisgah.—3G 137
Pishill.—3A 42
Pistyll.—1C 70
Pitagowan.—2F 145
Pitcairn.—3F 145
Pitcairngreen.—1C 138
Pitcalnie.—1C 160
Pitcaple.—1E 154
Pitchcombe.—2G 39
Pitchcott.—5E 53
Pitchford.—5H 73
Pitch Green.—2A 42
Pitch Place.—5A 30
Pitcombe.—5B 26
Pitcox.—2C 132
Pitcur.—5B 146
Pitfichie.—2D 154
Pitfour Castle.—1D 138
Pitgrudy.—4E 167
Pitkennedy.—3E 147
Pitlessie.—3F 139
Pitlochry.—3G 145
Pitmachie.—1D 154
Pitmaduthy.—1B 160
Pitmedden.—1F 155
Pitminster.—2F 13
Pitmuies.—4E 147
Pitnacree.—3G 145
Pitney.—1H 13
Pitroddie.—1E 138
Pitscottie.—2G 139
Pitsea.—2B 32
Pitsford.—1E 53
Pitsford Hill.—2C 23
Pitsmoor.—4D 88
Pitstone.—1C 42
Pitt.—1C 16
Pitt Court.—3F 39
Pittenheath.—1D 44
Pittentrail.—3E 166
Pittenweem.—3H 139
Pittington.—5G 117

Pitton.—4A 36
(West Glamorgan)
Pitton.—5H 27
(Wiltshire)
Pittswood.—1H 19
Pittulie.—2G 163
Pittville.—5D 50
Pitversie.—2D 138
Pityme.—2D 6
(Cornwall)
Pity Me.—5F 117
(Durham)
Pixey Green.—5E 69
Pixley.—4A 50
Place Newton.—2D 103
Plaidy.—4G 7
(Cornwall)
Plaidy.—3E 163
(Grampian)
Plain Dealings.—3D 34
Plains.—3A 130
Plainsfield.—5B 24
Plaish.—1C 60
Plaistow.—4A 50
(Hereford & Worcester)
Plaistow.—2B 18
(West Sussex)
Plaitford.—2A 16
Plas Llwyd.—3B 84
Plastow Green.—2D 28
Plas yn Cefn.—3C 84
Platt.—5H 31
Platt Bridge.—2D 86
Platt Lane.—2H 73
Platts Common.—2D 88
Platt's Heath.—5C 32
Platt, The.—2G 19
Plawsworth.—5F 117
Plaxtol.—5G 31
Playden.—3D 20
Playford.—3E 57
Play Hatch.—5A 42
Playing Place.—2F 5
Playley Green.—4B 50
Plealey.—5G 73
Pleasington.—3D 92
Pleasley.—1C 76
Pledgdon Green.—5E 55
Plenmeller.—3A 116
Pleshey.—1C 44
Plockton.—5H 157
Plocrapool.—8D 173
Ploughfield.—3F 49
Plowden.—2A 60
Ploxgreen.—5F 73
Pluckley.—1D 20
Plumbland.—1C 104
Plumgarths.—5F 105
Plumley.—5E 87
Plummers Plain.—3D 18
Plumpton.—1F 105
(Cumbria)
Plumpton.—4E 19
(East Sussex)
Plumpton.—3C 52
(Northamptonshire)
Plumptonfoot.—1F 105
Plumpton Green.—4E 19
Plumpton Head.—1G 105
Plumstead.—3F 31
(London)
Plumstead.—2D 80
(Norfolk)
Plumtree.—4D 76
Plumtree Park.—4D 76
Plungar.—4E 77
Plush.—3C 14
Plushabridge.—2H 7
Plwmp.—2C 46
Plymouth.—4A 8
Plymouth Airport.—3B 8
Plympton.—4B 8
Plymstock.—4B 8
Plymtree.—3D 12
Pockley.—1B 102

Pocklington.—1A 96
Pockthorpe.—3A 80
Pode Hole.—5B 78
Podimore.—1A 14
Podington.—1G 53
Podmore.—4B 74
Poffley End.—1E 41
Point Clear.—1G 45
Pointon.—4A 78
Pokesdown.—4G 15
Polbae.—2H 111
Polbain.—2D 165
Polbathic.—4H 7
Polbeth.—3D 130
Polbrock.—3E 6
Polchar, The.—3C 152
Polebrook.—4H 65
Pole Elm.—2C 50
Polegate.—5G 19
Pole Moor.—4A 94
Poles.—4E 167
Polesworth.—2G 63
Polgigga.—3E 165
Polgooth.—4D 6
Poling.—5B 18
Poling Corner.—5B 18
Polio.—1B 160
Polkerris.—4E 7
Polla.—3D 168
Pollard Street.—2F 81
Pollington.—4G 95
Polloch.—2B 142
Pollok.—3G 129
Pollokshaws.—3G 129
Pollokshields.—3G 129
Polmaily.—5G 159
Polmassick.—2G 5
Polmont.—2C 130
Polnessan.—3D 118
Polnish.—5F 149
Polperro.—4G 7
Polruan.—4F 7
Polscoe.—3F 7
Polsham.—4F 25
Polskeoch.—4F 119
Polstead.—4B 56
Polstead Heath.—3B 56
Poltesco.—5E 5
Poltimore.—4C 12
Polton.—3F 131
Polwarth.—4D 132
Polyphant.—1G 7
Polzeath.—2D 6
Ponde.—4D 48
Pondersbridge.—3B 66
Ponders End.—1E 31
Pond Street.—4D 54
Pondtail.—3G 29
Ponsanooth.—3E 5
Ponsongath.—5E 5
Ponsworthy.—2D 8
Pontamman.—1C 36
Pontantwn.—3H 172
Pontardawe.—2D 36
Pontardulais.—2B 36
Pont-ar-gothi.—5E 47
Pont ar Hydfer.—5A 48
Pontarllechau.—5G 47
Pontarsais.—2H 35
Pontblyddyn.—4E 85
Pontbren Llwyd.—2F 37
Pont Cyfung.—5G 83
Pontdolgoch.—1F 59
Pontefract.—3E 95
Ponteland.—2E 117
Ponterwyd.—2C 58
Pontesbury.—5F 73
Pontesford.—5G 73
Pontfadog.—2E 73
Pontfaen.—2E 73
(Clwyd)
Pontfaen.—1D 34
(Dyfed)
Pont-faen.—4B 48
(Powys)

Pontgarreg.—2C 46
Pont-Henri.—2A 36
Ponthir.—3B 38
Ponthirwaun.—3B 46
Pontllanfraith.—3H 37
Pontlliw.—2C 36
Pont Llogel.—4C 72
Pontlottyn.—2H 37
Pontlyfni.—5D 82
Pontneddfechan.—2F 37
Pont-newydd.—4D 84
(Clwyd)
Pont-newydd.—4H 35
(Dyfed)
Pontnewydd.—3A 38
(Gwent)
Pont Pen-y-benglog.—4F 83
Pontrhydfendigaid.—4C 58
Pont Rhyd-y-cyff.—4E 37
Pontrhydfen.—3D 36
Pontrhydygroes.—3C 58
Pontrhydyrun.—3A 38
Pont-Rhythallt.—4E 83
Pontrilas.—5F 49
Pontrilas Road.—5F 49
Pontrobert.—4D 72
Pont-rug.—4E 83
Ponts Green.—4A 20
Pontshaen.—3D 46
Pontshill.—5A 50
Pontsticill.—1G 37
Pont-Walby.—2C 37
Pontwelly.—4D 46
Pontwgan.—3G 83
Pontyates.—2A 36
Pontyberem.—1B 36
Pontybodkin.—5E 85
Pontyclun.—4G 37
Pontycymer.—3F 37
Pontyglazier.—1A 46
Pontygwaith.—3G 37
Pont-y-pant.—5G 83
Pontypool.—2A 38
Pontypridd.—4G 37
Pontywaun.—3A 38
Pooksgreen.—2B 16
Pool.—2D 4
(Cornwall)
Pool.—1A 4
(Isles of Scilly)
Pool.—1C 94
(West Yorkshire)
Poole.—4F 15
(Dorset)
Poole.—3E 95
(North Yorkshire)
Poole Green.—2A 74
Poole Keynes.—3A 40
Poolend.—2D 74
Poolewe.—5C 164
Pooley Bridge.—2F 105
Poolfold.—2C 74
Pool Head.—2H 49
Pool Hey.—1A 86
Poolhill.—5B 50
Poolmill.—5H 49
Pool o' Muckhart.—3B 138
Pool Quay.—4E 73
Poolsbrook.—5E 89
Pool Street.—4G 55
Pootings.—1F 19
Pope Hill.—3C 34
Pope's Hill.—1E 39
Popeswood.—2G 29
Popham.—4D 28
Poplar.—3E 31
Porchfield.—4C 16
Porin.—3F 159
Poringland.—2E 69
Porkellis.—3D 5
Porlock.—1E 23
Porlock Weir.—1E 23
Portachoillan.—4F 127
Port Ann.—1H 127
Port Appin.—4D 142
Port Askaig.—3C 126

Portavadie.—3H 127
Port Bannatyne.—3B 128
Portbury.—5D 38
Port Carlisle.—3D 114
Port Charlotte.—4A 126
Portchester.—2E 16
Port Clarence.—2B 108
Port Dinorwic.—4E 83
Port Driseach.—2A 128
Port Dundas.—3G 129
Port Ellen.—5B 126
Port Elphinstone.—1E 155
Portencross.—5C 128
Port Erin.—5A 110
Port Erroll.—5H 163
Porter's Fen Corner.—2E 67
Portesham.—5B 14
Portessie.—2B 162
Port e Vullen.—2D 110
Port Eynon.—4A 36
Portfield Gate.—3C 34
Portgate.—1A 8
Port Gaverne.—1E 6
Port Glasgow.—2E 128
Portgordon.—2A 162
Portgower.—2H 167
Porth.—3G 37
Porthallow.—4G 7
(nr. Looe, Corn.)
Porthallow.—4E 5
(nr. St Keverne, Corn.)
Porthcawl.—5E 36
Porthcothan.—2C 6
Porthcurno.—4A 4
Port Henderson.—1G 157
Porthgain.—1D 34
Porthgwarra.—4A 4
Porthill.—4G 73
Porthkerry.—5G 37
Porthleven.—4D 4
Porthmadog.—2E 71
Porth Mellin.—5D 4
Porthmeor.—3B 4
Porth Navas.—4E 5
Portholland.—3D 6
Porthoustock.—4F 5
Porthtowan.—2D 5
Porth-y-felin.—2B 82
Porthyrhyd.—1B 36
(nr. Carmarthen, Dyfed)
Porthyrhyd.—4G 47
(nr. Llandovery, Dyfed)
Porth-y-waen.—3E 73
Portincaple.—4B 136
Portington.—2H 95
Portinnisherrich.—2G 135
Portinscale.—2D 104
Port Isaac.—1D 6
Portishead.—5C 38
Portknockie.—2B 162
Port Lamont.—2B 128
Portlethen.—4G 155
Portlethen Station.—4G 155
Portling.—4F 113
Portloe.—3C 5
Port Logan.—5E 111
Portmahomack.—5G 167
Port Mary.—2E 135
Port Mead.—3C 36
Portmeirion.—2E 71
Portmellon.—2H 5
Port Mor.—1F 141
Portmore.—4B 16
Port Mulgrave.—3E 109
Portnacroish.—4D 142
Portnaguran.—4H 173
Portnahaven.—4A 126
Portnalong.—5C 156
Portnaluchaig.—5E 149
Portnancon.—2E 168
Portobello.—2G 131
(Lothian)
Portobello.—4D 94
(West Yorkshire)
Port of Menteith.—3E 137
Port of Ness.—1H 173

Porton.—5G 27
Portormin.—5D 170
Portpatrick.—4F 111
Port Quin.—1D 6
Port Ramsay.—4C 142
Portreath.—2D 4
Portree.—4D 157
Port St Mary.—5B 110
Portscatho.—3F 5
Portsea.—3E 17
Port Seton.—2H 131
Portskerra.—2A 170
Portskewett.—4D 28
Portslade-by-Sea.—5D 18
Portsmouth.—4E 17
(Hampshire)
Portsmouth.—3F 93
(West Yorkshire)
Port Soderick.—4C 110
Portsoy.—2C 162
Port Sunlight.—2F 85
Portswood.—2C 16
Port Talbot.—4D 36
Porttannachy.—2A 162
Port Tennant.—3C 36
Portuairk.—2F 141
Portvoller.—4H 173
Portway.—3G 49
(Hereford & Worcester)
Portway.—5E 63
(Warwickshire)
Port Wemyss.—4A 126
Port William.—5A 112
Portwrinkle.—4H 7
Poslingford.—3G 55
Postbridge.—2C 8
Postcombe.—3A 42
Post Green.—4E 15
Postling.—2F 21
Postlip.—5E 51
Post-mawr.—2D 46
Postwick.—2E 69
Potarch.—4D 154
Potsgrove.—4G 53
Potten End.—2D 42
Potter Brompton.—2E 103
Pottergate Street.—3D 68
Potterhanworth.—1H 77
Potterhanworth Booths.—1H 77
Potter Heigham.—4G 81
Potterne.—3E 27
Potterne Wick.—3E 27
Potternewton.—2D 94
Potters Bar.—2F 43
Potters Brook.—4D 99
Potters Cross.—4C 62
Potters Crouch.—2E 43
Potter's Forstal.—1C 20
Potter Somersal.—4F 75
Potterspury.—3E 53
Potter Street.—2A 44
Potterton.—2G 155
Potthorpe.—3B 80
Pottle Street.—4D 26
Potto.—4B 108
Potton.—3B 54
Pott Row.—5G 79
Pott Shrigley.—5G 87
Poughill.—3C 10
(Cornwall)
Poughill.—3B 12
(Devon)
Poulner.—3G 15
Poulshot.—3E 27
Poulton.—2C 40
Poulton-le-Fylde.—2A 92
Pound Bank.—5B 62
Poundfield.—2G 19
Poundgate.—3F 19
Pound Green.—3G 19
Pound Hill.—2D 19
Poundland.—1G 111
Poundon.—5D 52
Poundsgate.—2D 8

Poundstock.—4C 10
Pound Street.—2C 28
Pounsley.—3G 19
Powburn.—1E 121
Powderham.—5C 12
Powerstock.—4A 14
Powfoot.—3C 114
Powick.—2C 50
Powmill.—4C 138
Poxwell.—5C 14
Poyle.—3B 30
Poynings.—4D 18
Poyntington.—2B 14
Poynton.—4G 87
(Cheshire)
Poynton.—4H 73
(Shropshire)
Poynton Green.—4H 73
Poys Street.—5F 69
Poystreet Green.—2B 56
Praa Sands.—4C 4
Pratt's Bottom.—4F 31
Praze-an-Beeble.—3D 4
Prees.—2H 73
Preesall.—1A 92
Preesall Park.—1A 92
Prees Green.—2H 73
Prees Higher Heath.—2H 73
Prendergast.—3C 12
Prendwick.—3E 123
Pren-gwyn.—3D 46
Prenteg.—1E 71
Prenton.—2F 85
Prescot.—3B 86
Prescott.—2D 12
(Devon)
Prescott.—3G 73
(Shropshire)
Preshute.—2G 27
Pressen.—1C 122
Prestatyn.—2C 84
Prestbury.—5G 87
(Cheshire)
Prestbury.—5D 51
(Gloucestershire)
Presteigne.—4A 60
Presthope.—1C 60
Prestleigh.—4B 26
Preston.—4D 132
(Borders)
Preston.—2E 9
(Devon)
Preston.—5C 14
(Dorset)
Preston.—5E 19
(East Sussex)
Preston.—2B 40
(Gloucestershire)
Preston.—5A 54
(Hertfordshire)
Preston.—2D 97
(Humberside)
Preston.—4G 33
(nr. Canterbury, Kent)
Preston.—4E 32
(Faversham, Kent)
Preston.—3C 92
(Lancashire)
Preston.—2F 65
(Leicestershire)
Preston.—2B 132
(nr. East Linton, Lothian)
Preston.—2G 131
(Prestonpans, Lothian)
Preston.—2F 123
(Northumberland)
Preston.—4H 73
(Shropshire)
Preston.—2B 56
(Suffolk)
Preston.—5D 40
(nr. Aldbourne, Wilts.)
Preston.—5B 40
(nr. Lyneham, Wilts.)
Preston Bagot.—1F 51
Preston Bissett.—5D 52

Preston Bowyer.—1E 13
Preston Brockhurst.—3H 73
Preston Brook.—4C 86
Preston Candover.—1E 17
Preston Capes.—2C 52
Preston Cross.—4A 50
Preston Gubbals.—4G 73
Preston-le-Skerne.—2G 107
Preston Marsh.—3H 49
Prestonmill.—4G 113
Preston on Stour.—5G 51
Preston on the Hill.—4C 86
Preston on Wye.—3F 49
Prestonpans.—2G 131
Preston Plucknett.—2A 14
Preston-under-Scar.—5E 106
Preston upon the WealdMoors.
—1A 62
Preston Wynne.—3H 49
Prestwich.—2F 87
Prestwick.—2E 117
(Northumberland)
Prestwick.—2C 118
(Strathclyde)
Prestwick Airport.—2C 118
Prestwold.—5C 76
Prestwood.—2B 42
(Buckinghamshire)
Prestwood.—3F 75
(Staffordshire)
Price Town.—3F 37
Prickwillow.—4E 67
Priddy.—3F 25
Priestcliffe.—5B 88
Priesthill.—3G 129
Priest Hutton.—2E 99
Priestland.—1E 119
Priestweston.—1H 59
Priestwood.—5B 42
(Berkshire)
Priestwood.—4A 32
(Kent)
Primethorpe.—3C 64
Primrose Green.—4C 80
Primrose Hill.—4C 66
(Cambridgeshire)
Primrose Hill.—2B 76
(Derbyshire)
Primrose Hill.—2E 39
(Gloucestershire)
Primrose Hill.—2A 86
(Lancashire)
Primrose Valley.—2G 103
Primsidemill.—2C 122
Princes Gate.—3E 35
Princes Risborough.—2B 42
Princethorpe.—5B 64
Princetown.—2B 8
Prinsted.—3F 17
Prion.—4C 84
Prior Muir.—2H 139
Prior's Frome.—4H 49
Priors Halton.—3B 60
Priors Hardwick.—2B 52
Priorslee.—1B 62
Priors Marston.—2B 52
Priors Norton.—5C 50
Priory, The.—2B 28
Priory Wood.—3E 49
Priston.—2B 26
Pristow Green.—4D 68
Prittlewell.—2C 32
Privett.—1E 17
Prixford.—2B 22
Probus.—2F 5
Prospect.—5C 114
Provanmill.—3H 129
Prudhoe.—3D 117
Publow.—2B 26
Puckeridge.—5C 54
Puckington.—2G 13
Pucklechurch.—5E 39
Puckrup.—4C 50
Puddaven.—3D 9
Puddinglake.—1B 74

Puddington.—3F 85
(Cheshire)
Puddington.—2B 12
(Devon)
Puddlebrook.—1E 39
Puddledock.—3C 68
Puddletown.—4C 14
Pudleston.—2H 49
Pudsey.—2C 94
Pulborough.—4B 18
Puleston.—5B 74
Pulford.—5F 85
Pulham.—3C 14
Pulham Market.—4D 69
Pulham St Mary.—4E 69
Pulley.—5G 73
Pulloxhill.—4H 53
Pulverbatch.—5G 73
Pumpherston.—3D 130
Pumpsaint.—3F 47
Puncheston.—2D 34
Puncknowle.—5A 14
Punnett's Town.—3H 19
Purbrook.—3E 17
Purfleet.—3G 31
Puriton.—4D 24
Purleigh.—2E 45
Purley.—5H 41
(Berkshire)
Purley.—4E 31
(London)
Purlogue.—3H 59
Purls Bridge.—4D 67
Purse Caundle.—2B 14
Purslow.—2A 60
Purston Jaglin.—4E 95
Purtington.—3G 13
Purton.—2E 39
(nr. Lydney, Glos.)
Purton.—2E 39
(nr. Sharpness, Glos.)
Purton.—4B 40
(Wiltshire)
Purton Stoke.—3B 40
Pury End.—3E 52
Pusey.—3E 41
Putley.—4A 50
Putney.—3D 30
Putsborough.—1A 22
Puttenham.—1B 42
(Hertfordshire)
Puttenham.—1A 18
(Surrey)
Puttock End.—3A 56
Puttock's End.—1B 44
Puxton.—2E 25
Pwll.—2A 36
(Dyfed)
Pwll.—5D 72
(Powys)
Pwllcrochan.—4C 34
Pwll-glas.—5D 84
Pwllgoyw.—4C 48
Pwllheli.—2C 70
Pwllmeyric.—3D 38
Pwlltrap.—3F 35
Pwll-y-glaw.—3B 36
Pyecombe.—4D 19
Pye Corner.—4B 38
(Gwent)
Pye Corner.—1H 43
(Hertfordshire)
Pye Green.—1D 63
Pyewipe.—4E 97
Pyford.—5B 30
Pyle.—5C 16
(Isle of Wight)
Pyle.—4E 36
(Mid Glamorgan)
Pylle.—5B 26
Pymore.—4D 67
(Cambridgeshire)
Pymore.—4H 13
(Dorset)
Pyrton.—3H 41
Pytchley.—5F 65

Pyworthy.—3D 10

Quabbs.—2H 59
Quadring.—4B 78
Quadring Eaudike.—4B 78
Quainton.—5E 53
Quarley.—4A 28
Quarndon.—3H 75
Quarndon Common.—3H 75
Quarrendon.—1B 42
Quarrier's Homes.—3E 129
Quarrington.—3H 77
Quarrington Hill.—1G 107
Quarrybank.—4H 85
(Cheshire)
Quarry Bank.—4D 62
(West Midlands)
Quarry, The.—3F 39
Quarrywood.—2F 161
Quartalehouse.—4G 163
Quarter.—4A 130
(nr. Hamilton, S'clyde.)
Quarter.—3C 128
(nr. Largs, S'clyde.)
Quatford.—3B 62
Quatt.—4B 62
Quebec.—5E 117
Quedgeley.—1G 39
Queen Adelaide.—4E 67
Queenborough.—3D 32
Queen Camel.—1A 14
Queen Charlton.—2B 26
Queen Dart.—2B 12
Queenhill.—4C 50
Queen Oak.—5C 26
Queensbury.—2A 94
Queensferry.—4F 85
(Clwyd)
Queensferry.—2E 131
(Lothian)
Queenstown.—2A 92
Queen Street.—1A 20
(Kent)
Queen Street.—4B 40
(Wiltshire)
Queenzieburn.—2H 129
Quemerford.—2F 27
Quendale.—10E 175
Quendon.—4E 55
Queniborough.—1D 64
Quenington.—2C 40
Quernmore.—3E 99
Quethiock.—3H 7
Quick's Green.—5G 41
Quidenham.—4C 68
Quidhampton.—3D 28
(Hampshire)
Quidhampton.—5G 27
(Wiltshire)
Quidinish.—9C 173
Quilquox.—5G 163
Quina Brook.—2H 73
Quine's Hill.—4C 110
Quinton.—2E 53
(Northamptonshire)
Quinton.—4D 63
(West Midlands)
Quintrell Downs.—3C 6
Quixhill.—3F 75
Quoditch.—4E 11
Quorndon.—1C 64
Quothquan.—1B 120
Quoyloo.—5B 174

Rableyheath.—1F 43
Raby.—4C 114
(Cumbria)
Raby.—3F 85
(Merseyside)
Rachan Mill.—1D 120
Rachub.—4F 83
Rackenford.—2B 12
Rackham.—4B 18
Rackheath.—4E 81

Racks.—2B 114
Rackwick.—8B 174
(Hoy, Orkney)
Rackwick.—3D 174
(Westray, Orkney)
Radbourne.—4G 75
Radcliffe.—2E 87
(Manchester)
Radcliffe.—4G 123
(Northumberland)
Radcliffe on Trent.—4D 76
Radernie.—3G 139
Radford.—3B 26
(Avon)
Radford.—2E 51
(Hereford & Worcester)
Radford.—3C 76
(Nottinghamshire)
Radford.—4H 63
(West Midlands)
Radford Semele.—1H 51
Radipole.—5B 14
Radlett.—1C 30
Radley.—3G 41
Radnage.—3A 42
Radstock.—3B 26
Radstone.—3C 52
Radway.—3A 52
Radway Green.—2B 74
Radwell.—2H 53
(Bedfordshire)
Radwell.—4B 54
(Hertfordshire)
Radwinter.—4F 55
Radyr.—4H 37
Rafford.—3E 161
Ragdale.—1D 64
Ragdon.—1B 60
Ragged Appleshaw.—4B 28
Raggra.—4F 171
Raglan.—2C 38
Ragnall.—5A 90
Raigbeg.—1C 152
Rainford.—2B 86
Rainford Junction.—2B 86
Rainham.—4C 32
(Kent)
Rainham.—2G 31
(London)
Rainhill.—3B 86
Rainow.—5G 87
Rainton.—2G 101
Rainton Bridge.—5G 117
Rainworth.—2C 76
Raisbeck.—4H 105
Raise.—5A 116
Rait.—1E 139
Raithby.—4F 91
(nr. Louth, Lincs.)
Raithby.—1C 78
(nr. Spilsby, Lincs.)
Raithwaite.—3F 109
Rake.—1G 17
Rake End.—1E 63
Rakeway.—3E 75
Rakewood.—1G 87
Ralia.—4B 152
Ram Alley.—2H 27
Ramasaig.—4A 156
Rame.—3E 5
(nr. Falmouth, Corn.)
Rame.—5A 8
(nr. Torpoint, Corn.)
Ram Lane.—1D 20
Ramnageo.—2H 175
Rampisham.—3A 14
Rampside.—3B 98
Rampton.—1D 54
(Cambridgeshire)
Rampton.—5H 89
(Nottinghamshire)
Ramsbottom.—1E 87
Ramsburn.—3C 162
Ramsbury.—5D 40
Ramscraigs.—5D 170
Ramsdean.—1F 17

Ramsdell.—3D 28
Ramsden.—3D 42
(Hereford & Worcester)
Ramsden.—1E 41
(Oxfordshire)
Ramsden Bellhouse.—1B 32
Ramsden Heath.—1B 32
Ramsey.—4B 66
(Cambridgeshire)
Ramsey.—4E 57
(Essex)
Ramsey.—2D 110
(Isle of Man)
Ramsey Forty Foot.—4C 66
Ramsey Heights.—4B 66
Ramsey Mereside.—4B 66
Ramsey St Mary's.—4B 66
Ramsgate.—4H 33
Ramshorn.—3E 75
Ramsley.—4G 11
Ramsnest Common.—2A 18
Ranby.—5E 91
(Lincolnshire)
Ranby.—4G 89
(Nottinghamshire)
Rand.—5D 90
Randwick.—2G 39
Ranfurly.—3F 129
Rangag.—4D 170
Rangemore.—5F 75
Rangeworthy.—4E 39
Ranish.—5G 173
Rankinston.—3D 118
Rank's Green.—1D 44
Ranmore Common.—5C 30
Rann.—3E 93
Rannoch Station.—3B 144
Ranochan.—5G 149
Ranskill.—4G 89
Ranton.—5C 74
Ranton Green.—5C 74
Ranworth.—4F 81
Raploch.—4G 137
Rapness.—3E 174
Rapps.—2G 13
Rascal Moor.—2A 96
Rascarrel.—5E 113
Rase Hill.—2F 93
Rashfield.—1C 128
Rashwood.—1D 50
Raskelf.—2H 101
Rasmsgill.—2E 100
Rassau.—1H 37
Rastrick.—3B 94
Ratagan.—2B 150
Ratby.—2C 64
Ratcliffe Culey.—3H 63
Ratcliffe on Soar.—5B 76
Ratcliffe on the Wreake.—1D 64
Rathen.—2H 163
Rathfriland.—3D 10
Rathillet.—1F 139
Rathmell.—4B 100
Ratho.—2E 131
Ratho Station.—2E 131
Rathven.—2B 162
Ratley.—1B 16
(Hampshire)
Ratley.—3A 52
(Warwickshire)
Ratlinghope.—1B 60
Rattar.—1E 171
Ratten Row.—5E 115
(Cumbria)
Ratten Row.—1B 92
(Lancashire)
Rattery.—3D 8
Rattlesden.—2B 56
Ratten Village.—5G 19
Rattray.—3H 163
(Grampian)
Rattray.—4A 146
(Tayside)
Raughton.—5E 115

Raughton Head.—5E 115
Raunds.—5G 65
Ravenfield.—3E 89
Ravenglass.—5B 104
Ravenhills Green.—2B 50
Raveningham.—3F 69
Ravenscar.—4G 109
Ravenscraig.—2C 110
Ravensden.—2H 53
Ravenshead.—2C 76
Ravensmoor.—2A 74
Ravensthorpe.—5D 64
(Northamptonshire)
Ravensthorpe.—3C 94
(West Yorkshire)
Ravenstonedale.—4A 106
Ravenstone.—2F 53
(Buckinghamshire)
Ravenstone.—1B 64
(Leicestershire)
Ravenstown.—2C 98
Ravenstruther.—5C 130
Ravensworth.—4E 107
Raw.—4G 109
Rawcliffe.—3G 95
(Humberside)
Rawcliffe.—4A 102
(North Yorkshire)
Rawcliffe Bridge.—3G 95
Rawdon.—2C 94
Rawgreen.—4C 116
Rawmarsh.—3E 89
Rawnsley.—1E 63
Rawreth.—1B 32
Rawridge.—3F 13
Rawtenstall.—3F 93
Raydon.—4C 56
Rayleys.—5D 122
Rayleigh.—1C 32
Raymond's Hill.—4G 13
Rayne.—5G 55
Rayners Lane.—2C 30
Reach.—1E 55
Read.—2E 93
Reading.—5A 42
Reading Green.—5E 69
Reading Street.—2D 20
Readymoney.—4F 7
Reagill.—3H 105
Rea Hill.—4F 9
Rearquhar.—4E 167
Rearsby.—1D 64
Reasby.—5C 90
Rease Heath.—2A 74
Reaster.—2E 171
Reawick.—7E 175
Reay.—2B 170
Rechullin.—3A 158
Reculver.—4G 33
Redberth.—4D 35
Redbourn.—1E 43
Redbourne.—5B 96
Redbridge.—1F 31
Redbrook.—1H 73
(Clwyd)
Redbrook.—1D 38
(Gloucestershire)
Redburn.—4D 160
(Highland)
Redburn.—3A 116
(Northumberland)
Redcar.—2D 108
Redcastle.—4H 159
Redcliff.—4C 62
Redcliff Bay.—5C 38
Red Dial.—5D 114
Redding.—2C 130
Reddingmuirhead.—2C 130
Reddings, The.—5D 50
Reddish.—3F 37
Redditch.—1E 51
Rede.—2A 56
Redenhall.—4E 69
Redesdale Camp.—5C 122
Redesmouth.—1B 116

Redford.—4E 147
(Tayside)
Redford.—1G 17
(West Sussex)
Redfordgreen.—3F 121
Redgate.—3G 7
Redgrave.—5C 144
Redhill.—2E 25
(Avon)
Redhill.—3E 155
(Grampian)
Redhill.—4B 54
(Hertfordshire)
Redhill.—1B 62
(Shropshire)
Redhill.—5D 31
(Surrey)
Red Hill.—2F 51
(Warwickshire)
Red Hill.—3E 95
(West Yorkshire)
Redhouses.—3B 126
Redisham.—4G 69
Redland.—5D 39
(Avon)
Redland.—5C 174
(Orkney)
Redlingfield.—5D 69
Red Lodge.—1F 55
Redlynch.—5C 26
(Somerset)
Redlynch.—1H 15
(Wiltshire)
Redmain.—1C 104
Redmarley.—1B 50
Redmarley D'Abitot.—4B 50
Redmarshall.—2C 107
Redmile.—4E 77
Redmire.—5D 106
Rednal.—3F 73
Redpath.—1H 121
Redpoint.—2G 157
Red Post.—2C 10
Red Rock.—2C 86
Red Roses.—3F 35
Red Row.—5G 123
Redruth.—2E 5
Red Street.—2C 74
Redvales.—2F 87
Red Wharf Bay.—2E 83
Redwick.—4D 38
(Avon)
Redwick.—4C 38
(Gwent)
Redworth.—2F 107
Reed.—4C 54
Reed End.—4C 54
Reedham.—5C 90
(Lincolnshire)
Reedham.—5G 81
(Norfolk)
Reedness.—2G 95
Reeds Beck.—1B 78
Reef.—4D 173
Reemshill.—4E 163
Reepham.—5C 90
(Lincolnshire)
Reepham.—3C 80
(Norfolk)
Reeth.—5D 106
Regaby.—2D 110
Reghoul.—3C 160
Reiff.—2D 164
Reigate.—5D 30
Reighton.—2G 103
Reith.—2H 59
Reisque.—1F 155
Reiss.—3F 171
Rejerrah.—3C 6
Releath.—3D 4
Relubbus.—3C 4
Relugas.—4D 161
Remenham.—4A 42
Remenham Hill.—4A 42
Rempstone.—5C 76
Rendcomb.—2B 40
Rendham.—1F 57
Renfrew.—3G 129
Renhold.—2H 53

Renishaw.—5E 89
Rennington.—3G 123
Renton.—2E 129
Renwick.—5G 115
Repps.—4G 81
Repton.—5H 75
Rescarie.—4B 160
Rescassa.—2G 5
Rescobie.—3E 147
Rescorla.—2G 5
Resipole.—2B 142
Resolis.—2A 160
Resolven.—2E 37
Rest and be thankful.—3B 136
Reston.—3E 133
Restrop.—4B 40
Retew.—4D 6
Retire.—2E 5
Rettendon.—1B 32
Retyn.—4C 6
Revesby.—1B 78
Rew.—5D 8
Rewe.—4C 12
Rew Street.—4C 16
Rexon.—1A 8
Reybridge.—2E 27
Reydon.—5H 69
Reymerston.—2C 68
Reynalton.—4D 35
Reynoldston.—4A 36
Rezare.—2H 7
Rhadyr.—2B 38
Rhandirmwyn.—3G 47
Rhayader.—4F 59
Rheindown.—4H 159
Rhemore.—3G 141
Rhenetra.—3D 156
Rhenigidale.—7E 173
Rhewl-Mostyn.—2D 84
Rhewl.—1D 172
(nr. Llangollen, Clwyd)
Rhewl.—4D 84
(nr. Ruthin, Clwyd)
Rhewl.—2F 37
(Shropshire)
Rhian.—2C 166
Rhian Breck.—3C 166
Rhicarn.—1E 165
Rhiconich.—3C 168
Rhicullen.—1A 160
Rhidorroch.—4F 165
Rhifail.—4H 169
Rhigos.—2F 37
Rhilochan.—3E 167
Rhiroy.—5F 165
Rhitongue.—3G 169
Rhiw.—3B 70
Rhiwbina.—4H 37
Rhiwbryfdir.—1F 71
Rhiwderin.—4A 38
Rhiwlas.—2D 72
(Clwyd)
Rhiwlas.—2B 72
(nr. Bala, Gwynedd)
Rhiwlas.—4C 82
(nr. Bangor, Gwynedd)
Rhodes.—2F 87
Rhodesia.—4F 89
Rhodes Minnis.—1F 21
Rhodiad.—2A 34
Rhondda.—3F 37
Rhonehouse.—4E 113
Rhoose.—5G 37
Rhos.—4C 46
(Dyfed)
Rhos.—2D 36
(West Glamorgan)
Rhosaman.—1D 36
Rhoscefnhir.—3E 83
Rhoscolyn.—3B 82
Rhos Common.—4E 73
Rhoscrowther.—4C 34
Rhos-ddu.—2B 70
Rhosdylluan.—3A 72
Rhosesmor.—4E 84
Rhos-fawr.—2C 70

Rhosgadfan.—5E 83
Rhosgoch.—2D 82
(Gwynedd)
Rhosgoch.—3D 48
(Powys)
Rhos Haminiog.—1E 47
Rhos-hill.—3A 46
Rhoshirwaun.—3A 70
Rhoslan.—1D 71
Rhoslefain.—5E 71
Rhosllanerchrugog.—1E 73
Rhosmaen.—5F 47
Rhosmeirch.—3D 82
Rhosneigr.—3C 82
Rhos-on-Sea.—2H 83
Rhossili.—4A 36
Rhosson.—2A 34
Rhos, The.—3D 34
Rhostrehwfa.—3D 82
Rhostryfan.—5D 83
Rhostyllen.—1F 73
Rhoswiel.—2E 73
Rhosybol.—2D 82
Rhos-y-brithdir.—3D 72
Rhos-y-garth.—3B 58
Rhos-y-gwaliau.—2B 72
Rhos-y-llan.—2B 70
Rhos-y-meirch.—4H 59
Rhu.—1D 128
Rhuallt.—3C 84
Rhuddall Heath.—4H 85
Rhuddlan.—3C 84
Rhue.—4E 165
Rhulen.—3D 48
Rhunahaorine.—5F 127
Rhuthun.—5D 84
Rhuvoult.—3C 168
Rhyd.—1F 71
Rhydargaeau.—2H 35
Rhydcymerau.—4E 47
Rhydd.—3C 50
Rhyd-Ddu.—5E 83
Rhydding.—3D 36
Rhyddian.—3D 47
Rhydfelin.—4G 37
Rhydfudr.—4A 58
Rhydlanfair.—5H 83
Rhydlewis.—3C 46
Rhydlios.—2A 70
Rhyd-lydan.—5A 84
Rhyd-meirionydd.—2B 58
Rhydowen.—3D 46
Rhydrosser.—4A 58
Rhydspence.—3E 49
Rhydtalog.—5E 85
Rhyd-uchaf.—2B 72
Rhydwyn.—2C 82
Rhyd-y-clafdy.—2C 70
Rhydycroesau.—2E 73
Rhydyfelin.—3A 58
Rhyd-y-foel.—3B 84
Rhydyfro.—2D 36
Rhydymain.—3H 71
Rhyd-y-meirch.—2B 38
Rhyd-y-meudwy.—5D 84
Rhydymwyn.—4E 84
Rhyd-yr-onnen.—5F 71
Rhyd-y-sarn.—1F 71
Rhyl.—2C 84
Rhymney.—2H 37
Rhynd.—1D 138
Rhynie.—1B 154
Ribbesford.—5B 62
Ribbleton.—2F 92
Ribchester.—2D 92
Riber.—2H 75
Ribigill.—3F 169
Riby.—5D 97
Riccall.—2G 95
Riccarton.—1D 118
Richards Castle.—4B 60
Richborough Port.—4H 33
Riching's Park.—3B 30
Richmond.—4E 107
Richmond upon Thames.—3C 30
Rickarton.—5F 155

Rickerby.—4F 115
Rickerscote.—5D 74
Rickford.—3E 25
Rickham.—5D 8
Rickinghall Inferior.—5C 68
Rickinghall Superior.—5C 68
Rickleton.—4F 117
Rickling.—4D 55
Rickling Green.—5E 55
Rickmansworth.—1B 30
Riddings.—2B 110
Riddlecombe.—2G 11
Riddlesden.—1A 94
Ridge.—5E 15
(Dorset)
Ridge.—2F 43
(Hertfordshire)
Ridge.—5E 27
(Wiltshire)
Ridgebourne.—4F 59
Ridgehill.—2F 25
Ridge Lane.—3G 63
Ridgeway.—2A 76
(nr. Alfreton, Derbys.)
Ridgeway.—4E 88
(nr. Sheffield, Derbys.)
Ridgeway.—2C 74
(Staffordshire)
Ridgeway Cross.—3B 50
Ridgeway Moor.—4E 88
Ridgewell.—3G 55
Ridgewood.—4F 19
Ridgmont.—4G 53
Ridgwardine.—4A 74
Riding Mill.—3D 116
Ridley.—4H 31
(Kent)
Ridley.—3A 116
(Northumberland)
Ridlington.—2F 65
(Leicestershire)
Ridlington.—2F 81
(Norfolk)
Ridsdale.—1C 116
Riemore Lodge.—4H 145
Rienachait.—1E 165
Rievaulx.—1A 102
Rift House.—1B 108
Rigg.—3D 114
Riggend.—2A 130
Rigmaden Park.—1F 99
Rigsby.—5G 91
Rigside.—1A 120
Riley Green.—2E 92
Rileyhill.—1F 63
Rilla Mill.—2G 7
Rillington.—2D 102
Rimington.—1F 93
Rimpton.—1B 14
Rimsdale.—4H 169
Rimswell.—3F 97
Ringasta.—10E 175
Ringford.—4D 113
Ringing Hill.—1B 64
Ringinglow.—4C 88
Ringland.—4D 80
Ringlestone.—5C 32
Ringmer.—4F 19
Ringmore.—5C 8
(nr. Kingsbridge, Devon)
Ringmore.—2F 9
(nr. Teignmouth, Devon)
Ring O'Bells.—1B 86
Ring's End.—2C 66
Ringsfield.—4G 69
Ringsfield Corner.—4G 69
Ringshall.—1C 42
(Hertfordshire)
Ringshall.—2C 56
(Suffolk)
Ringshall Stocks.—2C 56
Ringstead.—3G 79
(Norfolk)
Ringstead.—5G 65
(Northamptonshire)
Ringwood.—3G 15

Ringwould.—1H 21
Rinmore.—2B 154
Rinnigill.—8C 174
Rinsey.—4C 4
Ripe.—4G 19
Ripley.—2A 76
(Derbyshire)
Ripley.—4G 15
(Hampshire)
Ripley.—3F 101
(North Yorkshire)
Ripley.—5B 30
(Surrey)
Riplingham.—2B 96
Riplington.—1E 17
Ripon.—2G 101
Rippingale.—5H 77
Ripple.—4C 50
(Hereford & Worcester)
Ripple.—1H 21
(Kent)
Ripponden.—1H 87
Rireavoch.—4E 165
Risabus.—5B 126
Risbury.—2H 49
Risby.—2C 96
(nr. Hull, Humberside)
Risby.—4B 96
(nr. Scunthorpe, Humberside)
Risby.—1A 56
(Suffolk)
Risca.—3A 38
Rise.—1D 96
Riseden.—2H 19
(East Sussex)
Riseden.—2B 20
(Kent)
Rise End.—2G 75
Risegate.—5B 78
Riseholme.—5B 90
Riseley.—1H 53
(Bedfordshire)
Riseley.—2F 29
(Berkshire)
Rishangles.—1D 56
Rishton.—2E 93
Rishworth.—1H 87
Risley.—3D 86
(Cheshire)
Risley.—4B 76
(Derbyshire)
Risplith.—3F 101
Rispond.—2E 169
Rivar.—2B 28
Rivenhall.—1E 45
Rivenhall End.—1E 45
River.—1H 17
River Bank.—1E 55
Riverhead.—5G 31
Rivington.—1D 86
Roach Bridge.—3C 92
Roachill.—3E 23
Roade.—2E 53
Road Green.—3E 69
Roadhead.—2G 115
Roadmeetings.—5B 130
Roadside.—2D 170
Roadside of Catterline.—1H 147
Roadside of Kinneff.—1H 147
Roadwater.—2G 23
Road Weedon.—2D 52
Roag.—4B 156
Roa Island.—3B 98
Roath.—5H 37
Roberton.—3G 121
(Borders)
Roberton.—2B 120
(Strathclyde)
Robertsbridge.—3B 20
Robertstown.—4G 161
(Grampian)
Robertstown.—2G 37
(Mid Glamorgan)
Roberttown.—3B 94
Robeston Back.—3D 35
Robeston Wathen.—3D 35

Robeston West.—4B 34
Robin Hood.—1C 86
(Lancashire)
Robin Hood.—3D 94
(West Yorkshire)
Robinhood End.—4G 55
Robin Hood's Bay.—4G 109
Roborough.—2F 11
(nr. Great Torrington, Devon)
Roborough.—3B 8
(nr. Plymouth, Devon)
Rob Roy's House.—2A 136
Roby.—3B 86
Roby Mill.—2C 86
Rocester.—4F 75
Roch.—2B 34
Rochdale.—1F 87
Roche.—3D 6
Rochester.—4B 32
(Kent)
Rochester.—5C 122
(Northumberland)
Rochford.—1C 32
Rock.—2D 6
(Cornwall)
Rock.—5B 62
(Hereford & Worcester)
Rock.—2G 123
(Northumberland)
Rock.—4C 18
(West Sussex)
Rockbeare.—4D 12
Rockbourne.—2G 15
Rockcliffe.—3E 115
(Cumbria)
Rockcliffe.—4F 113
(Dumfries & Galloway)
Rockcliffe Cross.—3E 115
Rock Ferry.—2F 85
Rockfield.—1C 38
(Gwent)
Rockfield.—5G 167
(Highland)
Rockford.—3G 15
Rockgreen.—3C 60
Rockhampton.—3E 39
Rockhead.—1E 7
Rock Hill.—1D 50
Rockingham.—3F 65
Rockland All Saints.—3B 68
Rockland St Mary.—2F 69
Rockland St Peter.—3B 68
Rockley.—5C 40
Rockwell End.—4A 42
Rockwell Green.—1E 13
Rodborough.—2G 39
Rodbourne.—4H 39
Rodd.—4A 60
Roddam.—2E 123
Rodden.—5B 14
Roddymoor.—1E 107
Rode.—3D 26
Rode Heath.—2C 74
(nr. Alsager, Ches.)
Rodeheath.—1C 74
(nr. Congleton, Ches.)
Roden.—4H 73
Rodenloft.—2D 119
Rodhuish.—2G 23
Rodington.—4H 73
Rodley.—1F 39
Rodmarton.—3H 39
Rodmell.—5F 19
Rodmersham.—4D 32
Rodmersham Green.—4D 32
Rodney Stoke.—4E 25
Rodsley.—3G 75
Rodway.—1A 62
(Shropshire)
Rodway.—4C 24
(Somerset)
Rodwell.—5B 14
Roecliffe.—3G 101
Roe Green.—4C 54
Roehampton.—3D 30

Roewen.—3G 83
Roffey.—2C 18
Rogart.—3E 167
Rogate.—16 17
Roger Ground.—5E 105
Rogerstone.—4A 38
Rogiet.—4C 38
Rogue's Alley.—2C 66
Roke.—3H 41
Rokemarsh.—3H 41
Roker.—4H 117
Rollesby.—4G 81
Rolleston.—2E 65
(Leicestershire)
Rolleston.—2E 77
(Nottinghamshire)
Rolleston.—5G 75
(Staffordshire)
Rolston.—1E 97
Rolvenden.—2C 20
Rolvenden Layne.—2C 20
Romaldkirk.—2C 106
Roman Bank.—4F 79
Romanby.—5G 107
Roman Camp.—2D 131
Romannobridge.—5E 131
Romansleigh.—3D 22
Romers Common.—4C 60
Romesdal.—3D 156
Romford.—3F 15
(Dorset)
Romford.—2G 31
(London)
Romiley.—3G 87
Romsey.—1B 16
Romsley.—5D 62
(Hereford & Worcester)
Romsley.—4B 62
(Shropshire)
Ronague.—4B 110
Rookhope.—5C 116
Rookley.—5D 16
Rooks Bridge.—3D 24
Rooksey Green.—2B 56
Rooks Nest.—2G 23
Rookwood.—4F 17
Roos.—2E 97
Roosebeck.—3B 98
Roosecote.—3B 98
Rootfield.—3H 159
Rootham's Green.—2A 54
Rootpark.—4C 130
Ropley.—5E 29
Ropley Dean.—5E 29
Ropsley.—4G 77
Rora.—3H 163
Rorandle.—2D 154
Rorrington.—5F 73
Rose.—4B 6
Roseacre.—2B 92
Rose Ash.—3D 23
Rosebank.—5B 130
Rosebush.—2D 35
Rosedale Abbey.—5E 109
Roseden.—2E 123
Rose Green.—5B 56
(Essex)
Rose Green.—3B 56
(Suffolk)
Rosehall.—3B 166
Rosehearty.—2G 163
Rose Hill.—4F 19
(East Sussex)
Rosehill.—4A 74
(nr. Market Drayton, Shrops.)
Rosehill.—4G 73
(nr. Shrewsbury, Shrops.)
Roseisle.—2F 161
Rosemarket.—4C 34
Rosemarkie.—3B 160
Rosemary Lane.—2E 13
Rosemount.—4A 146
Rosenannon.—3D 6
Roser's Cross.—3G 19
Rosevean.—4E 6

Rosewell.—3F 131
Roseworth.—2B 108
Roseworthy.—3D 4
Rosgill.—3G 105
Roshven.—1B 142
Roskhill.—4B 156
Roskorwell.—4E 5
Rosley.—5E 114
Roslin.—3F 131
Roslliston.—1G 63
Rosneath.—1D 128
Ross.—3F 133
(Borders)
Ross.—5D 112
(Dumfries & Galloway)
Ross.—1F 123
(Northumberland)
Ross.—1G 137
(Tayside)
Rossett.—5F 85
Rossington.—3G 89
Rosskeen.—2A 160
Rossland.—2F 129
Ross-on-Wye.—5A 50
Roster.—5E 171
Rostherne.—4E 87
Rostholme.—2F 89
Rosthwaite.—3D 104
Roston.—3F 75
Rosudgeon.—4C 4
Rosyth.—5D 138
Rothbury.—4E 123
Rotherby.—1D 64
Rotherfield.—3G 19
Rotherfield Greys.—4A 42
Rotherfield Peppard.—4A 42
Rotherham.—3E 89
Rothersthorpe.—2E 52
Rotherwick.—3F 29
Rothes.—4G 161
Rothesay.—3B 128
Rothienorman.—5E 162
Rothiesholm.—5F 174
Rothley.—1C 64
(Leicestershire)
Rothley.—1D 116
(Northumberland)
Rothwell.—3D 90
(Lincolnshire)
Rothwell.—4F 65
(Northamptonshire)
Rothwell.—3D 94
(West Yorkshire)
Rothwell Haigh.—3D 94
Rotsea.—4F 103
Rottal.—2C 146
Rotten End.—1F 57
Rottenhill.—3H 163
Rotten Row.—5G 41
(Berkshire)
Rotten Row.—4C 80
(Norfolk)
Rotten Row.—5F 63
(West Midlands)
Rottingdean.—5E 19
Rottington.—3A 104
Roud.—5D 16
Rougham.—3A 80
(Norfolk)
Rougham.—1B 56
(Suffolk)
Rougham Green.—1B 56
Rough Close.—4D 74
Rough Common.—5F 33
Roughcote.—3D 74
Rough Haugh.—4H 169
Rough Hay.—5G 75
Roughlee.—1F 93
Roughley.—3F 63
Roughsike.—2G 115
Roughton.—1B 78
(Lincolnshire)
Roughton.—2E 81
(Norfolk)
Roughton.—3B 62
(Shropshire)

Roundbush Green.—1B 44
Roundham.—3H 13
Roundhay.—2D 94
Round Hill.—3F 9
Roundhurst Common.—2A 18
Round Oak.—2A 60
Roundstreet Common.—3B 18
Roundthwaite.—4H 105
Roundway.—2F 27
Roundyhill.—3C 146
Rousdon.—4F 13
Rousham.—5B 52
Rous Lench.—2E 51
Routh.—1C 96
Rout's Green.—3A 42
Row.—4C 7
(Cornwall)
Row.—1D 98
(nr. Kendal, Cumbria)
Row.—1H 105
(nr. Penrith, Cumbria)
Rowanburn.—2F 115
Rowardennan.—4C 136
Rowarth.—4H 87
Row Ash.—1D 16
Rowberrow.—3E 25
Rowde.—2E 27
Rowden.—4G 11
Rowden Hill.—5H 39
Rowfoot.—3H 115
Row Green.—5C 55
Row Heath.—1H 45
Rowhedge.—5C 56
Rowhook.—2C 18
Rowington.—1G 51
Rowland.—5C 88
Rowland's Castle.—2F 17
Rowlands Gill.—4E 117
Rowledge.—4G 29
Rowley.—5D 117
(Durham)
Rowley.—2B 96
(Humberside)
Rowley.—5F 73
(Shropshire)
Rowley.—5F 75
(Staffordshire)
Rowley Hill.—4B 94
Rowley Regis.—4D 62
Rowlstone.—5F 49
Rowly.—1B 18
Rowner.—3D 16
Rowney Green.—5E 63
Rownhams.—2B 16
Rowrah.—3B 104
Rowsham.—1B 42
Rowsley.—1G 75
Rowson Green.—3A 76
Rowstock.—4F 41
Rowston.—2H 77
Rowton.—4G 85
(Cheshire)
Rowton.—2D 60
(nr. Ludlow, Shrops.)
Rowton.—1A 62
(nr. Shrewsbury, Shrops.)
Rowton.—4F 73
(nr. Telford, Shrops.)
Row Town.—4B 30
Roxburgh.—1A 122
Roxby.—4B 96
(Humberside)
Roxby.—3E 109
(North Yorkshire)
Roxton.—2A 54
Roxwell.—2C 44
Royal Leamington Spa.—1H 51
Royal Oak.—2F 107
(Durham)
Royal Oak.—2B 86
(Lancashire)
Royal Oak.—2G 103
(North Yorkshire)
Royal's Green.—3A 74
Royal Tunbridge Wells.—2G 19

Roybridge.—5E 151
Roydon.—1H 43
(Essex)
Roydon.—4C 68
(nr. Diss, Norf.)
Roydon.—5G 79
(nr. King's Lynn, Norf.)
Roydon Hamlet.—2H 43
Royston.—3C 54
(Hertfordshire)
Royston.—4D 94
(South Yorkshire)
Royston Water.—2F 13
Royton.—2G 87
Ruabon.—1F 73
Ruadh-phort Mor.—3C 126
Ruaig.—4B 140
Ruan High Lanes.—3G 5
Ruan Lanihorne.—2F 5
Ruan Minor.—5E 5
Ruarach.—1B 150
Ruardean.—1E 39
Ruardean Hill.—1E 39
Ruardean Woodside.—1E 39
Rubery.—5D 63
Rubha Stoer.—5A 168
Ruchazie.—3H 129
Ruckcroft.—5G 115
Ruckhall Common.—4G 49
Ruckinge.—2E 21
Ruckland.—5F 91
Rucklers Lane.—2D 42
Ruckley.—5H 73
Rudby.—4B 108
Ruddington.—4C 76
Rudford.—5B 50
Rudge.—3C 62
(Shropshire)
Rudge.—3D 26
(Somerset)
Rudge Heath.—3B 62
Rudgeway.—4E 39
Rudgwick.—2B 18
Rudhall.—5A 50
Rudheath.—5D 86
Rudley Green.—2E 45
Rudloe.—5G 39
Rudry.—4H 37
Rudston.—3F 103
Rudyard.—2D 74
Rufford.—1B 86
Rufforth.—4A 102
Rugby.—5C 64
Rugeley.—1E 63
Ruilick.—4H 159
Ruisaurie.—4G 159
Ruisgarry.—9B 173
Ruishton.—1F 13
Ruislip.—2B 30
Ruislip Common.—2B 30
Rumbling Bridge.—4C 138
Rumburgh.—4F 69
Rumford.—2C 130
(Central)
Rumford.—2C 6
(Cornwall)
Rumney.—5A 38
Rumwell.—1E 13
Runcorn.—4C 86
Runcton.—3G 17
Runcton Holme.—2F 67
Rundlestone.—2B 8
Runfold.—4G 29
Runhall.—2C 68
Runham.—4G 81
Runnington.—1E 12
Runshaw Moor.—1C 86
Runswick.—3F 109
Runtaleave.—2B 146
Runwell.—1B 32
Ruscombe.—5A 42
Rushall.—4H 57
(Hereford & Worcester)
Rushall.—4D 69
(Norfolk)

236 G.B. Handy

Rushall.—2F 63
(West Midlands)
Rushall.—3G 27
(Wiltshire)
Rushbrook.—1A 56
Rushbury.—1C 60
Rushden.—4C 54
(Hertfordshire)
Rushden.—1H 5
(Northamptonshire)
Rushford.—2A 8
(Devon)
Rushford.—4B 68
(Norfolk)
Rush Green.—5B 54
Rushlake Green.—4H 19
Rushmere.—4G 69
Rushmere St Andrew.—3D 57
Rushmoor.—4G 29
Rushock.—5C 62
Rusholme.—3F 87
Rushton.—4H 85
(Cheshire)
Rushton.—4F 65
(Northamptonshire)
Rushton.—2A 62
(Shropshire)
Rushton Spencer.—1D 74
Rushwick.—2C 50
Rushyford.—2F 107
Ruskie.—3F 137
Ruskington.—2H 77
Rusland.—1C 98
Rusper.—2D 8
Ruspidge.—1E 39
Russell's Water.—4A 42
Russel's Green.—5E 69
Russ Hill.—1D 18
Russland.—6C 174
Rusthall.—2G 19
Rustington.—5B 18
Ruston.—1E 103
Ruston Parva.—3F 103
Ruswarp.—4F 109
Rutherglen.—3H 129
Ruthernbridge.—3E 6
Ruthin.—5D 84
(Clwyd)
Ruthin.—5F 37
(South Glamorgan)
Ruthrieston.—3G 155
Ruthven.—4C 162
(Grampian)
Ruthven.—5C 160
(nr. Inverness, H'land.)
Ruthven.—4B 152
(nr. Kingussie, H'land.)
Ruthven.—4B 146
(Tayside)
Ruthvoes.—3D 6
Ruthwaite.—1D 104
Ruthwell.—3B 114
Ruxton Green.—1D 38
Ruyton-XI-Towns.—3F 73
Ryal.—2D 116
Ryall.—4H 13
(Dorset)
Ryall.—3C 50
(Hereford & Worcester)
Ryarsh.—5A 32
Rychraggan.—5G 159
Ryde.—4E 105
Ryde.—4D 16
Rye.—3D 20
Ryecroft Gate.—1D 74
Ryeford.—5A 50
Rye Foreign.—3C 20
Rye Harbour.—4D 20
Ryehill.—3F 97
Rye Street.—4B 50
Ryhall.—1H 65
Ryhill.—4D 94
Ryhope.—4H 117
Ryhope Colliery.—4H 117
Rylands.—4C 76
Rylstone.—4C 100

Ryme Intrinseca.—2A 14
Ryther.—2F 95
Ryton.—4B 50
(Gloucestershire)
Ryton.—2C 102
(North Yorkshire)
Ryton.—2B 62
(Shropshire)
Ryton.—3E 117
(Tyne & Wear)
Ryton.—4A 64
(Warwickshire)
Ryton-on-Dunsmore.—5A 64
Ryton Woodside.—3E 117

Saasaig.—3E 149
Sabden.—2E 93
Sacombe.—1G 43
Sacriston.—5F 117
Sadberge.—3G 107
Saddell.—2B 124
Saddington.—3D 64
Saddle Bow.—1F 67
Saddlescombe.—4D 18
Sadgill.—4F 105
Saffron Walden.—4E 55
Sageston.—4D 34
Saham Hills.—2B 68
Saham Toney.—2A 68
Saighton.—4G 85
St Abbs.—3F 133
St Agnes.—4B 6
St Albans.—2E 43
St Allen.—4C 6
St Andrews.—2H 139
St Andrews Major.—5H 37
St Annes.—3A 92
St Ann's.—5C 120
St Ann's Chapel.—2A 8
(Cornwall)
St Ann's Chapel.—5C 8
(Devon)
St Anthony.—4E 5
(nr. Helford, Corn.)
St Anthony.—3F 5
(nr. St Mawes, Corn.)
St Arvans.—3D 38
St Asaph.—3C 84
St Athan.—5G 37
St Austell.—4E 6
St Bartholomew's Hill.—1E 15
St Bees.—3A 104
St Blazey.—4E 7
St Blazey Gate.—4E 7
St Boswells.—1H 121
St Breock.—2D 6
St Breward.—2E 7
St Briavels.—2D 38
St Brides.—3B 34
St Bride's Major.—5E 37
St Bride's Netherwent.—4C 38
St Bride's-super-Ely.—5G 37
St Bride's Wentlooge.—4A 38
St Budeaux.—4A 8
Saintbury.—4F 51
St Buryan.—4B 4
St Catherine.—5F 39
St Catherines.—3A 136
St Clears.—3F 35
St Cleer.—3C 7
St Clement.—2F 5
St Clether.—1C 6
St Colmac.—3B 128
St Columb Major.—3D 6
St Columb Minor.—3C 6
St Columb Road.—4D 6
St Combs.—2H 163
St Cross.—1C 16
St Cross South Elmham.—4E 69
St Cyrus.—2G 147
St David's.—2A 34
(Dyfed)
St David's.—1B 138
(Tayside)

St Day.—2E 5
St Dennis.—4D 6
St Dogmaels.—3A 46
St Dominick.—3A 8
St Donats.—5F 37
St Edith's Marsh.—2E-27
St Endellion.—2D 6
St Enoder.—4C 6
St Erme.—2F 5
St Erney.—4H 7
St Erth.—3C 4
St Erth Praze.—3C 4
St Ervan.—2C 6
St Eval.—3C 6
St Ewe.—2C 5
St Fagans.—5H 37
St Fergus.—3H 163
St Fillans.—1F 137
St Florence.—4D 35
St Gennys.—4B 10
St George.—3B 84
St George's.—2D 24
(Avon)
St Georges.—5G 37
(South Glamorgan)
St Germans.—4H 7
St Giles in the Wood.—2F 11
St Giles on the Heath.—1D 10
St Giles's Hill.—1C 16
St Gluvias.—3E 5
St Harmon.—3E 59
St Helena.—2G 63
St Helen Auckland.—2E 107
St Helens.—1B 104
(Cumbria)
St Helen's.—4C 20
(East Sussex)
St Helens.—5E 17
(Isle of Wight)
St Helens.—3D 86
(Merseyside)
St Hilary.—3C 4
(Cornwall)
St Hilary.—5G 37
(South Glamorgan)
Saint Hill.—3D 12
(Devon)
Saint Hill.—2E 19
(West Sussex)
St Illtyd.—2A 38
St Ippollitts.—5A 54
St Ishmael.—4G 35
St Ishmael's.—4B 34
St Issey.—2D 6
St Ive.—3A 8
St Ives.—5C 66
(Cambridgeshire)
St Ives.—2C 4
(Cornwall)
St Ives.—3G 15
(Dorset)
St James End.—1E 53
St James South Elmham.—4F 69
St Jidgey.—3D 6
St John.—4A 8
St John's.—1D 106
(Durham)
St John's.—2C 50
(Hereford & Worcester)
St John's.—3B 110
(Isle of Man)
St John's Chapel.—3B 22
(Devon)
St John's Chapel.—1B 106
(Durham)
St John's Fen End.—1E 67
St John's Town of Dairy.
—1D 112
St Judes.—2C 110
St Just.—3F 5
(nr. Falmouth, Corn)
St Just.—3A 4
(nr. Penzance, Corn.)
St Justin Roseland.—3F 5
St Katharines.—5E 163
St Keverne.—4E 5

St Kew.—2E 6
St Kew Highway.—2E 7
St Keyne.—3G 7
St Lawrence.—3E 7
(Cornwall)
St Lawrence.—2F 45
(Essex)
St Lawrence.—5D 16
(Isle of Wight)
St Leonards.—2C 42
(Buckinghamshire)
St Leonards.—3G 15
(Dorset)
St Leonards.—5B 20
(East Sussex)
St Levan.—4A 4
St Lythans.—5H 37
St Mabyn.—2E 7
St Margarets.—4F 49
(Hereford & Worcester)
St Margarets.—1D 42
(nr. Hemel Hempstead, Herts.)
St Margarets.—1G 43
(nr. Hoddesdon, Herts.)
St Margarets.—2G 27
(Wiltshire)
St Margaret's at Cliffe.—1H 21
St Margaret's Hope.—8D 174
St Margaret South Elmham.
—4F 69
St Mark's.—4B 110
St Martin.—4D 5
St Martins.—2F 73
(Shropshire)
St Martins.—5A 146
(Tayside)
St Martin's Green.—4E 5
St Mary Bourne.—3C 28
St Marychurch.—3F 9
(Devon)
St Mary Church.—5G 37
(South Glamorgan)
St Mary Cray.—4F 31
St Mary Hill.—5F 37
St Mary in the Marsh.—3E 21
St Mary's.—7D 174
St Mary's Airport.—1B 4
St Mary's Bay.—3E 21
St Mary's Grove.—2E 25
St Mary's Hoo.—3C 32
St Maughan's Green.—1C 38
St Mawes.—3F 5
St Mawgan.—3C 6
St Mawgan Airport.—3C 6
St Mellion.—3H 7
St Mellons.—4A 38
St Merryn.—2C 6
St Mewan.—4D 6
St Michael Caerhays.—2G 5
St Michael Penkevil.—2F 5
St Michaels.—3E 9
(Devon)
St Michaels.—4C 60
(Hereford & Worcester)
St Michaels.—2C 20
(Kent)
St Michael's on Wyre.—1B 92
St Michael South Elmham.
—4F 69
St Minver.—2D 6
St Monance.—3H 139
St Neot.—3F 7
St Neots.—1A 54
St Nicholas.—1C 34
(Dyfed)
St Nicholas.—5G 37
(South Glamorgan)
St Nicholas at Wade.—4G 33
St Nicholas South Elmham.
—4F 69
St Ninians.—4G 137
St Olaves.—3G 69
St Osyth.—1H 45
St Osyth Heath.—1H 45
St Owen's Cross.—5H 49
St Paul's Cray.—4F 31

St Paul's Walden.—5A 54
St Peter's.—4H 33
St Peter the Great.—2C 50
St Petrox.—5C 34
St Pinnock.—3G 7
St Quivox.—2C 118
St Ruan.—5E 5
St Stephen.—4D 6
St Stephens.—1H 7
(nr. Launceston, Corn.)
St Stephens.—4A 8
(nr. Saltash, Corn.)
St Teath.—1E 7
St Thomas.—4C 12
(Devon)
St Thomas.—3C 36
(West Glamorgan)
St Tudy.—2E 7
St Twynnells.—5C 34
St Veep.—4F 7
St Vigeans.—4F 147
St Wenn.—3D 6
St Weonards.—5G 49
St Winnolls.—4H 7
Salcombe.—5D 8
Salcombe Regis.—5E 13
Salcott.—1F 45
Sale.—3E 87
Saleby.—5G 91
Sale Green.—2D 50
Salehurst.—3B 20
Salem.—2B 58
(nr. Aberystwyth, Dyfed)
Salem.—5F 47
(nr. Llandeilo, Dyfed)
Salem.—5E 83
(Gwynedd)
Salen.—2A 142
(Highland)
Salen.—4G 141
(Strathclyde)
Salesbury.—2D 93
Saleway.—2D 50
Salford.—1H 42
(Bedfordshire)
Salford.—3F 87
(Manchester)
Salford.—5G 51
(Oxfordshire)
Salford Priors.—2E 51
Salfords.—1D 19
Salhouse.—4F 81
Saligo.—3A 126
Saline.—4C 138
Salisbury.—5G 27
Salkeld Dykes.—1G 105
Sallachan.—2D 143
Sallachy.—5B 158
(nr. Dornie, H'land.)
Sallachy.—3C 166
(nr. Lairg, H'land.)
Salle.—3D 80
Salmonby.—5F 91
Salmond's Muir.—5E 147
Salperton.—5G 51
Salph End.—2H 53
Salsburgh.—3B 130
Salt.—5D 74
Salta.—5B 114
Saltash.—4A 8
Saltburn.—2B 160
Saltburn-by-the-Sea.—2D 108
Saltby.—5F 77
Saltcoats.—5B 104
(Cumbria)
Saltcoats.—5D 128
(Strathclyde)
Saltdean.—5E 19
Salter.—3F 99
Salterforth.—1F 93
Salters Lode.—2E 67
Salterswall.—1A 74
Salterton.—5G 27
Saltfleet.—3G 91
Saltfleetby All Saints.—3G 91
Saltfleetby St Clements.—3G 91

Saltfleetby St Peter.—4G 91
Saltford.—2B 26
Salthouse.—1C 80
Saltmarshe.—3H 95
Saltmead.—5H 37
Saltney.—4F 85
Saltoun.—2C 102
Saltrens.—3A 22
Saltwick.—2E 117
Saltwood.—2F 21
Salum.—4B 140
Salwarpe.—1C 50
Salwayash.—4H 13
Samala.—2C 172
Samalaman.—1A 142
Samborne.—1E 51
(Warwickshire)
Sambourne.—4D 26
(Wiltshire)
Sambrook.—5B 74
Samlesbury.—2C 92
Samlesbury Bottoms.—3D 92
Sampford Arundel.—2E 12
Sampford Brett.—1G 23
Sampford Courtenay.—3G 11
Sampford Peverell.—2D 12
Sampford Spiney.—2B 8
Samsonslane.—5F 174
Samuelston.—2A 132
Sanaigmore.—2A 126
Sancreed.—4B 4
Sancton.—2A 96
Sand.—4D 164
(Highland)
Sand.—4E 25
(Somerset)
Sandaig.—3F 149
Sandal.—5D 114
Sandal Magna.—4D 94
Sandavore.—5C 148
Sanday Airport.—3F 174
Sandbach.—1B 74
Sandbank.—1C 128
Sandbanks.—5F 15
Sandend.—2C 162
Sanderstead.—4E 31
Sandfields.—3D 36
Sandford.—3E 25
(Avon)
Sandford.—3A 106
(Cumbria)
Sandford.—3B 12
(Devon)
Sandford.—5E 15
(Dorset)
Sandford.—3G 15
(Hampshire)
Sandford.—5D 16
(Isle of Wight)
Sandford.—3F 73
(nr. Oswestry, Shrops.)
Sandford.—2H 73
(nr. Whitchurch, Shrops.)
Sandford.—5A 130
(Strathclyde)
Sandfordhill.—4H 163
Sandford-on-Thames.—2G 41
Sandford Orcas.—1B 14
Sandford St Martin.—5B 52
Sandgarth.—6E 174
Sandgate.—2G 21
Sandgreen.—4C 112
Sandhaven.—2G 163
Sandhead.—5F 111
Sandhill.—4E 67
Sandhills.—2B 14
(Dorset)
Sandhills.—2A 18
(Surrey)
Sandhoe.—3C 116
Sand Hole.—2A 96
Sandholme.—2A 96
(Humberside)
Sandholme.—4C 78
(Lincolnshire)

G.B. Handy 237

Shallowford.—1D 22
(Devon)
Shallowford.—5C 74
(Staffordshire)
Shalmsford Street.—5E 33
Shalstone.—4D 52
Shamley Green.—1B 18
Shandon.—1D 128
Shandwick.—1C 160
Shangton.—3E 64
Shankhouse.—2F 117
Shanklin.—5D 16
Shannochie.—3D 125
Shap.—3G 105
Shapwick.—3E 15
(Dorset)
Shapwick.—5E 25
(Somerset)
Sharcott.—3G 27
Shardlow.—4B 76
Shareshill.—2D 62
Sharlston.—4D 94
Sharlston Common.—4D 94
Sharnal Street.—3B 32
Sharnbrook.—2G 53
Sharneyford.—3F 93
Sharnford.—3B 64
Sharnhill Green.—3C 14
Sharoe Green.—2C 92
Sharow.—2G 101
Sharpenhoe.—4H 53
Sharperton.—4D 122
Sharpness.—2E 39
Sharp Street.—3F 81
Sharpthorne.—2E 19
Sharrington.—2C 80
Shatterford.—4B 62
Shatton.—4B 88
Shaugh Prior.—2B 8
Shavington.—2B 74
Shaw.—2C 28
(Berkshire)
Shaw.—2G 87
(Manchester)
Shaw.—2D 27
(Wiltshire)
Shawbost.—3E 173
Shawbury.—3H 73
Shawdon Hall.—3E 123
Shawell.—4C 64
Shawford.—1C 16
Shawforth.—3F 93
Shaw Green.—1C 86
Shawhead.—2F 113
Shaw Mills.—3F 101
Shawwood.—2E 119
Shear Cross.—4D 26
Shearington.—3B 114
Shearsby.—3D 64
Shearston.—5C 24
Shebbear.—3E 11
Shebdon.—5B 74
Shebster.—2C 170
Shedfield.—2D 16
Shedog.—2D 124
Sheen.—1F 75
Sheepbridge.—5D 88
Sheep Hill.—4E 117
Sheepscar.—2D 94
Sheepscombe.—1G 39
Sheepstor.—3B 8
Sheepwash.—3E 11
(Devon)
Sheepwash.—1F 117
(Northumberland)
Sheepway.—5C 38
Sheepy Magna.—2H 63
Sheepy Parva.—2H 63
Sheering.—1B 44
Sheerness.—3D 32
Sheerwater.—4B 30
Sheet.—1F 17
Sheffield.—4D 88
Sheffield Bottom.—2E 29
Sheffield Green.—3F 19
Shefford.—4A 54

Shefford Woodlands.—5E 41
Sheigra.—2B 168
Sheinton.—2A 62
Shelderton.—3B 60
Sheldon.—1F 75
(Derbyshire)
Sheldon.—3E 12
(Devon)
Sheldon.—4F 63
(West Midlands)
Sheldwich.—5E 32
Shelf.—3B 94
Shelfanger.—4D 68
Shelfield.—1F 51
(Warwickshire)
Shelfield.—2E 63
(West Midlands)
Shelford.—3D 76
(Nottinghamshire)
Shelford.—4B 64
(Warwickshire)
Shell.—2D 50
Shelley.—4C 56
(Suffolk)
Shelley.—4C 94
(West Yorkshire)
Shell Green.—4C 86
Shellingford.—3E 40
Shellow Bowells.—2C 44
Shelsley Beauchamp.—1B 50
Shelsley Walsh.—1B 50
Shelthorpe.—1C 64
Shelton.—1H 53
(Bedfordshire)
Shelton.—3E 68
(Norfolk)
Shelton.—3E 77
(Nottinghamshire)
Shelton.—4G 73
(Shropshire)
Shelton Green.—3E 69
Shelton Lock.—4A 76
Shelve.—1A 60
Shelwick.—3H 49
Shelwick Green.—3H 49
Shenfield.—1H 31
Shenington.—3A 52
Shenley.—2E 43
Shenley Brook End.—4F 53
Shenleybury.—2E 43
Shenley Church End.—4F 53
Shenmore.—4F 49
Shennanton.—3A 112
Shenstone.—5C 62
(Hereford & Worcester)
Shenstone.—2F 63
(Staffordshire)
Shenstone Woodend.—2F 63
Shenton.—2A 64
Shenval.—1G 153
Shepeau Stow.—1C 66
Shepherd's Bush.—2D 30
Shepherds Gate.—1E 67
Shepherd's Green.—4A 42
Shepherd's Port.—4E 79
Shepherdswell.—1G 21
Shepley.—2B 88
Sheppardstown.—4E 171
Shepperton.—4B 30
Shepreth.—3C 54
Shepshed.—1B 64
Shepton Beauchamp.—2H 13
Shepton Mallet.—4B 26
Shepton Montague.—5B 26
Shepway.—5B 32
Sheraton.—1B 108
Sherborne.—3F 25
(Avon)
Sherborne.—2B 14
(Dorset)
Sherborne.—1C 40
(Gloucestershire)
Sherborne Causeway.—1D 14
Sherborne St John.—3E 28

Sherbourne.—1G 51
Sherburn.—5G 117
(Durham)
Sherburn.—2E 103
(North Yorkshire)
Sherburn Hill.—5G 117
Sherburn in Elmet.—2E 95
Shere.—1B 18
Shereford.—3A 80
Sherfield English.—1A 16
Sherfield on Loddon.—3E 29
Sherford.—5D 9
(Devon)
Sherford.—4E 15
(Dorset)
Sheriffhales.—1B 62
Sheriff Hutton.—3B 102
Sheriffston.—2G 161
Sheringham.—1D 80
Sherington.—3F 53
Shermanbury.—4D 18
Shernal Green.—1D 50
Shernborne.—4G 79
Sherrington.—5E 27
Sherston.—4G 39
Sherwood.—3C 76
Sherwood Green.—3B 22
Sheshader.—4H 173
Shettleston.—3H 129
Shevington.—2C 86
Shevington Moor.—1C 86
Shevington Vale.—2C 86
Sheviock.—4H 7
Shiel Bridge.—2B 150
Shieldaig.—1H 157
(nr. Charlestown, H'land.)
Shieldaig.—3H 157
(Loch Shieldaig, H'land.)
Shieldhill.—2B 130
(Central)
Shieldhill.—1B 114
(Dumfries & Galloway)
Shieldhill.—5D 130
(Strathclyde)
Shieldmuir.—4A 130
Shielfoot.—2A 142
Shiemill.—3H 163
(Grampian)
Shielhill.—3D 146
(Tayside)
Shifnal.—2B 62
Shilbottle.—4F 123
Shilbottle Grange.—4G 123
Shildon.—2F 107
Shillford.—4F 129
Shillingford.—3F 23
(Devon)
Shillingford.—3G 41
(Oxfordshire)
Shillingford St George.—5C 12
Shillingstone.—2D 14
Shillington.—4A 54
Shillmoor.—4C 122
Shilton.—2D 40
(Oxfordshire)
Shilton.—4B 64
(Warwickshire)
Shilvinghampton.—5B 14
Shilvington.—1E 117
Shimpling.—4D 68
(Norfolk)
Shimpling.—2A 56
(Suffolk)
Shimpling Street.—2A 56
Shincliffe.—5F 117
Shiney Row.—4G 117
Shinfield.—2F 29
Shingay.—3C 54
Shingham.—2G 67
Shingle Street.—3F 57
Shinner's Bridge.—3D 9
Shinness.—2C 166
Shipbourne.—5G 31
Shipdham.—2B 68
Shipham.—3E 25
Shiphay.—3E 9

Shiplake.—5A 42
Shipley.—3B 76
(Derbyshire)
Shipley.—3F 123
(Northumberland)
Shipley.—3C 62
(Shropshire)
Shipley.—3C 18
(West Sussex)
Shipley.—2B 94
(West Yorkshire)
Shipley Bridge.—1E 19
Shipmeadow.—3F 69
Shippon.—3F 41
Shipston on Stour.—3G 51
Shipton.—5E 53
(Buckinghamshire)
Shipton.—1B 40
(Gloucestershire)
Shipton.—4A 102
(North Yorkshire)
Shipton.—1C 60
(Shropshire)
Shipton Bellinger.—4H 27
Shipton Gorge.—4H 13
Shipton Green.—4G 17
Shipton Moyne.—4G 39
Shipton-on-Cherwell.—1F 41
Shiptonthorpe.—1A 96
Shipton-under-Wychwood.
—1D 40
Shirburn.—1H 41
Shirdley Hill.—1A 86
Shire.—1H 105
Shirebrook.—1C 76
Shiregreen.—3D 88
Shirehampton.—5D 38
Shiremoor.—2G 117
Shirenewton.—3C 38
Shireoaks.—4F 89
Shires Mill.—5C 138
Shirkoak.—2D 20
Shirland.—2A 76
Shirley.—3G 75
(Derbyshire)
Shirley.—2C 16
(Hampshire)
Shirley.—5F 63
(West Midlands)
Shirleywich.—5D 75
Shirl Heath.—2G 49
Shirrell Heath.—2D 16
Shirwell.—2E 22
Shirwell Cross.—2B 22
Shiskine.—3D 124
Shobdon.—4A 60
Shobnall.—5G 75
Shobrooke.—3B 12
Shoby.—5D 76
Shocklach.—1G 73
Shoeburyness.—2D 32
Sholden.—5H 33
Sholing.—2C 16
Sholver.—2F 87
Shoot Hill.—4G 73
Shop.—2C 10
(nr. Bude, Corn.)
Shop.—2C 6
(nr. Padstow, Corn.)
Shop.—2D 11
(Devon)
Shopford.—2G 115
Shop Street.—1E 57
Shoreditch.—2E 31
(London)
Shoreditch.—1F 13
(Somerset)
Shoreham.—4G 31
Shoreham Airport.—5D 18
Shoreham Beach.—5D 18
Shoreham-by-Sea.—5D 18
Shoresdean.—5F 133
Shoreswood.—5F 133
Shore, The.—2E 139
Shorncote.—3B 40
Shorne.—3A 32

Shorne Ridgeway.—3A 32
Shortacombe.—4F 11
Shortbridge.—3F 19
Shortgate.—4F 19
Short Green.—4C 68
Shorthampton.—5H 51
Short Heath.—1H 63
(Derbyshire)
Short Heath.—3F 63
(nr. Erdington, W Midlands)
Short Heath.—2D 63
(nr. Wednesfield, W Midlands)
Shortlanesend.—2F 5
Shorton.—3E 9
Shortstown.—1H 53
Shortwood.—5E 39
Shorwell.—5C 16
Shoscombe.—3C 26
Shotesham.—3E 69
Shotgate.—1B 32
Shotley.—4E 57
Shotley Bridge.—4D 117
Shotleyfield.—4D 116
Shotley Gate.—4E 57
Shottenden.—5E 33
Shottermill.—5G 29
Shottery.—2F 51
Shotteswell.—3B 52
Shottisham.—3F 57
Shottle.—3H 75
Shotton.—4F 85
(Clwyd)
Shotton.—1B 108
(nr. Peterlee, Durham)
Shotton.—2G 107
(nr. Sedgefield, Northumb)
Shotton.—2F 117
(nr. Morpeth, Northmb.)
Shotton.—1C 122
(nr. Town Yetholm, Northmb.)
Shotton Colliery.—5G 117
Shotts.—3B 130
Shotwick.—3F 85
Shouldham.—2F 67
Shouldham Thorpe.—2F 67
Shoulton.—2C 50
Shrawardine.—4F 73
Shrawley.—1C 50
Shreding Green.—2B 30
Shrewley.—1G 51
Shrewsbury.—4G 73
Shrewton.—4F 27
Shripney.—3H 17
Shrivenham.—4D 40
Shropham.—3B 68
Shroton.—2D 14
Shrub End.—5B 56
Shucknall.—3H 49
Study Camps.—3F 55
Shulishader.—4H 173
Shulista.—1D 156
Shurdington.—1H 39
Shurlock Row.—5B 42
Shurrery.—3C 170
Shurton.—4C 24
Shustoke.—3G 63
Shute.—4F 13
(nr. Axminster, Devon)
Shute.—2F 12
(nr. Crediton, Devon)
Shutford.—3A 52
Shut Heath.—5C 74
Shuthonger.—4C 50
Shutlanehead.—3C 74
Shutlanger.—2E 53
Shutt Green.—2C 62
Shuttington.—2G 63
Shuttlewood.—5E 89
Shuttleworth.—1F 87
Siabost.—3G 173

Sibsey.—2C 78
Sibsey Fen Side.—2C 78
Sibson.—3H 65
(Cambridgeshire)
Sibson.—2A 64
(Leicestershire)
Sibster.—3F 171
Sibthorpe.—3E 77
Sibton.—1F 57
Sicklesmere.—1A 56
Sicklinghall.—1D 94
Sid.—5E 13
Sidbury.—4E 13
(Devon)
Sidbury.—4A 62
(Shropshire)
Sidcot.—3E 25
Sidcup.—3F 31
Siddick.—1B 104
Siddington.—5F 87
(Cheshire)
Siddington.—3B 40
(Gloucestershire)
Side of the Moor.—1E 87
Sidestrand.—2E 81
Sidford.—5E 13
Sidinish.—2D 172
Sidlesham.—4G 17
Sidley.—5B 20
Sidlowbridge.—1D 18
Sidmouth.—5E 13
Siefton.—2B 60
Sigford.—2D 9
Sigglesthorne.—1D 96
Sighthill.—2E 131
Siginstone.—5F 37
Signet.—1D 40
Silchester.—2E 29
Sileby.—1D 64
Silecroft.—1A 98
Silfield.—3D 68
Silian.—2E 47
Silkstone.—2C 88
Silkstone Common.—2C 88
Silksworth.—4G 117
Silk Willoughby.—3H 77
Silloth.—4C 114
Sills.—4C 122
Sillyearn.—3C 162
Silpho.—5G 109
Silsden.—1H 93
Silsoe.—4H 53
Silverbank.—4E 154
Silverburn.—3F 131
Silverdale.—2D 98
(Lancashire)
Silverdale.—3C 74
(Staffordshire)
Silverdale Green.—2D 98
Silver End.—1E 44
(Essex)
Silver End.—4D 62
(West Midlands)
Silvergate.—3D 80
Silverhillocks.—2E 163
Silverley's Green.—5E 69
Silverstone.—3D 52
Silverton.—3C 12
(Devon)
Silverton.—2F 129
(Strathclyde)
Silvington.—5A 62
Simm's Cross.—4C 86
Simm's Lane End.—2C 86
Simonburn.—2B 116
Simonsbath.—2D 22
Simonstone.—2E 93
Simprin.—5E 133
Simpson.—3B 34
Sinclairston.—3D 118
Sinclairtown.—4E 139
Sinderby.—1G 101
Sinderhope.—4B 116
Sindlesham.—2F 29
Sinfin.—4H 75
Singleborough.—4E 53

Singleton.—1D 20 (Kent)
Singleton.—2A 92 (Lancashire)
Singleton.—2G 17 (West Sussex)
Sinkhurst Green.—1C 20
Sinnahard.—2B 154
Sinnington.—1C 102
Sinton Green.—1C 50
Sipson.—3H 30
Sirhowy.—1H 37
Sissinghurst.—2B 20
Siston—5E 39
Sithney.—4D 4
Sittingbourne.—4D 32
Six Ashes.—4B 62
Six Bells.—2A 38
Six Hills.—5D 76 (Leicestershire)
Sixhills.—4D 90 (Lincolnshire)
Six Mile Bottom.—2E 55
Sixpenny Handley.—2E 15
Sizewell.—1G 57
Skail.—4H 169
Skaill.—7E 174
Skallary.—9B 172
Skares.—3E 119
Skateraw.—2D 132
Skaw.—5G 175
Skeabost.—4D 156
Skeeby.—4E 107
Skeffington.—2F 65
Skeffling.—4F 97
Skegby.—1B 76 (nr. Mansfield, Notts.)
Skegby.—5H 89 (nr. Tuxford, Notts.)
Skegness.—1E 79
Skelberry.—10E 175 (nr. Boddam, Shetland)
Skelberry.—3E 175 (nr. Housetter, Shetland)
Skelbo.—4E 167
Skelbo Street.—4E 167
Skelbrooke.—4F 95
Skeldyke.—4C 78
Skelfhill.—4G 121
Skellingthorpe.—5B 90
Skellister.—6F 175
Skellorn Green.—4G 87
Skellow.—4F 95
Skelmanthorpe.—4C 94
Skelmersdale.—2B 86
Skelmorlie.—3C 128
Skelpick.—3H 169
Skelton.—3D 108 (Cleveland)
Skelton.—1F 105 (Cumbria)
Skelton.—3H 95 (Humberside)
Skelton.—4D 107 (nr. Richmond, N Yorks.)
Skelton.—3G 101 (nr. Ripon, N Yorks.)
Skelton.—4A 102 (nr. York, N Yorks.)
Skelton Green.—3D 108
Skelwick.—3D 174
Skelwith Bridge.—4E 105
Skendleby.—1D 78
Skendleby Psalter.—5G 91
Skenfrith.—5G 49
Skerne.—4F 103
Skeroblingarry.—3B 124
Skerray.—2G 169
Skerricha.—3C 168
Skerton.—3D 98
Sketchley.—3B 64
Sketty.—3C 36
Skewen.—3D 36
Skewsby.—2B 102
Skeyton.—3E 81
Skeyton Corner.—3E 81

Skiall.—2C 170
Skidbrooke.—3G 91
Skidbrooke North End.—3G 91
Skidby.—2C 96
Skigersta.—1H 173
Skilgate.—3F 23
Skillington.—5F 77
Skinflats.—1C 130
Skinidin.—4B 156
Skinnet.—2F 169
Skinningrove.—2E 109
Skipness.—4H 127
Skiprigg.—5E 115
Skipsea.—4G 103
Skipsea Brough.—4G 103
Skipton.—4C 100
Skipton-on-Swale.—2G 101
Skipwith.—2G 95
Skirbeck.—3C 78
Skirbeck Quarter.—3C 78
Skirling.—1C 120
Skirmett.—3A 42
Skirpenbeck.—4C 102
Skirwith.—1H 105 (Cumbria)
Skirwith.—2G 99 (North Yorkshire)
Skirza.—2F 171
Skitby.—3F 115
Skitham.—1B 92
Skittle Green.—2A 42
Skulamus.—1E 149
Skullomie.—2G 169
Skyborry Green.—3H 59
Skye Green.—5A 56
Skye of Curr.—1D 153
Slack.—3G 93
Slackhall.—4A 88
Slack Head.—2D 99 (Cumbria)
Slackhead.—2B 162 (Grampian)
Slackholme End.—5H 91
Slacks of Cairnbanno.—4F 163
Slack, The.—2E 107
Slad.—2G 39
Slade.—1B 22 (Devon)
Slade.—4A 36 (West Glamorgan)
Slade End.—3G 41
Slade Field.—4C 66
Slade Green.—3G 31
Slade Heath.—2D 62
Slade Hooton.—4F 89
Sladesbridge.—2E 6
Slade, The.—2D 28
Slaggyford.—4H 115
Slaidburn.—4G 99
Slaid Hill.—1D 94
Slaithwaite.—4A 94
Slaley.—2G 75 (Derbyshire)
Slaley.—4C 116 (Northumberland)
Slamannan.—2B 130
Slapton.—5G 53 (Buckinghamshire)
Slapton.—5E 9 (Devon)
Slapton.—3D 52 (Northamptonshire)
Slattocks.—2F 87
Slaugham.—3D 18
Slaughterford.—5G 39
Slawston.—3E 65
Sleaford.—5G 29 (Hampshire)
Sleaford.—3H 77 (Lincolnshire)
Sleagill.—3G 105
Sleap.—3G 73
Sledmere.—3E 103
Sleightholme.—3C 106
Sleights.—4F 109

Slepe.—4E 15
Slerra.—1D 10
Slickly.—2E 171
Sliddery.—3D 124
Sligachan.—1C 148
Slimbridge.—2F 39
Slindon.—4C 74 (Staffordshire)
Slindon.—3H 17 (West Sussex)
Slinfold.—2C 18
Slingsby.—2B 102
Slip End.—1D 43
Slipton.—5G 65
Slitting Mill.—1E 63
Slochd.—1C 152
Slockavullin.—4F 135
Sloley.—3E 81
Sloncombe.—1D 8
Sloothby.—5G 91
Slough.—2A 30
Slough Green.—1F 13 (Somerset)
Slough Green.—3D 19 (West Sussex)
Sluggan.—1C 152
Slyne.—3D 99
Smailholm.—1A 122
Smallbridge.—1G 87
Smallbrook.—4B 12
Smallburgh.—3F 81
Smallburn.—2F 119
Smalldale.—5A 88
Small Dole.—4D 18
Smalley.—3B 76
Small Heath.—4E 63
Smallholm.—2B 114
Small Hythe.—2C 20
Smallrice.—4D 74
Smallridge.—3G 13
Smallwood Hey.—1A 92
Smallworth.—4C 68
Smannell.—4B 28
Smardale.—4A 106
Smarden.—1C 20
Smarden Bell.—1C 20
Smart's Hill.—1G 19
Smeatharpe.—2E 13
Smeeth.—2E 21
Smeeth, The.—1E 67
Smeeton Westerby.—3D 64
Smerclate.—7C 172
Smerral.—5D 170
Smestow.—3C 62
Smethwick.—4E 63
Smirisary.—1A 142
Smisby.—1H 63
Smitham Hill.—3F 25
Smith End Green.—2B 50
Smithfield.—3F 115
Smith Green.—4D 99
Smithies, The.—3A 62
Smithincott.—2D 12
Smith's Green.—5E 55
Smithstown.—1G 157
Smithton.—4B 160
Smithwood Green.—2B 56
Smithy Bridge.—1G 87
Smithy Green.—5E 87
Smithy Lane Ends.—1B 86
Smockington.—4B 64
Smyth's Green.—1F 45
Snaigow House.—4H 145
Snailbeach.—5F 73
Snailwell.—1F 55
Snainton.—1E 103
Snaith.—3G 95
Snape.—1F 101 (North Yorkshire)
Snape.—2F 57 (Suffolk)
Snape Green.—1A 86
Snarestone.—2H 63
Snarford.—4C 90
Snargate.—3D 20

Snave.—3E 20
Sneachill.—2D 50
Snead.—1A 60
Snead Common.—1B 50
Sneaton.—4F 109
Sneatonthorpe.—4G 109
Snelland.—4C 90
Snelston.—3F 75
Snetterton.—3B 68
Snettisham.—1F 79
Snibston.—1B 64
Snig's End.—5B 136
Snishival.—5C 172
Snitter.—4C 123
Snitterby.—3B 90
Snitterfield.—2C 51
Snitton.—3C 60
Snodhill.—3F 49
Snodland.—4B 32
Snods Edge.—4D 116
Snowshill.—4E 51
Snow Street.—4C 68
Snydale.—3E 94
Soake.—2E 17
Soar.—5F 47 (Dyfed)
Soar.—2F 71 (Gwynedd)
Soar.—4B 48 (Powys)
Soberton.—2E 16
Soberton Heath.—2E 16
Sockbridge.—2F 105
Sockburn.—4G 107
Sodom.—3C 84
Soham.—5E 67
Soham Cotes.—5E 67
Soldon Cross.—2D 10
Soldridge.—5E 29
Solent Breezes.—3D 16
Sole Street.—1E 21 (nr. Canterbury, Kent)
Sole Street.—4A 32 (nr. Gravesend, Kent)
Solihull.—5F 63
Sollas.—1D 172
Sollers Dilwyn.—2G 49
Sollers Hope.—4A 50
Sollom.—1B 86
Solva.—2A 34
Somerby.—1E 65 (Leicestershire)
Somerby.—5C 96 (Lincolnshire)
Somercotes.—2B 76
Somerford.—4G 15 (Dorset)
Somerford.—2C 62 (Staffordshire)
Somerford Keynes.—3B 40
Somerley.—4G 17
Somerleyton.—3G 69
Somersal Herbert.—4F 75
Somersby.—5F 91
Somersham.—5C 66 (Cambridgeshire)
Somersham.—3C 56 (Suffolk)
Somerton.—5B 52 (Oxfordshire)
Somerton.—1H 13 (Somerset)
Somerton.—2A 56 (Suffolk)
Sompting.—5C 18
Sonning.—5A 42
Sonning Common.—4A 42
Sookholme.—1C 76
Sopley.—4G 15
Sopworth.—4G 39
Sorbie.—5B 112
Sordale.—2D 170
Sorisdale.—2D 140
Sorn.—2E 119
Sornhill.—1E 119
Sortat.—2E 171

Sotby.—5E 91
Sots Hole.—1A 78
Sotterley.—4G 69
Soudley.—1B 60 (nr. Church Stretton, Shrops.)
Soudley.—5B 74 (nr. Market Drayton, Shrops.)
Soughton.—4E 85
Soulbury.—5F 53
Soulby.—3A 106 (nr. Appleby, Cumbria)
Soulby.—2F 105 (nr. Penrith, Cumbria)
Souldern.—4C 52
Souldrop.—1G 53
Sound.—7F 175
Soundwell.—5E 39
Sourhope.—2C 122
Sourin.—4D 174
Sourton.—4F 11
Soutergate.—1B 98
Southam.—5D 50 (Gloucestershire)
Southam.—1B 52 (Warwickshire)
South Ambersham.—1H 17
Southampton.—2C 16
Southampton Airport.—2C 16
Southannan.—4D 128
South Anston.—4F 89
South Ascot.—4A 30
South Baddesley.—4B 16
South Balfern.—4B 112
South Ballachulish.—3E 143
South Bank.—2C 108
South Barrow.—2C 70 (Gwynedd)
South Beach.—2G 117 (Northumberland)
South Benfleet.—2B 32
South Bents.—3H 17
South Bersted.—3H 17
South Boisdale.—7C 172
Southborough.—1G 19 (Dorset)
Southbourne.—4G 15 (Dorset)
Southbourne.—3F 17 (West Sussex)
South Brent.—3C 8
South Brewham.—5C 26
South Broomage.—1B 130
South Broomhill.—4G 123
Southburgh.—2B 68
South Burlingham.—2F 69
Southburn.—4C 103
South Cadbury.—1B 14
South Carlton.—5B 90
South Cave.—2B 96
South Cerney.—3B 40
South Chard.—3G 13
South Charlton.—2F 123
South Cheriton.—1B 14
South Church.—2F 107 (Durham)
Southchurch.—2D 32 (Essex)
South Cliffe.—2A 96
South Clifton.—5A 90
South Clunes.—4H 159
South Cockerington.—4F 91
South Collingham.—1F 77
South Common.—4E 19
South Cornelly.—4E 36
Southcott.—5G 53 (Bedfordshire)
Southcott.—2E 11 (nr. Great Torrington, Devon)
Southcott.—4F 11 (nr. Okehampton, Devon)

Southcott.—3G 27 (Wiltshire)
Southcourt.—1B 42
South Cove.—4G 69
South Creagan.—4D 143
South Creake.—2A 80
South Crosland.—4B 94
South Croxton.—1D 64
South Dalton.—1B 96
South Darenth.—4G 31
Southdean.—4A 122
South Dell.—1G 173
Southdown.—2F 17
South Duffield.—2G 95
Southease.—5F 19
South Elkington.—4E 91
South Elmsall.—4E 95
Southend.—5G 41 (Berkshire)
South End.—3B 98 (Cumbria)
Southend.—3F 39 (Gloucestershire)
South End.—3D 96 (Humberside)
Southend.—5A 124 (Strathclyde)
Southend Airport.—2C 32
Southend-on-Sea.—2C 32
Southerfield.—5C 114
Southerley.—1B 8
Southernden.—1C 20
Southerndown.—5E 37
Southerness.—4G 113
South Erradale.—1G 157
Southerton.—4D 12
Southery.—3F 67
Southey Green.—4G 55
South Fambridge.—1C 32
South Fawley.—4E 41
South Ferriby.—3B 96
South Field.—3C 96
South Galson.—2G 173
South Garvan.—1D 143
Southgate.—2A 58 (Dyfed)
Southgate.—1D 31 (London)
Southgate.—3D 80 (nr. Aylsham, Norf.)
Southgate.—4F 79 (nr. Dersingham, Norf.)
Southgate.—2A 80 (nr. Fakenham, Norf.)
Southgate.—4B 36 (West Glamorgan)
South Glendale.—7C 172
South Godstone.—1E 19
South Gorley.—2G 15
South Green.—1A 32 (Billericay, Essex)
South Green.—1G 45 (nr. Colchester, Essex)
South Green.—4C 32 (Kent)
South Hanningfield.—1B 32
South Harting.—2F 17
South Hayling.—4F 17
South Hazelrigg.—1E 123
South Heath.—2C 42 (Buckinghamshire)
South Heath.—1H 45 (Essex)
South Heighton.—5F 19
South Hetton.—5G 117
South Hiendley.—4D 94
South Hill.—2H 7 (Cornwall)
South Hill.—1H 13 (Somerset)
South Hinksey.—2G 41
South Hole.—1C 10
South Holme.—2C 102
South Holmwood.—1C 18
South Hornchurch.—2G 31

Stapleford.—5F 27
(Wiltshire)
Stapleford Abbotts.—1G 31
Stapleford Tawney.—1G 31
Staplegrove.—1F 13
Staplehay.—1F 13
Staplehurst.—1B 20
Staplers.—5D 16
Stapleton.—5E 39
(Avon)
Stapleton.—2G 115
(Cumbria)
Stapleton.—4A 60
(Hereford & Worcester)
Stapleton.—3B 64
(Leicestershire)
Stapleton.—3F 107
(North Yorkshire)
Stapleton.—5G 73
(Shropshire)
Stapleton.—1H 13
(Somerset)
Stapley.—2E 13
Staploe.—1A 54
Staplow.—3A 50
Star.—48 46
(Dyfed)
Star.—3F 139
(Fife)
Starbeck.—4G 101
Starbotton.—2C 100
Starcross.—5C 12
Stareton.—5H 63
Starkholmes.—2H 75
Starkigarth.—9F 175
Starling.—1E 87
Starling's Green.—4D 54
Starston.—4E 69
Start.—5E 9
Startforth.—3D 106
Start Hill.—5E 55
Startley.—4H 39
Stathe.—1G 13
Stathern.—4E 77
Station Town.—1B 108
Staughton Green.—1A 54
Staughton Highway.—1A 54
Staunton.—5B 50
(nr. Cheltenham, Glos.)
Staunton.—1D 38
(nr. Monmouth, Glos.)
Staunton in the Vale.—3F 77
Staunton on Arrow.—4A 60
Staunton on Wye.—3F 49
Staveley.—5F 105
(Cumbria)
Staveley.—5E 89
(Derbyshire)
Staveley.—3G 101
(North Yorkshire)
Staveley-in-Cartmel.—1C 98
Staverton.—3D 9
(Devon)
Staverton.—5C 50
(Gloucestershire)
Staverton.—1C 52
(Northamptonshire)
Staverton.—2D 26
(Wiltshire)
Stawell.—5D 24
Stawley.—3G 23
Staxigoe.—3F 171
Staxton.—2F 103
Staylittle.—1D 58
Staynall.—1A 92
Staythorpe.—2E 77
Stean.—2D 100
Stearsby.—2B 102
Steart.—4C 24
Stebbing.—5F 55
Stebbing Green.—5F 55
Stedham.—1G 17
Steel.—4C 116
Steel Cross.—2G 19
Steelend.—4C 138
Steele Road.—5H 121

Steen's Bridge.—2H 49
Steep.—1F 17
Steep Lane.—3H 93
Steeple.—5E 15
(Dorset)
Steeple.—2F 45
(Essex)
Steeple Ashton.—3E 27
Steeple Aston.—5B 52
Steeple Barton.—5B 52
Steeple Bumpstead.—3F 55
Steeple Claydon.—5D 52
Steeple Gidding.—4A 66
Steeple Langford.—5F 27
Steeple Morden.—3B 54
Steeton.—1H 93
Stein.—3B 156
Steinmanhill.—4E 163
Stelling Minnis.—1F 21
Stembridge.—1H 13
Stemster.—2D 171
(nr. Halkirk, H'land.)
Stemster.—2C 170
(nr. Westfield, H'land.)
Stenalees.—4E 6
Stenhill.—2D 12
Stenhouse.—2F 131
Stenhousemuir.—1B 130
Stenigot.—4E 91
Stenscholl.—2D 157
Stenson.—4H 75
Stenton.—2C 132
Stenwith.—4F 77
Stepaside.—4E 5
Stepford.—1F 113
Stepney.—2E 31
Steppingley.—mH 252
Stepps.—3H 129
Sterndale Moor.—1F 75
Sternfield.—1F 57
Stert.—3F 27
Stetchworth.—2F 55
Stevenage.—5B 54
Stevenston.—5D 128
Steventon.—4D 28
(Hampshire)
Steventon.—3F 41
(Oxfordshire)
Stevington.—2G 53
Stevington End.—3E 55
Stewartby.—3H 53
Stewarton.—4A 124
(nr. Campbeltown, S'clyde.)
Stewarton.—5F 129
(nr. Kilmarnock, S'clyde.)
Stewkley.—5F 53
Stewkley Dean.—5F 53
Stewley.—2G 13
Stewton.—4F 91
Steyning.—4C 18
Steynton.—4C 34
Stibb.—2C 10
Stibbard.—3B 80
Stibb Cross.—2E 11
Stibb Green.—2H 27
Stibbington.—3H 65
Stichill.—1B 122
Sticker.—4D 6
Stickford.—2C 78
Sticklepath.—4G 11
Sticklinch.—5F 25
Stickling Green.—4D 54
Stickney.—2C 78
Stidd.—2D 92
Stiffkey.—1B 80
Stifford's Bridge.—3B 50
Stileway.—4E 25
Stilligarry.—5C 172
Stillingfleet.—5A 102
Stillington.—2G 107
(Cleveland)
Stillington.—3A 102
(North Yorkshire)
Stilton.—4A 66
Stinchcombe.—3F 39
Stinsford.—4C 14

Stirchley.—2A 62
(Shropshire)
Stirchley.—4E 63
(West Midlands)
Stirling.—4G 137
(Central)
Stirling.—4H 163
(Grampian)
Stirton.—4C 100
Stisted.—5A 56
Stitchcombe.—2H 27
Stithians.—3E 5
Stittenham.—1A 160
Stivichall.—5H 63
Stixwould.—1A 78
Stoak.—3G 85
Stobo.—1D 120
Stobo Castle.—1D 120
Stoborough.—5E 15
Stobs Castle.—4H 121
Stobswood.—5G 123
Stock.—1A 32
Stockbridge.—5B 28
(Hampshire)
Stockbridge.—1A 94
(West Yorkshire)
Stockbury.—4C 32
Stockcross.—2C 28
Stockdalewaith.—5E 115
Stocker's Head.—5D 32
Stockerston.—3F 65
Stocking.—4A 50
Stockingford.—3H 63
Stocking Green.—4E 55
Stocking Pelham.—5D 54
Stockland.—3F 13
Stockland Bristol.—4C 24
Stockleigh English.—3B 12
Stockleigh Pomeroy.—3B 12
Stockley.—2F 27
Stocklinch.—2G 13
Stockport.—3F 87
Stocksbridge.—3C 88
Stocksfield.—3D 116
Stocks, The.—3D 20
Stockstreet.—5A 56
Stockton.—4C 60
(Hereford & Worcester)
Stockton.—3F 69
(Norfolk)
Stockton.—3B 62
(nr. Bridgnorth, Shrops.)
Stockton.—5E 73
(nr. Chirbury, Shrops.)
Stockton.—1B 62
(nr. Newport, Shrops.)
Stockton.—1B 52
(Warwickshire)
Stockton.—5E 27
(Wiltshire)
Stockton Brook.—2D 74
Stockton Cross.—4C 60
Stockton Heath.—4D 86
Stockton-on-Tees.—3B 108
Stockton on Teme.—1B 50
Stockton on the Forest.
      —4B 102
Stockwell Heath.—5E 75
Stockwood.—2B 26
(Avon)
Stock Wood.—2E 51
(Hereford & Worcester)
Stodmarsh.—4G 33
Stody.—2C 80
Stoer.—1E 165
Stoford.—2A 14
(Dorset)
Stoford.—5F 27
(Wiltshire)
Stogumber.—2G 23
Stogursey.—4C 24
Stoke.—1C 10
(Devon)
Stoke.—3C 28
(nr. Andover, Hants.)

Stoke.—3F 17
(nr. South Hayling, Hants.)
Stoke.—3C 32
(Kent)
Stoke.—5A 64
(West Midlands)
Stoke Abbott.—3H 13
Stoke Albany.—4F 65
Stoke Ash.—5D 68
Stoke Bardolph.—3D 76
Stoke Bliss.—1A 50
Stoke Bruerne.—3E 53
Stoke by Clare.—3G 55
Stoke-by-Nayland.—4B 56
Stoke Canon.—4C 12
Stoke Charity.—5C 28
Stoke Climsland.—2H 7
Stoke Cross.—2A 50
Stoke D'Abernon.—5C 30
Stoke Doyle.—4H 65
Stoke Dry.—3F 65
Stoke Edith.—3A 50
Stoke Farthing.—1F 15
Stoke Ferry.—3G 67
Stoke Fleming.—5E 9
Stokeford.—5D 14
Stoke Gabriel.—4E 9
Stoke Gifford.—5E 39
Stoke Golding.—3A 64
Stoke Goldington.—3F 53
Stokeham.—5H 89
Stoke Hammond.—5F 53
Stoke Heath.—5A 74
Stoke Holy Cross.—2E 69
Stokeinteignhead.—2F 9
Stoke Lacy.—3A 50
Stoke Lyne.—5C 52
Stoke Mandeville.—1B 42
Stokenchurch.—3A 42
Stoke Newington.—2E 31
Stokenham.—5E 9
Stoke on Tern.—5A 74
Stoke-on-Trent.—3C 74
Stoke Orchard.—5D 50
Stoke Pero.—1E 23
Stoke Poges.—2A 30
Stoke Prior.—1D 50
(nr. Bromsgrove, Here & Worcs.)
Stoke Prior.—2H 49
(nr. Leominster, Here & Worcs.)
Stoke Rivers.—2C 22
Stoke Rochford.—5G 77
Stoke Row.—4H 41
Stoke St Gregory.—1G 13
Stoke St Mary.—1F 13
Stoke St Michael.—4B 26
Stoke St Milborough.—2C 60
Stokesay.—2B 60
Stokesby.—4G 81
Stokesley.—4C 108
Stoke sub Hamdon.—2H 13
Stoke Talmage.—3H 41
Stoke Trister.—1C 14
Stolford.—4C 24
Stondon Massey.—2B 44
Stone.—1A 42
(Buckinghamshire)
Stone.—3E 39
(Gloucestershire)
Stone.—5C 62
(Hereford & Worcester)
Stone.—3G 31
(Kent)
Stone.—5F 25
(Somerset)
Stone.—4D 74
(Staffordshire)
Stonea.—3D 66
Stoneacton.—1C 60
Stone Allerton.—3E 25
Ston Easton.—3B 26
Stonebridge.—3D 25
(Avon)
Stonebridge.—1C 18
(Surrey)
Stone Bridge Corner.—2B 66

Stonebroom.—2B 76
Stonebyres.—5B 130
Stone Chair.—3B 94
Stone Cross.—5H 19
(East Sussex)
Stone Cross.—2G 19
(Kent)
Stone Cross.—3E 63
(West Midlands)
Stone-edge-Batch.—5C 38
Stoneferry.—2D 96
Stonefield.—4H 129
(Hamilton, S'clyde.)
Stonefield.—5D 142
(nr. Oban, S'clyde.)
Stonegate.—3A 20
(East Sussex)
Stonegate.—4E 109
(North Yorkshire)
Stonegrave.—2B 102
Stonehall.—3C 50
Stonehaugh.—2A 116
Stonehaven.—5F 155
Stone Heath.—4D 74
Stone House.—1G 99
(Cumbria)
Stonehouse.—2G 39
(Gloucestershire)
Stonehouse.—4H 115
(Northumberland)
Stonehouse.—5A 130
(Strathclyde)
Stone in Oxney.—3D 20
Stoneleigh.—5H 63
Stoneley Green.—2A 74
Stonely.—1A 54
Stonepits.—2E 51
Stoner Hill.—1F 17
Stonesby.—5F 77
Stonesfield.—1E 41
Stones Green.—5D 56
Stone Street.—5G 31
(Kent)
Stone Street.—4B 56
(nr. Boxford, Suff.)
Stone Street.—4F 69
(nr. Halesworth, Suff.)
Stonethwaite.—3D 104
Stoneybridge.—5C 172
Stoneyburn.—3C 130
Stoney Cross.—2A 16
Stoneygate.—2D 64
Stoneyhills.—1D 32
Stoney Middleton.—5E 89
Stoney Stanton.—3B 64
Stoney Stoke.—5C 26
Stoney Stratton.—5B 26
Stoney Stretton.—5F 73
Stoneywood.—2F 155
Stonham Aspal.—2D 56
Stonnall.—2E 63
Stonor.—4A 42
Stonton Wyville.—3E 65
Stony Cross.—2C 22
Stonybreck.—1B 174
Stony Cross.—3B 22
(Devon)
Stony Cross.—3B 50
(nr. Great Malvern, Here & Worcs.)
Stony Cross.—4C 60
(nr. Leominster, Here & Worcs.)
Stony Houghton.—1B 76
Stony Stratford.—3E 53
Stoodleigh.—2C 22
(nr. Barnstaple, Devon)
Stoodleigh.—2C 12
(nr. Tiverton, Devon)
Stopham.—4B 18
Stopsley.—5A 54
Stoptide.—2D 6
Storeton.—2F 85
Stornoway.—4G 173
Stornoway Airport.—4G 173
Storridge.—3B 50
Storrington.—4B 18
Storth.—1D 99

Storwood.—5C 102
Stotfield.—1G 161
Stotfold.—4B 54
Stottesdon.—4A 62
Stoughton.—2D 64
(Leicestershire)
Stoughton.—5A 30
(Surrey)
Stoughton.—2G 17
(West Sussex)
Stoul.—4F 149
Stoulton.—3D 50
Stourbridge.—4C 62
Stourpaine.—3D 14
Stourport-on-Severn.—5C 62
Stour Provost.—1C 14
Stour Row.—1D 14
Stourton.—4C 62
(Staffordshire)
Stourton.—4G 51
(Warwickshire)
Stourton.—2D 94
(West Yorkshire)
Stourton.—5C 26
(Wiltshire)
Stourton Caundle.—2C 14
Stoven.—4G 69
Stow.—5A 132
(Borders)
Stow.—4H 77
(nr. Billingborough, Lincs.)
Stow.—4A 90
(nr. Gainsborough, Lincs.)
Stow Bardolph.—2F 67
Stow Bedon.—3B 68
Stowbridge.—2F 67
Stow cum Quy.—1E 55
Stowe.—2C 60
(Gloucestershire)
Stowe.—3A 60
(Shropshire)
Stowe.—1F 63
(Staffordshire)
Stowe-by-Chartley.—5E 75
Stowell.—1B 14
Stowey.—3F 25
Stowford.—5D 12
(nr. Exmouth, Devon)
Stowford.—1A 8
(nr. Tavistock, Devon)
Stowlangtoft.—1B 56
Stow Longa.—5A 66
Stow Maries.—1C 32
Stowmarket.—2C 56
Stow-on-the-Wold.—5F 51
Stowting.—1F 21
Stowupland.—1C 56
Straad.—3B 128
Strachan.—4D 154
Strachur.—3H 135
Stradbroke.—5E 69
Stradbrook.—3E 27
Stradishall.—2G 55
Stradsett.—2F 67
Stragglethorpe.—2G 77
(Lincolnshire)
Stragglethorpe.—4D 76
(Nottinghamshire)
Straid.—5A 118
Straight Soley.—5E 40
Straiton.—3F 131
(Lothian)
Straiton.—4C 118
(Strathclyde)
Straloch.—2H 145
Stramshall.—4E 75
Strang.—4C 110
Strangford.—5H 49
Stranraer.—3F 111
Strata Florida.—4C 58
Stratfield Mortimer.—5E 29
Stratfield Saye.—2E 29
Stratfield Turgis.—3E 29
Stratford.—4C 50
Stratford St Andrew.—1F 57
Stratford St Mary.—4C 56

Sydenham Damerel.—2A 8
Syderstone.—2A 80
Sydling St Nicholas.—4B 14
Sydmonton.—3C 28
Sydnal Lane.—2C 62
Sydney.—2B 74
Syerston.—3E 77
Syke.—1F 87
Sykehouse.—4G 95
Sykes.—4F 99
Syleham.—5E 69
Sylen.—2B 36
Sylfaen.—5D 72
Symbister.—5C 175
Symington.—1B 120
  (nr. Biggar, S'clyde.)
Symington.—1C 118
  (nr. Kilmarnock, S'clyde.)
Symondsbury.—4H 13
Symonds Yat West.—1D 38
Synod Inn.—2D 46
Syre.—4G 169
Syreford.—3E 49
Syresham.—3D 52
Syston.—1D 64
  (Leicestershire)
Syston.—3G 77
  (Lincolnshire)
Sytchampton.—1C 50
Sywell.—1F 53

Tachbrook Mallory.—1H 51
Tackley.—5B 52
Tacolneston.—3D 68
Tadcaster.—1E 95
Taddington.—5B 88
  (Derbyshire)
Taddington.—4E 51
  (Gloucestershire)
Taddiport.—2E 11
Tadley.—2E 28
Tadlow.—3B 54
Tadmarton.—4A 52
Tadwick.—5F 39
Tadworth.—5D 30
Tafarnaubach.—1H 37
Tafarn-gelyn.—4D 84
Tafarn-y-bwlch.—4A 46
Taffs Well.—4H 37
Tafolwern.—5A 72
Tai-bach.—3D 72
  (Clwyd)
Taibach.—4D 36
  (West Glamorgan)
Tain.—2E 171
  (nr. Thurso, H'land.)
Tain.—5E 167
  (nr. Invergordon, H'land.)
Tai-nant.—1E 73
Tai'n Lon.—5D 82
Tairgwaith.—1D 36
Takeley.—5E 55
Takeley Street.—5E 55
Talachddu.—4C 48
Talacre.—2D 84
Talardd.—3A 72
Talaton.—4D 12
Talbenny.—3B 34
Talbot Green.—4G 37
Taleford.—4D 12
Talerddig.—5B 72
Talgarreg.—2D 46
Talgarth.—4D 48
Taliesin.—1B 58
Talisker.—5C 156
Talke.—2C 74
Talkin.—4G 115
Talladale.—1B 158
Talla Linnfoots.—2D 120
Tallaminnock.—5D 118
Tallarn Green.—1G 73
Tallentire.—1C 104
Talley.—4F 47
Tallington.—2H 65
Talmine.—2F 169

Talog.—2G 35
Talsarn.—2E 47
  (nr. Lampeter, Dyfed)
Talsarn.—5G 47
  (nr. Llandovery, Dyfed)
Talsarnau.—2F 71
Talskiddy.—3D 6
Talwrn.—1E 73
  (Clwyd)
Talwrn.—3D 83
  (Gwynedd)
Talybont.—2B 58
  (Dyfed)
Tal-y-bont.—3F 83
  (nr. Bangor, Gwynedd)
Tal-y-bont.—3E 71
  (nr. Barmouth, Gwynedd)
Tal-y-bont.—4G 83
  (nr. Dolgarrog, Gwynedd)
Talybont.—5D 48
  (Powys)
Tal-y-cafn.—3G 83
Tal-y-coed.—1C 38
Tal-y-llyn.—5G 71
  (Gwynedd)
Tallyllyn.—5D 48
  (Powys)
Talysarn.—5D 83
Tal-y-waenydd.—1F 71
Talywain.—2A 38
Talywern.—5H 71
Tamerton Foliot.—3A 8
Tamworth.—2G 63
Tamworth Green.—3C 78
Tandlehill.—3F 129
Tandridge.—5E 31
Tanerdy.—2H 35
Tanfield.—4E 117
Tanfield Lea.—4E 117
Tangasdale.—9B 172
Tang Hall.—4B 102
Tangiers.—3C 34
Tangley.—3B 28
Tangmere.—3H 17
Tangwick.—4D 175
Tankerness.—7E 174
Tankersley.—3D 88
Tankerton.—4F 33
Tan-lan.—4G 83
  (nr. Llanrwst, Gwynedd)
Tan-lan.—1F 71
  (nr. Penrhyndeudraeth, Gwynedd)
Tannach.—4F 171
Tannadice.—3D 147
Tanners Green.—5E 63
Tannington.—1E 57
Tannochside.—3A 130
Tan Office Green.—2G 55
Tansley.—2H 75
Tansley Knoll.—1H 75
Tansor.—3H 65
Tantobie.—4E 117
Tanton.—3C 108
Tanvats.—1A 78
Tanworth-in-Arden.—5F 63
Tan-y-bwlch.—1F 71
Tan-y-fron.—4B 84
  (nr. Denbigh, Clwyd)
Tanyfron.—5E 85
  (nr. Wrexham, Clwyd)
Tanygrisiau.—1F 71
Tan-y-groes.—3B 46
Tan-y-pistyll.—3C 72
Tan-yr-allt.—2C 84
Taplow.—2A 30
Tapton.—5D 88
Tarbert.—1E 127
  (Jura, S'clyde.)
Tarbert.—3G 127
  (Knapdale, S'clyde.)
Tarbert.—7D 173
  (Western Isles)
Tarbet.—4F 140
  (nr. Mallaig, H'land.)
Tarbet.—4B 168
  (nr. Scourie, H'land.)

Tarbet.—3C 136
  (Strathclyde)
Tarbock Green.—4B 86
Tarbolton.—2D 118
Tarbrax.—4D 130
Tardebigge.—1E 51
Tarfside.—1D 147
Tarland.—3B 154
Tarleton.—3B 92
Tarlogie.—5E 167
Tarlscough.—1B 86
Tarlton.—3A 40
Tarnbrook.—4E 99
Tarnock.—3D 25
Tarns.—5C 114
Tarporley.—4H 85
Tarr.—5B 24
Tarrant Crawford.—3E 15
Tarrant Gunville.—2E 15
Tarrant Hinton.—2E 15
Tarrant Keyneston.—3E 15
Tarrant Launceston.—2E 15
Tarrant Monkton.—3E 15
Tarrant Rawston.—3E 15
Tarrant Rushton.—3E 15
Tarrel.—5F 167
Tarring Neville.—5F 19
Tarrington.—3A 50
Tarsappie.—1D 138
Tarskavaig.—3D 149
Tarves.—5F 163
Tarvie.—3G 159
Tarvin.—4G 85
Tasburgh.—3D 69
Tasley.—3A 62
Taston.—5A 52
Tatenhill.—5G 75
Tathall End.—3F 53
Tatham.—3F 99
Tathwell.—4F 91
Tatling End.—2B 30
Tatsfield.—5F 31
Tattenhall.—5G 85
Tatterford.—3A 80
Tattersett.—3A 80
Tattershall.—2B 78
Tattershall Bridge.—2A 78
Tattershall Thorpe.—2B 78
Tattingstone.—4D 56
Tattingstone White Horse.
  —4D 56
Tatworth.—3G 13
Taunton.—1F 13
Taverham.—4D 80
Taverners Green.—1B 44
Tavernspite.—3E 35
Tavistock.—2A 8
Tavool House.—1B 134
Taw Green.—4G 11
Tawstock.—3B 22
Taxal.—4H 87
Tayinloan.—5E 127
Taynish.—1F 127
Taynton.—5B 50
  (Gloucestershire)
Taynton.—1D 40
  (Oxfordshire)
Taynuilt.—5E 143
Tayport.—1G 139
Tayvallich.—1F 127
Tealby.—3D 90
Teangue.—3E 149
Tebay.—4H 105
Tebworth.—5G 53
Tedburn St Mary.—4B 12
Teddington.—4D 50
  (Gloucestershire)
Teddington.—3C 30
  (London)
Tedsmore.—3F 73
Tedstone Delamere.—2A 50
Tedstone Wafre.—2A 50
Teesport.—2C 108
Teesside.—2C 108
Teesside Airport.—3A 108

Teeton.—5D 64
Teffont Evias.—5E 27
Teffont Magna.—5E 27
Tegryn.—4B 46
Teigh.—1F 65
Teigncombe.—1C 8
Teigngrace.—2F 9
Teignmouth.—2F 9
Telford.—1A 62
Telham.—4B 20
Tellisford.—3D 26
Telscombe.—5F 19
Telscombe Cliffs.—5E 19
Tempar.—3D 144
Templand.—1B 114
Temple.—2F 7
  (Cornwall)
Temple.—4G 131
  (Lothian)
Temple.—3G 129
  (Strathclyde)
Temple Balsall.—5G 63
Temple Bar.—1B 36
  (nr. Ammanford, Dyfed)
Temple Bar.—2E 47
  (nr. Lampeter, Dyfed)
Temple Cloud.—3B 26
Templecombe.—1C 14
Temple Ewell.—1G 21
Temple Grafton.—2F 51
Temple Guiting.—5E 51
Templehall.—4E 139
Temple Hirst.—3G 95
Temple Normanton.—1B 76
Temple Sowerby.—2H 105
Templeton.—2B 28
  (Berkshire)
Templeton.—2B 12
  (Devon)
Templeton.—3E 35
  (Dyfed)
Templetown.—5E 117
Tempsford.—2A 54
Tenandry.—2G 145
Tenbury Wells.—4C 60
Tenby.—4E 35
Tendring.—5D 56
Tendring Green.—5D 56
Ten Mile Bank.—3F 67
Tenterden.—2C 20
Terfyn.—3B 84
Terling.—1D 44
Ternhill.—4A 74
Terregles.—2G 113
Terrick.—2B 42
Terrington.—2D 102
Terrington St Clement.—5E 79
Terrington St John.—1E 67
Terry's Green.—5F 63
Teston.—5B 32
Testwood.—2B 16
Tetbury.—3G 39
Tetbury Upton.—3G 39
Tetchill.—2F 73
Tetcott.—4D 10
Tetford.—5F 91
Tetney.—5F 97
Tetney Lock.—5F 97
Tetsworth.—2H 41
Tettenhall.—2C 62
Teuchatcroft.—4D 146
Teversal.—1B 76
Teversham.—2D 55
Teviothead.—4G 121
Tewel.—5F 155
Tewin.—1F 43
Tewin Wood.—1F 43
Tewkesbury.—4C 50
Teynham.—4D 32
Thackthwaite.—2F 105
Thakeham.—4C 18
Thame.—2A 42
Thames Ditton.—4C 30
Thames Haven.—2B 32
Thamesmead.—2F 31
Thamesport.—3C 32

Thanington.—5F 33
Thankerton.—1B 120
Tharston.—3D 69
Thatcham.—2D 28
Thatto Heath.—3C 86
Thaxted.—4F 55
Theakston.—1G 101
Thealby.—4A 96
Theale.—5H 41
  (Berkshire)
Theale.—4E 25
  (Somerset)
Thearne.—2C 96
Theberton.—5G 57
Theddingworth.—4D 64
Theddlethorpe All Saints.
  —4G 91
Theddlethorpe St Helen.—4G 91
Thelbridge Barton.—2A 12
Thelnetham.—5C 68
Thelveton.—4D 68
Thelwall.—4D 86
Themelthorpe.—3C 80
Thenford.—3C 52
Therfield.—4C 54
Thetford.—1A 66
  (Lincolnshire)
Thetford.—4A 68
  (Norfolk)
Thethwaite.—5E 115
Theydon Bois.—1F 31
Thick Hollins.—4B 94
Thickwood.—5G 39
Thimbleby.—5E 91
  (Lincolnshire)
Thimbleby.—5B 108
  (North Yorkshire)
Thingwall.—2E 85
Thirkleby.—2H 101
Thirlby.—1H 101
Thirlestane.—5B 132
Thirn.—1F 101
Thirsk.—1H 101
Thirtleby.—2D 96
Thistleton.—2B 92
  (Lancashire)
Thistleton.—1G 65
  (Leicestershire)
Thistley Green.—5F 67
Thixendale.—3D 102
Thockrington.—2C 116
Tholomas Drove.—2C 66
Tholthorpe.—3H 101
Thomas Chapel.—4E 35
Thomas Close.—5F 115
Thomastown.—4E 162
  (Grampian)
Thomastown.—4G 37
  (Mid Glamorgan)
Thompson.—3B 68
Thomshill.—3G 161
Thong.—3A 32
Thongsbridge.—2B 88
Thoralby.—1D 100
Thoresby.—5G 89
Thoresway.—3D 90
Thorganby.—3E 91
  (Lincolnshire)
Thorganby.—5B 102
  (North Yorkshire)
Thorgill.—5E 109
Thorington.—5G 69
Thorington Street.—4C 56
Thorlby.—4C 100
Thorley.—1A 44
Thorley Street.—1A 44
  (Hertfordshire)
Thorley Street.—5B 16
  (Isle of Wight)
Thormanby.—2H 101
Thorn.—4H 59
Thornaby-on-Tees.—3B 108
Thornage.—2C 80
Thornborough.—4E 53
  (Buckinghamshire)

Thornborough.—2F 101
  (North Yorkshire)
Thornbury.—3E 39
  (Avon)
Thornbury.—3E 11
  (Devon)
Thornbury.—2A 50
  (Hereford & Worcester)
Thornby.—4D 114
  (Cumbria)
Thornby.—5D 64
  (Northamptonshire)
Thorncliffe.—2E 75
Thorncombe.—3G 13
  (nr. Beaminster, Dorset)
Thorncombe Street.—1A 18
Thorncote Green.—3A 54
Thorndon.—1D 56
Thorndon Cross.—4F 11
Thorne.—4G 95
Thornehill Head.—2E 11
Thorner.—1D 94
Thorne St Margaret.—3G 23
Thorney.—2B 66
  (Cambridgeshire)
Thorney.—5A 90
  (Nottinghamshire)
Thorney.—1H 13
  (Somerset)
Thorney Hill.—4G 15
Thorney Toll.—2C 66
Thornfalcon.—1F 13
Thornford.—2B 14
Thorngrafton.—3A 116
Thorngrove.—5D 24
Thorngumbald.—3E 97
Thornham.—3G 79
Thornham Magna.—5D 68
Thornham Parva.—5D 68
Thornhaugh.—2H 65
Thornhill.—4F 137
  (Central)
Thornhill.—4B 104
  (Cumbria)
Thornhill.—4B 88
  (Derbyshire)
Thornhill.—5A 120
  (Dumfries & Galloway)
Thornhill.—2C 16
  (Hampshire)
Thornhill.—4H 37
  (Mid Glamorgan)
Thornhill.—4C 94
  (West Yorkshire)
Thornhill Lees.—4C 94
Thornhills.—3B 94
Thornholme.—3G 103
Thornington.—1C 122
Thornley.—1G 107
  (nr. Durham, Durham)
Thornley.—1E 107
  (nr. Tow Law, Durham)
Thornley Gate.—4B 116
Thornliebank.—4G 129
Thornroan.—5F 163
Thorns.—2G 55
Thornsett.—4H 87
Thorns Flush.—1B 18
Thornthwaite.—2D 104
  (Cumbria)
Thornthwaite.—4E 101
  (North Yorkshire)
Thornton.—4E 53
  (Buckinghamshire)
Thornton.—3B 108
  (Cleveland)
Thornton.—4E 139
  (Fife)
Thornton.—5C 102
  (Humberside)
Thornton.—1A 92
  (Lancashire)
Thornton.—2B 64
  (Leicestershire)

Torry.—3G 155
Torryburn.—5C 138
Torthorwald.—2B 114
Tortington.—5B 18
Tortworth.—3F 39
Torvaig.—4D 157
Torver.—5D 104
Torwood.—1B 130
Torworth.—4G 89
Toscaig.—5G 157
Toseland.—1B 54
Tosside.—4G 99
Tostock.—1B 56
Totaig.—3B 156
Totardor.—5C 156
Tote.—4D 156
Totegan.—2A 170
Tothill.—4G 91
Totland.—5B 16
Totley.—5D 88
Totnell.—3B 14
Totnes.—3E 9
Toton.—4B 76
Totscore.—2C 156
Tottenham.—1E 31
Tottenhill.—1F 67
Tottenhill Row.—1F 67
Totteridge.—1D 30
Totternhoe.—5G 53
Tottington.—1E 87
Totton.—2B 16
Touchen-End.—5B 42
Touches.—3G 13
Toulvaddie.—5F 167
Towans, The.—3C 4
Toward.—3C 128
Towcester.—3D 52
Towednack.—3B 4
Tower End.—1F 67
Tower Hamlets.—2E 31
Towerhill.—4D 10
(Devon)
Tower Hill.—2B 86
(Merseyside)
Tower Hill.—3C 18
(West Sussex)
Towersey.—2A 42
Towie.—2B 154
Towiemore.—4A 162
Tow Law.—1E 107
Town End.—3D 66
(Cambridgeshire)
Town End.—4F 105
(nr. Ambleside, Cumbria)
Town End.—2H 105
(nr. Appleby, Cumbria)
Town End.—1D 98
(nr. Lindale, Cumbria)
Town End.—1C 98
(nr. Newby Bridge, Cumbria)
Town End.—4B 86
(Merseyside)
Townend.—2F 129
(Strathclyde)
Townfield.—5C 116
Towngate.—5G 115
(Cumbria)
Towngate.—1A 66
(Lincolnshire)
Town Green.—2B 86
Town Head.—4E 105
(nr. Grasmere, Cumbria)
Town Head.—3H 105
(nr. Great Asby, Cumbria)
Townhead.—1G 105
(nr. Lazonby, Cumbria)
Townhead.—1B 104
(nr. Maryport, Cumbria)
Townhead.—1H 105
(nr. Ousby, Cumbria)
Townhead.—5D 113
(Dumfries & Galloway)
Townhead of Greenlaw.—3E 113
Townhill.—5D 138
(Fife)

Townhill.—3C 36
(West Glamorgan)
Town Kelloe.—1G 107
Town Littleworth.—4F 19
Town Row.—2G 19
Towns End.—3D 28
(Hampshire)
Townsend.—2E 43
(Hertfordshire)
Townshend.—3C 4
Town Street.—4G 67
Town Yetholme.—2C 122
Towthorpe.—3D 103
(Humberside)
Towthorpe.—4B 102
(North Yorkshire)
Towton.—2E 95
Towyn.—3B 84
Toxteth.—4A 86
Toynton All Saints.—1C 78
Toynton Fen Side.—1C 78
Toynton St Peter.—1D 78
Toy's Hill.—5F 31
Trabboch.—2D 118
Traboe.—4E 5
Tradespark.—3C 160
Trafford Park.—3E 87
Trallong.—5B 48
Tranent.—2H 131
Tranmere.—2F 85
Trantlebeg.—3A 170
Trantlemore.—3A 170
Tranwell.—1E 117
Trapp.—1C 36
Traquair.—1F 121
Trash Green.—2E 29
Trawden.—2G 93
Trawscoed.—4C 48
Trawsfynydd.—2G 71
Trawsgoed.—3B 58
Treaddow.—5H 49
Trealaw.—3G 37
Treales.—2B 92
Trearddur Bay.—3B 82
Treaslane.—3C 156
Treator.—2D 6
Trebanog.—3G 37
Trebanos.—2D 36
Trebarber.—3C 6
Trebartha.—2G 7
Trebarwith.—1E 7
Trebetherick.—2D 6
Treborough.—2G 23
Trebudannon.—3H 7
Trebullett.—2H 7
Treburley.—2H 7
Treburrick.—2C 6
Trebyan.—3E 7
Trecastle.—5A 48
Trecenydd.—4H 37
Trecott.—3G 11
Trecwn.—1C 34
Trecynon.—2F 37
Tredaule.—1G 7
Tredegar.—2H 37
Trederwen.—4E 73
Tredington.—5D 50
(Gloucestershire)
Tredington.—3G 51
(Warwickshire)
Tredinnick.—3F 7
(nr. Bodmin, Corn.)
Tredinnick.—4G 7
(nr. Looe, Corn.)
Tredinnick.—2D 6
(nr. Padstow, Corn.)
Tredogan.—5G 37
Tredomen.—4D 48
Tredrissi.—3A 46
Tredunnock.—3B 38
Tredustan.—4D 48
Treen.—4A 4
(nr. Land's End, Corn.)
Treen.—3B 4
(nr. St Ives, Corn.)
Treeton.—4E 89

Trefasser.—1B 34
Trefdraeth.—3D 82
Trefecca.—4D 48
Trefechan.—2G 37
Trefeglwys.—1E 59
Trefeitha.—4D 48
Treffgarne.—2C 34
Treffynnon.—2B 34
Trefil.—1H 37
Trefilan.—2E 47
Treflach.—3E 73
Trefnant.—3C 84
Trefonen.—3E 73
Trefor.—1C 70
(nr. Caernarfon, Gwynedd)
Trefor.—2C 82
(nr. Holyhead, Gwynedd)
Treforest.—4G 37
Trefriw.—4G 83
Trefynwy.—1D 38
Tregada.—1H 7
Tregadillett.—1G 7
Tregare.—1C 38
Tregarne.—4E 5
Tregaron.—2F 47
Tregarth.—4F 83
Tregear.—4C 6
Tregeare.—1G 7
Tregeiriog.—2D 70
Tregele.—1C 82
Tregiskey.—2H 5
Tregole.—4B 10
Tregonetha.—3D 6
Tregonhawke.—4A 8
Tregony.—2G 5
Tregoodwell.—1F 7
Tregorrick.—4E 6
Tregoss.—3D 6
Tregowris.—4E 5
Tregoyd.—4D 48
Tregrehan Mills.—4E 7
Tre-groes.—3D 46
Tregullon.—3E 7
Tregurrian.—3C 6
Tregynon.—1F 59
Trehafod.—3G 37
Trehan.—4A 8
Treharris.—3G 37
Tre-Herbert.—3E 47
(Dyfed)
Treherbert.—3F 37
(Mid Glamorgan)
Trehunist.—3H 7
Trekenner.—2H 7
Trekenning.—3D 6
Treknow.—1E 7
Trelan.—5E 5
Trelash.—4B 10
Trelassick.—4C 6
Trelawnyd.—3C 84
Trelech.—4B 46
Trelech a'r Betws.—2G 35
Treleddyd-fawr.—2A 34
Trelewis.—3H 37
Treligga.—1E 7
Trelights.—2D 6
Trelill.—2E 7
Trelissick.—3F 5
Trelleck.—2D 38
Trelleck Grange.—2C 38
Trelogan.—2F 85
Trelystan.—5E 73
Tremadog.—1E 71
Tremail.—1F 7
Tremain.—3B 46
Tremaine.—1G 7
Tremar.—3G 7
Trematon.—4H 7
Tremeirchion.—3C 84
Tremore.—3E 6
Tremorfa.—5A 38
Trenance.—5D 4
(nr. Helston, Corn.)
Trenance.—3C 6
(nr. Newquay, Corn.)

Trenance.—2D 6
(nr. Padstow, Corn.)
Trenarren.—2H 5
Trench.—1A 62
Trencreek.—3C 6
Trendeal.—4C 6
Trenear.—3D 5
Treneglos.—1G 7
Trenewan.—4F 7
Trenfenter.—4B 58
Trengune.—4B 10
Trent.—2A 14
Trentham.—3C 74
Trentishoe.—1C 22
Trentlock.—4B 76
Treoes.—5F 37
Treorchy.—3F 37
Tre'r-ddol.—1B 58
Trerule Foot.—4H 7
Tresaith.—2B 46
Trescott.—3C 62
Trescowe.—3C 4
Tresham.—3F 39
Tresillian.—2F 5
Tresinney.—1F 7
Treskinnick Cross.—4C 10
Tresmeer.—1G 7
Tresparrett.—4B 10
Tresparrett Posts.—4B 10
Tressady.—3D 166
Tressait.—2F 145
Tresta.—6E 175
Treswell.—5H 89
Treswithian.—2D 4
Trethomas.—4H 37
Trethosa.—4D 6
Trethurgy.—4E 7
Tretio.—2A 34
Tretire.—3H 7
Tretower.—5D 48
Treuddyn.—5E 85
Trevadlock.—2G 7
Trevalga.—4A 10
Trevalyn.—5F 85
Trevance.—2D 6
Trevanger.—2D 6
Trevanson.—2D 6
Trevarrack.—3B 4
Trevarren.—3D 6
Trevarrian.—3C 6
Trevarrick.—2H 5
Tre-vaughan.—2H 35
(nr. Carmarthen, Dyfed)
Trevaughan.—3F 35
(nr. Whitland, Dyfed)
Treveighan.—2E 7
Trevellas.—4B 6
Trevelmond.—3G 7
Treverva.—3E 5
Trevescan.—4A 4
Trevethin.—2A 38
Trevia.—1E 7
Trevigro.—3H 7
Treviscoe.—4D 6
Trevivian.—1F 7
Trevone.—2C 6
Trevor.—1E 73
(Clwyd)
Trevor (Trefor).—1C 70
(Gwynedd)
Trevor Uchaf.—1E 73
Trew.—4D 4
Trewalder.—1E 7
Trewarlett.—1H 7
Trewarmett.—1E 7
Trewassa.—1F 7
Treween.—1G 7
Trewellard.—3A 4
Trewen.—1G 7
Trewennack.—4D 5
Trewern.—4E 73
Trewetha.—1E 6
Trewidland.—3G 7
Trewint.—4B 10

Trewithian.—3F 5
Trewoofe.—4B 4
Trewoon.—4D 6
Treworthal.—3F 5
Treyarnon.—2C 6
Treyford.—2G 17
Triangle.—2E 63
(Staffordshire)
Triangle.—3H 93
(West Yorkshire)
Trickett's Cross.—3F 15
Triffleton.—2C 34
Trimdon.—1G 107
Trimdon Colliery.—1G 107
Trimdon Grange.—1G 107
Trimingham.—2E 81
Trimley.—4E 57
Trimley Heath.—4E 57
Trimley Lower Street.—4E 57
Trimpley.—5B 62
Trimsaran.—2A 36
Trimstone.—1B 22
Trinafour.—2E 144
Trinant.—3A 38
Tring.—1C 42
Trinity.—2F 131
(Lothian)
Trinity.—2F 147
(Tayside)
Trislaig.—1E 143
Trispen.—4C 6
Tritlington.—5G 123
Trochry.—5G 145
Troed-rhiw-dalar.—2B 48
Troedrhiwfwch.—2H 37
Troedrhiw-gwair.—2H 37
Troedyraur.—3C 46
Troedyrhiw.—2G 37
Trondavoe.—4E 175
Troon.—3D 4
(Cornwall)
Troon.—1C 118
(Strathclyde)
Troqueer.—2G 113
Troston.—5A 68
Trottiscliffe.—4H 31
Trotton.—1G 17
Troutbeck.—4F 105
(nr. Ambleside, Cumbria)
Troutbeck.—2E 105
(nr. Penrith, Cumbria)
Troutbeck Bridge.—4F 105
Troway.—5D 88
Trowbridge.—3D 26
Trowell.—4B 76
Trowle Common.—3D 26
Trowley Bottom.—1D 43
Trowse Newton.—2E 69
Trudoxhill.—4C 26
Trull.—1F 13
Trumaisgarry.—1D 172
Trumpan.—2B 156
Trumpet.—4A 50
Trumpington.—2D 54
Trumps Green.—4A 30
Trunch.—2E 81
Trunnah.—1A 92
Truro.—2F 5
Trusham.—1E 9
Trusley.—4G 75
Trusthorpe.—4H 91
Tryfil.—2D 82
Trysull.—3C 62
Tubney.—3F 41
Tuckenhay.—4E 9
Tuckhill.—4B 62
Tuckingmill.—2D 4
Tuckton.—4G 15
Tuddenham.—3D 57
(nr. Ipswich, Suff.)
Tuddenham.—5G 67
(nr. Mildenhall, Suff.)
Tudeley.—1H 19
Tudhoe.—1F 107
Tudhoe Grange.—1F 107
Tudorville.—5H 49

Tudweiliog.—2B 70
Tuesley.—1A 18
Tuffley.—1G 39
Tufton.—2D 34
(Dyfed)
Tufton.—4C 32
(Hampshire)
Tugby.—2E 65
Tugford.—2C 60
Tughall.—2G 123
Tulchan.—1B 138
Tullibardine.—2B 138
Tullibody.—4A 138
Tullich.—4B 158
(nr. Lochcarron, H'land.)
Tullich.—1C 160
(nr. Tain, H'land.)
Tullich Muir.—1B 160
Tulliemet.—3H 145
Tulloch.—5F 163
(Grampian)
Tulloch.—4D 166
(nr. Bonar Bridge, H'land.)
Tulloch.—5F 151
(nr. Fort William, H'land.)
Tulloch.—2D 153
(nr. Grantown-on-Spey, H'...)
Tulloch.—1C 138
(Tayside)
Tullochgorm.—4G 135
Tullybeagles Lodge.—5H 14...
Tullymurdoch.—3A 146
Tullynessle.—2C 154
Tumble.—1B 36
Tumbler's Green.—5A 56
Tumby.—2B 78
Tumby Woodside.—2B 78
Tummel Bridge.—3E 145
Tunbridge Wells.—2G 19
Tungate.—3E 81
Tunley.—3B 26
Tunstall.—2F 97
(Humberside)
Tunstall.—4C 32
(Kent)
Tunstall.—2F 99
(Lancashire)
Tunstall.—2G 69
(Norfolk)
Tunstall.—5F 107
(North Yorkshire)
Tunstall.—5B 74
(nr. Eccleshall, Staffs.)
Tunstall.—2C 74
(nr. Stoke-on-Trent, Staffs...)
Tunstall.—2F 57
(Suffolk)
Tunstall.—4G 117
(Tyne & Wear)
Tunstead.—5B 88
(Derbyshire)
Tunstead.—3E 81
(Norfolk)
Tunstead Milton.—4H 87
Tunworth.—4E 29
Tupsley.—3H 49
Tupton.—1A 76
Turfholm.—1H 119
Turfmoor.—3F 13
Turgis Green.—3E 29
Turkdean.—1C 40
Turkey Island.—2D 16
Tur Langton.—3E 64
Turleigh.—2D 26
Turlin Moor.—4E 15
Turnant.—5F 49
Turnastone.—4F 49
Turnberry.—4B 118
Turnchapel.—4B 8
Turnditch.—3G 75
Turners Hill.—2E 19
Turners Puddle.—4D 14
Turnhouse.—2E 131
Turnworth.—3D 14
Turriff.—4E 163
Tursdale.—1G 107

n Bottoms.—1E 87
ry.—4C 162
s Green.—5E 63
—2G 53
ile.—3A 42
le Heath.—3A 42
eston.—4D 52
elaw.—3F 121
ry.—1C 75
ll.—5D 63
ill.—3D 38
ngton.—3E 81
Clump.—5G 41
ell.—1E 7
rd.—5H 89
—5B 174
kney)
—6E 175
etland)
har.—2A 130
dale.—2B 62
lmouth.—4F 133
smuir.—2C 120
reheads.—2E 5
nlow Green.—1B 74
ty.—5A 78
on.—2C 26
kenham.—3C 30
worth.—5C 50
eham.—4D 18
noe.—3C 26
stead.—4A 56
stead Green.—4A 56
s Green.—3D 86
on.—1F 93
chen.—2D 23
ron)
chen.—3A 60
opshire)
Bridges.—2C 8
ron)
Bridges.—2E 39
oucestershire)
Dales.—1G 75
Gates.—2G 63
Mile Oak Cross.—3E 9
ross.—2H 63
ord.—5A 42
rkshire)
ord.—5D 52
ckinghamshire)
ord.—5H 75
byshire)
ord.—2D 14
set)
ord.—1C 16
mpshire)
ord.—1E 65
cestershire)
ord.—3C 80
folk)
ord Common.—4H 49
carno.—2H 37
holm.—4D 112
ce.—4C 50
ing Green.—4D 50
llanan.—5G 47
-mynydd.—1C 36
y-Sheriff.—2C 38
rell.—5G 65
ton.—4F 49
n.—3F 63
—3C 80
es.—1C 36
vyn.—4D 72
Gote.—1G 66
St Giles.—1D 66
St Giles.—1D 66
—3F 17
reen.—5G 55
Braintree, Essex)
reen.—4E 55
Saffron Walden, Essex)
reen.—5E 55
r. Stansted Mountfitchet,
al.—2B 94

Ty-isaf.—2D 72
Tyldesley.—2E 87
Tyle.—5F 47
Tyler Hill.—4F 33
Tylers Green.—1A 30
(Buckinghamshire)
Tyler's Green.—2B 44
(Essex)
Tylorstown.—3G 37
Tylwch.—2E 59
Ty-nant.—1B 72
Tyndrum.—5H 143
Tyneham.—5D 15
Tynehead.—4G 131
Tynemouth.—3G 117
Tyneside.—3F 117
Tynewydd.—3F 37
Tyninghame.—2C 132
Tynribbie.—4D 142
Tynron.—5H 119
Tyn'y-bryn.—4G 37
Tyn-y-celyn.—2D 72
Tyn-y-coedcae.—4H 37
Tyn-y-cwm.—2C 36
Tyn-y-ffridd.—2D 72
Tynygongl.—2E 83
Ty'nygraig.—4B 58
Tyn-y-groes.—3G 83
Tyn-yr-eithin.—4B 58
Tyn-y-rhyd.—4C 72
Tyn-y-wern.—3C 72
Tyringham.—3F 53
Tythecott.—2E 11
Tythegston.—5E 37
Tytherington.—4E 39
(Avon)
Tytherington.—5G 87
(Cheshire)
Tytherington.—4C 26
(Somerset)
Tytherington.—4E 27
(Wiltshire)
Tytherleigh.—3G 13
Tywardreath.—4E 7
Tywardreath Highway.—4E 7
Tywyn.—3G 83
(nr. Llandudno, Gwynedd)
Tywyn.—5C 71
(nr. Machynlleth, Gwynedd)

Uags.—5G 157
Ubbeston Green.—5F 69
Ubley.—3F 25
Uckerby.—4F 107
Uckfield.—3F 19
Uckinghall.—4C 50
Uckington.—5D 50
(Gloucestershire)
Uckington.—4H 73
(Shropshire)
Uddingston.—3H 129
Uddington.—1A 120
Udimore.—4C 20
Udny Green.—1F 155
Udny Station.—1G 155
Udston.—4H 129
Udstonhead.—5A 130
Uffcott.—5C 40
Uffculme.—2D 12
Uffington.—2H 65
(Lincolnshire)
Uffington.—4E 40
(Oxfordshire)
Uffington.—4H 73
(Shropshire)
Ufford.—2H 65
(Cambridgeshire)
Ufford.—2E 57
(Suffolk)
Ufton.—1A 52
Ufton Nervet.—2E 29
Ugadale.—3B 124
Ugborough.—4C 8
Ugford.—5F 27
Uggeshall.—5G 69

Ugglebarnby.—4F 109
Ugley.—5E 55
Ugley Green.—5E 55
Ugthorpe.—3E 109
Uidh.—9B 172
Uig.—3A 156
(nr. Dunvegan, H'land.)
Uig.—2C 156
(Glen Uig, H'land.)
Uigshader.—4D 156
Uisken.—2A 134
Ulbster.—4F 171
Ulcat Row.—2F 105
Ulceby.—4D 96
(Humberside)
Ulceby.—5G 91
(Lincolnshire)
Ulceby Skitter.—4D 96
Ulcombe.—1C 20
Uldale.—1D 104
Uley.—3F 39
Ulgham.—5G 123
Ullapool.—5C 168
Ullenhall.—1F 51
Ulleskelf.—5A 102
Ullesthorpe.—4C 64
Ulley.—4E 89
Ullingswick.—2H 49
Ullinish.—5C 156
Ullock.—2B 104
Ulpha.—5C 104
Ulrome.—4G 103
Ulsta.—4F 175
Ulting.—2E 44
Ulva House.—5F 141
Ulverston.—2B 98
Ulwell.—5F 15
Umberleigh.—3C 22
Unapool.—5C 168
Underbarrow.—5F 105
Undercliffe.—2B 94
Underdale.—4H 73
Underriver.—5G 31
Under Tofts.—4D 88
Underton.—3A 62
Underwood.—4B 8
(Devon)
Underwood.—2B 76
(Nottinghamshire)
Undley.—4F 67
Undy.—4C 38
Union Mills.—4C 110
Union Street.—2B 20
Unst Airport.—1H 175
Unstone.—5D 88
Unstone Green.—5D 88
Unthank.—5E 115
(nr. Carlisle, Cumbria)
Unthank.—5H 115
(nr. Gamblesby, Cumbria)
Unthank.—1F 105
(nr. Penrith, Cumbria)
Unthank End.—1F 105
Upavon.—3G 27
Up Cerne.—3B 14
Upchurch.—4C 32
Upcott.—3F 11
(Devon)
Upcott.—2F 49
(Hereford & Worcester)
Upend.—2C 55
Up Exe.—3C 12
Upgate.—4D 80
Upgate Street.—3C 68
Uphall.—2D 130
Uphall Station.—2D 130
Upham.—3B 12
(Devon)
Upham.—1D 16
(Hampshire)
Uphampton.—4A 60
(nr. Leominster, Here & Worcs)
Uphampton.—1C 50
(nr. Worcester, Here & Worcs.)
Up Hatherley.—5D 50
Uphill.—3D 24

Up Holland.—2C 86
Uplawmoor.—4F 129
Upleadon.—5B 50
Upleatham.—3D 108
Uplees.—4D 32
Uploders.—4A 14
Uplowman.—2D 12
Uplyme.—4G 13
Up Marden.—2F 17
Upminster.—2G 31
Up Nately.—3E 29
Uppottery.—3F 13
Uppat.—3F 167
Upper Affcot.—2B 60
Upper Arley.—4B 62
Upper Armley.—2C 94
Upper Arncott.—1H 41
Upper Astrop.—4C 52
Upper Badcall.—4B 168
Upper Bangor.—3E 83
Upper Barvas.—2F 173
Upper Basildon.—4G 41
Upper Batley.—3C 94
Upper Bayble.—4H 173
Upper Beeding.—4C 18
Upper Benefield.—4G 65
Upper Bentley.—1D 51
Upper Bighouse.—3A 170
Upper Boddam.—5D 162
Upper Boddington.—2B 52
Upper Booth.—4B 88
Upper Borth.—2B 58
Upper Boyndlie.—2G 163
Upper Brailes.—4H 51
Upper Breakish.—1E 149
Upper Breinton.—3G 49
Upper Broadheath.—2C 50
Upper Broughton.—5D 76
Upper Brynamman.—1D 36
Upper Bucklebury.—2D 28
Upper Bullington.—4C 28
Upper Burgate.—2G 15
Upper Caldecote.—3A 54
Upper Canterton.—2A 16
Upper Carloway.—3E 173
Upper Catesby.—2C 52
Upper Chapel.—3C 48
Upper Cheddon.—1F 13
Upper Chicksgrove.—1E 15
Upper Church Village.—4G 37
Upper Chute.—3A 28
Upper Clatford.—4B 28
Upper Clynnog.—1D 70
Upper Coberley.—1A 40
Upper Coedcae.—2A 38
Upper Cokeham.—5C 18
Upper Coll.—4G 173
Upper Cound.—5H 73
Upper Cudworth.—2D 88
Upper Cumberworth.—2C 88
Upper Cuttlehill.—4B 162
Upper Cwmbran.—2A 38
Upper Dallachy.—2A 162
Upper Dean.—1H 53
Upper Denby.—2C 88
Upper Derraid.—5E 157
Upper Diabaig.—2H 157
Upper Dicker.—5G 19
Upper Dinchope.—2B 60
Upper Dochcarty.—2H 159
Upper Dounreay.—2B 170
Upper Dovercourt.—4F 57
Upper Dunsforth.—3G 99
Upper Dunsley.—1C 42
Upper Eastern Green.—4G 63
Upper Elkstone.—5F 85
Upper Ellastone.—3F 75
Upper End.—5A 88
Upper Enham.—4B 28
Upper Farringdon.—5F 29
Upper Framilode.—1F 39
Upper Froyle.—4F 29
Upper Gills.—1F 171
Upper Glenfintaig.—5E 151
Upper Godney.—4E 25
Upper Gravenhurst.—4A 54

Upper Green.—2B 28
(Berkshire)
Upper Green.—4D 54
(Essex)
Upper Green.—3C 94
(West Yorkshire)
Upper Grove Common.—5H 49
Upper Hackney.—1G 75
Upper Hale.—4G 29
Upper Halliford.—4B 30
Upper Halling.—4A 32
Upper Hambleton.—2G 65
Upper Hardwick.—2G 49
Upper Hartfield.—2F 19
Upper Haugh.—3E 89
Upper Hayton.—2C 60
Upper Heath.—2C 60
Upper Hellesdon.—4E 79
Upper Helmsley.—4B 102
Upper Hengoed.—2E 73
Upper Hergest.—2E 49
Upper Heyford.—2D 52
(Northamptonshire)
Upper Heyford.—5B 52
(Oxfordshire)
Upper Hill.—2G 49
Upper Hindhope.—4B 120
Upper Hopton.—4B 94
Upper Howsell.—3B 50
Upper Hulme.—1E 75
Upper Inglesham.—3D 40
Upper Kilcott.—4F 39
Upper Killay.—3B 36
Upper Kirkton.—5E 163
(Grampian)
Upper Kirkton.—4C 128
(Strathclyde)
Upper Knockando.—4F 161
Upper Knockchoilum.—2G 151
Upper Lambourn.—4E 40
Upper Langford.—3E 25
Upper Langwith.—1C 76
Upper Largo.—3G 139
Upper Latheron.—5D 171
Upper Layham.—4E 75
Upper Leigh.—4E 75
Upper Lenie.—1H 151
Upper Lochton.—4D 154
Upper Longdon.—1E 63
Upper Longwood.—2A 62
Upper Lybster.—5E 171
Upper Lydbrook.—1E 39
Upper Lye.—4A 60
Upper Maes-coed.—4F 49
Upper Midway.—2G 87
Upper Millichope.—2C 60
Upper Milovaig.—4A 156
Upper Minety.—3B 40
Upper Mitton.—5C 62
Upper Nash.—4D 34
Upper Netchwood.—3A 62
Upper Nobut.—4E 75
Upper North Dean.—3B 42
Upper Norwood.—2H 17
Upper Nyland.—1C 14
Upper Ollach.—5E 157
Upper Outwoods.—5G 75
Upper Padley.—5C 88
Upper Pennington.—4B 16
Upper Poppleton.—4A 102
Upper Quinton.—3F 51
Upper Rochford.—1A 50
Upper Rusko.—3C 112
Upper Sandaig.—2F 149
Upper Sanday.—7E 174
Upper Sapey.—1A 50
Upper Seagry.—4H 39
Upper Shelton.—3G 53
Upper Sheringham.—1D 80
Upper Skelmorlie.—3C 128
Upper Slaughter.—5F 51
Upper Sonachan.—1H 135
Upper Soudley.—1E 39
Upper Staploe.—2A 54
Upper Stoke.—2E 69
Upper Stondon.—4A 54

Upper Stowe.—2D 52
Upper Street.—2G 15
(Hampshire)
Upper Street.—4F 81
(nr. Horning, Norf.)
Upper Street.—4F 81
(nr. Hoveton, Norf.)
Upper Street.—4D 56
(Suffolk)
Upper Strensham.—4D 50
Upper Studley.—3D 26
Upper Sundon.—5H 53
Upper Swell.—5F 51
Upper Tankersley.—3D 88
Upper Tean.—4E 75
Upperthong.—2B 88
Upperthorpe.—2H 89
Upper Tillyrie.—4D 37
Upperton.—1H 17
Upper Tooting.—3D 31
Upper Town.—2F 25
(Avon)
Uppertown.—1H 75
(nr. Ashover, Derbys.)
Upper Town.—2G 75
(nr. Bonsall, Derbys.)
Upper Town.—2G 75
(nr. Hognaston, Derbys.)
Upper Town.—3H 49
(Hereford & Worcester)
Uppertown.—1F 171
(Highland)
Uppertown.—2A 116
(Northumberland)
Uppertown.—8D 174
(Orkney)
Upper Tysoe.—3H 51
Upper Upham.—3B 32
Upper Upnor.—3B 32
Upper Urquhart.—3D 138
Upper Wardington.—3B 52
Upper Weald.—4F 53
Upper Weedon.—2D 52
Upper Wellingham.—4F 19
Upper Whiston.—4E 89
Upper Wield.—5E 29
Upper Winchendon.—1A 42
Upperwood.—2G 75
Upper Woodford.—5G 27
Upper Wootton.—3D 28
Upper Wraxall.—5G 39
Upper Wyche.—3B 50
Uppincott.—3B 12
Uppingham.—3F 65
Uppington.—5H 73
Upsall.—1H 101
Upsettlington.—5E 133
Upshire.—2H 43
Up Somborne.—5B 28
Upstreet.—4G 33
Up Sydling.—3B 14
Upthorpe.—5B 68
Upton.—3A 30
(Berkshire)
Upton.—1A 42
(Buckinghamshire)
Upton.—5A 66
(nr. Huntingdon, Cambs.)
Upton.—2A 66
(nr. Peterborough, Cambs.)
Upton.—4G 85
(Cheshire)
Upton.—3C 10
(nr. Bude, Corn.)
Upton.—2G 7
(nr. Liskeard, Corn.)
Upton.—1E 104
(Cumbria)
Upton.—3D 12
(nr. Honiton, Devon)
Upton.—5D 8
(nr. Kingsbridge, Devon)
Upton.—4E 15
(nr. Poole, Dorset)
Upton.—5C 14
(nr. Weymouth, Dorset)

Upton.—4D 34
(Dyfed)
Upton.—3B 28
(nr. Andover, Hants.)
Upton.—2B 16
(nr. Southampton, Hants.)
Upton.—4G 103
(Humberside)
Upton.—4O 16
(Isle of Wight)
Upton.—3A 64
(Leicestershire)
Upton.—4A 90
(Lincolnshire)
Upton.—2C 85
(Merseyside)
Upton.—4F 81
(Norfolk)
Upton.—1E 52
(Northamptonshire)
Upton.—5H 89
(nr. East Retford, Notts.)
Upton.—2C 77
(nr. Southwell, Notts.)
Upton.—4C 46
(Oxfordshire)
Upton.—1H 13
(nr. Somerton, Som.)
Upton.—3F 23
(nr. Wiveliscombe, Som.)
Upton.—2F 51
(Warwickshire)
Upton.—4E 95
(West Yorkshire)
Upton.—5D 26
(Wiltshire)
Upton Bishop.—5A 50
Upton Cheney.—5E 39
Upton Cressett.—3A 62
Upton Crews.—5A 50
Upton Cross.—2C 7
Upton End.—4A 54
Upton Grey.—4E 29
Upton Heath.—4E 85
Upton Hellions.—3B 12
Upton Lovell.—4E 27
Upton Magna.—4H 73
Upton Noble.—5C 26
Upton Pyne.—4C 12
Upton St Leonards.—1G 39
Upton Scudamore.—4D 26
Upton Snodsbury.—2D 50
Upton upon Severn.—3C 50
Upton Warren.—1D 50
Upwaltham.—2H 17
Upware.—5E 67
Upwell.—2F 67
Upwey.—5B 14
Upwick Green.—5D 54
Upwood.—4B 66
Urafirth.—4E 175
Uragaig.—4A 134
Urchany.—4C 160
Urchfont.—3F 27
Urdimarsh.—3H 49
Ure.—3D 175
Ure Bank.—2G 101
Urgha.—8D 173
Urlay Nook.—3B 108
Urmston.—3E 87
Urquhart.—2G 161
Urra.—4C 108
Urray.—3H 159
Usan.—3G 147
Ushaw Moor.—5F 117
Usk.—2B 38
Usselby.—3C 90
Usworth.—4G 117
Uton.—4B 12
Utterby.—3F 91
Uttoxeter.—4E 75
Uwchmynydd.—3A 70
Uxbridge.—2B 30
Uyeasound.—1G 175
Uzmaston.—3C 34

Valley.—3B 82
Valley End.—4A 30
Valley Truckle.—1E 7
Valtos.—2E 157
(Highland)
Valtos.—4C 173
(Western Isles)
Van.—2E 59
Vange.—2B 32
Varteg.—2A 38
Vatersay.—9B 172
Vatten.—4B 156
Vaul.—4B 140
Vaynol.—4E 83
Vaynor.—1G 37
Veensgarth.—7F 175
Velindre.—4A 46
(nr. Newport, Dyfed)
Velindre.—4D 48
(Powys)
Velindre (Felindre).—4C 46
(nr. Newcastle Emlyn, Dyfed)
Vellow.—2G 23
Velly.—1C 10
Venhay.—2A 12
Venn.—5D 8
Venngreen.—2D 11
Vennington.—5F 73
Venn Ottery.—4D 12
Venn's Green.—3H 49
Venny Tedburn.—4B 12
Venterdon.—2F 7
Ventnor.—5D 16
Vernham Dean.—3B 28
Vernham Street.—3B 28
Vernolds Common.—2B 60
Verwig (Ferwig).—3A 46
Verwood.—3F 15
Veryan.—3G 5
Veryan Green.—2G 5
Vicarage.—5F 13
Vickerstown.—3A 98
Victoria.—3D 6
Vidlin.—5F 175
Viewpark.—3A 130
Vigo.—2G 63
Vigo Village.—4H 31
Vinehall Street.—3B 20
Vine's Cross.—4G 19
Viney Hill.—2E 39
Virginia Water.—4A 30
Virginstow.—4D 11
Vobster.—4C 26
Voe.—5F 175
Vole.—1G 24
Vowchurch.—4F 49
Vulcan Village.—3C 86

Wackerfield.—2E 107
Wacton.—3D 69
Wadborough.—3D 50
Waddesdon.—1A 42
Waddeton.—4E 9
Waddicar.—3A 86
Waddingham.—3B 90
Waddington.—1E 93
(Lancashire)
Waddington.—1G 77
(Lincolnshire)
Waddon.—2E 9
Wadebridge.—2D 6
Wadeford.—2G 13
Wadenhoe.—4H 65
Wadesmill.—1G 43
Wadhurst.—2H 19
Wadshelf.—1G 30
Wadsley.—3D 88
Wadsley Bridge.—3D 88
Wadswick.—2D 26
Wadwick.—3C 28
Wadworth.—3F 89

Waen.—4C 84
(nr. Bodfari, Clwyd)
Waen.—4D 84
(nr. Llandyrnog, Clwyd)
Waen.—4B 84
(nr. Nantglyn, Clwyd)
Waen.—1E 59
(Powys)
Waen Fach.—4E 72
Waen Goleugoed.—3C 84
Wag.—1H 167
Wainfleet All Saints.—2D 79
Wainfleet Bank.—2D 78
Wainfleet St Mary.—2D 79
Wainhouse Corner.—4B 10
Wainscott.—3B 32
Wainstalls.—3H 93
Waitby.—4A 106
Waithe.—5E 97
Wakefield.—3D 94
Wakerley.—3G 65
Wakes Colne.—5A 56
Walberswick.—5G 69
Walberton.—3H 17
Walbottle.—3E 117
Walby.—3F 115
Walcombe.—4F 25
Walcot.—3A 96
(Humberside)
Walcot.—4H 77
(Lincolnshire)
Walcot.—4H 73
(Shropshire)
Walcot.—2F 51
(Warwickshire)
Walcot.—4C 40
(Wiltshire)
Walcote.—4C 64
Walcot Green.—4D 68
Walcott.—2A 78
(Lincolnshire)
Walcott.—2F 81
(Norfolk)
Walden.—1D 100
Walden Head.—1C 100
Walden Stubbs.—4F 95
Walderslade.—4B 32
Walderton.—2F 17
Walditch.—4H 13
Waldley.—4F 75
Waldridge.—4F 117
Waldringfield.—3E 57
Waldron.—4G 19
Wales.—4E 89
Walesby.—3D 90
(Lincolnshire)
Walesby.—5G 89
(Nottinghamshire)
Walford.—3A 60
(nr. Leintwardine, Here & Worcs.)
Walford.—5H 49
(nr. Ross-on-Wye, Here &
Worcs.)
Walford.—3G 73
(Shropshire)
Walford.—4C 74
(Staffordshire)
Walford Heath.—4G 73
Walgherton.—3A 74
Walgrave.—5F 65
Walhampton.—4B 16
Walkden.—2E 87
Walker.—3F 117
Walkerburn.—1F 121
Walker Fold.—1D 92
Walkeringham.—3H 89
Walkerith.—3H 89
Walkern.—5B 54
Walker's Green.—3H 49
Walkerton.—3E 139
Walkerville.—5F 107
Walkford.—4H 15
Walkhampton.—3B 8
Walkington.—2B 96
Walkley.—4D 88
Walk Mill.—3F 93

Wall.—3D 4
(Cornwall)
Wall.—3C 116
(Northumberland)
Wall.—2F 63
(Staffordshire)
Wallaceton.—1F 113
Wallacetown.—2C 118
(Ayr, S'clyde.)
Wallacetown.—4B 118
(nr. Dailly, S'clyde.)
Wallands Park.—4F 19
Wallasey.—1E 85
Wallaston Green.—4C 34
Wallbrook.—3D 62
Wallcrouch.—2A 20
Wall End.—1B 98
(Cumbria)
Wallend.—3C 32
(Kent)
Wall Heath.—4C 62
Wallingford.—4H 41
Wallington.—3D 16
(Hampshire)
Wallington.—4B 54
(Hertfordshire)
Wallington.—4D 31
(London)
Wallis.—2D 34
Wallisdown.—4F 15
Walliswood.—2C 18
Wall Nook.—5F 117
Walls.—7D 175
Wallsend.—3F 117
Wallsworth.—5C 50
Wall under Heywood.—1C 60
Wallyford.—2G 131
Walmer.—5H 33
Walmer Bridge.—3B 92
Walmersley.—1F 87
Walmley.—3F 63
Walnut Grove.—1D 138
Walpole.—5F 69
Walpole Cross Keys.—1E 67
Walpole Gate.—1E 67
Walpole Highway.—1E 67
Walpolelane.—5F 69
Walpole Marsh.—1D 67
Walpole St Andrew.—1E 67
Walpole St Peter.—1E 67
Walsall.—2E 63
Walsall Wood.—2E 63
Walsden.—3G 93
Walsgrave-on-Sowe.—4A 64
Walsham le Willows.—5B 68
Walshaw.—1E 87
Walshford.—4H 101
Walsoken.—1D 67
Walston.—5D 130
Walsworth.—4A 54
Walterstone.—5G 37
Walterstone.—5F 49
Waltham.—5E 97
(Humberside)
Waltham.—1F 21
(Kent)
Waltham Abbey.—2G 43
Waltham Chase.—2D 16
Waltham Cross.—2G 43
Waltham Forest.—1E 31
Waltham on the Wolds.—5F 77
Waltham St Lawrence.—5B 42
Waltham's Cross.—4F 55
Walthamstow.—2E 31
Walton.—4F 53
(Buckinghamshire)
Walton.—2A 66
(Cambridgeshire)
Walton.—3G 115
(Cumbria)
Walton.—1A 76
(Derbyshire)
Walton.—4C 64
(Leicestershire)
Walton.—3A 86
(Merseyside)

Walton.—2E 49
(Powys)
Walton.—4H 73
(Shropshire)
Walton.—5E 25
(Somerset)
Walton.—5C 74
(nr. Eccleshall, Staffs.)
Walton.—4C 74
(nr. Stone, Staffs.)
Walton.—4E 57
(Suffolk)
Walton.—2G 51
(Warwickshire)
Walton.—4D 94
(nr. Wakefield, W Yorks.)
Walton.—1E 95
(nr. Wetherby, W Yorks.)
Walton Cardiff.—4D 50
Walton East.—2D 34
Walton Elm.—2C 14
Walton-in-Gordano.—5C 38
Walton-le-Dale.—3C 92
Walton-on-Thames.—4C 30
Walton-on-the-Hill.—5D 74
(Staffordshire)
Walton on the Hill.—5D 30
(Surrey)
Walton on the Naze.—5E 57
Walton on the Wolds.—1C 64
Walton-on-Trent.—1G 63
Walton Park.—5C 38
Walton West.—3B 34
Walwick.—2C 116
Walworth.—3F 107
Walworth Gate.—2F 107
Walwyn's Castle.—3B 34
Wambrook.—3F 13
Wampool.—4D 114
Wanborough.—1A 18
(Surrey)
Wanborough.—4D 40
(Wiltshire)
Wandel.—2E 120
Wandsworth.—3D 30
Wangford.—4G 67
(nr. Lakenheath, Suff.)
Wangford.—5G 69
(nr. Southwold, Suff.)
Wanlip.—1D 64
Wanlockhead.—3A 120
Wannock.—5G 19
Wansford.—3H 65
(Cambridgeshire)
Wansford.—4F 103
(Humberside)
Wanshurst Green.—1B 20
Wanstead.—2F 31
Wanstrow.—4C 26
Wanswell.—2E 39
Wantage.—4F 41
Wapley.—5F 39
Wappenbury.—1A 52
Wappenham.—3D 52
Warbleton.—4H 19
Warblington.—3F 17
Warborough.—3G 41
Warboys.—4C 66
Warbreck.—2A 92
Warbstow.—4C 10
Warburton.—4D 87
Warcop.—3A 106
Warden.—3C 32
(Kent)
Warden.—3C 116
(Northumberland)
Ward End.—4F 63
Ward Green.—1C 56
Wardhedges.—4H 53
Wardhouse.—5C 162
Wardington.—3B 52
Wardle.—2A 74
(Cheshire)
Wardle.—1G 87
(Manchester)

Wardley.—2F 65
(Leicestershire)
Wardley.—1G 17
(West Sussex)
Wardlow.—5B 88
Wardsend.—4G 87
Wardy Hill.—4D 66
Ware.—1G 43
(Hertfordshire)
Ware.—4G 33
(Kent)
Wareham.—5E 15
Warehorne.—2D 20
Warenford.—2F 123
Waren Mill.—1F 123
Warenton.—1F 123
Wareside.—1G 43
Waresley.—2B 54
(Cambridgeshire)
Waresley.—5C 62
(Hereford & Worcester)
Warfield.—5B 42
Warfleet.—4E 9
Wargate.—4B 78
Wargrave.—5C 42
Warham.—1B 80
Wark.—1C 122
(nr. Coldstream, Northmb.)
Wark.—2B 116
(nr. Hexham, Northmb.)
Warkleigh.—3C 22
Warkton.—5F 65
Warkworth.—3B 52
(Northamptonshire)
Warkworth.—4G 123
(Northumberland)
Warlaby.—5G 107
Warland.—3G 93
Warleggan.—3F 7
Warlingham.—5E 31
Warmanbie.—3C 114
Warmfield.—3D 94
Warmingham.—1B 74
Warminghurst.—4C 18
Warmington.—3H 65
(Northamptonshire)
Warmington.—3B 52
(Warwickshire)
Warminster.—4D 27
Warmley.—5E 39
Warmsworth.—2F 89
Warmwell.—5C 14
Warndon.—2C 50
Warners End.—2D 42
Warnford.—1E 16
Warnham.—2C 18
Warningcamp.—5B 18
Warninglid.—3D 18
Warren.—5F 87
(Cheshire)
Warren.—5C 34
(Dyfed)
Warrenby.—2C 108
Warren Corner.—4G 29
(nr. Aldershot, Hants.)
Warren Corner.—1F 17
(nr. Petersfield, Hants.)
Warren Row.—4B 42
Warren Street.—5D 32
Warrington.—2F 53
(Buckinghamshire)
Warrington.—4D 86
(Cheshire)
Warsash.—3C 16
Warse.—1F 171
Warslow.—2E 75
Warsop.—1C 76
Warsop Vale.—1C 76
Warter.—4D 102
Warthermarske.—2F 101
Warthill.—4B 102
Wartling.—5A 20
Wartnaby.—5E 76
Warton.—2D 99
(nr. Carnforth, Lancs.)

Westdean.—5G 19
(East Sussex)
West Dean.—2G 17
(West Sussex)
West Dean.—1A 16
(Wiltshire)
West Deeping.—2A 66
West Derby.—3B 86
West Dereham.—2F 67
West Down.—1B 22
Westdowns.—1E 7
West Drayton.—3B 30
(London)
West Drayton.—5H 89
(Nottinghamshire)
West Dunnet.—1E 171
West Ella.—3C 96
West End.—2E 25
(nr. Nailsea, Avon)
West End.—4F 39
(nr. Yate, Avon)
West End.—2G 53
(Bedfordshire)
West End.—5B 42
(Berkshire)
West End.—3D 66
(Cambridgeshire)
West End.—3E 15
(Dorset)
West End.—2C 70
(Gwynedd)
West End.—2C 16
(Hampshire)
West End.—4E 51
(Hereford & Worcester)
West End.—2F 43
(Hertfordshire)
West End.—3F 103
(nr. Kilham, Humberside)
West End.—2D 97
(nr. Preston, Humberside)
West End.—2B 96
(nr. South Cave, Humberside)
West End.—4G 103
(nr. Ulrome, Humberside)
West End.—4F 33
(Kent)
West End.—3C 78
(Lincolnshire)
West End.—4G 81
(Norfolk)
West End.—4E 101
(North Yorkshire)
West End.—5C 130
(Strathclyde)
West End.—4A 30
(Surrey)
West End.—1E 15
(Wiltshire)
West End Green.—2E 29
Westenhanger.—2F 21
Wester Aberchalder.—2H 151
Wester Balgedie.—3D 138
Wester Brae.—2A 160
Wester Culbeuchly.—2D 162
Westerdale.—3D 170
(Highland)
Westerdale.—4D 108
(North Yorkshire)
Wester Dechmont.—2D 130
Wester Fearn.—5D 166
Westerfield.—3D 68
Wester Galcantray.—4C 160
Westergate.—3H 17
Wester Gruinards.—4C 166
Westerham.—5F 31
Westerhope.—3E 117
Westerleigh.—5E 39
Westerloch.—3F 171
Wester Mandally.—3E 151
Westermill.—8D 174
Wester Parkgate.—1B 114
Wester Pencaitland.—3H 131
Wester Rarichie.—1C 160
Wester Slumbay.—5A 158

Westerton.—1F 107
(Durham)
Westerton.—3F 147
(Tayside)
Westerton.—3G 17
(West Sussex)
Westerwick.—7D 175
West Farleigh.—5B 32
West Farndon.—2C 52
West Felton.—3F 73
Westfield.—3B 26
(Avon)
Westfield.—2A 104
(Cumbria)
Westfield.—4C 20
(East Sussex)
Westfield.—2C 170
(Highland)
Westfield.—2C 130
(Lothian)
Westfield.—2B 68
(Norfolk)
Westfields.—3C 14
Westfields of Rattray.—4A 146
West Firle.—5F 19
West Fleetham.—2F 123
West Garforth.—2D 94
West Ginge.—4F 41
West Grafton.—2H 27
West Green.—3F 29
West Grimstead.—1H 15
West Grinstead.—3C 18
West Haddlesey.—3F 95
West Haddon.—5D 64
West Hagbourne.—4G 41
West Hagley.—4C 62
West Hall.—3G 115
(Cumbria)
Westhall.—4G 69
(Suffolk)
West Hallam.—3B 76
Westhall Terrace.—5D 146
West Halton.—3B 96
Westham.—5B 14
(Dorset)
Westham.—5H 19
(East Sussex)
West Ham.—2F 31
(London)
Westham.—4E 25
(Somerset)
Westhampnett.—3G 17
West Handley.—5D 88
West Hanney.—3F 41
West Hanningfield.—1B 32
West Hardwick.—4E 94
West Harnham.—1G 15
West Harptree.—3F 25
West Harting.—1F 17
West Harton.—3G 117
West Hatch.—1F 13
Westhay.—4E 25
Westhead.—2B 86
(Lancashire)
West Head.—2E 67
(Norfolk)
West Heath.—3D 28
(nr. Basingstoke, Hants.)
West Heath.—3G 29
(nr. Farnborough, Hants.)
West Helmsdale.—2H 167
West Hendred.—4F 41
West Heslerton.—2E 103
West Hewish.—2D 25
West Hide.—3H 49
West Hill.—5C 38
(Avon)

West Hill.—4D 12
(Devon)
Westhill.—3F 155
(Grampian)
Westhill.—4B 160
(Highland)
West Hill.—3G 103
(Humberside)
West Hill.—2E 19
(West Sussex)
West Hoathly.—2E 19
West Holme.—5D 15
Westhope.—2G 49
(Hereford & Worcester)
Westhope.—2B 60
(Shropshire)
West Horndon.—2H 31
Westhorp.—2C 52
Westhorpe.—4B 78
(Lincolnshire)
Westhorpe.—1C 56
(Suffolk)
West Horrington.—4F 25
West Horsley.—5B 30
West Horton.—1E 123
West Hougham.—1G 21
Westhoughton.—2D 86
Westhouse.—2F 99
West Howe.—4F 15
West Humble.—5C 30
West Huntspill.—4D 24
West Hyde.—1B 30
West Hythe.—2F 21
West Ilsley.—4F 41
West Inchmichael.—1E 139
West Itchenor.—3F 17
West Keal.—1C 78
West Kennett.—2G 27
West Kilbride.—5D 128
(Strathclyde)
West Kilbride.—7C 172
(Western Isles)
West Kingsdown.—4G 31
West Kington.—5G 39
West Kirby.—2E 84
West Knapton.—2D 103
West Knighton.—5C 14
West Knoyle.—5D 26
West Kyloe.—5G 133
Westlake.—4C 8
West Lambrook.—2H 13
West Langdon.—1H 21
West Langwell.—3D 166
West Lavington.—1G 17
(West Sussex)
West Lavington.—3F 27
(Wiltshire)
West Layton.—4E 107
West Leake.—3C 76
West Learmouth.—1C 122
Westleigh.—3A 22
(nr. Bideford, Devon)
Westleigh.—2D 12
(nr. Tiverton, Devon)
West Leigh.—3G 11
(nr. Winkleigh, Devon)
Westleigh.—2D 86
(Manchester)
West Leith.—1C 42
Westleton.—1G 57
West Lexham.—4A 80
Westley.—5F 73
(Shropshire)
Westley.—1A 56
(Suffolk)
Westley Waterless.—5F 55
West Lilling.—3B 102
Westlington.—1A 42
West Linton.—4E 131
(Borders)
Westlinton.—3E 115
(Cumbria)
West Littleton.—5F 39
West Looe.—4G 7
West Lulworth.—5D 14
West Lutton.—3E 103

West Lydford.—5F 25
West Lynn.—1F 67
West Mains.—2B 138
West Malling.—5A 32
West Malvern.—3B 50
Westmancote.—4D 50
West Marden.—2F 17
West Markham.—5H 89
West Marsh.—5E 97
(Humberside)
Westmarsh.—4G 33
(Kent)
West Marton.—4B 100
West Meon.—1E 17
West Mersea.—1G 45
Westmeston.—4E 19
West Mill.—4A 54
(Hitchin, Herts.)
West Milton.—4A 14
Westminster.—3D 31
West Molesey.—4C 30
West Monkton.—1F 13
Westmoor End.—1C 104
West Moors.—3F 15
West Morden.—4E 15
West Muir.—2E 147
(nr. Brechin, Tayside)
Westmuir.—3C 146
(nr. Kirriemuir, Tayside)
West Murkle.—2D 170
West Ness.—2B 102
Westnewton.—5C 114
(Cumbria)
West Newton.—2D 97
(Humberside)
West Newton.—5F 79
(Norfolk)
Westnewton.—1D 122
(Northumberland)
West Norwood.—3E 31
Westoe.—3G 117
West Ogwell.—2E 9
Weston.—2C 26
(Avon)
Weston.—5E 41
(Berkshire)
Weston.—2B 74
(nr. Crewe, Ches.)
Weston.—5B 87
(Macclesfield, Ches.)
Weston.—4C 86
(Runcorn, Ches.)
Weston.—5E 13
(Devon)
Weston.—5A 14
(Dorset)
Weston.—1F 17
(Hampshire)
Weston.—2F 49
(Hereford & Worcester)
Weston.—4B 54
(Hertfordshire)
Weston.—5B 78
(Lincolnshire)
Weston.—3C 52
(Northamptonshire)
Weston.—1B 94
(North Yorkshire)
Weston.—1E 77
(Nottinghamshire)
Weston.—1C 60
(nr. Bridgnorth, Shrops.)
Weston.—3A 60
(nr. Knighton, Shrops.)
Weston.—3H 73
(nr. Wem, Shrops.)
Weston.—5D 75
(Staffordshire)
Weston.—5D 130
(Strathclyde)
Weston Bampfylde.—1B 14
Weston Beggard.—3H 49
Westonbirt.—4G 39
Weston by Welland.—3E 65

Weston Colville.—2F 55
Westoncommon.—3G 73
Weston Coyney.—3D 74
Weston Ditch.—5F 67
Weston Favell.—1E 53
Weston Green.—2F 55
(Cambridgeshire)
Weston Green.—4D 80
(Norfolk)
Weston Heath.—1B 62
Weston Hills.—1B 66
Weston in Arden.—4A 64
Westoning.—2F 53
Weston-in-Gordano.—5C 38
Weston Jones.—5B 74
Weston Longville.—4D 80
Weston Lullingfields.—3G 73
Weston-on-Avon.—2F 51
Weston-on-the-Green.—1G 41
Weston-on-Trent.—5B 76
Weston Patrick.—4E 29
Weston Rhyn.—2E 73
Weston Subedge.—3F 51
Weston-super-Mare.—2D 24
Weston Town.—4C 26
Weston Turville.—1B 42
Weston under Lizard.—1C 62
Weston under Penyard.—5A 50
Weston under Wetherley.
—1A 52
Weston Underwood.—2F 53
(Buckinghamshire)
Weston Underwood.—3G 75
(Derbyshire)
Westonzoyland.—5D 24
West Orchard.—2E 14
West Overton.—2G 27
Westow.—3C 102
West Park.—1B 108
West Parley.—4F 15
West Peckham.—5H 31
West Pelton.—4F 117
West Pennard.—5F 25
West Pentire.—3B 6
West Perry.—1A 54
West Pitcorthie.—3H 139
West Plean.—1B 130
West Poringland.—2E 69
West Porlock.—1E 23
Westport.—2G 13
West Putford.—2D 10
West Quantoxhead.—4B 24
Westra.—5H 37
West Rainton.—5G 117
West Rasen.—4C 90
West Ravendale.—3E 91
Westray Airport.—2D 174
West Raynham.—3A 80
Westrigg.—3C 130
West Rounton.—4B 108
West Row.—5F 67
West Rudham.—3A 80
West Runton.—1D 81
Westruther.—4C 132
Westry.—3C 66
West Saltoun.—3A 132
West Sandford.—3B 12
West Sandwick.—3F 175
West Scrafton.—1D 100
Westside.—4C 174
West Sleekburn.—1F 117
West Somerton.—4G 81
West Stafford.—5C 14
West Stockwith.—3H 89
West Stoke.—3G 17
West Stonesdale.—4B 106
West Stoughton.—4E 25
West Stour.—1C 14
West Stourmouth.—4G 33
West Stow.—5A 68
West Stowell.—2G 27
West Strathan.—2F 169
West Stratton.—4D 28
West Street.—5D 32
West Tanfield.—2F 101
West Taphouse.—3F 7

West Tarbert.—3G 127
West Thirston.—5F 123
West Thorney.—3F 17
West Thurrock.—3G 31
West Tilbury.—3A 32
West Tisted.—1E 17
West Tofts.—3A 68
West Torrington.—4D 90
West Town.—2E 25
(nr. Backwell, Avon)
West Town.—2F 25
(nr. Blagdon, Avon)
West Town.—4F 17
(Hampshire)
West Tytherley.—1A 16
West Tytherton.—5H 39
West View.—1B 108
Westville.—3C 76
West Walton.—1D 66
West Walton Highway.—1D!
Westward.—5D 114
Westward Ho.—3A 22
Westwell.—1D 20
(Kent)
Westwell.—2D 40
(Oxfordshire)
Westwell Leacon.—1D 20
West Wellow.—2A 16
West Wemyss.—4F 76
West Wick.—2D 24
(Avon)
Westwick.—1D 54
(Cambridgeshire)
Westwick.—3D 106
(Durham)
Westwick.—3E 81
(Norfolk)
West Wickham.—3F 55
(Cambridgeshire)
West Wickham.—4E 31
(London)
West Williamston.—4D 34
West Willoughby.—3G 77
West Winch.—1F 67
West Winterslow.—5H 27
West Wittering.—4F 17
West Witton.—1D 100
Westwood.—3A 66
(Cambridgeshire)
Westwood.—4D 12
(Devon)
Westwood.—4H 33
(Kent)
Westwood.—4H 129
(Strathclyde)
Westwood.—3D 26
(Wiltshire)
West Woodburn.—1B 116
West Woodhay.—2B 28
West Woodlands.—4C 26
West Woodside.—5E 114
(Cumbria)
Westwoodside.—3H 89
(Humberside)
West Worldham.—5F 29
West Worlington.—2A 12
West Worthing.—5C 18
West Wratting.—2F 55
West Wycombe.—3B 42
West Wylam.—3E 117
West Yatton.—5G 39
West Yell.—3F 175
West Youlstone.—2C 10
Wetheral.—4F 115
Wetherby.—1E 94
Wetherden.—1C 56
Wetheringsett.—1D 56
Wethersfield.—4G 55
Wethersta.—5E 175
Wetherup Street.—1D 56
Wetley Rocks.—3D 74
Wettenhall.—1A 74
Wetton.—2F 75
Wetwang.—4E 103
Wetwood.—4B 74
Wexcombe.—3A 28

ham Street.—2A 30
hourne.—1D 80
orfolk)
bourne.—4G 29
urrey)
bread.—4E 69
bridge.—4B 30
croft.—4G 13
dale.—2D 170
hill.—4B 28
mouth.—5B 14
thel.—2E 49
ddon.—4F 53
uckinghamshire)
ddon.—3C 54
mbridgeshire)
ddon.—1G 39
oucestershire)
ddon.—1G 15
iltshire)
le.—2G 105
lecombe.—4D 34
ley.—5F 89
ley Bridge.—4H 87
ley Thorns.—5F 89
lley.—2E 93
say Airport.—5H 175
ton.—1E 117
m.—3G 99
ness.—7B 174
plode.—5C 78
plode Drove.—1C 66
plode St Catherine.—5C 78
rfe.—3G 99
rles.—2B 92
rley End.—3G 53
rncliffe Side.—3C 88
rram-le-Street.—3D 102
ton.—1A 74
mbria)
ton.—2H 49
ereford & Worcester)
shton.—4E 107
sset.—1E 99
ttcote.—3H 51
teley.—3G 63
tfield.—3C 56
tley.—3G 13
Chard, Som.)
tley.—4C 26
tley.—1H 99
Frome, Som.)
tmore.—5A 62
tlington.—4B 20
ttmore.—5A 62
tton.—4E 77
uphill.—5B 112
w.—4C 106
atacre.—3G 69
atcroft.—2H 75
athampstead.—1E 43
athill.—4A 62
atley.—4B 12
avon)
atley.—4F 29
ampshire)
atley.—2G 41
rfordshire)
atley.—3A 94
t Yorkshire)
atley Hill.—1G 107
atley Lane.—2F 93
atley Park.—7F 89
aton Aston.—1C 62
atstone Park.—2C 42
ddon Cross.—2F 23
aelerstreet.—1A 18
elock.—2B 74
elock Heath.—2B 74
ddon.—3D 92
drake.—5B 102
ford.—3C 40
pley Hill.—2C 42
po.—1E 104
ston.—3E 84
nby.—3B 102
ostead.—2A 56

Wherstead.—3D 56
Wherwell.—4B 28
Wheston.—5B 88
Whetsted.—1A 20
Whetstone.—3C 64
(Leicestershire)
Whetstone.—1D 30
(London)
Whicham.—1A 98
Whichford.—4H 51
Whickham.—3F 117
Whiddon.—3E 11
Whiddon Down.—4G 11
Whigstreet.—4D 147
Whilton.—1D 52
Whimble.—3D 10
Whimple.—4D 12
Whimpwell Green.—3F 81
Whinburgh.—2C 68
Whin Lane End.—1A 92
Whinnyfold.—5H 163
Whinny Hill.—3G 107
Whippingham.—4D 16
Whipsnade.—1D 42
Whipton.—4C 12
Whirlow.—4D 88
Whisby.—1G 77
Whissendine.—1F 65
Whissonsett.—3B 80
Whisterfield.—5F 87
Whistley Green.—5A 42
Whiston.—3B 88
(Merseyside)
Whiston.—1F 53
(Northamptonshire)
Whiston.—3E 89
(South Yorkshire)
Whiston.—3E 75
(nr. Cheadle, Staffs.)
Whiston.—1C 62
(nr. Penkridge, Staffs.)
Whiston Cross.—2B 62
Whiston Eaves.—3E 75
Whitacre Heath.—3G 63
Whitbeck.—1A 98
Whitbourne.—5B 60
Whitburn.—3C 130
(Lothian)
Whitburn.—3H 117
(Tyne & Wear)
Whitburn Colliery.—3H 117
Whitby.—5F 85
(Cheshire)
Whitby.—3F 109
(North Yorkshire)
Whitbyheath.—3F 85
Whitchester.—4D 132
Whitchurch.—2B 26
(Avon)
Whitchurch.—5F 43
(Buckinghamshire)
Whitchurch.—2A 8
(Devon)
Whitchurch.—2A 34
(Dyfed)
Whitchurch.—4C 28
(Hampshire)
Whitchurch.—1D 38
(Hereford & Worcester)
Whitchurch.—5H 41
(Oxfordshire)
Whitchurch.—1H 73
(Shropshire)
Whitchurch.—5H 37
(South Glamorgan)
Whitchurch Canonicorum.
—4G 13
Whitchurch Hill.—5H 41
Whitcombe.—5C 14
Whitcot.—1A 60
Whitcott Keysett.—2H 59
Whiteash Green.—4G 55
Whitebog.—2H 160
Whitebridge.—2G 151
Whitebrook.—2D 38
Whitecairns.—2G 155

White Chapel.—1C 92
Whitechurch.—4A 46
White Colne.—5A 56
White Coppice.—1D 86
White Corries.—3G 143
Whitecraig.—2G 131
Whitecroft.—2E 39
Whitecross.—2C 130
(Central)
White Cross.—4D 5
(Cornwall)
White End.—4B 50
Whiteface.—5E 166
Whitefaulds.—4B 118
Whitefield.—4E 15
(Dorset)
Whitefield.—2F 87
(Manchester)
Whitefield.—3G 23
(Somerset)
Whiteford.—1E 154
Whitegate.—1A 74
Whitehall.—2E 12
(Devon)
Whitehall.—3F 29
(Hampshire)
Whitehall.—5F 174
(Orkney)
Whitehall.—3C 18
(West Sussex)
Whitehaven.—3A 104
Whitehill.—5F 29
(Hampshire)
Whitehill.—4D 128
(Strathclyde)
Whitehills.—2D 162
(Grampian)
Whitehills.—3D 146
(Tayside)
White Horse Common.—3F 81
Whitehough.—4H 87
Whitehouse.—2D 36
(Grampian)
Whitehouse.—3G 127
(Strathclyde)
Whiteinch.—3G 129
Whitekirk.—1B 132
White Kirley.—1D 106
White Lackington.—4C 14
(Dorset)
Whitelackington.—2G 13
(Somerset)
White Ladies Aston.—2D 50
White Lee.—3C 94
Whiteley Bank.—5D 16
Whiteley Village.—4B 30
Whitemans Green.—3E 19
White Mill.—5D 46
Whitemire.—3D 161
Whitemoor.—4D 6
Whitenap.—1B 16
Whiteness.—7E 175
White Notley.—1D 44
Whiteoak Green.—1E 41
Whiteparish.—1H 15
White Pit.—5F 91
Whiterashes.—1F 155
White Rocks.—5G 49
White Roding.—1B 44
Whiterow.—3E 161
(Grampian)
Whiterow.—4F 171
(Highland)
Whiteshill.—2G 39
Whiteside.—3C 130
(Lothian)
Whiteside.—3A 116
(Northumberland)
Whitesmith.—4G 19
Whitestaunton.—2F 13
Whitestone.—4B 12
(Devon)
Whitestone.—4D 154
(Grampian)
White Stone.—3H 49
(Hereford & Worcester)

Whitestones.—3F 163
Whitestreet Green.—4B 56
Whitewall Corner.—3C 102
White Waltham.—5B 42
Whiteway.—1H 39
Whitewell.—1D 92
Whiteworks.—2C 8
Whitewreath.—3G 161
Whitfield.—3E 39
(Avon)
Whitfield.—1H 21
(Kent)
Whitfield.—4D 52
(Northamptonshire)
Whitfield.—4A 116
(Northumberland)
Whitfield.—5D 146
(Tayside)
Whitford.—3D 84
(Clwyd)
Whitford.—4F 13
(Devon)
Whitgift.—3A 96
Whitgreave.—5C 74
Whithorn.—5D 112
Whiting Bay.—3E 125
Whitington.—3G 67
Whitkirk.—2D 94
Whitland.—3F 35
Whitleigh.—3A 8
Whitletts.—2C 118
Whitley.—5A 42
(Berkshire)
Whitley.—3F 95
(North Yorkshire)
Whitley.—2D 27
(Wiltshire)
Whitley Bay.—2G 117
Whitley Bridge.—3F 95
Whitley Chapel.—4C 116
Whitley Heath.—5C 74
Whitley Lower.—4C 94
Whitley Thorpe.—3F 95
Whitlocks End.—5F 63
Whitminster.—2F 39
Whitmore.—3F 15
(Dorset)
Whitmore.—3C 74
(Staffordshire)
Whitnage.—2D 12
Whitnash.—1H 51
Whitney.—3E 49
Whitrigg.—4D 114
(nr. Kirkbride, Cumbria)
Whitrigg.—1D 104
(nr. Torpenhow, Cumbria)
Whitsbury.—2G 15
Whitsome.—4E 133
Whitson.—4B 38
Whitstable.—4F 33
Whitstone.—4C 10
Whittingham.—3E 123
Whittingslow.—2B 60
Whittington.—5D 88
(Derbyshire)
Whittington.—5E 51
(Gloucestershire)
Whittington.—2C 50
(Hereford & Worcester)
Whittington.—2F 99
(Lancashire)
Whittington.—2F 73
(Shropshire)
Whittington.—4C 62
(nr. Kinver, Staffs.)
Whittington.—2F 63
(nr. Lichfield, Staffs.)
Whittington.—3G 63
(Warwickshire)
Whittington Barracks.—2F 63
Whittlebury.—3D 52
Whittleford.—3H 63
Whittle-le-Woods.—3C 92
Whittlesey.—3B 66
Whittlesford.—3D 54
Whittlestone Head.—1E 87

Whitton.—2B 122
(Borders)
Whitton.—2G 107
(Cleveland)
Whitton.—3B 96
(Humberside)
Whitton.—4E 123
(Northumberland)
Whitton.—4H 59
(Powys)
Whitton.—3C 60
(Shropshire)
Whitton.—3D 56
(Suffolk)
Whittonditch.—5D 40
Whittonstall.—4D 116
Whitway.—3C 28
Whitwell.—5F 89
(Derbyshire)
Whitwell.—5A 54
(Hertfordshire)
Whitwell.—5D 16
(Isle of Wight)
Whitwell.—2G 65
(Leicestershire)
Whitwell.—5F 107
(North Yorkshire)
Whitwell-on-the-Hill.—3C 102
Whitwick.—1B 64
Whitwood.—3E 94
Whitworth.—1F 87
Whixall.—2H 73
Whixley.—4H 101
Whoberley.—5B 60
Whorlton.—3E 107
(Durham)
Whorlton.—4B 108
(North Yorkshire)
Whygate.—2A 116
Whyle.—4C 60
Whyteleafe.—5E 31
Wibdon.—3D 38
Wibtoft.—4B 64
Wichenford.—5F 63
Wichling.—5D 32
Wick.—5F 39
(Avon)
Wick.—4G 15
* (Dorset)
Wick.—3D 50
(Hereford & Worcester)
Wick.—3F 171
(Highland)
Wick.—5F 37
(Mid Glamorgan)
Wick.—4C 24
(nr. Bridgewater, Som.)
Wick.—3D 24
(nr. Burnham-on-Sea, Som.)
Wick.—1H 13
(nr. Somerton, Som.)
Wick.—5B 18
(West Sussex)
Wick.—1G 15
(Wiltshire)
Wick Airport.—3F 171
Wicken.—5E 67
(Cambridgeshire)
Wicken.—4E 53
(Northamptonshire)
Wicken Bonhunt.—4D 55
Wickenby.—4C 90
Wickersley.—3E 89
Wicker Street Green.—3B 56
Wickford.—1B 32
Wickham.—5E 41
(Berkshire)
Wickham.—2D 16
(Hampshire)
Wickham Bishops.—1E 45
Wickhambreaux.—5G 33
Wickhambrook.—2G 55
Wickhamford.—3E 51
Wickham Green.—1C 56
Wickham Heath.—2C 28
Wickham Market.—2F 57

Wickhampton.—2G 69
Wickham St Paul.—4A 56
Wickham Skeith.—1C 56
Wickham Street.—1C 56
Wick Hill.—2F 29
Wicklewood.—2C 68
Wickmere.—2D 80
Wick St Lawrence.—2D 24
Wickwar.—4F 39
Widdington.—4E 55
Widdrington.—5G 123
Widdrington Station.—5G 123
Widecombe in the Moor.—2D 8
Widegates.—4G 7
Widemouth Bay.—3C 10
Wide Open.—2F 117
Widewall.—8D 174
Widford.—2C 44
(Essex)
Widford.—1H 43
(Hertfordshire)
Widham.—4B 40
Widmer End.—3B 42
Widmerpool.—5D 76
Widnes.—4C 86
Widworthy.—4F 13
Wigan.—2C 86
Wigbeth.—3F 15
Wiggaton.—4E 12
Wiggenhall St Germans.—1E 67
Wiggenhall St MaryMagdalen.
—1E 67
Wiggenhall St Mary theVirgin.
—1E 67
Wiggenhall St Peter.—1F 67
Wiggenhall St. Germans.—1E 67
Wiggens Green.—3F 55
Wigginton.—1C 42
(Hertfordshire)
Wigginton.—4A 102
(North Yorkshire)
Wigginton.—4A 52
(Oxfordshire)
Wigginton.—2G 63
(Staffordshire)
Wigglesworth.—4B 100
Wiggonby.—4D 114
Wiggonholt.—4B 18
Wighill.—1E 95
Wighton.—2B 80
Wightwick.—2C 62
Wigley.—2B 16
Wigmore.—4B 60
(Hereford & Worcester)
Wigmore.—4C 32
(Kent)
Wigsley.—5A 90
Wigsthorpe.—4H 65
Wigston.—3D 64
Wigtoft.—4B 78
Wigtown.—4B 112
Wigtwizzle.—3C 88
Wike.—1D 94
Wilbarston.—4F 65
Wilberfoss.—4C 102
Wilburton.—5D 67
Wilby.—4C 68
(Norfolk)
Wilby.—1F 53
(Northamptonshire)
Wilby.—5E 69
(Suffolk)
Wilcot.—2G 27
Wilcott.—4F 73
Wildboarclough.—1D 75
Wilden.—2H 53
(Bedfordshire)
Wilden.—5C 62
(Hereford & Worcester)
Wildern.—2C 16
Wilderspool.—4D 86
Wilde Street.—5E 67
Wildhearn.—3B 28
Wildmoor.—5D 62
Wildsworth.—3A 90

G.B. Handy 251

Wildwood.—5D 74
Wilford.—4C 76
Wilkesley.—3A 74
Wilkhaven.—5G 167
Wilkieston.—3E 131
Wilksby.—1B 78
Willand.—2D 12
Willaston.—2A 74
(nr. Crewe, Ches.)
Willaston.—3F 85
(nr. Neston, Ches.)
Willaston.—4C 110
(Isle of Man)
Willen.—1F 53
Willenhall.—5A 64
(Coventry, W Midlands)
Willenhall.—3D 62
(nr. Wolverhampton,
W Midlands)
Willerby.—2C 96
(Humberside)
Willerby.—2F 103
(North Yorkshire)
Willersey.—4F 51
Willersley.—3F 49
Willesborough.—1E 20
Willesborough Lees.—1E 21
Willesden.—2D 30
Willesley.—4G 39
Willet.—5B 24
Willey.—3A 62
(Shropshire)
Willey.—4B 64
(Warwickshire)
Willey Down.—5A 30
Williamscot.—3B 52
Willian.—4B 54
Willingale.—2B 44
Willingdon.—5G 19
Willingham.—5D 66
Willingham by Stow.—4A 90
Willingham Green.—2F 55
Willington.—3A 54
(Bedfordshire)
Willington.—5G 75
(Derbyshire)
Willington.—1E 107
(Durham)
Willington.—3G 117
(Tyne & Wear)
Willington.—4G 51
(Warwickshire)
Willington Corner.—4H 85
Willisham Tye.—2C 56
Willitoft.—2H 95
Williton.—1G 23
Willoughbridge.—3B 74
Willoughby.—5G 91
(Lincolnshire)
Willoughby.—1C 52
(Warwickshire)
Willoughby on the Wolds.
—5D 76
Willoughby Waterleys.—3C 64
Willoughton.—3B 90
Willow Green.—2B 50
Willows Green.—1D 44
Willsbridge.—5E 39
Willslock.—4E 75
Willsworthy.—1B 8
Wilmcote.—2F 51
Wilmington.—2B 26
(Avon)
Wilmington.—4F 13
(Devon)
Wilmington.—5G 19
(East Sussex)
Wilmington.—3G 31
(Kent)
Wilmslow.—4F 87
Wilnecote.—2G 63
Wilney Green.—4C 68
Wilpshire.—2D 93
Wilsden.—2A 94
Wilsford.—3H 77
(Lincolnshire)

Wilsford.—4G 27
(nr. Amesbury, Wilts.)
Wilsford.—3F 27
(nr. Devizes, Wilts.)
Wilsill.—3E 101
Wilsley Green.—2B 20
Wilson.—5H 49
(Hereford & Worcester)
Wilson.—5B 76
(Leicestershire)
Wilsontown.—4C 130
Wilstead.—3H 53
Wilsthorpe.—3G 103
(Humberside)
Wilsthorpe.—1H 65
(Lincolnshire)
Wilstone.—1C 42
Wilton.—3G 121
(Borders)
Wilton.—3C 108
(Cleveland)
Wilton.—3B 104
(Cumbria)
Wilton.—1D 102
(North Yorkshire)
Wilton.—2A 28
(nr. Marlborough, Wilts.)
Wilton.—5F 27
(nr. Salisbury, Wilts.)
Wimbish.—4E 55
Wimbish Green.—4F 55
Wimblebury.—1E 63
Wimbledon.—3D 30
Wimblington.—3D 66
Wimborne Minster.—4F 15
Wimborne St Giles.—2F 15
Wimbotsham.—2F 67
Wimpstone.—3G 51
Wincanton.—1C 14
Winceby.—1C 78
Wincham.—5D 87
Winchburgh.—2D 131
Winchcombe.—5E 51
Winchelsea.—4D 20
Winchelsea Beach.—4D 20
Winchester.—1C 16
Winchet Hill.—1B 20
Winchfield.—3F 29
Winchmore Hill.—1A 30
(Buckinghamshire)
Winchmore Hill.—1E 31
(London)
Wincle.—1D 74
Windermere.—5F 105
Winderton.—3H 51
Windhill.—4H 159
Windle Hill.—3F 85
Windlesham.—4A 30
Windley.—3H 75
Windmill.—5B 88
Windmill Hill.—4H 19
(East Sussex)
Windmill Hill.—2G 13
(Somerset)
Windrush.—1C 40
Windsor.—3A 30
Windsor Green.—2A 56
Windyedge.—4F 155
Windygates.—3F 139
Windyharbour.—5F 87
Windyknowe.—3C 130
Wineham.—3D 18
Winestead.—3F 97
Winfarthing.—4D 68
Winford.—2F 25
(Avon)
Winford.—5D 16
(Isle of Wight)
Winforton.—3E 49
Winfrith Newburgh.—5D 14
Wing.—5F 53
(Buckinghamshire)
Wing.—2F 65
(Leicestershire)
Wingate.—1G 107

Wingates.—2D 86
(Manchester)
Wingates.—5F 123
(Northumberland)
Wingerworth.—1A 76
Wingfield.—5H 53
(Bedfordshire)
Wingfield.—5E 69
(Suffolk)
Wingfield.—3D 26
(Wiltshire)
Wingfield Park.—2A 76
Wingham.—5G 33
Wingmore.—1F 21
Wingrave.—1B 42
Winkburn.—2E 76
Winkfield.—3A 30
Winkfield Row.—5B 42
Winkhill.—2E 75
Winkleburn.—3E 28
Winkleigh.—3G 11
Winksley.—2F 101
Winkton.—4G 15
Winlaton.—3E 117
Winlaton Mill.—3E 117
Winless.—3F 171
Winmarleigh.—1B 92
Winnall.—4G 49
Winnersh.—5A 42
Winnington.—5D 86
(Cheshire)
Winnington.—4B 74
(Staffordshire)
Winnothdale.—3E 75
Winscales.—2B 104
Winscombe.—3E 25
Winsford.—1A 74
(Cheshire)
Winsford.—2F 23
(Somerset)
Winsham.—2B 22
(Devon)
Winsham.—3G 13
(Somerset)
Winshill.—5G 75
Winsh-wen.—3C 36
Winskill.—1G 105
Winslade.—4E 29
Winsley.—2C 26
Winslow.—5E 53
Winson.—2B 40
Winson Green.—4E 63
Winsor.—2B 16
Winster.—5F 105
(Cumbria)
Winster.—1G 75
(Derbyshire)
Winston.—3E 107
(Durham)
Winston.—1D 57
(Suffolk)
Winstone.—2A 40
Winswell.—2E 11
Winterborne Clenston.—3D 14
Winterborne Herringston.
—5B 14
Winterborne Houghton.—3D 14
Winterborne Kingston.—4D 14
Winterborne Monkton.—5B 14
Winterborne Stickland.—3D 14
Winterborne Whitchurch.
—5B 14
Winterborne Zelston.—4D 15
Winterbourne.—4E 39
(Avon)
Winterbourne.—5F 41
(Berkshire)
Winterbourne Abbas.—4B 14
Winterbourne Bassett.—5C 40
Winterbourne Dauntsey.—5G 27
Winterbourne Earls.—5G 27
Winterbourne Gunner.—5G 27
Winterbourne Monkton.—5C 40
Winterbourne Steepleton.
—5B 14
Winterbourne Stoke.—4F 27

Winterbrook.—4H 41
Winterburn.—4C 100
Winter Gardens.—2B 32
Winteringham.—3B 96
Winterley.—2B 74
Wintersett.—4D 94
Winterslow.—5H 27
Winterton.—4B 96
Winterton-on-Sea.—4G 81
Winthorpe.—1E 79
(Lincolnshire)
Winthorpe.—2F 77
(Nottinghamshire)
Winton.—3A 106
(Cumbria)
Winton.—4F 15
(Dorset)
Winton.—5G 19
(East Sussex)
Wintringham.—2D 103
Winwick.—4A 66
(Cambridgeshire)
Winwick.—3D 86
(Cheshire)
Winwick.—5D 64
(Northamptonshire)
Wirksworth.—2G 75
Wirswall.—1H 73
Wisbech.—2D 66
Wisbech St Mary.—2D 66
Wisborough Green.—3B 18
Wiseton.—4H 89
Wishaw.—4A 130
(Strathclyde)
Wishaw.—3F 63
(Warwickshire)
Wisley.—5B 30
Wispington.—5E 91
Wissenden.—1D 20
Wissett.—5F 69
Wistanstow.—2B 60
Wistanswick.—5A 74
Wistaston.—2A 74
Wiston.—3D 34
(Dyfed)
Wiston.—1B 120
(Strathclyde)
Wiston.—4C 18
(West Sussex)
Wistow.—4B 66
(Cambridgeshire)
Wistow.—2F 95
(North Yorkshire)
Wiswell.—2E 93
Witcham.—4D 200
Witchampton.—3E 15
Witchford.—5E 67
Witham.—1E 44
Witham Friary.—4C 26
Witham on the Hill.—1H 65
Withcall.—4E 91
Witherenden Hill.—3H 19
Withergate.—3E 81
Witheridge.—2B 12
Witheridge Hill.—4H 41
Withern.—3H 63
Withernsea.—3F 97
Withernwick.—1D 97
Withersdale Street.—4E 69
Withersfield.—3F 55
Witherslack.—1D 98
Withiel.—3D 6
Withiel Florey.—2F 23
Withington.—1C 74
(Cheshire)
Withington.—1B 40
(Gloucestershire)
Withington.—3H 49
(Hereford & Worcester)
Withington.—3F 87
(Manchester)
Withington.—4H 73
(Shropshire)

Withington.—4E 75
(Staffordshire)
Withington Green.—5F 87
Withington Marsh.—3H 49
Withleigh.—2C 12
Withnell.—3D 92
Withnell Fold.—3D 92
Withybrook.—4B 64
Withycombe.—1G 23
Withycombe Raleigh.—5D 12
Withyham.—2F 19
Withypool.—2E 23
Witley.—2A 18
Witnesham.—2D 57
Witney.—1E 41
Wittering.—2H 65
Wittersham.—3C 20
Witton.—1C 50
(Hereford & Worcester)
Witton.—2F 69
(Norfolk)
Witton Bridge.—2F 81
Witton Gilbert.—5F 117
Witton le Wear.—1E 107
Witton Park.—1E 107
Wiveliscombe.—3G 23
Wivelrod.—5E 29
Wivelsfield.—3E 19
Wivelsfield Green.—4E 19
Wivenhoe.—5C 56
Wiveton.—1C 80
Wix.—5D 56
Wixford.—2E 51
Wixhill.—3H 73
Wixoe.—3G 55
Woburn.—4G 53
Woburn Sands.—4G 53
Woking.—5B 30
Wokingham.—2G 29
Wolborough.—2E 9
Woldingham.—5E 31
Wold Newton.—2F 103
(nr. Bridlington, Humberside)
Wold Newton.—3E 91
(nr. Grimsby, Humberside)
Wolferlow.—1A 50
Wolferton.—5F 79
Wolfhill.—5A 146
Wolf's Castle.—2C 34
Wolfsdale.—2C 34
Wolgarston.—1D 62
Wollaston.—1G 53
(Northamptonshire)
Wollaston.—4F 73
(Shropshire)
Wollaston.—4C 62
(West Midlands)
Wollaton.—3C 76
Wollerton.—4A 74
Wollescote.—4D 62
Wollpit.—1B 56
Wolseley.—5E 75
Wolsingham.—1D 106
Wolstanton.—3C 74
Wolston.—5B 64
Wolsty.—4C 114
Wolterton.—2D 80
Wolvercote.—2F 41
Wolverhampton.—3D 62
Wolverley.—5C 62
(Hereford & Worcester)
Wolverley.—2G 73
(Shropshire)
Wolverton.—3F 53
(Buckinghamshire)
Wolverton.—3D 28
(Hampshire)
Wolverton.—1G 51
(Warwickshire)
Wolverton.—5C 26
(Wiltshire)
Wolverton Common.—3D 28
Wolvesnewton.—3C 38
Wolvey.—4B 64
Wolvey Heath.—4B 64
Wolviston.—2B 108

Womaston.—4H 59
Wombleton.—1B 102
Wombourne.—3C 62
Wombwell.—2D 88
Womenswold.—5G 33
Womersley.—4F 95
Wonersh.—1B 18
Wonson.—1C 8
Wonston.—5C 28
Wooburn.—2A 30
Wooburn Green.—2A 30
Wood.—2B 34
Woodacott.—3D 11
Woodale.—2D 100
Woodall.—4E 89
Woodbank.—3F 85
Woodbastwick.—4F 81
Woodbeck.—5H 89
Woodborough.—3D 76
(Nottinghamshire)
Woodborough.—3G 27
(Wiltshire)
Woodbridge.—4E 13
(Devon)
Woodbridge.—2C 14
(Dorset)
Woodbridge.—3E 57
(Suffolk)
Wood Burcote.—3D 52
Woodbury.—5D 12
Woodbury Salterton.—5D 1?
Woodchester.—2G 39
Woodchurch.—2D 20
(Kent)
Woodchurch.—2E 85
(Merseyside)
Woodcock Heath.—5E 75
Woodcombe.—1F 23
Woodcote.—4H 41
(Oxfordshire)
Woodcote.—1B 62
(Shropshire)
Woodcote Green.—5D 62
Woodcott.—3C 28
Woodcroft.—3D 38
Woodcutts.—2E 15
Wood Dalling.—3C 80
Woodditton.—2F 55
Woodeaton.—1G 41
(Oxfordshire)
Wood Eaton.—1C 62
(Staffordshire)
Woodend.—4C 86
(Cheshire)
Woodend.—5C 104
(Cumbria)
Wood End.—5C 54
(Hertfordshire)
Woodend.—3D 52
(Northamptonshire)
Woodend.—5F 75
(Staffordshire)
Wood End.—4G 63
(nr. Bedworth, Warwicks.)
Wood End.—3G 63
(nr. Dordon, Warwicks.)
Wood End.—5F 63
(nr. Tanworth-in-Arden,
Warw?
Woodend.—3G 17
(West Sussex)
Wood Enderby.—1B 78
Woodend Green.—5C 54
Woodfalls.—1G 15
Woodfield.—5C 52
Woodfields.—2D 93
Woodford.—2C 10
(Cornwall)
Woodford.—4D 9
(nr. Dartmouth, Devon)
Woodford.—4B 8
(nr. Plymouth, Devon)
Woodford.—3E 39
(Gloucestershire)

252 G.B. Handy

ford.—1F 31
ndon)
lford.—4F 87
anchester)
lford.—5G 65
rthamptonshire)
lford Green.—1F 31
lford Halse.—2C 52
gate.—1D 50
eford & Worcester)
gate.—4C 80
rfolk)
dgate.—4D 63
st Midlands)
dgate.—3H 17
st Sussex)
lgreen.—2G 15
mpshire)
l Green.—1E 31
ndon)
l Hall.—2D 96
mberside)
thall.—1B 78
ncolnshire)
thall.—5C 106
rth Yorkshire)
hall.—2E 129
athclyde)
tham.—4B 30
tham Ferrers.—1B 32
tham Mortimer.—2E 44
tham Walter.—2E 44
shaven.—1G 139
l Hayes.—2D 62
head.—2F 163
Fraserburgh, Grampian)
head.—5E 163
Fyvie, Grampian)
head.—3E 75
affordshire)
hill.—5C 38
on)
hill.—4B 62
ropshire)
thorn.—1F 117
thouse.—1C 64
cestershire)
house.—4E 88
uth Yorkshire)
house.—2C 94
eds, W Yorks.)
house.—3A 30
rmanton, N Yorks.)
house Eaves.—1C 64
houses.—3G 85
eshire)
houses.—2G 87
Failsworth, Manchester)
houses.—3E 87
Sale, Manchester)
houses.—1F 63
affordshire)
huish.—4F 9
hurst.—5C 66
dingdean.—5E 19
dland.—3D 9
von)
dland.—2D 106
rham)
dland Head.—4A 12
dlands.—3F 15
rset)
dlands.—4E 155
ampian)
dlands.—2B 16
mpshire)
dlands.—4G 31
nt)
dlands.—4G 101
rth Yorkshire)
dlands.—2F 89
uth Yorkshire)
dlands St. Mary.—5E 41
dlane.—5A 74
ropshire)

Woodlane.—5F 75
(Staffordshire)
Woodleigh.—5D 8
Woodlesford.—3D 94
Woodley.—5A 42
(Berkshire)
Woodley.—3G 87
(Manchester)
Woodmancote.—5D 50
(nr. Cheltenham, Glos.)
Woodmancote.—2B 40
(nr. Cirencester, Glos.)
Woodmancote.—3F 39
(Dursley, Glos.)
Woodmancote.—3D 50
(Hereford & Worcester)
Woodmancote.—3F 17
(nr. Chichester, W Suss.)
Woodmancote.—4D 18
(nr. Henfield, W Suss.)
Woodmancott.—4D 28
Woodmansey.—2C 96
Woodmansgreen.—1G 17
Woodmansterne.—5D 31
Woodmancton.—5D 12
Woodmill.—5F 75
Woodminton.—1F 15
Woodnesborough.—5H 33
Woodnewton.—3H 65
Woodnook.—4G 77
Wood Norton.—3C 80
Woodplumpton.—2C 92
Woodrising.—2B 68
Woodrow.—5D 114
(Cumbria)
Woodrow.—3C 14
(Dorset)
Wood Row.—3D 94
(West Yorkshire)
Woods Eaves.—3E 49
(Hereford & Worcester)
Woodseaves.—4A 74
(Shropshire)
Woodseaves.—5B 74
(Staffordshire)
Woodsend.—5D 40
Woodsetts.—4F 89
Woodsford.—4C 14
Wood's Green.—2H 19
(Berkshire)
Woodside.—1B 104
(Cumbria)
Woodside.—3A 76
(Derbyshire)
Woodside.—2B 114
(Dumfries & Galloway)
Woodside.—2E 107
(Durham)
Woodside.—3G 139
(Fife)
Woodside.—3G 155
(Grampian)
Woodside.—2F 43
(Hertfordshire)
Woodside.—5B 146
(Tayside)
Wood Stanway.—4E 51
Woodstock.—1F 41
Woodstock Slop.—2D 34
Woodston.—3A 66
Wood Street.—5A 30
Woodthorpe.—5E 89
(Derbyshire)
Woodthorpe.—1C 64
(Leicestershire)
Woodthorpe.—4G 91
(Lincolnshire)
Woodthorpe.—5A 102
(North Yorkshire)
Woodton.—3E 69
Woodtown.—3A 22
(nr. Bideford, Devon)
Woodtown.—3A 22
(nr. Littleham, Devon)
Woodvale.—1A 86

Woodville.—1H 63
Wood Walton.—4B 66
Woodyates.—2F 15
Woody Bay.—1C 22
Woofferton.—4C 60
Wookey.—4F 25
Wookey Hole.—4F 25
Wool.—5D 14
Woolacombe.—1A 22
Woolage Green.—1G 21
Woolaston.—3D 39
Woolavington.—4D 24
Woolbeding.—1G 17
Woolcotts.—2F 23
Wooldale.—2B 88
Wooler.—2D 123
Woolfardisworthy.—1D 10
(nr. Bideford, Devon)
Woolfardisworthy.—3B 12
(nr. Crediton, Devon)
Woolfords.—4D 130
Woolgarston.—5E 15
Woolhampton.—2D 28
Woolhope.—4A 50
Woolland.—3C 14
Woollard.—2B 26
(Avon)
Woolley.—2C 26
(Avon)
Woolley.—5A 66
(Cambridgeshire)
Woolley.—2C 10
(Cornwall)
Woolley.—1A 76
(Derbyshire)
Woolley.—4D 94
(West Yorkshire)
Woolley Green.—2D 26
Woolmere Green.—1D 50
Woolmer Green.—1F 43
Woolminstone.—3H 13
Woolridge.—5C 50
Woolscott.—3B 52
Woolsington.—3E 117
Woolstaston.—5H 60
Woolsthorpe.—5G 77
(nr. Colsterworth, Lincs.)
Woolsthorpe.—4F 77
(nr. Grantham, Lincs.)
Woolston.—4D 86
(Cheshire)
Woolston.—5D 8
(Devon)
Woolston.—2C 16
(Hampshire)
Woolston.—2B 60
(nr. Church Stretton, Shrops.)
Woolston.—3F 73
(nr. Oswestry, Shrops.)
Woolston.—1B 14
(Somerset)
Woolstone.—4D 50
(Gloucestershire)
Woolstone.—4D 40
(Oxfordshire)
Woolston Green.—3D 9
Woolton.—4B 86
Woolton Hill.—2C 28
Woolverstone.—4D 57
Woolverton.—3C 26
Woolwich.—3F 31
Woonton.—2F 49
(nr. Kington, Here & Worcs.)
Woonton.—4C 60
(nr. Leominster, Here & Worcs.)
Wooperton.—2E 123
Woore.—3B 74
Wootton.—4B 62
(Bedfordshire)
Wootton.—3H 53
(Bedfordshire)
Wootton.—4H 15
(Hampshire)
Wootton.—4C 96
(Humberside)
Wootton.—4D 16
(Isle of Wight)

Wootton.—1G 21
(Kent)
Wootton.—2E 53
(Northamptonshire)
Wootton.—2F 41
(nr. Abingdon, Oxon)
Wootton.—1F 41
(nr. Woodstock, Oxon)
Wootton.—3B 60
(nr. Ludlow, Shrops.)
Wootton.—3F 73
(nr. Oswestry, Shrops.)
Wootton.—5C 74
(nr. Eccleshall, Staffs.)
Wootton.—3F 75
(nr. Ellastone, Staffs.)
Wootton Bassett.—4B 40
Wootton Bridge.—4D 16
Wootton Common.—4D 16
Wootton Courtenay.—1F 23
Wootton Fitzpaine.—4G 13
Wootton Rivers.—2G 27
Woottons.—4E 75
Wootton St Lawrence.—3D 28
Wootton Wawen.—1F 51
Worcester.—2C 50
Worcester Park.—4D 30
Wordsley.—4C 62
Worfield.—3B 62
Workhouse Green.—4B 56
Workington.—2A 104
Worksop.—5F 89
Worlaby.—4C 96
World's End.—5F 41
(Berkshire)
Worlds End.—2E 17
(Hampshire)
Worldsend.—1B 60
(Shropshire)
Worlds End.—4F 63
(West Midlands)
World's End.—4E 19
(West Sussex)
Worle.—2D 24
Worleston.—2A 74
Worley.—3G 39
Worlingham.—4G 69
Worlington.—5F 67
Worlingworth.—1E 57
Wormbridge.—4G 49
Wormegay.—1F 67
Wormelow Tump.—4G 49
Wormhill.—5B 88
Wormiehills.—5F 147
Wormingford.—4B 56
Worminghall.—2H 41
Wormington.—4E 51
Worminster.—4F 25
Wormit.—1F 139
Wormleighton.—2B 52
Wormley.—2G 43
(Hertfordshire)
Wormley.—2A 18
(Surrey)
Wormshill.—5C 32
Wormsley.—3G 49
Worplesdon.—5A 30
Worrall.—3D 88
Worsbrough.—2D 88
Worsley.—2E 87
Worstead.—3F 81
Worsthorne.—2F 93
Worston.—1E 93
Worth.—5H 33
(Kent)
Worth.—2D 19
(West Sussex)
Wortham.—5C 68
Worthen.—5F 73
Worthenbury.—1G 73
Worthing.—4B 80
(Norfolk)
Worthing.—5C 18
(West Sussex)
Worthington.—5B 76
Worth Matravers.—5E 15

Worting.—3E 28
Wortley.—3F 39
(Gloucestershire)
Wortley.—3F 89
(South Yorkshire)
Wortley.—2C 94
(West Yorkshire)
Worton.—5C 106
(North Yorkshire)
Worton.—3E 27
(Wiltshire)
Wortwell.—4E 69
Wotherton.—5E 73
Wothorpe.—2H 65
Wotter.—3B 8
Wotton.—1G 39
(Gloucestershire)
Wotton.—1C 18
(Surrey)
Wotton-under-Edge.—3F 39
Wotton Underwood.—1H 41
Wouldham.—4B 32
Wrabness.—4D 57
Wrafton.—2A 22
Wragby.—5D 90
(Lincolnshire)
Wragby.—4E 94
(West Yorkshire)
Wramplingham.—2D 68
Wrangbrook.—4E 95
Wrangle.—2D 78
Wrangle Lowgate.—2D 78
Wrangway.—2E 13
Wrantage.—1G 13
Wrawby.—5C 96
Wraxall.—5C 38
(Avon)
Wraxall.—3A 14
(Dorset)
Wraxall.—5B 26
(Somerset)
Wray.—3F 99
Wraysbury.—3B 30
Wrayton.—2F 99
Wrea Green.—2A 92
Wreay.—5F 115
(nr. Carlisle, Cumbria)
Wreay.—2F 105
(nr. Penrith, Cumbria)
Wrecclesham.—4G 29
Wrecsam.—5F 85
Wrekenton.—4F 117
Wrelton.—1C 102
Wrenbury.—1H 73
Wreningham.—3D 68
Wrentham.—4G 69
Wrenthorpe.—3D 94
Wrentnall.—5G 73
Wressle.—2H 95
(nr. Goole, Humberside)
Wressle.—5B 96
(nr. Scunthorpe, Humberside)
Wrestlingworth.—3B 54
Wretham.—3B 68
Wretton.—3F 67
Wrexham.—5F 85
Wrexham Industrial Est.—1F 73
Wrickton.—4A 62
Wrightington Bar.—1C 86
Wright's Green.—1B 44
Wrinehill.—3B 74
Wrington.—2E 25
Writtle.—2C 44
Wrockwardine.—1A 62
Wroot.—2H 89
Wrotham.—5H 31
Wrotham Heath.—5H 31
Wroughton.—4C 40
Wroxall.—5D 16
(Isle of Wight)
Wroxall.—5C 63
(Warwickshire)
Wroxeter.—5H 73
Wroxham.—4E 81
Wroxton.—3B 52

Wyaston.—3F 75
Wyatt's Green.—1G 31
Wyberton.—3C 78
Wyboston.—2A 54
Wybunbury.—3A 74
Wychbold.—1D 50
Wych Cross.—2F 19
Wychnor.—1F 63
Wychnor Bridges.—1F 63
Wyck.—5F 29
Wyck Hill.—5F 51
Wyck Rissington.—5F 51
Wycliffe.—3E 107
Wycombe Marsh.—3B 42
Wyddial.—4C 54
Wye.—1E 21
Wyesham.—1D 38
Wyfold Grange.—4H 41
Wyfordby.—1E 65
Wyke.—4B 12
(Devon)
Wyke.—1C 14
(Dorset)
Wyke.—2A 62
(Shropshire)
Wyke.—5A 30
(Surrey)
Wyke.—3B 94
(West Yorkshire)
Wyke Champflower.—5B 26
Wykeham.—5B 78
(Lincolnshire)
Wykeham.—2D 102
(nr. Malton, N Yorks.)
Wykeham.—1E 103
(nr. Scarborough, N Yorks.)
Wyken.—3B 62
(Shropshire)
Wyken.—4A 64
(West Midlands)
Wyke Regis.—5B 14
Wyke, The.—2B 62
Wykey.—3F 73
Wykin.—3B 64
Wylam.—3E 117
Wylde Green.—3F 63
Wylye.—5F 27
Wymering.—3E 17
Wymeswold.—5D 76
Wymington.—1G 53
Wymondham.—1F 65
(Leicestershire)
Wymondham.—2D 68
(Norfolk)
Wyndham.—3F 37
Wynford Eagle.—4A 14
Wyre Piddle.—3D 50
Wysall.—5D 76
Wyson.—4C 60
Wythall.—5E 63
Wytham.—2F 41
Wythburn.—3E 105
Wythenshawe.—4F 87
Wyton.—5B 66
(Cambridgeshire)
Wyton.—2D 96
(Humberside)
Wyverstone.—1C 56
Wyverstone Street.—1C 56
Wyville.—5F 77
Wyvis Lodge.—1G 159

Yaddlethorpe.—5A 96
Yafford.—5C 16
Yafforth.—5G 107
Yalberton.—4E 9
Yalding.—5A 32
Yanley.—2F 25
Yanwath.—2G 105
Yanworth.—1B 40
Yapham.—4C 102
Yapton.—3H 17
Yarburgh.—3F 91
Yarcombe.—1F 13

Yard.—3D 22
(Devon)
Yard.—2G 23
(Somerset)
Yardley.—4F 63
Yardley Gobion.—3E 53
Yardley Hastings.—2F 53
Yardley Wood.—5F 63
Yardro.—2E 48
Yarhampton.—1B 50
Yarkhill.—3A 50
Yarlet.—5D 74
Yarley.—4F 25
Yarlington.—1B 14
Yarm.—3B 108
Yarmouth.—5B 16
Yarnbrook.—3D 26
Yarnfield.—4C 74
Yarnscombe.—3B 22
Yarnton.—1F 41
Yarpole.—4B 60
Yarrow.—2F 121
(Borders)
Yarrow.—1A 116
(Northumberland)
Yarrow.—4D 25
(Somerset)
Yarrow Feus.—2F 121

Yarrow Ford.—1G 121
Yarsop.—3G 49
Yarwell.—3H 65
Yate.—4F 39
Yateley.—2G 29
Yatesbury.—5B 40
Yattendon.—5G 41
Yatton.—2E 25
(Avon)
Yatton.—4B 60
(Hereford & Worcester)
Yatton Keynell.—5G 39
Yaverland.—5E 16
Yawl.—4G 13
Yaxham.—4C 80
Yaxley.—3A 66
(Cambridgeshire)
Yaxley.—5D 68
(Suffolk)
Yazor.—3G 49
Y Dref.—2D 71
Y Drenewydd.—1G 59
Yeading.—2C 30
Yeadon.—1C 94
Yealand Conyers.—2E 99
Yealand Redmayne.—2E 99
Yealmpton.—4B 8
Yearby.—2D 108

Yearngill.—5C 114
Yearsett.—2B 50
Yearsley.—2A 102
Yeaton.—4G 73
Yeaveley.—3F 75
Yeavering.—1D 122
Yedingham.—2D 103
Yelden.—1H 53
Yeldersley Hollies.—3G 75
Yelford.—2E 41
Yelling.—1B 54
Yelstead.—4C 32
Yelvertoft.—5C 64
Yelverton.—3B 8
(Devon)
Yelverton.—2E 69
(Norfolk)
Yenston.—1C 14
Yeoford.—4A 12
Yeolmbridge.—1H 7
Yeo Mill.—3E 23
Yeovil.—2A 14
Yeovil Marsh.—2A 14
Yeovilton.—1A 14
Yerbeston.—4D 34
Yetlington.—4E 123
Yetminster.—2A 14
Yett.—2D 118
(nr. Ayr, S'clyde.)

Yett.—4A 130
(nr. Motherwell, S'clyde.)
Yettington.—5D 12
Yetts o' Muckhart.—3C 138
Y Fenni.—1B 38
Y Ffor.—2C 70
Yieldshields.—4B 130
Yiewsley.—2B 30
Yinstay.—6E 174
Ynysboeth.—3G 37
Ynysddu.—3H 37
Ynysforgan.—3C 36
Ynyshir.—3G 37
Ynyslas.—1B 58
Ynysmaerdy.—4G 37
(Mid Glamorgan)
Ynysmaerdy.—3D 36
(West Glamorgan)
Ynysmeudwy.—2D 36
Ynystawe.—2C 36
Ynys-wen.—3F 37
(Mid Glamorgan)
Ynyswen.—1E 37
(Powys)
Ynysybwl.—3G 37
Yockenthwaite.—2C 100
Yockleton.—4E 123
Yokefleet.—3A 96
Yoker.—3G 129

Yonder Bognie.—4C 162
York.—4A 102
Yorkletts.—4E 33
Yorkley.—2E 39
Yorton.—3H 73
Yorton Heath.—3H 73
Youlgreave.—1G 75
Youlthorpe.—4C 102
Youlton.—3H 101
Young's End.—1D 44
Young Wood.—5D 90
Yoxall.—1F 63
Yoxford.—1F 57
Yr Wyddgrug.—4E 85
Ysbyty Cynfyn.—3C 58
Ysbyty Ifan.—1H 71
Ysbyty Ystwyth.—3C 58
Ysceifiog.—3D 84
Yspitty.—3B 36
Ystalyfera.—2D 36
Ystrad.—3F 37
Ystrad Aeron.—2E 47
Ystradfellte.—1F 37
Ystradffin.—3G 47
Ystradgynlais.—1D 36
Ystrad Meurig.—4C 58
Ystrad-Mynach.—3H 37
Ystradowen.—1D 36
(Dyfed)

Ystradowen.—5G 37
(South Glamorgan)
Ystumtuen.—3C 58
Ythanbank.—5G 163
Y Trallwng.—5E 72

Zeal Monachorum.—3H 11
Zeals.—5C 26
Zelah.—4C 6
Zennor.—3B 4
Zouch.—5C 76

Maps printed in Great Britain by
Jarrold Printing, Whitefriars, Norwich, NR3 1SH